The Concept of Universal Crimes in International Law

Terje Einarsen

2012
Torkel Opsahl Academic EPublisher
Oslo

To the memory of my father Einar, who died in December 2011, and to my mother Mary.

Thanks for imprinting a sense of justice.

We the Peoples of the United Nations Determined

> *to reaffirm faith in fundamental human rights, in the dignity and worth of the human person, in the equal rights of men and women and of nations large and small, and*

> *to establish conditions under which justice and respect for obligations arising from treaties and other sources of international law can be maintained*

Charter of the United Nations (1945)

The definition of a crime cannot, however, be made to depend on which nation commits the act. I am not willing to charge as a crime against a German official acts which would not be crimes if committed by officials of the United States.

Justice Robert H. Jackson (1945)
Chief Prosecutor at Nuremberg

ACKNOWLEDGEMENTS

This book is the product of a research project meant to address certain issues of complicity in international criminal law. It started after a street encounter in 2007 with Dean Asbjørn Strandbakken of the Law Faculty, University of Bergen (UiB), who encouraged me to apply for a postdoctoral position. I was at the time enjoying my professional life as a judge at the Gulating High Court for the western parts of Norway. I was generously granted leave for three and a half years by the chief justice of Gulating, Bjørn Solbakken, and by the Norwegian Court Administration, to undertake the project. The research formed part of a larger project at the Law Faculty (UiB), financed by the Research Council of Norway and led by Professor Erling Johannes Husabø. I am grateful to several people at the Law Faculty for their continuous support during the research period. I am also happy to have had the chance to visit the international courts in The Hague and to take a most interesting trip to Arusha, Tanzania, to visit the Rwanda tribunal. At the tribunal I was well taken care of by Judge Erik Møse and his staff, as well as by acting chief of prosecutions Richard Karegyesa, Iain Morley, and several of their colleagues.

I am deeply indebted to those who at different stages read and critically commented on various parts of the manuscript. They include Dr. Joseph Rikhof, senior counsel at the Crimes against Humanity and War Crimes Section of the Canadian Department of Justice and professor of international criminal law at the University of Ottawa; Professor Erling Johannes Husabø of UiB; Dr. Elin Skaar, senior researcher at the Chr. Michelsen Institute in Bergen; and Dr. William Minter, Washington, DC. Judge Elizabeth Baumann at the Stavanger District Court and PhD candidate at UiB, and Kjetil Skjerve, PhD candidate at UiB, also offered helpful comments on draft chapters. At the early stages of this research I was capably and kindly assisted by law student Stein Are Mikkelsen in collecting and organising relevant sources. During the summer of 2011, I was fortunate to enjoy enthusiastic and competent research assistance from lawyer Catalina Vallejo.

I would like to warmly thank Cathy Sunshine for her invaluable editorial expertise, intelligence, sense of humour, and professional care for the book. Many thanks also to Professor Morten Bergsmo, Editor-in-

Chief of Torkel Opsahl Academic Epublisher, for believing in the project and being willing to publish this book. Alf Butenschøn Skre, Senior Editorial Assistant, provided kind and competent support at the final stages of the publication process. In addition, I would like to thank the (to me unknown) peer reviewers for their comments.

Last but not least, my warmest thanks go to those who have accompanied me throughout this long book project, especially to my dear Elin for enduring my many late nights with the manuscript, and to my parents Einar and Mary for always being supportive.

Terje Einarsen
Bergen, February 2012

PREFACE

Despite the ambiguities of international law in general and international criminal law in particular, serious crimes committed, organised, or tolerated by representatives of different kinds of power structures are now of concern to the world community. These crimes may occur in the context of war or form part of a larger pattern of aggressive behaviour by powerful actors within a society. They are often directly linked to abuse of political or military systems or to an absence of effective state institutions. Such 'international crimes', which might also be referred to as 'universal crimes' because of their inherent gravity and violation of universal values and interests, are also attacks on the rule of law. They typically constitute transgressions of various social and moral norms, including human rights. Human rights are universal in the sense that every person has and should enjoy them in a modern society. Similarly, no person should be exposed to universal crimes. However, these aspirations do not always correspond to legally binding rights and obligations or to mechanisms of enforcement under current international law. We are still living in an age of uncertainty regarding which specific types of crimes are punishable directly under international law and might also be prosecuted on a regular basis before international courts.

This book is the first in a four-part series entitled "Rethinking the Essentials of International Criminal Law and Transitional Justice". It concentrates on the concept of universal crimes and the general issues involved in classifying certain offences. Other issues, such as the scope of liability for different kinds of participation in universal crimes and the direct legal consequences of these crimes, are not discussed in detail in this book, but are reserved for later volumes. The forthcoming second volume focuses on punishable participation in universal crimes. The third and fourth volumes shift attention to the legal consequences of universal crimes: book three focuses on accountability and jurisdiction as important aspects of universal crimes, while the fourth and final book in the series is about fair trial in universal crime cases. The basic research ideas underlying this comprehensive universal crimes project have been developed by the author of this book. The other books are to be published in cooperation with other analysts; the next volume will be co-authored with Dr. Joseph Rikhof.

A first research aim of this book is to explore the complex issue of which crimes are covered by international law according to theoretical and historical perspectives, academic debates, the works of the International Law Commission, and legal practice in international tribunals. The second aim is to examine different ways of classifying international crimes and then to develop a set of necessary and sufficient conditions that should be used when defining and classifying punishable crimes under international law. Using these criteria as a framework for identification and evaluation of relevant crimes, the book's third aim is to compile a comprehensive list of crimes under international law *lex lata*, followed by crimes *lex ferenda* that fulfil some, but not all, of the criteria and which might later be elevated to the sphere of *lex lata*. The enumerative crime definition in this book includes 150 crime types. The final aim is to examine whether it may be useful to gradually replace the concept of international crimes with the concept of universal crimes in further academic analysis and legal debates.

The principal purpose of this study is thus to clarify and specify the concept of universal crimes with a view to providing a common framework for understanding important features of the complex field of law concerned with the most serious crimes. Central issues to be explored include the following: What are the relevant crimes that may give rise to direct criminal liability under international law? Are they currently limited to certain core international crimes? Why should certain crimes be included whereas other serious offences should not? Should specific legal bases be considered more compelling than others for selection of crimes?

This work is addressed to all with an interest in international criminal law and related disciplines like human rights, humanitarian law, and transitional justice. Hopefully it will prove to be a modest contribution to a more coherent and practical understanding of international criminal law.

ABBREVIATIONS

AU	African Union
CIL	customary international law
ECCC	Extraordinary Chambers in the Courts of Cambodia
ECHR	European Court of Human Rights
ECJ	European Court of Justice
EU	European Union
GA	United Nations General Assembly
HRL	human rights law
IACHR	Inter-American Court of Human Rights
ICC	International Criminal Court
ICC-OTP	ICC Office of the Prosecutor
ICCPR	International Covenant on Civil and Political Rights
ICJ	International Court of Justice
ICL	international criminal law
ICTR	International Criminal Tribunal for Rwanda
ICTY	International Criminal Tribunal for the former Yugoslavia
IHL	international humanitarian law
ILC	International Law Commission
IMT	International Military Tribunal (also called the Nuremberg Tribunal)
NGO	non-governmental organisation
NMT	Nuernberg Military Tribunals
PCIJ	Permanent Court of International Justice
SC	United Nations Security Council
SCSL	Special Court for Sierra Leone
STL	Special Tribunal for Lebanon
TCL	transnational criminal law
TRC	Truth and Reconciliation Commission (South Africa)

UDHR	Universal Declaration of Human Rights
UN	United Nations
UNCLOS	United Nations Convention on the Law of the Sea
VCLT	Vienna Convention on the Law of Treaties

TABLE OF CONTENTS

Acknowledgements i

Preface iii

Abbreviations v

1. *Universal Law versus Grave Crimes* 1
    1.1. Overture: Obama's Nobel Lecture 1
    1.2. The Subject Matter of Universal Crimes 4
    1.3. Chapter Previews 15

2. *Universal Crimes in Perspective* 19
    2.1. The Nature of Universal Crimes 19
        2.1.1. Crimes, Criminal Law, and International Criminal Law . 19
        2.1.2. Preliminary Definition of Universal Crimes 21
        2.1.3. Crimes that Shock Humanity and Civilised Societies 23
    2.2. Universal Crimes in a Normative and Political Context 24
        2.2.1. Respecting Human Dignity through Criminal Liability .. 24
        2.2.2. The Rule of Law and Accountability for Leaders and
                Others 28
        2.2.3. The United Nations Paradigm of International Law 38
        2.2.4. Importance of the Shifting Political Context 51
        2.2.5. Justice and Peace 56
    2.3. Special Features of Universal Crimes 62
        2.3.1. Legal Foundation and Attached Competences
                and Duties 62
        2.3.2. Grave Breaches of International Law 66
        2.3.3. Crimes Committed, Organised, or Tolerated
                by Powerful Persons 68
        2.3.4. Gravity Assessment 73
        2.3.5. Universal Crimes Require Retributive Criminal Justice.. 83

3. *Legal Bases of Universal Crimes Norms* 87
    3.1. Methodological Challenges 87
    3.2. The Fragmented Nature of International Criminal Law 89

3.3. The Legal Bases 97
    3.3.1. The Framework of International Law-Creating
         Sources 97
    3.3.2. Multilateral Treaties 100
    3.3.3. Customary International Law 104
    3.3.4. General Principles as International Law 108
    3.3.5. Legislative Security Council Resolutions 119
    3.3.6. Establishing Universal Crimes Norms with
         Multiple Legal Bases 125
3.4. Interpretative Sources, Priority Principles 129
    3.4.1. Various Interpretive Sources 129
    3.4.2. The Priority Principles: *Lex Superior, Lex Specialis,*
         and *Lex Posterior* 130
3.5. *Lex Lata* and *Lex Ferenda* 133

4. *Reconceptualising International Crimes* 135
4.1. Identifying Crimes under International Law 135
4.2. Different Conceptualisations of International Crimes 137
4.3. International Crimes in the Statutes
    of International Institutions 145
4.4. Concepts of International Crimes in the Literature 150
    4.4.1. Zahar and Sluiter 2008 150
    4.4.2. Cassese 2008 151
    4.4.3. Werle 2009 152
    4.4.4. Bassiouni 2008 154
    4.4.5. Schabas 2010 156
    4.4.6. Cryer, Friman, Robinson, and Wilmhurst 2010 158
    4.4.7. Ratner, Abrams, and Bischoff 2009 160
    4.4.8. Currie 2010 163
4.5. Statements of the International Law Commission 168
    4.5.1. International Law Context 168
    4.5.2. The First Rapporteur, Jean Spiropoulos (1949–1951) ... 171
    4.5.3. 1954 Draft Code of Offences against the Peace and
         Security of Mankind 174
    4.5.4. Special Rapporteur Doudou Thiam (1981–1991) 181
    4.5.5. 1991 Provisional Draft Code 185
    4.5.6. 1994 Draft Statute for an International Criminal Court. 188
    4.5.7. The Relationship between the Statute and the Code 196
    4.5.8. 1996 Draft Code of Crimes against the Peace
         and Security of Mankind 200
    4.5.9. The Work of the ILC on the Obligation to Extradite
         or Prosecute (2004–2010) 202

4.6. Anyone Better? The Hostage Case (1948) 206
4.7. The New Definition of Aggression in the Rome Statute (2010) 209
    4.7.1. International Law and Statutory Context:
            The Most Serious Crimes 209
    4.7.2. The Definition Adopted at the Review Conference....... 213
4.8. Classifying International Crimes 217
    4.8.1. Different Kinds of Definitions of International
            Crimes.. 217
    4.8.2. Different Levels of Generality of Definitions of
            International Crimes 221
    4.8.3. Delimitation by Non-international Crimes 225
4.9. Classifying International Crimes within a Universal Crimes
    Framework.. 231
    4.9.1. Necessary and Sufficient Conditions of International
            Crimes.. 231
            4.9.1.1. General Remarks on the Conditions and
                     Legal Consequences of International Crimes. 231
            4.9.1.2. Necessary and Sufficient Conditions 236
            4.9.1.3. Formulating a Proposed Legal Definition
                     of International Crimes................................... 248
    4.9.2. Developing an Enumerative Definition of
            International Crimes 249
            4.9.2.1. General Remarks on the Typology................. 249
            4.9.2.2. Requirement for a Gravity Clause................. 253
            4.9.2.3. The Relevance of Conditions of War
                     or Peace 255
            4.9.2.4. The Crime Status of Terrorism....................... 266
            4.9.2.5. A Brief Note on the Status of Other
                     Possible Crimes under International Law 274
    4.9.3. Consolidated List of International Crimes..................... 275
4.10. From International Crimes to Universal Crimes 286

5. *Towards a Concept of Universal Crimes*...................................... 289
5.1. Crimes with Uncertain Status under International Law 289
5.2. Conceptualising Universal Crimes 295
    5.2.1. Seeking a Theoretical Definition of Universal Crimes.. 295
    5.2.2. Distilling the Essentials of Universal Crimes 301
    5.2.3. Illustrating the Notion and Application of
            the Inherent Gravity Clauses 306
5.3. Developing a United Nations Declaration on Universal Crimes 313

Appendix I: Consolidated List of Universal Crimes 319

Appendix II: Court Cases 329

Appendix III: Figures 335

Bibliography 337

Index 347

Torkel Opsahl Academic EPublisher 357

Also in the FICHL Publication Series 359

1

Universal Law versus Grave Crimes

1.1. Overture: Obama's Nobel Lecture

In his remarks at the Nobel Peace Prize ceremony in Oslo on 10 December 2009, US President Barack Obama asserted that war is justified only "if it is waged as a last resort or in self-defense; if the force used is proportional; and if, whenever possible, civilians are spared from violence". He focused not only on the option of war, but also on its relationship with "the peace that we seek [...] based on the inherent rights and dignity of every individual".[1] His speech seemed to mark a significant shift in American rhetoric about the world community, signalling greater recognition of international norms on universal interests and values. Those universal norms are the subject matter at the heart of this book.

Obama stressed that efforts should always be made, first and foremost, to avoid the tragic choice of war, and he suggested ways for the world to build a just and lasting peace that eventually should make resort to war unnecessary. In particular, he pointed to the implementation of universal rights as a precondition for a just peace:

> It was this insight that drove drafters of the Universal Declaration of Human Rights after the Second World War. In the wake of devastation, they recognized that if human rights are not protected, peace is a hollow promise.[2]

To make such protection of rights effective, Obama said, we must "develop alternatives to violence that are tough enough to actually change behavior", because "if we want a lasting peace, then the words of the international community must mean something". He added that "regimes that break the rules must be held accountable" and that the subsequent sanctions "must exact a real price".[3] Accountability for breaking fundamental rules, therefore, becomes a key to a just international order.

---

[1] "Obama's Nobel Remarks", transcript reprinted in *New York Times*, 10 December 2009, available at http://www.nytimes.com/2009/12/11/world/europe/11prexy.text .html, last accessed 6 June 2011.

[2] *Ibid.*

[3] *Ibid.*

Obama made clear that the rules in question include the Geneva Conventions, and that the same principle of accountability applies to those who violate international law by brutalising their own people.[4] Although Obama did not further specify his understanding of accountability, it may be taken to include individual criminal liability on the part of political and military leaders.[5] One indication of a genuine shift in the United States position was the affirmative US vote in the United Nations Security Council in 2011 in favour of referring the repression of the uprising in Libya to the prosecutor of the International Criminal Court.[6]

It is important to note that Obama did not exempt the United States or any other country from these common international standards. Indeed, he explicitly said that the United States should be "a standard bearer in the conduct of war".[7] It seems reasonable to interpret his speech to mean that universal standards with regard to protection of human rights, justice, and – arguably – accountability must apply universally. Under this interpretation, Obama's Nobel speech would undoubtedly be one of the most powerful and carefully balanced expressions in support of the United Nations project of international law and international relations put forward by an American president since the end of World War II.[8]

However, there are also other plausible and less far-reaching interpretations of Obama's speech, given the *de facto* continuity in US policy. To date, the United States continues to resist any political or legal move at the international level which might entail holding US leaders or military

---

[4] *Ibid.*

[5] Four days later, on 14 December 2009, US Secretary of State Hillary Rodham Clinton delivered a speech at Georgetown University entitled "Remarks on the Human Rights Agenda for the 21st Century". She stated, "We know that all governments and all leaders sometimes fall short. So there have to be internal mechanisms of accountability when rights are violated". Note that Clinton only referred to 'internal mechanisms' and not, for instance, to 'international courts'. Speech available at http://www.state.gov/secretary/rm/2009a/12/133544.htm, last accessed 28 June 2011.

[6] UN Security Council Resolution 1970 (2011), 26 February 2011, paras. 4 and 5.

[7] "Obama's Nobel Remarks", *supra* note 1.

[8] At the beginning of the twenty-first century, in contrast, US policies had led to doubt about "how far the USA is deliberately posing a challenge to the whole UN system and to the existing international legal order, or whether it is operating within the system, even if manipulating the rules for its own end". Christine Gray, *International Law and the Use of Force*, Oxford University Press, Oxford, UK, 2008, p. 4.

personnel accountable for international crimes before an international or foreign court. In that respect, at least, the United States has been reluctant to accept the idea that no country or person is above international law.[9] Given the US government's tenacious distinction between friends and foes and its attempt to uphold a certain international order, there is the risk that it might extend such an exemption to other nations considered friendly or important to special US interests. This would run contrary to the more general interests of the world community and to the principle of equality between nations. A case in point is the controversy surrounding the report of the United Nations Fact Finding Mission on the Gaza Conflict in 2009,[10] accompanied by the firm resistance of US leaders to establishing an international criminal law mechanism to pursue accountability for possible Israeli and Palestinian war crimes.

What Obama did in his Nobel lecture, nevertheless, was to take a careful first step to confirm key common values and suggest a principled way forward for the international community. Importantly for the direction of the further process, Obama did not suggest backing away from humanitarian law, human rights law, or international criminal law. A reasonable inference is that his administration may be prepared to place more emphasis on core universal standards. Active US support would be especially important for the implementation and enforcement of criminal liability under international law. If China, Russia, and the United States were all to join the International Criminal Court in the future, this would be several giant steps forward.[11] Without universal accountability for serious crimes, along with strict adherence to other principles of justice such as non-discrimination and fair criminal procedures, international criminal law will surely not fulfil its true potential.

---

[9] Gray states, "Thus the question arises whether US lip service to international law on the use of force is meaningless or to be welcomed as indicating continued adherence to the Charter system? Are the USA's assertions that it is acting multilaterally and in the interests of the international community of any value? Or is the USA actually claiming special rights exercisable exclusively by it as the only remaining super power?" (*ibid*).

[10] See United Nations, *Human Rights in Palestine and other Occupied Arab Territories*, A/HRC/12/48, 15 September 2009.

[11] See Rome Statute of the International Criminal Court (hereafter, Rome Statute), 27 July 1998. As of 30 June 2011, the treaty had 116 states parties, including two permanent members of the United Nations Security Council (France and the United Kingdom).

International efforts to combat impunity for regime leaders and others suspected of having committed grave international crimes require non-biased support from the most powerful states. While this is not easily reconciled with the traditional realist thinking and self-interest of a super-power, there may be significant long-term advantages in providing such support, even for the United States. Lasting and just peace in conflict-ridden parts of the world may one day be worth the price for all states in an increasingly interconnected world. Conceivably, far-sighted US leaders might even acknowledge that a stronger international legal order could help curb abuses of democracy within the United States itself.

1.2. The Subject Matter of Universal Crimes

Some crimes are particularly grave offences of concern to the world community as a whole. They may occur in the context of war or as part of a larger pattern of aggressive behaviour by powerful actors within a society. These crimes are often directly linked to abuse of political or military systems or to a lack of effective state institutions. Such crimes, which can be referred to as universal crimes, are also attacks on the rule of law and on human dignity. They typically constitute transgressions of various social and moral norms, including human rights. Human rights are universal in the sense that every person has and should enjoy them in a modern society. Similarly, no person should be exposed to universal crimes. However, these aspirations do not always correspond to legally binding rights and obligations, or to mechanisms of enforcement under international law.

The main purpose of this study is to further specify the concept of universal crimes as a way of providing a common framework for understanding important features of the complex field of law concerned with the most serious crimes. The central legal issues to be explored include the following: What are the relevant crimes that may give rise to direct criminal liability under international law? Are they limited to certain core international crimes? Why should certain crimes be put on the list whereas other serious offences should not? Should specific legal bases be considered more compelling than others for such determination?

A complicating factor when trying to answer such questions is the increasingly fragmented nature of international criminal law. It comprises several new sub-regimes, including international or internationalised criminal courts that apply similar, but to some extent also different, substantive rules and may use different methodological approaches. The material jurisdictions of these courts have often been more limited than that which international law arguably allows. Consequently, while the legal status of certain crimes has been clarified, the status of other grave crimes remains controversial. Gradual expansion and diversification is a general problem within the broad field of international law, and the International Law Commission has therefore put 'fragmentation' on its formal agenda.[12] In proposing 'universal crimes' as a new and comprehensive concept, with the potential to provide a unified perspective on international criminal law, this study attempts to offer a response to the problem of fragmentation. This is based on the understanding that there is much more common ground within this field of law than is generally recognised. When systematically considered, this concept of universal crimes may serve to meet the pressing need for synthesising seemingly isolated bits and pieces of international criminal law.

This project to advance the concept of universal crimes should therefore be seen in light of the reasoning of the International Law Commission, which claimed in 2006 that international law is a legal system and that its rules and principles "should be interpreted against the background of other rules and principles".[13] A special regime, even a subregime, may prevail over general law as *lex specialis* within its particular field of operation.[14] In addition, the role of general international law is also relevant to special regimes, as will be discussed later.[15]

If one can identify a legal mega-norm, or a cluster of international rules, underpinned by general principles of law and common legal values, it may be possible to find coherence among seemingly separate fragments of international criminal law. Such a development, of course, would in no way guarantee an international rule of law in which impunity for universal

---

[12] See International Law Commission (ILC), *Fragmentation of International Law. Difficulties Arising from the Diversification and Expansion of International Law*, in ILC, *Analytical Guide to the Work of the International Law Commission 1949–1997*, 1998.

[13] ILC, *Conclusions of the Work of the Study Group on the Fragmentation of International Law: Difficulties Arising from the Diversification and Expansion of International Law*, 2006, conclusion no. 1, reprinted in *Yearbook of the International Law Commission, 2006*, vol. II, part II.

[14] This is also recognised by the ILC in *ibid.*, conclusion no. 14.

[15] See, *e.g.*, Chapter 3, section 3.2.

crimes is the exception rather than the norm. But this study contends that there are significant advantages in including the concept of universal crimes in international law terminology as a complement to, or perhaps even as a replacement for, the more traditional concept of international crimes. As will be explained in more detail in the following chapters, the concept of international crimes is more commonly defined by enumeration than by conceptual criteria, and it is defined differently by different scholars. The concept of universal crimes, while it is not yet precisely defined in legal terms, is more conducive to facilitating common understandings, a better informed dialogue among the different actors in the field, and sharper analysis of the law and its potential for development on the core issues mentioned above.

In later chapters, this study will lay out more precise wording to define the legal concept. Beginning with common usage, however, we can initially define 'universal crimes' as certain acts, or kinds of inhuman behaviour, that are proscribed by norms that ultimately apply and might be implemented and enforced universally. Everyone is expected to refrain from such acts insofar as they are incompatible with obligations assumed to be respected by every human being regardless of location, nationality, religion, or other status. This should not be understood as implying that the norms in question are timeless or unchanging. But, like universal human rights, the concept of universal crimes implies norms that need to be respected and implemented in modern societies in order to promote fundamental interests of the world community and uphold humane values.

The norms establishing universal crimes may have an additional moral or national legal basis, or both, and perhaps a religious or philosophical basis. Essential to lawyers, however, is the fact that most of the norms of direct interest for the present study already have an independent legal foundation in international law. In addition, one may claim that certain norms that are *not* part of current international criminal law *ought* to be so, because they meet the required moral and policy-oriented criteria for being part of the legal body of universal crimes.

In examining the concept of universal crimes, it will be necessary to consider both 'soft' and 'hard' law, a distinction which also occurs in human rights law. Soft law principles are legally relevant but not binding, whereas hard law is legally binding. The reason is that soft law norms do not originate from a recognised 'law-creating source of international law', but rather from another legally relevant source. By definition, only certain sources are capable of creating binding rules of law on their own. These sources include treaties, international custom, general principles of law, and legislative United Nations Security Council resolutions.[16] A declaration of the United Nations General Assembly on a legally relevant subject matter, on the other hand, is regarded as soft law rather than hard law that is binding; the Universal Declaration of Human Rights is the most important example. Whether a specific norm is 'soft' or 'hard', may be subject to contention and legal development. Several of the norms expressed in the UDHR are thus today recognised as binding customary international law.

In addition, even binding rules may be soft in *substance* if not in legal form. For instance, treaty provisions may be so vague or uncertain with respect to their content that they are best considered guidelines that cannot on their own determine legal rights or obligations. This consideration applies even more frequently to rules emerging as 'general principles of law',[17] which are often soft, at least in some respects. Because of the legality principle in criminal law,[18] the issue of a sufficient legal basis is crucial when analysing universal crimes. While soft international norms do not establish criminal liability, however, they still need to be taken into account, since they may exert substantial influence on the hard law-making processes.[19]

Although 'universal crimes' is not yet commonly used legal terminology, the concept is nevertheless closely tied in historical and legal terms to the establishment and continuation of the United Nations paradigm.[20] Acts of aggression, war crimes, crimes against humanity, and genocide, for example, are among the typical crimes that can be considered universal crimes.

The universality of a crime, one may venture as a working thesis, is directly related to the nature and gravity of the crime, which in turn is based on factors such as the character of the acts, the scale of the crime,

---

[16] See Chapter 3, sections 3.3.2–3.3.5.
[17] Consider, *e.g.*, Alan Boyle and Christine Chinkin, *The Making of International Law*, Oxford University Press, Oxford, UK, 2006, pp. 222–225 and 285–289.
[18] See Kenneth S. Gallant, *The Principle of Legality in International and Comparative Criminal Law*, Cambridge University Press, Cambridge, UK, 2009.
[19] See Chapter 3, sections 3.3–3.4.
[20] On the meaning of the phrase 'UN paradigm of international law', see, *e.g.*, Chapter 2, section 2.2.3, and Chapter 3, section 3.3.1.

and the involvement in the crime of state leaders or other powerful entities in society. The nature and gravity of the crimes in question establishes them as acts that should be outlawed in any public order claiming legitimacy as a legal order, especially legal orders adhering to the principles of human rights and the rule of law. This means that there is a kind of circular relationship between the notions of universal crimes and the rule of law.[21]

A related but not identical concept is that of *jus cogens*, referring to norms conceived as superior to other rules of international law on account of the importance of their subject matter content as well as the universal acceptance of their superiority.[22] *Jus cogens* norms govern certain aspects of life within the international community, and if binding, cannot be contracted away; that is, they are 'peremptory norms'.[23] Closely connected are rules classified as obligations owed to the international community as a whole: the obligations *erga omnes* of a state. Any state may invoke the responsibility of a state that is violating such obligations.[24] Note that all obligations established by *jus cogens* norms are also obligations *erga omnes*.[25] Frequently cited examples of relevant *jus cogens* norms are "the prohibition of aggression, slavery and the slave trade, genocide, racial discrimination apartheid and torture, as well as basic rules of international humanitarian law applicable in armed conflict".[26] Breaches of *jus cogens* rules cannot be justified by reference to conflicting norms at lower levels of the hierarchy of international norms. A conflict between different *jus cogens* norms is, however, theoretically conceivable. Thus one can envisage modification of a *jus cogens* norm by a subsequent norm of international law having the same character.[27]

It is important to note that a norm having the possible character of *jus cogens*, because of its content and broad acceptance, must still be

---

[21] On the rule of law concept and its relationship to universal crimes, see Chapter 2, section 2.2.2.

[22] See ILC, 2006, conclusion no. 32, *supra* note 13.

[23] For an in-depth survey, see Alexander Orakhelashvili, *Peremptory Norms in International Law*, Oxford University Press, Oxford, UK, 2008.

[24] Consider ILC, 2006, conclusion no. 37, *supra* note 13.

[25] The reverse is not necessarily true. See *ibid.*, conclusion no. 38.

[26] *Ibid.*, conclusion no. 33.

[27] The latter possibility is explicitly foreseen by the United Nations in the Vienna Convention on the Law of Treaties, 1969, Article 53.

'formatted' through a law-creating process of international law in order to be legally binding. If it is not, the norm cannot be 'superior law' since it has not yet become hard law. Therefore, one cannot conclude at a conceptual level that certain universal crimes norms are binding and superior norms of international law (*jus cogens*), without additional evidence that they have been incorporated into hard law.[28]

There are two distinct analytical options for use of the term *jus cogens*. One is to apply the term to both binding law (hard law) and non-binding norms (soft law), on the understanding that each may have an implied *jus cogens* 'character'. The second is to reserve the concept of *jus cogens* for norms that have both elements: the required character with regard to specific content and universal acceptance as a norm, *and* the legal status of binding law.

The first and broader approach implies that the concept of *jus cogens* is relevant to dynamic legal processes rather than being only a name for the end result. It also implies the need for great care in drawing the sometimes fine line between binding and non-binding norms of international law. Such a conceptual clarification does not solve the practical problem when a norm appears to be emerging as a customary rule or a binding general principle of international law.[29] In any case, one cannot simply start a legal reasoning by declaring a norm to be *jus cogens* and then deduce that the norm has superior legal force in conflict with other binding legal norms. The concrete use of the *jus cogens* stamp requires that sufficient inquires first be undertaken, both on the substance of the norm and on its binding legal status. It goes without saying that both aspects of possible *jus cogens* norms are often disputed within the international community and by commentators, precisely because they trump other legal, moral, and political arguments.

The concept of *jus cogens* may not be essential to the study of universal crimes, since the norms underlying these crimes already have the required character in terms of content and universality. But establish-

---

[28] On the same track, see Nina H. B. Jørgensen, *The Responsibility of States for International Crimes*, Oxford University Press, Oxford, UK, 2000: "There is no automatic or necessary link between *jus cogens* and international crimes except to the extent that public policy and the protection of certain moral values and imperatives within the international community overlap with the concept of crime" (p. 91).

[29] See Chapter 3, sections 3.3.3–3.3.4.

ing their superiority to other rules also depends on demonstrating that they are founded on at least one law-creating source of international law.

Proscriptions of acts constituting universal crimes may accordingly be found in different sources of international law, which may complement each other.[30] For many purposes it is sufficient to interpret and apply one particular legal basis, for instance, an international criminal court statute presumed to be in line with international law, without having resort to other rules. In principle, and sometimes for practical reasons as well, one may need to proceed beyond a single source. The gravity and, even more, the universal character of certain crimes cannot be assessed only with reference to abstract categorisations of the crimes. In practical legal work, it is not sufficient to identify the category of crimes being committed in a certain situation, for example, 'war crimes' or 'crimes against humanity'. It is also necessary to identify more specific crime types as well, for example, 'killing' or 'torture' in the particular context. Methods for the assessment of gravity, with a view to prioritising crimes, concrete crime scenes, and criminal acts, are also necessary for such purposes as prosecutorial decision-making.[31] In particular, it is important to determine whether a particular assessment of gravity, prescribed by some form of a 'gravity clause', is essential to the concept of universal crimes in international law.[32]

Given its potential, it is perhaps surprising that 'universal crimes' has not figured as a significant term in the international law literature. Searches by this author in June 2011 show interesting results. For instance, a search for the exact phrase 'universal crimes' using the Questia Library search engine listed 14 books, 13 journal articles, three magazine articles, and one newspaper article. A similar search in Google Scholar produced 476 matches, while HeinOnline displayed 305 matches (both searches were confined to journal articles). The oldest publication found was an article on extradition of criminals in the *Albany Law Journal* from 1872. The 25 oldest publications according to HeinOnline spanned more than a century, 1872–1982, whereas the 25 most recent publications were published in just the last three years, 2008–2011.

---

[30] A particular question is whether universal law can emerge through a combination of several legal bases without necessarily fulfilling all the criteria of any specific legal basis; see Chapter 3, section 3.3.6.

[31] See Chapter 4, section 4.3.4.

[32] See Chapter 4, section 4.9.2.2, and Chapter 5, sections 5.2.2–5.2.3.

Changing the exact search phrase from 'universal crimes' to 'universal crime' resulted in even more matches, with Google Scholar giving the largest number, 613. However, none of the books or articles use the term universal crime(s) in the title, except for one article published in 1998.[33] Even in that article the authors do not define the term precisely or discuss it in any detail.[34]

These numbers are far lower than those produced by comparable searches for the more familiar term 'international crime'. Another Google Scholar search in June 2011 revealed 20,800 matches for journal articles containing the phrase 'international crime', including 753 articles with that phrase in the title. Various other expressions have been used for similar phenomena, *inter alia*, 'core international crimes' (or just 'core crimes'), 'the most serious international crimes', 'grave international crimes', '*jus cogens* crimes', or 'crimes of serious international concern'; all had frequencies similar to that for 'universal crimes'.[35] Needless to say, the terms mentioned are not necessarily identical or interchangeable, nor do they convey the same meaning to different authors or actors in international law.[36]

This indicates that the concept of universal crimes has not been analysed in depth, nor has it been considered a distinct concept of international law. In most cases, the term seems to have been used loosely and interchangeably with 'international crimes' or similar expressions. It seems to occur most commonly in articles concerned with universal jurisdiction, suggesting that some authors are linking the conditions of certain acts classified as 'universal crimes' with the particular legal consequences

---

[33] Colleen Enache-Brown and Ari Fried, "Universal Crime, Jurisdiction and Duty: The Obligation of *Aut Dedere Aut Judicare* in International Law", in *McGill Law Journal*, 1998, vol. 43, pp. 613–633.

[34] The article is still interesting, though, as it points to linkages between gross violations of human rights, universal crimes, and universal jurisdiction: "Once an act which falls within the category of 'universal crime' is committed, irrespective of where the act is committed or who the victims are, the ability of all states to exert jurisdiction logically follows" (*ibid.*, p. 625).

[35] Compare the 476 matches at Google Scholar for 'universal crimes' with 374 matches for 'core crimes', 334 for 'the most serious international crimes', 229 for 'core international crimes', 209 for '*jus cogens* crimes', 160 for 'grave international crimes', and just 5 for 'crimes of serious international concern' (search run in June 2011).

[36] See Chapter 4, sections 4.4–4.7, with regard to 'international crimes'.

of 'universal jurisdiction'.[37] In the current restatement of foreign relations law of United States, from 1987, a similar linkage, although not the specific term, appears in §404, "Universal Jurisdiction to Define and Punish Certain Offenses". The text declares that a state under international law has "jurisdiction to define and prescribe punishment for *certain offenses recognized by the community of nations as of universal concern*, such as piracy, slave trade, attacks on or hijacking of aircraft, genocide, war crimes, and perhaps certain acts of terrorism",[38] even when no other basis of jurisdiction applies.

The existence of many similar terms raises the question of why a new concept should be introduced. Preliminary answers have already been suggested by reference to an informed dialogue and sharper analysis of the law. This will, however, require not only specification of the concept of universal crimes but also clarification of its relationship to the concept of international crimes. In preliminary summary terms, 'international crimes' will be defined as types of crimes for which there is criminal liability under international criminal law.

From a practical legal perspective, a crucial question is whether a certain act may – depending on the factual circumstances – incur direct criminal liability under international law. If it does, a number of specific legal consequences may follow. The answer to the question is quite clear with respect to the crime of genocide and crimes against humanity. In many other cases the answer is debatable. In general, however, when direct criminal liability under international law is deemed to exist within the normative dimension for the kind of offence committed, the corresponding crime type might be termed an 'international crime'. What

---

[37] Some recent articles listed by Google Scholar in response to a search on the term 'universal crimes' include William S. Dodge, "Alien Tort Litigation and the Prescriptive Jurisdiction Fallacy", in *Harvard International Law Journal Online*, 2010, vol. 51, pp. 35–46; Eugene Kontorovich and Steven Art, "An Empirical Examination of Universal Jurisdiction for Piracy", in *American Journal of International Law*, 2010, vol. 104, no. 3, pp. 436–453; Barry Hart Dubner and Karen Greene, "On the Creation of a New Legal Regime to Try Sea Pirates", in *Journal of Maritime Law and Commerce*, 2010, vol. 39, no. 3, pp. 439–464; and Itamar Mann, "The Dual Foundation of Universal Jurisdiction: Towards a Jurisprudence for the 'Court of Critique'", in *Transnational Legal Theory*, 2010, vol. 1, no. 4, pp. 485–521.

[38] *Restatement of the Law Third, Foreign Relations Law of the United States,* section 404, American Law Institute, 1987 (emphasis added).

needs to be explained in detail is why such liability exists for some offences and not for others, even though the damaging effect for victims may not differ much. This topic requires an extensive analysis of how international crimes are and should be identified and distinguished from other international offences and non-international crimes. For that reason, the longest chapter in this book (Chapter 4) is devoted to the identification and classification of international crimes.

Whether or not one adopts the new terminology of 'universal crimes' or uses the more familiar term 'international crimes', it is necessary to go beyond simply identifying such crimes to analyse the assumptions underlying contemporary international law which justify their special treatment. The conception of universal crimes set forth in this book may provide a framework for understanding this, whichever term is ultimately applied.

If the facts on the ground fit all the elements of a particular crime identified as an international crime under international law, one may conclude that a universal crime has been committed. Prosecutors and others must be able to identity a concrete crime, taking into account both law and facts. One option considered in the earlier stages of this project was to use the concept of universal crimes for the concrete crimes corresponding to international crimes. On reflection, however, it appears that this distinction, based on the common duality of the concept of crimes as both norms proscribing a certain conduct and criminal acts committed in real life, is better applied to both the international crimes and universal crimes terminology. As is the case in domestic law, whether one is referring to abstract norms or concrete acts should be clear from the context.

The complexity of universal crimes, however, raises particular challenges for international decision-makers in drawing the connection between abstract law and the reality of acts of crime on the ground. Because of the particular 'systemic' nature of universal crimes, they often involve many different participants within a multifaceted power structure, even entire collective entities.[39] Therefore, it may be a challenging task for prosecutors, judges, and the drafters of international court statutes to distinguish the types of crimes appropriately considered to be international or universal crimes, as well as to determine the scope of

---

[39] See, *e.g.*, André Nollkaemper and Harmen van der Wilt (eds.), *System Criminality in International Law*, Cambridge University Press, Cambridge, UK, 2009.

jurisdiction, investigation, prosecution, and finally conviction. International prosecutors in particular need to be aware of the extent of discretion they have and the expectations to be met in prosecutorial decision-making in light of the available resources.

A central factor in such decisions will often be the issue of assessment of the gravity of the crime. The concept of universal crimes may provide some assistance in this respect, as well as serving as a conceptual basis for justifying or critiquing current laws and practice. It is important to make clear, however, that the assessment of gravity of a crime in order to determine whether it should be classified as a universal crime, on the one hand, and the practical processes of selection and prioritizing crimes for the purpose of prosecution within the available options and resources, on the other, are two separate issues involving consideration of similar but also different factors. This will be discussed in greater depth later.[40]

This book, the first in a four-part series, concentrates on the concept of universal crimes and the general issues involved in classifying certain offences, whether the term used is international crimes or universal crimes. Other issues, such as the scope of liability for different kinds of participation in universal crimes and the direct legal consequences of universal crimes, are not discussed in detail in this book, but are reserved for later volumes. The forthcoming second volume concerns punishable participation in universal crimes. The third and fourth books shift attention to the legal consequences of universal crimes. Book three focuses on accountability and jurisdiction as important aspects of universal crimes, while the fourth and final book in the series is about fair trial in universal crimes cases.

This book is addressed to all with an interest in international criminal law and related disciplines like human rights, humanitarian law, and transitional justice, as well as to those involved in internationalised criminal law at the regional and national levels. Hopefully, it will prove to be a modest contribution to a more coherent and practical understanding of international criminal law.

---

[40] See Chapter 2, section 2.3.4.

1.3. Chapter Previews

Chapter 2, entitled "Universal Crimes in Perspective", provides a preliminary and contextual examination of the concept of universal crimes. It explores the nature and special features of universal crimes, as well as the normative and political context of these crimes. An important part of this context is the contemporary United Nations paradigm of international law. The chapter argues that the concept of universal crimes can only be understood within this particular legal, political, and community framework. It theorises that the phenomenon of universal crimes requires consistent retributive justice in compliance with the rule of law, particularly with respect to leaders. This requires a distinction between offences that are properly identified as universal crimes and other offences. The chapter provides a preliminary analysis of the issue of gravity, which is central to the identification of universal crimes. It contends that universal crimes consistently require retributive justice, even if other restorative mechanisms are also needed for societal reconciliation and even if such justice may be temporarily delayed for the sake of successful peace negotiations.

Chapter 3, "Legal Bases of Universal Crimes Norms", confronts methodological issues and discusses in particular the legal basis of universal crimes. It notes the fragmented character of current international criminal law and suggests that the concept of universal crimes may contribute to a more coherent understanding of the existing legal framework. The chapter explains the need to keep in mind a clear, principled distinction between the law as it is (*lex lata*) and the law as it should be (*lex ferenda*). The law-creating sources of international law are thus distinguished from other interpretative sources of international law.

Chapter 4, "Reconceptualising International Crimes", lays out a process for identifying the relevant crimes under international law, making use of the concept of international crimes. For historical, political, and legal reasons, the matter is extremely multifaceted and thus analytically complicated.

In domestic criminal law a primary source of law is legislation. This creates problems at the international level, since the space for international criminal legislation is limited, and some would even say non-existent from a strictly legal point of view. At the same time, within the UN paradigm of international law, there has always been an urgent need for universal crimes norms as well as mechanisms for their enforcement. This situation has created great legal tensions. Making it even more difficult from a systemic point of view, the principle of legality requires a clear legal basis before criminal liability under international law can be applied to any person. Before an international criminal court, the legality requirement is generally twofold: the court must have material jurisdiction over the subject matter based on its statutes, and the substantive criminal provisions of the statutes must be founded in already existing international law. In addition, the law must have been accessible and individual criminal liability foreseeable to potential perpetrators when the relevant acts were committed.

In practice, these problems have not prevented the effective operation of international criminal law and its gradual development in cases where action has been supported politically by states through the UN system. As we know, much progress has been made on this front in recent decades, particularly since the end of the Cold War, symbolised by the fall of the Berlin Wall in November 1989. The decisions of the United Nations Security Council to establish the International Criminal Tribunal for the former Yugoslavia (ICTY) in 1993 and the International Criminal Tribunal for Rwanda (ICTR) in 1994 were important and visible steps in that regard,[41] as was the establishment of the International Criminal Court by the Rome Statute in 1998.[42] Still, it is not at all clear why certain offences under international law gain recognition as international crimes, sometimes quite suddenly, whereas norms proscribing other kinds of serious offences do not attain the same level of international attention or legal status.

Chapter 4 accordingly surveys the concept of international crimes through the statutes of international courts, positions taken by the Inter-

---

[41] See UN Security Council Resolution 827 (1993), para. 2: "Decides hereby to establish an international tribunal for the sole purpose of prosecuting persons responsible for serious violations of international humanitarian law committed in the territory of the former Yugoslavia between 1 January 1991 and a date to be determined by the Security Council [...]"; and UN Security Council, Resolution 955 (1994), para 1: "Decides hereby [...] to establish an international tribunal for the sole purpose of prosecuting persons responsible for genocide and other serious violations of international humanitarian law committed in the territory of Rwanda and Rwandan citizens responsible for genocide and other such violations committed in the territory of neighbouring States, between 1 January 1994 and 31 December 1994 [...]".

[42] See Rome Statute, *supra* note 11.

national Law Commission over the last 60 years, and selected additional analyses of the concept in scholarly literature. In addition, it considers in detail a statement from the Nuremberg Tribunal in the Hostage Case and the new definition of aggression adopted by the Review Conference on the Rome Statute of the International Criminal Court, held in Kampala in 2010. International crimes are then classified on the basis of these empirical studies, making use of the universal crimes framework proposed. Towards the end of the chapter, a normative definition is offered, including both the generally 'necessary and sufficient conditions' of international crimes and an enumerative definition that lists the relevant crime types. The notion of a common gravity clause, applicable to all international or universal crimes, is introduced here. In conclusion, it is suggested that international crimes might usefully be reconceived as universal crimes.

Chapter 5, "Towards a Concept of Universal Crimes", summarises the results from the preceding analysis and proposes steps forward for the international community with respect to the concept of universal crimes. It notes the uncertain status of several crime types and advances the thesis that there is a need for a new conceptual framework for identification and evaluation of grave crimes in international law. The concept of universal crimes, the chapter contends, may fill this need. By emphasizing the notion of universality within the field of international criminal law, this concept may serve as a counterweight to fragmentation.

After a review of essential components of the universal crimes concept and related crime classifications, a theoretical definition of universal crimes is proposed, with clarification of its relationship to the legal definition of universal crimes. Two components of the legal concept of universal crimes are distinguished: the component of the underlying crimes (for example, killing or torture) and the component of a specific gravity clause. A distinction is also proposed between 'universal crime scenes', corresponding to the concrete parameters of the underlying acts of crime committed in real life, and 'universal crime scenarios', corresponding to the legally relevant context of those crimes. With regard to accountability for universal crimes, the theme of a later volume, it is suggested that the concept of universal crimes may allow for prosecutorial discretion as well as for alternative or complementary justice mechanisms to retributive justice.

The book concludes by calling for further clarification and academic inquiry into the concept of universal crimes as part of broader and better-informed public debate on the future direction of international criminal law. It suggests that developing a draft United Nations Declaration on Universal Crimes could be a useful instrument for these purposes.

2

Universal Crimes in Perspective

2.1. The Nature of Universal Crimes

2.1.1. Crimes, Criminal Law, and International Criminal Law

A typical dictionary definition of 'crime' is "an offence for which one may be punished by law".[1] Universal crimes obviously differ from common crimes in several ways. To begin with, they have different legal bases: universal crimes must have a foundation not only in law, but also in international law. One option for identifying these types of serious crimes for analysis would be to list those acts and kinds of conduct labelled as crimes in humanitarian treaties and statutes of international criminal tribunals. Although such an exercise might be practical, it would not explain why some crimes are on the list and others are not. A similar list could also be compiled based on whether certain behaviour is considered a crime under other sources of international law. In a later chapter, these approaches are used for the closely related concept of 'international crimes', resulting in enumeration and classification of such crimes.[2] This chapter, by contrast, takes a step back to consider the basic notions of a 'crime' and 'criminal law' and then seeks a rationale for the characterisation of some crimes as 'universal crimes'.

'Criminal law' is usually the name of a body of substantive rules designated by state institutions. How unlawful conduct is labelled by governments and judicial institutions has specific legal consequences. The use of the word 'crime' indicates not only that a certain act of behaviour would violate a rule, but also that formalised punishment is expected for such a violation.[3] In domestic law, 'criminal law' is thus usually taken as

---

[1] *Oxford Advanced Learner's Dictionary of Current English, Encyclopedic Edition*, Oxford University Press, Oxford, UK, 1992, s.v. 'crime'.

[2] See Chapter 4.

[3] At least under a liberal approach to the rule of law, criminal law is fundamentally act-based, as opposed to attitude-based or actor-based, in that it places the commission of a crime at the centre of inquiry. See George P. Fletcher, *The Grammar of Criminal Law: American, Comparative, and International*, vol. 1, *Foundations*, Oxford University Press, Oxford, UK, 2007, pp. 28–37.

the designation for a body of substantive rules formulated by the legislative body or bodies of a state to proscribe certain categories of conduct within its jurisdiction. The term also encompasses the more general principles for attributing criminal liability, as well as proportionality and concrete practices related to sentencing that have to be taken into account before a criminal act can be fairly translated into a particular sanction against the suspect. Substantive or material criminal law is often distinguished from criminal procedural law, which concerns rules related to the investigative phases and to the proceedings before national courts.

Since the birth of the nation-state, criminal law has often been considered a prerogative of state legislators and national criminal courts. The monopoly on enforcement of criminal law by public authorities has even been considered a defining feature of the national state, although forms of parallel 'traditional' justice based on local customs or minority-specific practices are known in several states. This prevailing image of criminal law as exclusively 'state justice' has, however, never been completely correct in a narrow sense. International and national principles of criminal jurisdiction have allowed for competing or overlapping state jurisdiction with regard to some crimes, and there has also been a long tradition of extradition treaties and other kinds of international cooperation among states for criminal law purposes. Especially after World War II, there have emerged some parts of criminal law which are primarily founded in international rather than national law.

Today, international criminal law (ICL) is an established part of public international law (hereafter, international law), although it is, according to Cassese, "a relatively new branch of international law' and 'still a very rudimentary branch of law".[4] ICL can, according to Werle, be said to encompass "all norms that establish, exclude or otherwise regulate responsibility for crimes under international law".[5] Norms regulating 'responsibility' would seem to correspond to international law in a substantive (material) sense, leaving out or placing less emphasis on pro-

---

[4] Antonio Cassese, *International Criminal Law*, Oxford University Press, Oxford, UK, 2003, pp. 16–17. The same characterisations are upheld in Antonio Cassese, *International Criminal Law*, 2nd ed., Oxford University Press, Oxford, UK, 2008, p. 4.

[5] Gerhard Werle, *Principles of International Criminal Law*, TMC Asser Press, The Hague, 2005, p. 25; upheld in Gerhard Werle, *Principles of International Criminal Law*, 2nd ed., TMC Asser Press, The Hague, 2009, p. 29.

cedural, jurisdictional, and institutional rules. Furthermore, this definition does not specify which substantive crimes are included.

The solution to the problem preferred by some authors has been to stipulate a shortlist of international crimes, typically war crimes, crimes against humanity, genocide, and the crime of aggression.[6] One reason for this approach might be the recognition that it remains controversial as to whether other crimes also involve direct individual responsibility under international law, and that the development of international law in that regard might still be in flux. It would thus seem almost impossible to draw further lines with sufficient precision in terms of *lex lata*, for example with regard to crimes such as terrorism, torture, piracy, and trafficking of narcotics or human beings. Chapter 4 of this book, however, argues that it is in fact possible to identify international crimes in much more detail.[7]

Despite the title of this chapter, the perspectives offered here are generally limited to the normative dimensions. The gruesome history of universal crimes committed over the centuries in various parts of the world is an indispensable part of the context, although beyond the scope of this text.

2.1.2. Preliminary Definition of Universal Crimes

This section sets forth a first definition of 'universal crimes' in order to explore certain ideas and facts about international criminal law. As noted earlier, 'universal crimes' is not a completely new expression in the literature, but it does not figure as a significant legal term, nor has it been analysed in depth.[8] It is simply too early, it seems, to find a meaningful descriptive definition, especially in common legal parlance.[9] This first definition is accordingly a stipulative definition, a normative definition of the language used in this book.

Later, after exploring the related concept of international crimes, a more comprehensive normative definition is also proposed.[10] Whether the

---

[6]   One example is Werle, 2009, p. 26, *supra* note 5. On different notions of international crimes in the literature, see Chapter 4, section 4.4.

[7]   See especially Chapter 4, section 4.9.

[8]   See Chapter 1, section 1.2.

[9]   On different kinds of definitions, see Chapter 4, section 4.8.1.

[10]   See Chapter 4, section 4.9.

concept of universal crimes can ultimately be defined theoretically as well remains to be seen. Such a theoretical definition could help us understand how the concept should be used in all cases. That is, just as a theoretical definition of 'justice' would not simply report usage of the word but would attempt to make a theoretical argument for a particular conception of justice, so too a theoretical definition of 'universal crimes' would elaborate a theoretical justification for a particular understanding of universal crimes.

At this stage of analysis, the need is for a working definition that can convey some of the key elements of the underlying notion of universal crimes. No legal conclusions are drawn in this chapter, and the legal justification for the concept of universal crimes in international law will only be clear following more detailed legal exposition later in this book, and, ultimately, from its use in practice.

The following, then, is a preliminary definition:

> 'Universal crimes' are certain identifiable acts that constitute grave breaches of rules of conduct; and that are committed, organised or tolerated by powerful actors; and that, according to contemporary international law, are punishable whenever and wherever they are committed; and that require prosecution and punishment through fair trials, or in special cases, some other kind of justice, somewhere at some point.

This definition is based on several criteria distinguishing universal crimes from other crimes, and it may not precisely match generally accepted shortlists of core international crimes or grave crimes. A significant feature of the proposed definition is the linking of grave breaches of rules of conduct to powerful actors, typically political or military leaders of a state or leaders of other powerful organisations in a society. This connection is also the reason that universal crimes are especially dangerous to many victims and to both small and large societies. While abuses of any list of human rights may serve as a list of the principal 'standard threats' to human dignity in a given era,[11] universal crimes can be considered to constitute 'extreme threats' to both individuals and communities.

---

[11] Compare Jack Donnelly, *Universal Human Rights in Theory and Practice*, 2nd ed., Cornell University Press, Ithaca, NY, 2003, p. 57 (with further reference to Henry Shue, *Basic Rights: Subsistence, Affluence, and U.S. Foreign Policy*, Princeton University Press, Princeton, NJ, 1980, pp. 29–34).

The subject matter of universal crimes may be part of a country's national criminal law and procedures. This is particularly relevant to the territorial state where the crime scene is located, to the states of perpetrators or victims, and to states operating under the doctrine of universal jurisdiction for prosecution of crimes committed by foreigners in a foreign land. However, even if these crimes are not incorporated into national law, the underlying justifications for including crimes in these categories are primarily and independently grounded in international law as such. As a point of departure, that means that the substantive norms proscribing the conduct can be derived from at least one of the legal sources capable of creating binding norms of international law, that is, treaties, customary law, the general principles of international law, and, more arguably, law-creating resolutions of the UN Security Council.[12]

2.1.3. Crimes that Shock Humanity and Civilised Societies

A philosophical starting point for identifying universal crimes is that some crimes are of such magnitude or gravity that they shock the consciousness of human beings wherever they live and regardless of their connection to the victims or to the place where the crimes were committed. The crimes might thus be considered 'universal' because they reflect a core of common moral perceptions and normative standards. The preamble to the Rome Statute of the International Criminal Court (ICC) refers to "atrocities that deeply shock the conscience of humanity".[13]

The notion of crimes that shock the consciousness of humanity is not based on empirical data collected and analysed by public opinion researchers or psychologists. But neither is it based only on moral and philosophical considerations. Rather, the language, however imprecise, reflects the reality of widely observed, strong psychological reactions to real events taking place in the modern world. Why such a vague phrase remains instrumental in shaping legal thinking on certain kinds of criminal behaviour may be hard to explain rationally, yet almost any rational person will intuitively understand why some crimes shock fellow human beings. It seems that there are fundamental common values ('community

---

[12] See Chapter 3, section 3.3.

[13] Rome Statute of the International Criminal Court (hereafter, Rome Statute), 17 July 1998, preamble, para. 2: "Mindful that during this century millions of children, women and men have been victims of unimaginable atrocities that deeply shock the conscience of humanity [...]".

values') that many people intuitively and/or intellectually are able to identify, at least in the sense that they understand when such a value is being totally ignored or crushed.

In a broad sense, it might be best to use the phrase 'crimes against humanity' for these crimes to make clear that the concept is not primarily based on evidence or assumptions as to what may shock human beings around the globe. But since the concept of 'crimes against humanity' is used in legal discourse with a more restricted meaning, it seems better to opt for the phrases 'crimes that shock humanity' and 'crimes that shock civilised societies' – the former understood as referring to common human reactions, and the latter as referring to societies in which collective memories and common notions of grave criminal behaviour have been shaped by the rule of law and internalised in social, legal, and moral norms. The ability of individuals and communities to be shocked by grave crimes, regardless of the nationality of the perpetrators or their victims, and then to demand that justice be served in fair proceedings, may be considered in some senses as a defining characteristic of true civilisation. The term 'civilised' in international law, it should be noted, has no direct connection to any specific religion or alleged superior culture, nor to any particular stage of economic development. While the phrases suggested above may be too vague at the operational level to serve as a characterisation of unlawful conduct for criminal law purposes, they may provide a general philosophical guide. That is, they highlight the fact that grave crimes inherently violate common human values and the fundamental interests of society. The ICC Rome Statute, for example, asserts "that such grave crimes threaten the peace, security and well-being of the world".[14] As a result, certain crimes can provoke diplomatic reactions or other international actions when they go unpunished.

2.2. Universal Crimes in a Normative and Political Context

2.2.1. Respecting Human Dignity through Criminal Liability

International law for a long time failed to seriously address the issue of criminal liability. Inter-state relations, as well as jurisdiction over individuals not part of a state's leadership, were in general considered prerogatives of nation-states for the purpose of international law. Attempts

---

[14] Rome Statute, preamble, para. 3, *supra* note 13.

were made after World War I, especially under the auspices of the League of Nations, to provide protection to minorities, stateless persons, and refugees by means of treaties and other international measures, but these efforts were often ineffective and did not fundamentally change the structure of international law.

Despite occasional diplomatic criticism of crimes committed or tolerated by governments, such as Turkey's crimes against the Armenians, international law had little to offer. It has even been claimed that Hitler's observation of the impunity for the Armenian massacres bolstered his confidence in proceeding with the Holocaust.[15] The Treaty of Versailles in Article 227 provides for a special criminal tribunal to try the former German emperor, William II of Hohenzollern, for "a supreme offence against international morality and the sanctity of treaties".[16] But the tribunal was never established, apparently because the Netherlands refused to extradite the Kaiser on the grounds that the offence charged was unknown in Dutch law[17] and thus constituted retroactive criminal law.[18] Articles 228–229 of the same treaty provided that other persons accused of "acts in violation of the laws and customs of war" could be brought before the military tribunals of the state to which the victims belonged, but only when the acts were committed "against the nationals of one of the Allied and Associated Powers". These clauses were not used, but a limited number of Germans were tried by German courts.[19] The Treaty of Sevres, in 1920, also envisaged prosecutions of persons accused of having committed acts contrary to the laws and customs of war (Articles 227 and 229), and it even required Turkey to extradite persons "responsible for the massacres committed" (Article 230).[20] This treaty, however, was never formally adopted.

---

[15] See Alexander Orakhelashvili, *Peremptory Norms in International Law*, Oxford University Press, Oxford, UK, 2008, p. 576.

[16] Versailles Treaty of 28 June 1919.

[17] See Alan Boyle and Christine Chinkin, *The Making of International Law*, Oxford University Press, Oxford, UK, 2007, p. 11; Ellen L. Lutz, "Prosecutions of Heads of State in Europe", in Ellen L. Lutz and Caitlin Reiger (eds.), *Prosecuting Heads of State*, Cambridge University Press, Cambridge, UK, 2009, pp. 25–26.

[18] See William A. Schabas, *The International Criminal Court: A Commentary on the Rome Statute*, Oxford University Press, Oxford, UK, 2010, p. 2.

[19] *Ibid.*, pp. 2–3.

[20] Peace Treaty of Sevres of 10 August 1920.

Arguably, the most important contribution in defining proscribed conduct in the classic inter-state period of international law was made within the field of peace initiatives, humanitarian protection, and aid to victims during war. This work, which started with the founding of the International Red Cross in 1864, resulted in several conventions, including the Convention for the Pacific Settlement of International Disputes and Convention (IV) Respecting the Laws and Customs of War on Land, both adopted by a conference of plenipotentiaries at The Hague in 1907. The famous Martens Clause was first introduced in the preamble to the 1899 Hague Convention and was included in slightly different form in the 1907 Convention Respecting the Laws and Customs of War on Land. It suggests that, in addition to the regulations adopted, there may exist "the protection and empire of the principles of international law, as they result from the usages established between civilized nations, from the laws of humanity and the requirements of the public conscience". Whatever its legal effects,[21] the Martens Clause constituted a significant pointer towards what the goal of international criminal law should be.

It was only after World War II, however, that the protection of human rights and the demands of justice were expressly formulated by the United Nations as aspirations of the new world organisation and as desired components of international law. Today it is fair to conclude that we are at the end of a long period of development which has culminated in broad international consensus on the value of a real possibility for all human beings to lead a dignified life, that is, a life worthy of a human being in a contemporary society.

The best expression of this consensus is the success of the human rights movement in defining international norms. It is now widely recognised that internationally agreed human rights, based on a moral vision of human nature, should set the limits and requirements of social action, especially by state institutions. Human rights are at once a utopian ideal and a realistic prescription for political and legal practices that uphold the ideal of human dignity. As the American author Donnelly has succinctly pointed out, human rights can be seen as a self-fulfilling moral prophecy: "Treat people like human beings – see attached list – and you will get

---

[21] The interpretation of the Martens Clause has been disputed. See, *e.g.*, Rupert Ticehurst, "The Martens Clause and the Laws of Armed Conflict", *International Review of the Red Cross*, no. 317, 1997, pp. 125–134.

truly human beings".[22] In effect, if taken seriously, human rights promote a particular model of human dignity within the modern state, in essence a liberal or democratic state based on the rule of law and on viable institutions that serve the rule of law. The model implies social and legal changes (or preservation of the necessary structures) in order to strike a balance between individual freedom and the interests of societies writ large. This in turn requires continuously pursuing enumerated human rights, including freedom of political and religious expression, division of state power, accountability for leaders and remedies for serious violation of human rights, independent courts, enforcement of equality and non-discrimination, special protection of minorities and vulnerable groups, and, realistically speaking, principles of fair and representative participation in political processes and conditioned majority rule. Most governments of the world have now accepted human rights in principle, if not necessarily the full consequences for political and legal systems.

The corollary of this line of thought is that blatant disrespect for human rights generally, or for the complementary humanitarian rules of conduct during armed conflicts, is deemed to create conditions which are an affront to human dignity and which increase the risk of multiple chain reactions of inhuman behaviour and, possibly, universal crimes. In some cases, violent conflict might follow a criminal conspiracy or denial of justice to victims of grave crimes at the national level. Experience has shown that international peace and security, as well as the preconditions for national reconciliation, may be threatened in situations where respect for human dignity is seriously undermined by governments or violent groups. The UN General Assembly and Security Council have affirmed this on several occasions. Likewise, the preamble to the ICC Rome Statute claims – as already mentioned – that grave crimes threaten the peace, security, and well-being of the world. The fight against impunity for grave crimes is thus not just an important human rights issue for victim groups and the society at large, but also an essential component of the modern development of international relations more generally and a driving force behind the renewed interest in ICL since the early 1990s.[23]

The needs for effective prevention and suppression of certain crimes and for promotion of respect for victim groups through mech-

---

[22] Donnelly, 2003, p. 15, *supra* note 11.

[23] Rome Statute, preamble, para. 5, *supra* note 13. The states parties affirm their determination "to put an end to impunity for the perpetrators of these crimes".

anisms of truth seeking and justice will undoubtedly raise sensitive questions for powerful states and for decision makers in peace processes. What must be understood, and increasingly seems to have been understood by the international community, is the close relationship between acceptance of the inherent dignity of human beings and protection of human rights, on the one hand, and the development of peaceful societies, on the other. One may see the contours of an emerging international consensus: to preserve the dignity of human beings in the contemporary world requires both widespread respect for human rights and humanitarian standards and relentless enforcement of responsibility for serious violations of the same norms. This is particularly the case when these crimes are committed by powerful leaders, because of the great dangers such criminality entails.

Echoing Donnelly's assertion, one could say that criminal liability for universal crimes can be seen as a self-fulfilling prophecy: "Treat leaders and others as human beings responsible for their participation in universal crimes – see attached definition – and you will get truly responsible leaders and societies".

2.2.2.   The Rule of Law and Accountability for Leaders and Others

The concept of 'rule of law' or '*Das Rechtsstaatsprinzip*' has many interpretations; there is no generally agreed definition. The principal contrasting views are the formal and substantive approaches. A strict formal definition focuses only upon the formal aspects of law: the law must be prospective, well known, and have the characteristics of generality and certainty. Such a formal approach allows laws to protect deliberative democracy, equality, and individual rights, but it does not require any additional substantive features of the law, including provision for fair procedures. A substantive definition holds that, in addition, the rule of law must include equal protection and application of the law, certain procedural and institutional safeguards, and due respect for fundamental human rights. However, there is no single, clear-cut distinction between the two approaches, as some proponents of a formal definition may include requirements of equal protection and even basic procedural guarantees.

Whether a substantive definition also requires a democratic constitutional framework in the sense of a 'majoritarian' political system at the level of the national state is debatable, since in some contexts such a requirement might raise constitutional and highly politicised issues.[24] The relationship between the rule of law and democracy also allows for different uses of terminology. For instance, in the Norwegian language, the solution has been to use the expression '*demokratisk rettsstat*', analogous to the German '*democratische rechtsstaat*', but this expression is difficult to translate properly into English without resorting to a hybrid expression ('democratic *Rechtsstaat*') or a literal construct ('democratic law state'). The advantage of the Germanic formula is that it keeps the two concepts, rule of law and democracy, separate yet closely connected, making it suitable for analytical, descriptive, and argumentative purposes.

In this book, the focus is not on the possible relationships between democracy and the rule of law but rather on the substantive rule of law concept. In the opinion of the author, a substantive rule of law notion is to some degree inherent in contemporary international law and can probably be derived as a general principle of international law, although its exact meaning and field of application – as well as its status as 'hard' or 'soft' law – remain open for discussion.

Historically, the concept of rule of law dates back to the Greek philosophers such as Aristotle and Plato.[25] An important feature of the idea of a state based on law, as highlighted by Aristotle, was that law should govern and that those in power should be servants of the law. This implied that even members of the government might be held accountable for breaking the law, a feature which is inherent in the substantive but not the formal definition of rule of law. Since the times of the American Revolution in 1776, the notion that no one is above the law has gained international popularity, especially during the twentieth century.[26] In the Nuremberg Judgment after World War II, this particular element was

---

[24] Consider, *e.g.,* the discussion and affirmative answer by Roberto Gargarella, "The Majoritarian Reading of the Rule of Law", in José María Maravall and Adam Prze-worski (eds.), *Democracy and the Rule of Law*, Cambridge University Press, Cambridge, UK, 2003, pp. 147–167.

[25] See, *e.g.*, references to Aristotle, *Politics*, and to Plato, *Laws*, in Ronald A. Cass, *The Rule of Law in America*, Johns Hopkins University Press, Baltimore, MD, 2001, p. 1.

[26] In the United States the perception persists that no one is above the law, "as can be found in the discourse attending the impeachment of President William Clinton as the sands ran out on the twentieth century". Cass, 2001, p. xii., *supra* note 25.

fully endorsed by the Tribunal and contrasted to the dreadful consequences of the '*Führerprinzip*'.[27]

At the London conference leading up to the Nuremberg Charter in 1945, Justice Robert H. Jackson, head of the American delegation and later prosecutor at the Nuremberg trials, underscored another important point. In order to satisfy the requirement of 'law', the definition of international crimes must be universally applicable and thus independent of the nationality, religion, political opinion, or other personal status of the perpetrator. This requirement does not necessarily imply that the crimes committed are universally enforced at a given point in time, because the jurisdiction of courts raises other institutional and prosecutorial issues. In a formal note, Jackson argued successfully in favour of general substantive laws to be applied at Nuremberg:

> The Jurisdiction of this Tribunal, of course, is limited to trial of those of the European Axis Powers. The definition of a crime cannot, however, be made to depend on which nation commits the act. I am not willing to charge as a crime against a German official acts which would not be crimes if committed by officials of the United States. I think no one will respect any conviction that rests on such a legal foundation.[28]

This particular notion of legality as generality is fundamental to equality and the rule of law in international affairs, and it should be kept separate from the formal legality requirements of a clear legal basis and prohibition of *ex post facto* laws.[29] Generality is thus an obvious and necessary feature of universal crimes norms.

---

[27] According to the *Führerprinzip* (*Führer* principle) "power was to reside in a Führer from whom sub-leaders were to derive authority in a hierarchical order, each sub-leader to owe unconditional obedience to his immediate superior but to be absolute in his own sphere of jurisdiction; and the power of the leadership was to be unlimited, extending to all phases of public and private life". International Military Tribunal (IMT), *Trial of the Major War Criminals before the International Military Tribunal: Nuremberg, 14 November 1945 – 1 October 1946*, Nuremberg, 1947 (hereafter, *Trial of the Major War Criminals*), vol. I, p. 31.

[28] Robert H. Jackson (United States Representative to the International Conference on Military Trials, London, 31 July 1945), *Notes on Proposed Definition of 'Crimes'*, 1945, published by the Avalon Project of Yale University Law School, available at http://avalon.law.yale.edu/imt/imtconst.asp, last accessed 8 June 2011.

[29] On the international legality principle, see Chapter 3, sections 3.3.2 and 3.3.4.

Although the rule of law concept has most frequently been discussed in relation to the internal affairs of states, it is also of great relevance to contemporary international affairs. The moral purpose of the United Nations was to promote the rule of law in international relations, viewed against the background of World War II and the associated history of barbarism.[30] This fact has significant legal repercussions because of the actual construction of the UN and its goals as stated in the UN Charter. A simple definition of 'rule of law' does not exist and might never be generally agreed, given the distinction between formal and substantive views. It is a difficult concept since it involves elements derived from a variety of sources, including legal philosophy, political science, constitutional theory, international law, and historical experiences. Nevertheless, some key elements of a substantive rule of law concept can be identified.

As an operational definition, useful for an assessment of the quality of particular legal institutions and norms ('legal regimes'), the five elements suggested by Brownlie constitute a robust platform:

1) Powers exercised by officials must be based upon authority conferred by law.

2) The law itself must conform to certain standards of justice, both substantial and procedural.

3) There must be a substantial separation of powers between the executive, the legislature and the judicial function [...].

4) The judiciary should not be subject to the control of the executive.

5) All legal persons are subject to rules of law, which are applied on the basis of equality.[31]

To those elements Brownlie adds the following: "the Rule of Law implies the absence of wide discretionary powers in the Government which may encroach on personal liberty, rights of property or freedom of contract".[32] Whether this 'practical concept'[33] suggested by Brownlie fully

---

[30] Ian Brownlie, *The Rule of Law in International Affairs*: *International Law at the Fiftieth Anniversary of the United Nations*, Kluwer Law International, Alphen aan den Rijn, Netherlands, 1998, p. 1.

[31] *Ibid.*, pp. 213–214. Although not discussed explicitly by Brownlie, the features suggested imply a substantive rule of law definition.

[32] *Ibid.*, p. 214.

[33] *Ibid.*, p. 213.

corresponds with the normative definition as grounded in general principles of international law is perhaps debatable, especially with regard to the requirement of "a substantial separation of powers" (element 3). In international law, at least, there is no general legislature, no general executive branch, and no court with general jurisdiction. The primarily horizontal structure of international law puts states at the forefront. Most legal norms have traditionally been – and still are – created by means of treaties made, and customs developed, among states. However, the rise of international institutions in the twentieth century and the subsequent emergence of special ('self-contained') regimes[34] challenges the perception of international law as a collection of rules and principles that only further more or less arbitrary state interests and would be distinct in this respect from a modern domestic legal system.[35]

For analytical and evaluative purposes, one should distinguish between the subjects of a normative 'rule of law' definition and the obligations attached to it. Are the subjects only the national legal regimes, as represented by individual states, or are other actors in the international legal order included as well, most notably the UN regime? The scope of the definition presented by Brownlie may not be absolutely clear in this respect, although it follows from the rest of his book that he also deems the concept relevant to international law as a legal system, with its various special regimes. This seems logical: if a normative, substantive definition of 'rule of law' applies to an analysis and evaluation of the legal frameworks of states, why should not the same standard also apply in principle to the framework of the international legal order?

As already suggested, it is clear that a system of generally competent and accountable executive, legislative, and judicial institutions has never been fully implemented at the international level – not even

---

[34] "A group of rules and principles concerned with a particular subject matter may form a special regime ('Self-contained regime') and be applicable as *lex specialis*. Such special regimes often have their own institutions to administer the relevant rules". International Law Commission (ILC), *Conclusions of the Work of the Study Group on Fragmentation of International Law: Difficulties Arising from the Diversification and Expansion of International Law*, 2006, conclusion no. 11, reprinted in *Yearbook of the International Law Commission, 2006*, vol. II, part II.

[35] *Ibid.*, conclusion no. 1. "International law is a legal system. Its rules and principles (*i.e.* its norms) act in relation to and should be interpreted against the background of other rules and principles. As a legal system, international law is not a random collection of such norms".

within the UN. That would in fact require something like a federal world state. To the contrary, the decentralised and fragmented nature of international law has often been noted, although that is not the full picture either. However, the difference between the system of international law and the legal system of a state should not imply wholly different standards for the rule of law. Rather, this difference can be accommodated through specific modifications at the international level to fit the present structures of international law.

This is the case, for example, with respect to the principle of legality, which is a necessary component of any formal or substantive notion of the rule of law. This principle is inherent in the second requirement proposed by Brownlie, that the law itself must conform to certain standards of justice. The question is whether modifications of the requirements of prior legislative notification and foreseeability, which are common in national criminal laws adhering to the rule of law, and indeed part of human rights law as well, are necessary and justified in inter-national criminal law to the same extent, perhaps especially with regard to universal crimes. Since international law, like any other living body of law, is not static, one possibility is that in recent years the principle of legality has moved more to the centre of international criminal law, thus reducing the possible differences between the substantive content of the rule of law at the international and national levels.

With the success of international criminal law as an enterprise, the need for strict enforcement of legality increases rather than decreases. Furthermore, "retroactive crime creation [...] is dangerous, and fortunately, incompatible with international law as it now stands".[36] Although this may at first sound convincing and straightforward, the complexity of international law making and its law-creating sources raises several questions, most notably the requirements for creation of a new crime under international law. For instance, is there a core of universal crimes embodied independently in the general principles of law, which could serve as a legal basis already containing existing universal crimes norms that states, or even the UN Security Council, may lawfully utilise when an international criminal court is being established or when states choose to *implement* international criminal law retroactively in domestic

---

[36] Kenneth S. Gallant, *The Principle of Legality in International and Comparative Criminal Law*, Cambridge University Press, Cambridge, UK, 2009, p. 405.

proceedings? If so, the distinction between unreasonable retroactive law creation, which is prohibited, and retroactive law enforcement, which is permissible, may need further clarification.[37]

The substantive rule of law notion requires fairness in all respects, in particular with respect to severe punishment. This may assist in the evaluation of the effectiveness of the legality principle. Doubts have been raised, for example, as to whether the legality principle has served as a guarantee of 'fair labelling' in criminal proceedings before international courts. The question, in other words, is whether descriptions of the alleged crimes and modes of participation – supposed to match the actual behaviour and criminal intent of the suspects – have always been made sufficiently clear in the indictments and judgments.[38] The problem may stem in part from the origin of the legality principle in constitutional law. For historic reasons, it has primarily been concerned with division of powers and due process rights of individuals who commit common crimes and who are prosecuted in the clear interest of the state, usually the state where the crime has been committed. With regard to universal crimes, the situation is different because a deliberate decision by the state to allow impunity is often a real risk following such crimes. As noted by Drumbl, "the apparatus of the state often encourages, coordinates, or even compels extraordinary international crimes".[39] It is thus not obvious that a unifying theory of strict legality, encompassing legality for both international crimes and ordinary common crimes, is possible and desirable.[40] That is, the special features of universal crimes must be taken into account if a fair balance is to be struck between the interests of the victims and the fundamental value of a sense of justice, on the one hand, and the interests of the suspects and the fundamental value of legality, on the other. For example, does the nature of mass atrocity sometimes justify a less technical approach to prosecution, for instance with regard to the specific labelling of a particular mode of participation in the indictment or the

---

[37] See Chapter 5, section 5.3.

[38] See Heikelina Verrijn Stuart, "Int'l Criminal Justice under Pressure", *International Justice Tribune*, May 5, 2010, no. 105, p. 1, available at http://sites.rnw.nl/pdf/ijt/IJT 105.pdf, last accessed 8 June 2011.

[39] Mark A. Drumbl, "The Principle of Legality in International and Comparative Criminal Law, by Kenneth S. Gallant, Book Review", in *Human Rights Quarterly*, August 2009, vol. 31, no. 3, pp. 801–806, p. 804.

[40] *Ibid.*, p. 805.

verdict? How to apply the principle of legality is thus important to this work, and the question of its weight or impact naturally arises as a problematic issue.[41]

For this project, the most important aspect of the rule of law definition proposed by Brownlie is point (5): all legal persons (including natural persons) are subject to rules of law applied on the basis of equality. Accountability of political and military leaders, with effective and fair 'head of state trials' as symbols of that accountability, is considered both a part of and a vehicle for strengthening the rule of law.[42] The 'accountability principle' implies that every person is held responsible in criminal matters, regardless of the *de jure* or *de facto* position of the suspect in society. Enforcement on this basis now seems to be spreading around the globe; one study showed that between January 1990 and May 2008, 67 heads of state or government from 43 countries had been formally charged with or indicted for serious criminal offences (32 defendants from Latin America, 16 from Africa, 10 from Europe, seven from Asia, and two from the Middle East).[43] The cases were almost evenly divided between human rights and corruption cases. Among the former, several cases seem to have concerned possible 'universal crimes'. If conducted transparently and in a way that inspires the general population's confidence in the process, head of state trials can contribute to ending pervasive traditions of impunity and demonstrate that no one is above the law, no matter how far up the political or military chain of command the individual might be.[44]

The accountability principle is of paramount legal and practical importance because political, military, and other leaders within a society are often involved in the planning and directing of complex universal crimes. The most senior leaders are, in many cases, the ones most responsible for the crimes. Therefore, accountability for leaders seems to be a necessary component of a normative concept of the rule of law, and having a rule of law framework in place appears a necessary condition for actually holding leaders accountable. This is, of course, implicitly recognised in constitutional law. More importantly, prosecutions before international (and internationalised) criminal tribunals since Nuremberg

---

[41] See Chapter 3, sections 3.3.2 and 3.3.4.
[42] See, *e.g.*, Lutz and Reiger, 2009, pp. 285 and 291, *supra* note 17.
[43] *Ibid.*, p. 12.
[44] *Ibid.*, p. 285.

and Tokyo have focused consistently, even if not exclusively, on the leaders alleged to be responsible.[45] With respect to the International Criminal Tribunal for the former Yugoslavia (ICTY) and the International Criminal Tribunal for Rwanda (ICTR), the UN Security Council at one point explicitly reminded the prosecutors at the tribunals "in reviewing and confirming any new indictments, to ensure that any such indictments concentrate on the most senior leaders suspected of being most responsible for crimes within the jurisdiction of the relevant Tribunal as set out in resolution 1503 (2003)".[46] Other examples include, but are not limited to, the trial of the former president of the Republic of Liberia, Charles Taylor, before the Special Court for Sierra Leone[47]; the arrest warrant by the ICC for the president of the Republic of Sudan, Omar al-Bashir[48]; and

---

[45] See, *e.g.*, IMT, *Trial of the Major War Criminals*, 1947, vol. I, p. 29, *supra* note 27: "All the defendants, with divers other persons, during a period of years preceding 8 May 1945, participated as leaders, organizers, instigators, or accomplices in the formulation or execution of a common plan or conspiracy to commit, or which involved the commission of, Crimes against Peace, War Crimes, and Crimes against Humanity". Also see International Military Tribunal for the Far East, *Araki et al.*, Judgment, 12 November 1948 (Annex 6 Indictment, Count 1, first sentence), p. 32: "All the Defendants together with divers other persons, between the 1st January, 1928 and the 2nd September, 1945, participated as leaders, organizers, instigators, or accomplices in the formulation or execution of a common plan or conspiracy, and are responsible for all acts performed by themselves or by any other person in execution of such plan".

[46] UN Security Council Resolution 1534 (2004), para. 5.

[47] Special Court for Sierra Leone (SCSL), *Prosecutor v. Taylor*, SCSL-03-01-PT, Prosecution's Second Amended Indictment, 29 May 2007. As of 1 July 2011, the prosecutor and the defence had submitted final trial briefs. See *Prosecutor v. Taylor*, SCSL-03-01-T, Prosecution Final Trial Brief, 8 April 2011, and Defence Final Trial Brief, 23 May 2011 (pleading not guilty on all accounts; see conclusion at p. 560).

[48] International Criminal Court (ICC), Pre-Trial Chamber I, Situation in Darfur, Sudan, *Decision on the Prosecution's Application for a Warrant of Arrest against Omar Hassan Ahmad Al Bashir*, Warrant of Arrest for Omar Hassan Ahmad Al Bashir, ICC-02/05-01/09, 4 March 2009. The Pre-Trial Chamber confirmed reasonable grounds to believe that the accused was criminally responsible for war crimes and crimes against humanity. See also ICC, Pre-Trial Chamber I, Situation in Darfur, Sudan, *Case of the Prosecutor v. Omar Hassan Ahmad Al Bashir ("Omar Al Bashir")*, Second Warrant of Arrest for Omar Hassan Ahmad Al Bashir, ICC-02/05-01/09, 12 July 2010. The Pre-Trial Chamber confirmed reasonable grounds to believe that the accused is also criminally responsible for genocide by killing, genocide by causing serious bodily or mental harm, and genocide by deliberately inflicting conditions of life calculated to bring about physical destruction (pp. 8–9).

---

the ICC arrest warrants for Muammar Gaddafi and two alleged co-perpetrators among the Libyan leadership.[49]

Practical legal issues, such as the responsibility of heads of state and the labelling of unlawful participation in universal crimes, are thus closely connected to a concept of the rule of law and to the accountability principle. On the other hand, most punishable participants are in fact intermediate leaders and low-level personnel, who in fact may never be charged with universal crimes, at least not before an international tribunal such as the ICC. This may pose the risk that a criminal law perspective from 'below' might be somewhat overlooked in the current and future literature on international criminal law, if it is not taken into account that international criminal law increasingly is being implemented by states domestically. Rikhof highlights the facts that "43 countries have become involved in the prosecutions of perpetrators of international crimes in the last 15 years" and that "more than 10,000 perpetrators have been brought to justice in such countries compared to 145 persons convicted by the five international institutions".[50] What might be even more surprising to many international criminal lawyers, however, is the extent to which immigration law and international refugee law (see, *inter alia*, the 1951 Refugee Convention, Article 1F), are being utilised in refugee law and practice to address many issues of war crimes and other international crimes in the context of national exclusion procedures. In a number of articles, Rikhof has addressed this point as well.[51] In many such cases, therefore, ICL is

---

[49] ICC, Pre-Trial Chamber I, Situation in the Libyan Arab Jamahiriya, *Decision on the Prosecutor's Application Pursuant to Article 58 as to Muammar Mohammed Abu Minyar Gaddafi, Seif Al-Islam Gaddafi and Abdullah Al-Senussi*, ICC-01/11, 27 June 2011. The Pre-Trial Chamber found reasonable grounds to believe that crimes against humanity had been committed and that the accused were criminally responsible.

[50] Joseph Rikhof, "Fewer Places to Hide? The Impact of Domestic War Crimes Prosecutions on International Impunity", in Morten Bergsmo (ed.), *Complementarity and the Exercise of Universal Jurisdiction for Core International Crimes*, FICHL Publication Series No. 7, Torkel Opsahl Academic Epublisher, Oslo, 2010, p. 80. Not included in the figures are the approximately 60,000 persons tried outside regular criminal courts in Rwanda, in the specialised *gacaca* proceedings (p. 44).

[51] See, *e.g.*, Joseph Rikhof, "War Criminals Not Welcome: How Common Law Countries Approach the Phenomenon of International Crimes in the Immigration and Refugee Context", in *International Journal of Refugee Law*, 2009, vol. 21, no. 3, pp. 453–507. See also Joseph Rikhof, *Exclusion at a Crossroads: The Interplay between International Criminal Law and Refugee Law in the Area of Extended Liability*, UN-

being applied to suspected low-level perpetrators and accomplices, often focusing on ways and means of participation other than those featured in the trials of political and military leaders at international tribunals. Such a complementary perspective, taking into account participants below the ranks of high-level leaders, is also needed to conceptualise the full extent of punishable participation in universal crimes and the potential reach of ICL.[52]

There are important connections between the concept of the rule of law as explained above and the legal frameworks for the prosecution of universal crimes. On the one hand, systematic impunity for such crimes may lead to a lower score on any rule of law index. On the other hand, accountability for such crimes, especially in relation to leaders and others bearing the greatest responsibility, has the potential to uphold and further develop the rule of law in international affairs. Upon closer examination, the issue becomes quite complex. A further assessment depends on a number of factors, including how the regime of international criminal law is conceived by state actors and is developed over time by the main stakeholders in the field. At this point it is sufficient to stress that such a relationship does exist, and that the strengthening or weakening of respect for the rule of law will probably affect the extent to which the most responsible persons are held accountable.

2.2.3. The United Nations Paradigm of International Law

The subject of universal crimes cannot be considered without due recognition of the particular legal order constituted by the UN. Although state actors will ultimately decide the future of international law, the UN plays an important role, not only as a subject of international law but as an institution defining a distinct legal order intertwined with international law. At the very least, the UN provides an organised framework for dis-cussions and decision-making in this field. During most of the classical inter-state period of international law before World War II, governments considered the issue of accountability for criminal acts to concern only the internal affairs of states or the legal relationship between sovereign states.

HCR Legal and Protection Policy Research Series, no. 22, June 2011, available at http://www.unhcr.org/pages/4d22f95f6.html, last accessed 1 August 2011.

[52] See preface to this book.

Formally established by the Charter of the United Nations of 26 June 1945, the UN through its powers, norm setting, and institutions was designed to substantially change international law and relations, especially in order to "save future generations from the scourge of war" and "maintain international peace and security".[53] Its founding documents confirmed faith in "fundamental human rights" and "the dignity and worth of the human person", as well as in "the equal rights of men and women and of nations large and small".[54] Another explicit goal of the UN was to "establish conditions under which justice and respect for obligations arising from treaties and other sources of international law can be maintained".[55]

The organisation was shaped by the experience of World War II (1939–1945), including flagrant breaches of the peace, terrible war crimes and crimes against humanity committed especially by the Hitler and Hirohito regimes, and the hard-won defeat of the Nazis and their partners. 'Never again' was not only a slogan: it was undoubtedly meant seriously by many of the founders of the new world organisation. Despite its shortcomings, the UN has to a large extent remained the dominant 'social paradigm' of international and human affairs that it was meant to be. The UN is based on a specific set of experiences, institutional beliefs, and values that affect the way state governments, the media, non-governmental organisations (NGOs), and ordinary people from every part of the world perceive internationally relevant events and respond to those perceptions. The UN paradigm has not been challenged seriously by competing international legal orders with conflicting interests and purposes. The UN Charter has been universally accepted by states, and Article 103 of the UN Charter determines that in the event of "a conflict between the obligations [of member states] under the present Charter and their obligations under any other international agreement, their obligations under the present Charter shall prevail". Any rule nominally applicable to

---

[53] See UN Charter preamble. Also consider, *e.g.*, Article 1(1) and 1(2), Article 2(4), and Articles 39–51.

[54] *Ibid.* Also consider Article 1(3), Article 13(1)(b), and Article 55(c).

[55] *Ibid.* Also consider Article 1(1): "to bring about by peaceful means, and in conformity with the principles of justice and international law, [...] settlement of international disputes or situations which might lead to a breach of the peace".

a UN member state which is incompatible with its UN obligations thus becomes inapplicable and void to the extent of such incompatibility.[56]

In short, the UN has become the dominant system for promoting human rights, social and legal justice, and peace and security at a global (universal) level, relevant to all states and peoples. It does not follow, as we know, that the targets have been met or that the UN is necessarily an effective organisation. Neither can one contend that the UN is an independent political and physical power comparable with a major state, or that international relations have been totally transformed since the founding of the UN.[57] One should also note that the UN does not exist in isolation from the world it is attempting to serve, including sovereign states, which remain the fundamental units of international law.[58]

Rather, the UN paradigm consists of a comprehensive mix of political, diplomatic, bureaucratic, and moral frameworks, primarily for the attempted exercise of concerted state powers. The intention is to enable states to solve problems which reach beyond national borders and which immediately, or in the long term, may threaten international peace and security, as well as, it might be added, social progress and the rule of law. There is no competing paradigm of relevance to international law at the global level, and no states have found it in their interest to refuse to acknowledge this social, political, and legal reality – not even the world's greatest powers, including the United States. In principle, this paradigm requires cooperation for progress in all fields concerned with fundamental common international interests and values. It is thus interesting that the Obama administration has recently recognised openly that a similar 'strategic wisdom' applies both historically and to the challenges ahead.[59]

---

[56] See, *e.g.*, ILC, 2006, conclusions nos. 41–42, *supra* note 34.

[57] See Thomas G. Weiss and Sam Daws, "World Politics: Continuity and Change since 1945", in Thomas G. Weiss and Sam Daws (eds.), *The Oxford Handbook on the United Nations*, Oxford University Press, Oxford, UK, 2008, p. 4.

[58] *Ibid.*

[59] White House, "National Security Strategy", Washington, DC, May 2010, pp. 12–13, 40, and 46–48, available at http://www.whitehouse.gov/sites/default/files/rss_viewer/national_security_strategy.pdf, last accessed 8 June 2011. Looking to the past: "We succeeded in the post-World War II era by pursuing our interests within multilateral forums like the United Nations – not outside of them. […] Indeed, the basis for international cooperation since World War II has been an architecture of international institutions, organizations, regimes, and standards that establishes certain rights and responsibilities for all sovereign nations" (pp. 12–13). Looking to the future: "In recent

While many observers have proposed reforms in some parts of existing UN structures, they have not suggested abandonment of the fundamental UN paradigm of international law. This project only considers such reforms as might be directly relevant to normative clarification of international crimes[60] or to the implementation of accountability for universal crimes.[61] But it is important to stress that it is only within the existing UN paradigm of international law that the subject matter of universal crimes in international law can be properly understood.

Although the full potential of the UN with respect to peace, justice, and human rights has never been realised,[62] the achievements under its auspices over the last 65 years have no doubt been substantial in many fields. Already in the early years, there was a promising start on a two-pronged platform for enhancing universal human dignity through the international promotion of human rights, on the one hand, and accountability for violations rising to the level of crimes that shock civilised societies, on the other. The two pillars were built simultaneously as the UN came into existence.

The first attempts to set up international criminal tribunals date to the aftermath of World War I.[63] But it was not until after World War II that the idea materialised in the form of the Nuremberg and Tokyo Tribunals to judge the grave crimes committed by the Nazis in Europe

---

years America's frustration with international institutions has led us at times to engage the United Nations (U.N.) system on an ad hoc basis. But in a world of transnational challenges, the United States will need to invest in strengthening the international system, working from inside international institutions and frameworks to face their imperfections head on and to mobilize transnational cooperation" (p. 13). "We need a U.N. capable of fulfilling its founding purpose - maintaining international peace and security, promoting global cooperation, and advancing human rights. To this end, we are paying our bills" (p. 46).

[60] See Chapter 5, section 5.3.

[61] See preface to this book.

[62] For a blunt critique of the current status of international human right law, as unfortunately misconstrued by states in several important respects, see Mark Gibney, *International Human Rights Law: Returning to Universal Principles*, Rowman and Littlefield, Lanham, MD, 2008. Interestingly, Gibney (pp. 85–113) proposes four concrete steps for reconstructing human rights law, one of which is a more aggressive emphasis on accountability for human rights violations, in line with the intentions behind the Universal Declaration of Human Rights.

[63] For a brief, informative overview, see, *e.g.*, Cassese, 2008, pp. 317–319, *supra* note 4.

and by the Japanese in Asia.[64] The single most important case was the first Nuremberg trial – *the* Nuremberg trial – of Nazi leaders and persons assumed to be closely associated with the Nazi regime, resulting in the famous Nuremberg Judgment of 1946. The 12 subsequent Nuremberg war crimes trials held pursuant to Allied Control Council Law No. 10, as well as some of the Tokyo war crimes trials at the International Military Tribunal for the Far East, are also interesting for the purpose of this project.

Several points are particularly relevant. First, the Nuremberg trial was based on the Agreement for the Prosecution and Punishment of the Major War Criminals of the European Axis, concluded 8 August 1945 between France, the Soviet Union, United Kingdom, and the United States, with formal adherence by 19 other states. According to the preamble of the agreement, the parties to the treaty were 'acting in the interests of all the United Nations'. At that time the UN had already been established, and there is ample evidence that the trial was in conformity with and in fact formed part of the emerging UN paradigm of international law.

Second, the Nuremberg trial was formally based on postulated substantive norms of international criminal law rather than on the national laws of the Allied powers.

Third, the legal bases for the applicable international law consisted of international treaties, customary law, and general principles of law recognised by civilised nations. A distinction was made between the terms establishing the jurisdiction of the Nuremberg International Military Tribunal (IMT), as prescribed by its Charter, and the material norms of international law that were presumed to exist prior to and independent of the IMT Charter (often called the Nuremberg Charter).

Fourth, it was generally assumed that individual responsibility for the crimes could be attributed to persons with several different positions

---

[64] For several different, partly practical reasons, the Tokyo trial has not received the same worldwide academic attention as the Nuremberg trial. In particular, compared with the Nuremberg trial, there is little written in English on the Tokyo trial. It has, however, been much discussed by Japanese scholars. For instructive introductions to the legacy of the Tokyo trial, see Yuma Totani, *The Tokyo War Crimes Trial: The Pursuit of Justice in the Wake of World War II*, Harvard University Press, Cambridge, MA, 2009; and Madoka Futamura, *War Crimes Tribunals and Transitional Justice: The Tokyo Trial and the Nuremberg Legacy*, Routledge, London, 2009.

in the power structure of Nazi Germany, for a variety of concrete acts and for quite different modes of participation in the crimes.

The Nuremberg precedents are important for two principal reasons. First, the Nuremberg trial and the legal principles that can be extracted from it are still, with some modification, at the heart of the UN paradigm. Although UN and other international practices have not always been in compliance with these principles, the many breaches of the substantive norms in many states and the inconsistent adherence to a norm of *de jure* accountability for grave crimes have not changed the core principles. In general, breaches of international law do not constitute a new legal norm, even if such breaches are widespread. Significantly, the International Court of Justice (ICJ) has upheld certain norms relevant to international criminal law as having a superior legal status (*jus cogens*),[65] constituting 'intransgressible principles',[66] and implying obligations *erga omnes* (owed by everybody to all).[67]

Second, there are important normative linkages between the Nuremberg Principles and the interpretation of contemporary international criminal law.[68] The present study contends that there is still more to be learned from the historical experiences of transitional justice in the aftermath of World War II, for example, with regard to the issue of the scope of punishable participation in universal crimes. This point will be discussed in more detail in another volume in this series.

---

[65] On *jus cogens*, see also Chapter 1, section 1.2, and Chapter 3, section 3.4.3.

[66] ICJ, *Legality of the Threat or Use of Nuclear Weapons*, Advisory Opinion, *I.C.J. Reports 1996*, p. 257, at para. 79. The expression 'intransgressible principles' seems at one level to be just another word for binding *jus cogens* principles, but at another level it is arguably a more precise term with regard to behaviour that is clearly rule-breaking and blameworthy under international law. See also, *e.g.*, ICJ, *Legal Consequences of the Construction of a Wall in the Occupied Palestinian Territory*, Advisory Opinion, *I.C.J. Reports 2004*, p. 136.

[67] See, *e.g.*, ICJ, *Barcelona Traction, Light and Power Company, Limited* (Belgium v. Spain), Judgment, *I.C.J. Reports 1970*, p. 3; ICJ, *East Timor* (Portugal v. Australia), Judgment, *I.C.J. Reports 1995*, p. 90; ICJ, *Wall* case, p. 199, *supra* note 66. In the latter, consider especially para. 155: "The Court would observe that the obligations violated by Israel include certain obligations *erga omnes*. [...] The obligations *erga omnes* violated by Israel are the obligation to respect the right of the Palestinian people to self-determination, and certain of its obligations under international humanitarian law".

[68] See also Chapter 3, sections 3.3.4 and 3.3.6.

During the years immediately following the Nuremberg Judgment, other major developments of international law included the formulation of the Nuremberg Principles by the International Law Commission in 1950,[69] in compliance with General Assembly Resolution 177 (II). That resolution had directed the Commission to "formulate the principles of international law recognized in the Charter of the *Nürnberg* Tribunal and in the judgement of the Tribunal" and to "prepare a draft code of offences against the peace and security of mankind, indicating clearly the place to be accorded to the [*Nürnberg*] principles".[70] In Resolution 95 (I) of 11 December 1946, the General Assembly had already *affirmed* "the principles of international law recognized by the Charter of the *Nürnberg* Tribunal and the judgment of the Tribunal" and directed the committee dealing with the subject "to treat as a matter of primary importance plans for the formulation, in the context of a general codification of offences against the peace and security of mankind, or of an International Criminal Code, of the principles recognized in the Charter of the *Nürnberg* Tribunal and in the judgment of the Tribunal".[71] Of particular interest are the following principles, as formulated and adopted by the International Law Commission in 1950:

I) Any person who commits an act which constitutes a crime under international law is responsible therefor and liable to punishment.

II) The fact that internal law does not impose a penalty for an act which constitutes a crime under international law does not relieve the person who committed the act from responsibility under international law.

III) The fact that a person who committed an act which constitutes a crime under international law acted as Head of State or responsible Government official does

---

[69] See ILC, *Principles of International Law Recognized in the Charter of the Nürnberg Tribunal and in the Judgment of the Tribunal*, 1950. This text was submitted to the General Assembly as a part of the Commission's report covering the work of that session. The report, which also contains commentaries on the principles, is reprinted in *Yearbook of the International Law Commission, 1950*, vol. II, para. 97.

[70] See UN General Assembly Resolution 177 (II), "Formulation of the Principles Recognised in the Charter of the *Nürnberg* Tribunal and in the Judgment of the Tribunal", 21 November 1947.

[71] See UN General Assembly Resolution 95 (I), "Affirmation of the Principles of International Law Recognized by the Charter of the *Nürnberg* Tribunal", 11 December 1946.

not relieve him from responsibility under international law.

IV) The fact that a person acted pursuant to order of his Government or of a superior does not relieve him from responsibility under international law, provided a moral choice was in fact possible to him.

V) Any person charged with a crime under international law has the right to a fair trial on the facts and law.

VI) The crimes hereinafter set out are punishable as crimes under international law: (a) Crimes against peace: (i) Planning, preparation, initiation or waging of a war of aggression or a war in violation of international treaties, agreements or assurances; (ii) Participation in a common plan or conspiracy for the accomplishment of any of the acts mentioned under (i). (b) War crimes [...] (c) Crimes against humanity [...].

VII) Complicity in the commission of a crime against peace, a war crime, or a crime against humanity as set forth in Principle IV is a crime under international law.[72]

Principles I and III have a direct bearing on the issue of the rule of law and accountability of leaders, whereas principles VI and VII concern the definition of the crimes and complicity as a presumably broad category of punishable participation in the same crimes. The UN adoption of the Nuremberg Principles clearly indicates that the war crimes trials after World War II and the laws they were based upon formed an important part of the UN paradigm of international law as it was established from the start. There is thus a presumption that subsequent international criminal law has reinforced rather than replaced the Nuremberg Principles.[73] This presumption will be examined in more detail later in this book.[74]

In 1948 the General Assembly adopted the Universal Declaration of Human Rights (UDHR). This declaration is no doubt an important part of the UN paradigm of international law, but it may be argued that its

---

[72] ILC, 1950, *supra* note 69.

[73] Consider Werle, 2009, p. 7, *supra* note 5: "Today the Nuremberg principles are recognized as customary law, and they form the nucleus of substantive international criminal law".

[74] See Chapter 3, section 3.3.4., on general principles of law and Chapter 4, section 4.5., on statements of the International Law Commission.

relative impact has been reduced by more recent human rights law. A better interpretation, however, would be that the human rights stated in the UDHR have been reinforced by subsequent law.

The preamble to the UDHR affirms that "recognition of the inherent dignity and of the equal and inalienable rights of all members of the human family is the foundation of freedom, justice and peace in the world". The point here is the triangular relationship between individual freedom (rights), peace, and justice, which is implicit in various other parts of the UDHR as well. For example, Article 14(1) states "that everyone has the right to seek and to enjoy in other countries asylum from persecution", but Article 14(2) makes an exception "in the case of prosecutions genuinely arising from non-political crimes or from acts contrary to the purposes and principles of the United Nations". This implies a connection to the Nuremberg Principles: some persons are first and foremost liable to punishment under international law, and should receive a fair trial instead of asylum.

Much the same principle can be found in international refugee law. Work on an international refugee convention had already started in 1946, two years before the UDHR was enacted, and culminated in the adoption by the UN of the 1951 Convention Relating to the Status of Refugees. Drafting of the Refugee Convention was much influenced by the persecutions that had taken place in Europe after World War I, especially of the Jews and other groups by Nazi Germany before and during World War II.[75] The phrase "persecutions on political, racial, or religious grounds" was previously used in Article 6(c) of the Nuremberg Charter, and the term 'persecution' can be found in numerous places in the Nuremberg Judgment.[76] The concept of persecution therefore became the key com-

---

[75] See Terje Einarsen, "Drafting History of the 1951 Refugee Convention and the 1967 Protocol", in Andreas Zimmermann (ed.), *The 1951 Refugee Convention Relating to the Status of Refugees and Its 1967 Protocol*, Oxford University Press, Oxford, UK, 2011, pp. 37–73.

[76] See IMT, *Trial of the Major War Criminals*, 1947, vol. I, *supra* note 27. Among the relevant passages in the document: "The persecution of the Jews at the hands of the Nazi Government has been proved in the greatest detail before the Tribunal" (p. 247); "The policy of persecution, repression, and murder of civilians in Germany before the war in 1939, who were likely to be hostile to the Government, was most ruthlessly carried out" (p. 254); "The Gestapo and SD were used for purposes which were criminal under the Charter involving the persecution and extermination of the Jews" (p. 267), "Göring persecuted the Jews" (p. 282); "Streicher's incitement to murder and

ponent in the general definition of a refugee in Article 1A(2) of the Refugee Convention. At the same time, Article 1F expressly excluded from refugee status "any person with respect to whom there are serious reasons for considering that: (a) he has committed a crime against peace, a war crime, or a crime against humanity, as defined in the international instruments drawn up to make provision in respect of such crimes" or "(c) he has been guilty of acts contrary to the purposes and principles of the United Nations".[77] It has always been clear that the 'international instruments' referenced are not confined to those already drawn up when the Refugee Convention was adopted, but also include all future international instruments for the same purpose. The content of international exclusion law, especially Article 1F(a), should as far as possible be interpreted in accordance with current international criminal law.[78]

The four Geneva Conventions specify protection of civilians in times of war and of prisoners of war and other members of the armed forces in need of special protection. Formally negotiated under the auspices of the Swiss Federal Council and the Red Cross, they are nevertheless very much a part of the UN paradigm of international law. They were adopted in 1949 and registered with the UN Secretariat. The parties are obliged to "enact any legislation necessary to provide effective penal sanctions for persons committing, or ordering to be committed, any of the grave breaches of the present Convention" – 'grave breaches' being defined with reference to enumerated acts, including but not limited to "wilful killing, torture or inhuman treatment" (see, for example, Articles 146 and 147 of the Fourth Geneva Convention Relative to the Protection of Civilian Persons in Time of War).

---

extermination at the time when Jews in the East were being killed under the most horrible conditions clearly constitutes persecution on political and racial grounds in connection with War Crimes, as defined by the Charter, and constitutes a Crime against Humanity" (p. 304).

[77] There is a vast literature on Article 1F of the Refugee Convention, but for a comprehensive introduction and overview, see, *e.g.*, Peter J. van Krieken (ed.), *Refugee Law in Context: The Exclusion Clause*, TMC Asser Press, The Hague, 1999.

[78] See Andreas Zimmermann and Philipp Wennholz, "Article 1 F", in Zimmermann, 2011, pp. 609–610, *supra* note 75: "Given the establishment of instruments such as the Rome Statute and a fairly extensive amount of jurisprudence by international and domestic tribunals in that regard, Art. 1 F (a) should be applied and interpreted taking this dynamic development into account".

The UN Convention on the Prevention and Punishment of the Crime of Genocide of 1948 was premised on the normative fact that "genocide is a crime under international law, contrary to the spirit and aims of the United Nations and condemned by the civilized world", as noted in its preamble. Two years earlier, in 1946, the General Assembly had in Resolution 96(I) on "The Crime of Genocide" affirmed that "genocide is a crime under international law which the civilized world condemns, and for the commission of which principals and accomplices – whether private individuals, public officials or statesmen, and whether the crime is committed on religious, racial, political or any other grounds – are punishable".[79] It is thus noteworthy that the Genocide Convention of 1948 did not make genocide a crime. It was, rather, the other way around: the Genocide Convention was drafted in order "to prevent and to punish" that crime, which was already understood to exist as such (see Article I).

This simple observation, which arises directly from the text of the Genocide Convention, is extremely important for the proper understanding of international criminal law. It raises the following question: if the Genocide Convention did not constitute the legal basis for the specific crime of genocide in international law, what was its legal basis? Obviously it was neither other treaties nor customary international law, since nobody had ever been convicted of the crime of genocide prior to the Genocide Convention.[80] It was also quite a new concept, invented a few years earlier by the Polish jurist Raphael Lemkin.[81] Although the

---

[79] UN General Assembly Resolution 96 (I), "The Crime of Genocide", 11 December 1946.

[80] See Cassese, 2008, p. 127, *supra* note 4. Cassese notes that in dealing with the extermination of the Jews and other ethnic, racial, or religious groups during World War II, the Nuremberg Tribunal referred in its judgment to the crime of persecution, and while the extermination of the Jews as a crime against humanity was also discussed in some other cases, and the word "genocide" was sometimes used to describe the criminal conduct, the crime of genocide was not elevated "to a distinct category of criminality". He mentions in particular "*Hoess*, decided by a Polish court in 1947 (at 12–18), and *Greifelt and others*, heard in 1948 by a US Military Tribunal (at 2–36)". The literature on the Genocide Convention is vast and includes William A. Schabas, *Genocide in International Law*, 2nd ed., Cambridge University Press, Cambridge, UK, 2009, as well as Paola Gaeta (ed.), *The UN Genocide Convention: A Commentary*, Oxford University Press, Oxford, UK, 2009.

[81] Raphael Lemkin, *Axis Rule in Occupied Europe: Laws of Occupation, Analysis of Government, Proposals for Redress*, Carnegie Endowment for International Peace, Washington, DC, 1944, pp. 79–95. Before Nuremberg, Lemkin had further elaborated

---

word "genocide" was indeed used in the indictment of the Nuremberg trial,[82] and defined as deliberate and systematic terrorising and extermination of particular civilian groups in occupied territories,[83] the concept as such was not applied or even discussed by the Nuremberg Tribunal. The reason, most likely, was that the judges did not find the concept necessary in addition to 'war crimes' and 'crimes against humanity', which had been made explicit legal bases for the prosecution in the Nuremberg Charter – the latter concept being employed for the first time in an actual criminal case. In the judgment, 'war crimes' and 'crimes against humanity' are not strictly separated in the legal discussions of these crimes;[84] hence the need for a particular concept of 'genocide' was diminished.[85] Still, as noted above, a few months after the Nuremberg

---

on the term in two other works: "Genocide – A Modern Crime", in *Free World*, April 1945, vol. 4, pp. 39–43, and "Genocide", in *American Scholar*, April 1946, vol. 15, no. 2, pp. 227–230.

[82] IMT, *Trial of the Major War Criminals*, 1947, vol. I, pp. 43–44, *supra* note 27.

[83] *Ibid.*, p. 43. "Throughout the period of their occupation of territories overrun by their armed forces the defendants, for the purpose of systematically terrorizing the inhabitants, murdered and tortured civilians, and ill-treated them, and imprisoned them without legal process. [...] They conducted systematic genocide, viz., the extermination of racial and national groups, against the civilian populations of certain occupied territories in order to destroy particular races and classes of people and national, racial, or religious groups, particularly Jews, Poles and Gypsies and others".

[84] *Ibid.*, pp. 226–255.

[85] One of the reasons why the two categories were discussed together probably also had to do with the *jurisdictional* limitation in the Nuremberg Charter with regard to crimes against humanity. See *Trial of the Major War Criminals* (*ibid.*): "With regard to Crimes against Humanity there is no doubt whatever that political opponents were murdered in Germany before the war, and that many of them were kept in concentration camps in circumstances of great horror and cruelty. The policy of terror was certainly carried out on a vast scale, and in many cases was organized and systematic. The policy of persecution, repression, and murder of civilians in Germany before the war of 1939, who were likely to be hostile to the Government, was most ruthlessly carried out. The persecution of Jews [...] is established beyond all doubt. To constitute Crimes against Humanity, the acts relied on before the outbreak of war must have been in execution of, or in connection with, [other] crime[s] within the jurisdiction of the Tribunal. The Tribunal is of the opinion that revolting and horrible as many of these crimes were, it has not been satisfactorily proved that they were done in execution of, or in connection with, any such [other] crime. The Tribunal therefore cannot make a general declaration that the acts before 1939 were Crimes against Humanity *within the meaning of the Charter* [...]" (p. 254, emphasis added). The same limitation did not apply to Control Council Law No. 10 of December 1945, which established jurisdiction in the subsequent Nuremberg trials. In the Justice Case, the tribunal

Judgment the General Assembly was already prepared to affirm that genocide was ('is') a crime under international law.

That seems to leave us with the 'general principles' of international law as the primary – or possibly an independent – legal foundation of genocide as an international crime. This finding has important repercussions for one thesis of this project: it indicates that within the prevailing UN paradigm some acts or behaviour might at some time again be considered, as in Nuremberg, a universal crime under international law by the international community through its established courts and institutions – that is, by personnel acting independently in their individual capacity as judges or commissioners – even though no clear prior legal basis exists either in a treaty or in customary international law.[86]

Such a thesis has implications for different aspects of the rule of law and presumes a moral foundation for international law[87] that reaches beyond classical legal positivism and the emphasis on rules deriving directly from state consent.[88] The argument is that the existing UN paradigm of international law allows for, and indeed may require, legal reasoning within the field of ICL that may include input from 'soft-law' principles and other different interpretative sources as well as possibly existing 'hard-law' general principles. Throughout this book, evidence will be provided to show that this is a realistic account of the process of law.

Under this understanding of potential sources of international law, an analysis of accountability for participation in universal crimes should not be confined only to enumerated crimes or modes of participation in crime as spelled out in existing treaties or statutes of certain international

---

made clear that crimes against humanity were autonomous crimes under international law: "certain crimes against humanity committed by Nazi authority against German nationals constituted violations not alone of statute but also of common international law". Nuernberg Military Tribunals, "The Justice Case", in *Trials of War Criminals before the Nuernberg Military Tribunals under Control Council Law No. 10*, vol. III, US Government Printing Office, Washington, DC, 1951, p. 979.

[86] On the law-creating sources of international criminal law, see Chapter 3, section 3.3.

[87] See, *e.g.*, the idea of a moral theory of international law set forth by Allen Buchanan, *Justice, Legitimacy and Self-determination: Moral Foundations for International Law*, Oxford University Press, Oxford, UK, 2007.

[88] The notion of 'legal positivism', like the concepts of 'legal idealism' and 'natural law thinking' and others, of course includes different positions and approaches to international legal theory. See, *e.g.*, Boyle and Chinkin, 2007, pp. 10–19, *supra* note 17.

tribunals at a certain point in time. By implication, the scope of punishable participation in universal crimes might be more open-ended in some respects and perhaps more closed in other respects than is generally acknowledged. Moreover, this perspective is also relevant to the possible need for revision of treaties and statutes relating to universal crimes and the present international criminal law regimes, in conformity with more general norms, as noted in Article 53 of the Vienna Convention on the Law of Treaties on "[t]reaties conflicting with a peremptory norm of general international law ('*jus cogens*')".

On the other hand, no court or institution has international law-making powers independent of the law-creating sources of the legal order. That would contradict the principle of legality and especially the element of *non-retroactivity of crimes and punishment*, which may itself have emerged as a *jus cogens* standard.[89] Therefore there may exist a substantial tension between the legitimate demands of justice and the ideal of strict adherence to legality, which, it may be argued, are both based on community values rooted in the rule of law in international affairs. Such tensions should be faced and dealt with in a principled and analytical manner, not excluding by definition any relevant international rule or legal materials.

2.2.4. Importance of the Shifting Political Context

In an ideal world, one might presume that informed politicians would take a very serious interest in the prosecution of the most heinous crimes, regardless of geography or the identity of the persons most responsible. At least one would expect that to be the case for politicians in democracies who run on a platform of fighting crimes and corruption. In the real world, such politicians, including those who are engaged principally with foreign policy issues, often do not seem to be much interested in crimes committed outside their own state borders.

In many cases, those politicians who take an interest in the matter do so not to ensure appropriate prosecution, but for other reasons. There have often been strong transnational state interests in covering up the truth or even facilitating impunity in the form of blanket amnesties for the most responsible perpetrators. The most important reason for this rather unfortunate situation is as simple as it is ugly: both historically and

---

[89] See generally Gallant, 2009, pp. 399–402, *supra* note 36.

currently, leading politicians in many countries have been among the most notorious persons responsible for such crimes. Their colleagues who are not similarly implicated nevertheless are aware that they too might some day come under scrutiny and that in any case they need to maintain good relations with other powerful political figures. In a world divided into sovereign states with inherently competing interests, each state responsible primarily for the welfare of its own citizens, leaders often presume the legitimacy of other strong leaders, as they also derive legitimacy from the state system. International political responses even to probable cases of genocide have often been slow and reluctant.[90] This underlying assumption may itself pave the way for 'system criminality' of direct relevance to international criminal law.[91]

States may be agents for community values and human rights. At the same time, however, they pursue preservation of the power of the state itself, and leaders of states pursue their own ambitions for power or economic self-interests. The construction of territorial sovereignty in itself implies substantial centralisation of powers. If such sovereignty is not

---

[90] For an account of European political failures in this regard, see Karen E. Smith, *Genocide and the Europeans*, Cambridge University Press, Cambridge, UK, 2010. She concludes pessimistically, "Thus we are left with the unhappy conclusion that implementation of the social norm against genocide faces both countervailing economic and geopolitical interests on the one hand, and professed respect for multilateral practices and principles on the other. Further, the legal norm is not enough to enable action to prevent, much less stop, genocide. 'Never again' is quite likely to be a hollow promise, for all the moral agonising this produces" (p. 253). This echoes an earlier account of acts of genocide and US responses to them by Samantha Power in *"A Problem from Hell": America and the Age of Genocide*, Perennial, New York, 2002. Power was appointed by President Obama to the National Security Council, where she was reported to have argued in favour of humanitarian intervention in Libya in 2011. See Sheryl Gay Stolberg, "Still Crusading, but Now on the Inside", *New York Times*, 29 March 2011, available at http://www.nytimes.com/2011/03/30/world/30 power.html.

[91] The concept of 'system criminality' is thoroughly analysed in André Nollkaemper and Harmen van der Wilt, *System Criminality in International Law*, Cambridge University Press, Cambridge, UK, 2009, p. 16. It is defined in the book as "a situation where collective entities order or encourage international crimes to be committed, or permit or tolerate the committing of international crimes". The authors, contending that system criminality requires more than just individual criminal liability, "favour a synthesis of both individual and collective responsibility" (p. 347). This interesting question of future international criminal law accountability *lex ferenda* is not further addressed here; see preface to this book.

---

established or breaks down due to civil war or internal strife over economic resources, anarchy and generalised violence might follow, often resulting in universal crimes by powerful armed groups. On the other hand, a seemingly well-functioning state apparatus is also open to abuse if a ruling elite consolidates its control gradually or though a coup d'état, or if rule of law mechanisms are not in place. Even democratically elected leaders may engage in internal or foreign affairs for dubious purposes that entail the risk of crime.

Another rationale for failure to prosecute grave crimes may be the fear of consequences that threaten international peace and security. Public expressions of such concern may be a deceitful cover for quite other considerations, but in practice this is difficult to judge. For instance, when some Arab and African leaders reacted strongly against the ICC because of the indictment of Sudanese President al-Bashir in 2009,[92] it was hard to know to what extent the protests were motivated by the leaders' concerns about disrupting fragile peace processes in Sudan or by fear of their own vulnerability to similar prosecution. The Libyan leader Gaddafi, for instance, described the indictment and arrest warrant of al-Bashir as "First World terrorism".[93] The African Union (AU) also condemned the arrest warrant and later applauded al-Bashir's leadership on peace issues.[94] When the ICC later issued an arrest warrant for Gaddafi as well,[95] the AU announced that its members would not execute it, and expressed no criticism of the Libyan leader.[96] It remains to be seen whether these institutional conflicts will in the end seriously discredit the ICC, the AU, or both.

With respect to the real chances for necessary support of international investigations and prosecutions of universal crimes, the political context is always important. There is ample evidence for this in the often

---

[92] See ICC, *Bashir* case, 2009, *supra* note 48.

[93] See France 24, "Bashir in Doha before Start of the Arab Summit", 29 March 2009, http://www.france24.com/en, last accessed 3 July 2011.

[94] See African Union, "The African Union Applauds the Success of the Referendum in Southern Sudan", press release, Addis Ababa, 8 February 2011: "The Chairperson applauds the leadership and unswerving commitment to peace of President Omar Hassan al Bashir and First Vice President Salva Kiir Mayardit that have made possible this triumph".

[95] ICC, Situation in the Libyan Arab Jamahiriya, 27 June 2011, *supra* note 49.

[96] See France 24, "Gaddafi's Fate is Notable Absentee in AU Peace Plan", 3 July 2011, http://www.france24.com/en, last accessed 3 July 2011.

inconsistent decision-making processes of the UN Security Council with regard to universal crimes. When the Security Council established the ICTY in 1993 and the ICTR in 1994, the threat to peace and security in the respective regions was invoked as a reason. In other cases since 1945 where it is suspected that grave crimes have been committed on a large scale, the Security Council has not established any new international special court, although threats to international peace and security have also existed in other places, for instance in the Middle East. Nevertheless, the UN has acted jointly with concerned states to establish a number of so-called internationalised tribunals or hybrid courts for grave crimes committed in countries like Sierra Leone, Lebanon, Cambodia, Bosnia, Kosovo, Iraq, and East Timor.[97] After adoption of the ICC treaty and its entry into force in 2002, the Security Council in 2005 referred the situation in Darfur, Sudan, since 1 July 2002 to the prosecutor of the ICC.[98] The same was done in 2011 with respect to the situation in Libya after 15 February 2011.[99] In addition, as of July 2011, the ICC has used other mechanisms to investigate four other formally defined situations: Northern Uganda (2004–);[100] the Democratic Republic of Congo (2004–);[101] the Central African Republic (2005–);[102] and the Republic of Kenya (2009–).[103] The ICC prosecutor has also requested authorisation to open an investigation in the Republic of Côte d'Ivoire (2011–).[104] In several

---

[97] See also Chapter 3, section 3.2, and Chapter 4, section 4.3.

[98] UN Security Council Resolution 1593 (2005), 31 March 2005.

[99] UN Security Council Resolution 1970 (2011), 26 February 2011.

[100] See *e.g.*, ICC, *Prosecutor v. Joseph Kony*, ICC-02/04-01/05, 27 September 2005; ICC, *Prosecutor v. Vincent Otti*, ICC-02/04, 8 July 2005; ICC, *Prosecutor v. Okut Odhiambo*, ICC-02/04, 8 July 2005; ICC, *Prosecutor v. Dominic Ongwen*, ICC-02/04, 8 July 2005.

[101] See *e.g.*, ICC, *Prosecutor v. Thomas Lubango Dyilo*, ICC-01/04-01/06, 29 January 2007; ICC, *Prosecutor v. Callixte Mbarushimana*, ICC-01/04-01/10, 28 September 2010; ICC, *Prosecutor v. Bosco Ntaganda*, ICC-01/04-02/06, 22 August 2006; ICC, *Prosecutor v. Germain Katanga and Mathieu Ngudjolo Chui*, ICC-01/04-01/07, 30 September 2008.

[102] See *e.g.*, ICC, *Prosecutor v. Jean-Pierre Bemba Gombo*, ICC-01/05-01/08, 15 June 2009.

[103] See *e.g.*, ICC, Decision Pursuant to Article 15 of the Rome Statute on the Authorization of an Investigation into the Situation in the Republic of Kenya, ICC-01/09, 31 March 2010.

[104] See ICC, *Situation in the Republic of Côte d'Ivoire, Request for Authorization of an Investigation Pursuant to Article 15*, ICC-02/11, 23 June 2011.

---

other instances where grave crimes may have taken place, notably in Israel and the Gaza strip in 2008/2009[105] and in Sri Lanka in 2008/2009,[106] the Security Council has not taken similar action. But it is too early to draw final conclusions with regard to inequality. For example, the ICC has made public that Afghanistan, Colombia, Georgia, Guinea, Honduras, Korea, Nigeria, and Palestine remain under preliminary examination.[107]

Despite the importance of the causes and effects from a sociological perspective, and despite the decisive influence of power politics on the enforcement and development of international criminal law, these considerations are not directly relevant to the legal considerations *strictu sensu*. From the viewpoint of substantive law, it does not matter whether a friend or foe commits the crimes, or whether an enforcement mechanism is put in place. Just as a domestic crime is a crime whether or not it is enforced, a universal crime is a universal crime.

If the long-term political goal is a viable and legitimate system of international criminal law, the principle of equal treatment is essential. No criminal law and legal procedure can be upheld as part of 'law' in the long run if the system is inconsistently applied in practice. Instead it risks becoming part of an unjust and potentially repressive power structure, a characterisation which might arguably apply to the current international order. International lawyers and human rights activists, as well as journalists and social scientists, should be aware of these risks. Scepticism about an uneven criminal justice system due to political interference or a reasoned critique of current rules or decisions of international law should not be understood as implying opposition to the system of international law itself.

Realistically, one must assume that many politicians cannot be counted on to support equal enforcement of international criminal law. Indeed, in many cases, they have been more a part of the problem than part of the solution. The work towards equal international justice is thus bound to be uneven and frustrating for those who are committed to this

---

[105] See United Nations, *Human Rights in Palestine and other Occupied Arab Territories*, A/HRC/12/48, 15 September 2009.

[106] See United Nations, *Report of the Secretary-General's Panel of Experts on Accountability in Sri Lanka*, 31 March 2011.

[107] ICC, Office of the Prosecutor, "Communications, Referrals and Preliminary Examinations", available at http://www.icc-cpi.int/Menus/ICC/Structure+of+the+Court/Office+of+the+Prosecutor/Comm+and+Ref/, last accessed 1 July 2011.

goal. Nevertheless, important steps have been taken during the last two decades, mainly because some crimes have been too grave to be ignored by broad public coverage and social media networks in an increasingly globalised world. This has resulted in the establishment of international and national mechanisms of transitional justice, and allowed official searches for truth in places where this would before have been unthinkable.

Despite the difficult tasks that have confronted the international courts and the mistakes that have been made, there has been significant success. The first firm steps have been taken to ensure accountability for universal crimes. The ICTY and the ICTR have shown the world that it is possible to establish responsibility on the part of leaders and other high-ranking personnel, as well as other perpetrators. Whether this trend will continue or be reversed in the coming years depends on the future successes and failures of the other international tribunals and hybrid courts so far established, and especially on how influential actors and media receive and communicate the work of the ICC.

2.2.5. Justice and Peace

As already noted, the preamble to the ICC Rome Statute recognises the link between peace and justice, declaring that "grave crimes threaten the peace, security and well-being of the world". It affirms that the parties are "determined to put an end to impunity for the perpetrators of these crimes and thus to contribute to the prevention of such crimes". Despite increasing recognition of the link between justice and peace, the opposing view – that in practice, it is necessary to choose between the two – is also common. Although it is generally recognised that peace and justice complement each other in the long term, tensions have arisen in the short term, or at least have been perceived to have arisen, between efforts to secure peace and efforts to ensure accountability for international crimes.[108]

---

[108] See the point of departure taken by the Bureau of the Assembly of States Parties to the ICC, in ICC, *Report of the Bureau on Stocktaking: Peace and Justice*, ASP/8/52, resumed 8th session, New York, 20 March 2010.

The relationship between peace and justice has been much discussed, especially within the field of transitional justice.[109] Whereas international criminal law is about the international rules, institutions, and judgments concerned with universal crimes, and is mainly studied by lawyers, transitional justice as an academic field is focused more on victim groups, political processes, regime changes, and other aspects of different justice mechanisms. The two fields are, however, concerned with much the same crimes.[110] Transitional justice refers to the set of judicial and non-judicial measures that have been implemented by different countries to redress the legacies of massive human rights abuses. The measures relevant to this field thus include criminal prosecutions and proceedings, both international and domestic, as well as truth commissions, reparations programs, and institutional reforms. Transitional justice can also be seen as a practical response to systematic or widespread violations of human rights, seeking recognition for victims and promoting possibilities for peace, reconciliation, and democracy through a holistic approach.[111]

One should readily admit that the causal connection between international peaceful settlements of conflict on the one hand and international criminal justice on the other hand, based on the historical record, may not fit any simple theory. Traditionally, many academics, politicians, diplomats, and journalists seem to have assumed that efforts to achieve peace and justice often contradict each other, and that in such cases peace must take precedence. Following this perspective, the goals of international law have frequently been perceived as promoting peace and mitigating the miseries of war rather than as achieving justice.[112] Thus there

---

[109] The concept of transitional justice consists of "both judicial and non-judicial processes and mechanisms, such as truth-seeking, prosecution initiatives, reparations programmes, institutional reform, or an appropriate combination thereof". UN General Assembly, *Annual Report of the United Nations High Commissioner for Human Rights: Analytical Study on Human Rights and Transitional Justice*, A/HCR/12/18, 6 August 2009, p. 4, para. 3.

[110] As academic disciplines, both have been growing fast. A Google Scholar search in June 2011 revealed 11,900 matches for journal articles containing the exact phrase 'transitional justice', as compared to 17,700 for 'international criminal law' and 20,800 for 'international crime'.

[111] See International Center for Transitional Justice, "What Is Transitional Justice?" 2009, available at http://ictj.org/publication/what-transitional-justice, last accessed 13 July 2011.

[112] See Buchanan, 2007, pp. 76–82, *supra* note 87.

has often been a perceived dilemma in choosing between securing peace with the cooperation of perpetrators of universal crimes or addressing justice at the cost of perpetuating conflict.

Although one should assume that justice in a meaningful sense of the word uncovers truth, enforces human rights, and enhances peace, thus preparing the ground for long-term reconciliation, in the short term peace agreements and political transitions may sometimes require deals guaranteeing impunity for all or some of the parties involved in grave crimes. This dilemma seems to have been recognised in national court jurisprudence with respect to the legality of amnesty laws in transitional processes with the aim of securing impunity for grave crimes committed by a former regime.[113]

The presumed need for such short-term measures raises the question of the timing of international criminal investigations and indictments. A common assumption is that trials are inherently risky in the aftermath of transitions, when peace or democracy is not yet fully consolidated. In other words, enforcement of justice might directly threaten ongoing or potential peace processes and thus reduce the short-term chances for improving humanitarian conditions for ordinary people on the ground.[114] Others have argued that it is possible to find the right time for justice in any particular circumstance, even though it may be difficult to lay out a general rule regarding the right time to prosecute.[115] It might also be that, in some circumstances, measures other than traditional retributive justice could lead to similar or even better results for peace and political transition, establishment of the historical truth, and future reconciliation. This has been the rationale behind alternative or complementary 'restorative' measures such as truth commissions, institutional reform, memorial sites, and economic compensation to

---

[113] See Louise Mallinder, *Amnesty, Human Rights and Political Transition: Bridging the Peace and Justice Divide*, Hart Publishing, Oxford, UK, 2008, pp. 239–246.

[114] For example, the indictment of President Omar al-Bashir of Sudan on charges of genocide, crimes against humanity, and war crimes in July 2008 generated an intense debate on the timing and political consequences of the indictment. For an interesting discussion, see Jacqueline Geis and Alex Mundt, "When to Indict? The Impact of Timing of International Criminal Indictments on Peace Processes and Humanitarian Action", paper prepared for the World Humanitarian Studies Conference, Groningen, Netherlands, February 2009.

[115] See Lutz and Reiger, 2009, p. 286, *supra* note 17.

victims, sometimes combined with amnesty laws providing impunity for past atrocities.

From the perspective of international law, however, empirical facts indicating the likely outcome of criminal justice proceedings to deliver peace may not be the decisive factor in determining the preferable course of action. The purpose of law is not determined by a review of historical facts, such as a review to evaluate the number of cases in which justice contributed to or detracted from the prospects of peace. In addition to the uncertainty surrounding results of such studies, the role of international law is to change social facts by altering the actual behaviour of people and governments, often gradually over many years, thus contributing to future peace and the reduction of grave crimes, both generally and in a particular country. The prevention of new universal crimes requires changes in the mentality of powerful institutions and persons in societies, changes that cannot easily be assessed through comparative historical studies. It may not be difficult to assess whether or not international criminal indictments have had an immediate deterrent effect on the proscribed behaviour in a certain country at a certain time. What is much more difficult to assess, and often ignored in the discourse on peace versus justice,[116] are more general and long-term deterrent effects on other actors who have no direct connections to the indictment and who may even be political and military leaders in other countries.[117]

---

[116] See the very premature conclusion by Geis and Mundt, 2009, p. 18, *supra* note 114. After having reviewed just a few cases of contested indictments by the ICC, these authors conclude that "there is little empirical evidence to suggest that the possibility of international criminal indictments for mass atrocity crimes serve as a deterrent or moderating force on government and rebel leaders".

[117] This seems to be the case to some extent even in the well-researched collaborative effort of Naomi Roht-Arriaza and Javier Mariezcurrena (eds.), *Transitional Justice in the Twenty-First Century: Beyond Truth versus Justice*, Cambridge University Press, Cambridge, UK, 2006. See the conclusions drawn by Ellen Lutz in "Transitional Justice: Lessons Learned and the Road Ahead" in the same volume, pp. 325–341. The book recognises preventive goals, including "preventing past perpetrators from reasserting power or discouraging future perpetrators" (p. 325), but one gets the impression that the preventive effects of criminal justice and other transitional justice mechanisms are understood as confined to the particular situation in each country studied. Compare Chapter 2, section 2.3.5, asserting that the deterrent effects of retributive justice for universal crimes, when imposed on a regular international and national basis, may extend to potentially new perpetrators in all states of the world.

Such studies would at minimum require a long time perspective and would have to use comparable cases, which would be difficult to find. For example, how would one measure the full impact of transitional justice in Germany and Japan after World War II? And can those two cases, taken as singular examples, be compared with two other cases in which transitional criminal justice was absent? The problem with the first question is that it depends on a counterfactual alternative which is inherently unknowable, namely, what would have been the results in those countries and in international law if these legal processes had not been imposed upon those two countries after World War II. The problem with the second question is that there are unlikely to be cases that are sufficiently comparable. Nevertheless, both scientific analysis and common sense would probably conclude that the establishment of a scheme of transitional justice, with emphasis on prosecution, did indeed make a difference in the history of modern Germany and Japan, in conjunction with other legal instruments that were imposed, such as new constitutions and general legal reforms. The precedent set by the trials of persons who were among the most responsible for the atrocities committed during World War II had a number of other effects as well, including a significant impact on the development of international human rights and humanitarian law.

The experiences of many modern states, as well as common sense, support the conclusion that the relationship between a stable social order (internal peace and security) and accountability for serious crimes (justice) is not contradictory. Rather, these objectives reinforce each other within the routine practice of well-functioning state institutions. In addition to these considerations, there are demands from victims and their spokespersons, as well as from society at large through the media and democratic politicians, that the regime of criminal law be capable of functioning so that at least the most serious crimes are investigated, the truth established, and suspects held accountable in fair procedures.

If this applies with respect to domestic crimes, then the question arises as to whether the same kind of relationship should not also be expected to apply to universal crimes and international peace and security. One possible response is that universal crimes are of a different and much more complex character, making investigation and prosecution infeasible. While this argument is relevant, it is not compelling. There is substantial evidence from real-world examples that victim groups and others expect investigation of universal crimes and that such crimes can be fairly prosecuted given sufficient resources and international determination. Another consideration often noted is that those individuals most responsible for universal crimes may enjoy so much power in a society that a trade-off is necessary for the sake of peace and regime transition. While this might be true in some cases, as noted above, such considerations apply primarily to the timing of investigation and prosecution rather than to whether they take place at all, and such compromises should be considered as exceptions rather than standard practice. One should also consider that the argument that justice most often undermines peace is a hypothesis rather than a result confirmed by a substantial body of research. At least one analysis of the impact of the ICC on three situations in Africa suggests that judicial intervention may be more likely to prevent atrocities than to impede peace, even if arrest warrants cannot be executed.[118] And although it is not possible to demonstrate with any certainty that the indictment of Sudan's President al-Bashir has had an effect on preventing further atrocities in Darfur, it has been suggested that that highly controversial indictment at least may not have exacerbated the situation.[119]

The experiences of the United Nations suggest that despite tensions between the themes of peace and justice, these must ultimately be considered as complementary rather than contradictory. For example, in 2009 the Office of the United Nations High Commissioner for Human Rights, recalling that the office over the years has been involved in complex discussions regarding the relationship between justice and peace, stated that the assumed tension between justice and peace has "gradually dissolved": "The United Nations now recognizes that, when properly pursued, justice and peace can promote and sustain one another".[120] The report noted that

---

[118] See Payam Akhavan, "Are International Criminal Tribunals a Disincentive to Peace? Reconciling Judicial Romanticism with Political Realism", in *Human Rights Quarterly*, August 2009, vol. 31, no. 3, pp. 624–654.

[119] *Ibid.*, p. 651. In the case of Côte d'Ivoire, Akhavan suggests that the "mere threats of ICC prosecutions may have resulted in the termination of hate broadcasts on the state-sponsored radio at a crucial point of escalating tensions" (p. 637). With regard to the Lord's Resistance Army in Uganda, he claims that the ICC's stigmatization of those responsible for mass atrocities eroded their political influence and military capabilities (p. 641).

[120] See UN General Assembly, 2009, p. 16, para. 51, *supra* note 109.

this point of view is reflected in current international law and in United Nations policy on amnesties.[121]

2.3.   Special Features of Universal Crimes

2.3.1.   Legal Foundation and Attached Competences and Duties

Universal crimes, this study contends, should be understood as those crimes against which human beings and societies must be protected by the norms and institutions of the international community. Within the UN paradigm of international law there is, arguably, a universal 'responsibility to protect',[122] which can also be said to include an obligation to facilitate prevention and suppression of certain crimes if necessary through international criminal prosecution.[123] The underlying universal crimes norms may have the character of *jus cogens*:[124] if binding international law proscribes the unlawful conduct, the norms will be superior legal norms from which no derogation is permitted.[125] These

---

[121]   *Ibid.*, p. 17, para. 52.

[122]   The concept of 'Responsibility to Protect' (R2P) originated from a challenge by UN Secretary-General Kofi Annan to the Millennium General Assembly in April 2000 and a subsequent initiative by the Canadian government to establish an ad hoc international commission on the matter; see International Commission on Intervention and State Sovereignty (ICISS), *The Responsibility to Protect*, International Development Research Centre, Ottawa, 2001. See also Gareth Evans, *The Responsibility to Protect: Ending Mass Atrocity Crimes Once and For All*, Brookings Institution Press, Washington, DC, 2008. The main focus of R2P discussions has been on the disputed right of humanitarian intervention: the question of when, if ever, it is appropriate for states to take coercive – and in particular, military – action against another state for the purpose of protecting people at risk in that other state. On this classical issue, see generally, *e.g.*, Nicholas J. Wheeler, *Saving Strangers: Humanitarian Intervention in International Society*, Oxford University Press, Oxford, UK, 2000.

[123]   International criminal prosecution is recognised as an element of the R2P doctrine both as prevention before the crisis ('responsibility to prevent') and as a rebuilding tool thereafter ('responsibility to rebuild'). See Evans, 2008, *supra* note 122, pp. 99–100 and 166–168.

[124]   On *jus cogens*, see Chapter 1, section 1.2, and Chapter 3, section 3.3.4.

[125]   See also Guy Goodwin-Gill, "Crime and International Law: Expulsion, Removal and the Non-Derogable Obligation", in Stefan Talmon and Guy Goodwin-Gill (eds.), *The Reality of International Law: Essays in Honour of Ian Brownlie*, Oxford University Press, Oxford, UK, 1999, p. 213. Goodwin-Gill states that such crimes are "indeed distinguished by [their] foundation in a rule of *jus cogens*". The issue of 'foundation'

---

crimes, in the words of Orakhelashvili, "entail objective illegality whose redress is a matter of community interest despite the attitudes of or prejudices to individual states".[126] The norms are also peremptory in the sense that a treaty is void if it conflicts with such a norm at the time of its conclusion (under the terms of the 1969 Vienna Convention on the Law of Treaties, Article 53).

Some interests are so fundamental to the international legal order that the international community as a whole has recognised their breaches as crimes. Hence there are certain essential obligations that must be honoured by states, international organisations, non-state actors, and even individuals. If those obligations are not met, there may be legal responsibility, including possible individual criminal liability. If a universal humanitarian obligation *erga omnes* (owed to all) exists to protect human beings and societies from universal crimes, the next question is what that obligation entails. Is it an obligation to intervene by physical means, to seek prevention by means of legislative acts or agreements, or is it also deterrence and justice by means of prosecution and punishment? Enactments of binding norms for the common good and fair prosecution of serious crimes are peaceful means, presumably at the core of a substantive rule of law, as noted above in the discussion of rule of law. Efforts to avoid impunity for perpetrators and to seek justice for victims of the most serious crimes are certainly also in compliance with the UN paradigm of international law. Peaceful means should always be regarded as principal tools, and military operations – including just wars – as the last resort, as pointed out by US President Obama in his Nobel lecture.[127] It follows that the community of states should at the very least consider establishing international institutions with adequate competence and resources to undertake investigations of concrete allegations of universal crimes and prosecutions in fair trials. Since the beginning of the 1990s, following the end of the Cold War, a number of such initiatives have been

---

is, however, in principle a different issue than the hierarchical status of a norm; see Chapter 1, section 1.2, and Chapter 3, section 3.4.2.

[126] Orakhelashvili, 2008, p. 288, *supra* note 15. A case in point is the initial responses by states such as the United States and Israel in fall 2009 to the UN report on the alleged universal crimes committed in Gaza and Israel in 2008–2009, before, during and after Operation Cast Lead. See United Nations, 2009, *supra* note 105.

[127] "Obama's Nobel Remarks", transcript reprinted in *New York Times*, 10 December 2009, available at http://www.nytimes.com/2009/12/11/world/europe/11prexy.text .html, last accessed 6 June 2011.

taken, leading to the establishment of the ICC and several international ad hoc tribunals. How exactly the content of a possible *obligation* to this end could be formulated, including the legal consequences for breaches of this obligation, is not an easy question to answer.[128]

These international obligations may have a single or multiple legal foundations in law, that is, they may be grounded in one or more law-creating sources of international law.[129] As noted above, *genocide* was considered unlawful by states before the Genocide Convention was formally adopted, and even before true customary international law had time to emerge, since the specific concept and crime of genocide was not elaborated in the Nuremberg Judgment or applied in other war crimes trials after World War II. At that time, therefore, its legal basis must have been its existence as a crime in the general principles of law. Today, the proscription of genocide has multiple foundations within ICL. The prohibition on genocide is no doubt a *jus cogens* norm.[130] Prevention and punishment of genocide are explicit obligations for the states parties to the Genocide Convention.[131] These obligations now apply to all states, however, on the basis of customary international law and/or general principles of international law.

Universal competences and duties to investigate and prosecute enumerated universal crimes may also be delegated by states and the international community to an international tribunal, typically with secondary obligations laid upon states to cooperate with the tribunal, as in the cases of the ICTY and the ICTR. Another example is the obligation to prevent and punish torture. It is part of the Convention Against Torture and Other Cruel, Inhuman or Degrading Treatment or Punishment, but the same obligation may have a complementary foundation in customary international law. Duties to enact legislation and penal sanctions for the purpose of deterring grave breaches of humanitarian law in times of war

---

[128] The issue of community and state duties relating to universal crimes is not discussed in any detail here, as it concerns the topic of accountability and jurisdiction in general. See preface to this book.

[129] See Chapter 3.

[130] See (with further references) Orna Ben-Naftali, "The Obligations to Prevent and to Punish Genocide", in Gaeta, 2009, p. 36, *supra* note 80.

[131] The obligation to prevent genocide is violated by omission. See ICJ, *Application of the Convention on the Prevention and Punishment of the Crime of Genocide* (Bosnia and Herzegovina v. Serbia and Montenegro), Judgment, *I.C.J. Reports 2007*, p. 223, at para. 432.

and armed conflict follow from the four Geneva Conventions and the two 1977 Protocols. Similar duties with regard to preventing and suppressing the crime of genocide, crimes against humanity, and war crimes might be considered an implicit part of the statutes of the ICC.[132]

Whether prosecution is a legal *duty* or not, it is a special feature of universal crimes that all states are *entitled* at any time to prosecute in good faith such crimes, whether or not there are any treaty-based obligations to do so. The principle of universal jurisdiction in the sense of a competence for all states to extradite or prosecute (*aut dedere, aut judicare*) a suspected perpetrator of grave international crimes undoubtedly forms part of general international law.[133] The underlying substantive norm of the prohibited conduct and a concomitant right to punish participation in universal crimes is therefore founded in customary international law and the general principles of international law, at least the latter, or at least the former when considered in conjunction with the general principles and treaties. This seems to have been the *opinio juris* of the prosecutors and judges at the Nuremberg Tribunal and in the subsequent trials after World War II. The Nuremberg Judgment thus contains several references to the general principles of law as being part of the legal basis for the crimes set out in the Nuremberg Charter.

Among the special features of universal crimes, therefore, are that their proscription tends to have multiple legal foundations in international law, that the general principles of international law might at some stage of a dynamic development constitute a foundation,[134] and that certain secondary rights and duties to prosecute are inherently attached to the actual primary norms.[135]

---

[132] See preamble to the Rome Statute: "Affirming that the most serious crimes of concern to the international community as a whole must not go unpunished and that their effective prosecution must be ensured by taking measures at the national level and by enhancing international cooperation [...] Recalling that it is the duty of every State to exercise its criminal jurisdiction over those responsible for international crimes [...]". On the meaning of the arguable legal duty of states to prosecute under the Rome Statute, see Schabas, 2010, pp. 45–47, *supra* note 18.

[133] On the International Law Commission's work on the obligation to extradite or prosecute, see Chapter 4, section 4.5.9.

[134] See Chapter 3, section 3.3, especially 3.3.3, 3.3.4, and 3.3.6.

[135] See Chapter 4, sections 4.5.9 and 4.9, although this subject is not discussed in any detail in this book.

2.3.2. Grave Breaches of International Law

Another feature of universal crimes is almost self-evident: they consist of grave breaches of international law which endanger entire communities as well as individual persons. The concept of 'grave breaches' was articulated with authority in the Geneva Conventions of 1949. These draw a contrast between grave breaches and other less severe breaches of these conventions by enumerating specific acts that are considered to be grave breaches. The same method is applied in the statutes of international tribunals: certain crimes are set forth by categories and defined as international crimes for the purpose of prosecution. This was already true of the Nuremberg Charter, which in Article 6 enumerates 'crimes against peace', 'war crimes', and 'crimes against humanity'. The same method was used by later international tribunals, although the exact lists and definitions of the crimes show some variation.

The crime of aggression ('crimes against peace') was initially, for political or practical reasons, not part of the operational ICC Rome Statute, despite being formally included within the Court's jurisdiction according to Article 5(1)(d). Similarly, this crime has not been included in the statutes of other international tribunals apart from the Nuremberg and Tokyo tribunals. However, the crime of aggression was defined and included in operational terms in the amended Rome Statute at the Kampala Review Conference in May 2010.[136]

On the other hand, 'genocide' (except in the Nuremberg and Tokyo tribunals), 'crimes against humanity', and 'war crimes' have always been included, as have some grave breaches of the Geneva Conventions (see, for example, Article 4 of the Statute for the International Tribunal for Rwanda: "serious violations of Article 3 common to the Geneva Conventions of 12 August 1949 for the Protection of War Victims, and of Additional Protocol II thereto of 8 June 1977"). These examples show that that the gravity of the crimes in question matters and may constitute a distinguishing element in the enterprise of UN-based international crime proscription and enforcement.

Such examples, however, should not be used to conclude that international criminal law is limited to three or four kinds of grave crimes, at a maximum five or six. The question cannot be resolved so easily.

---

[136] See Chapter 4, section 4.7.

Since treaties are part of international law, and complex multilateral treaties under the auspices of the UN may to some extent provide a substitute for world community legislation, new treaty-based crimes may be added as international cooperation focuses on deterrence of highly undesirable acts, which are often organised and are seen to have consequences in more than one state.

Such new developments in international criminal law can be seen, for example, in the evolution of thinking on 'acts of terrorism' in the years since 9/11.[137] This has thus far followed a separate track, although it converges with other parts of international criminal law and with traditional core international crimes. The UN Security Council has outlawed terrorism, but prosecution has generally not been raised from the national to the international level, except for acts of terror that might *also* be subsumed under headings such as 'war crimes' or 'crimes against humanity' in the jurisdictional clauses of international tribunals.[138]

How terrorism more generally may fit or not fit within the notions of universal crimes is addressed in Chapter 4. Another example is the crime of piracy. Piracy which is directed against commercial vessels may not *a priori* be comparable to core international crimes. In specific cases, however, acts of piracy such as those off the coast of Somalia might cause serious enough problems and arouse enough international attention to be seen as warranting prosecutions by an international tribunal. Hence there seems to be a need for criteria other than reference to a few recognised 'core crimes' or to a generic definition of 'international criminal law' in order to distinguish grave breaches from other criminal acts.

In summary, although being 'grave breaches' of international law clearly seems to be a required feature of the crimes examined in this

---

[137] On the status of terrorist crimes under current international law, see Chapter 4, section 4.9.2.

[138] An interesting development is, however, taking place at some of the international 'hybrid' tribunals. At the Special Court for Sierra Leone, former president Taylor of the Republic of Liberia is indicted on charges of "terrorizing the civilian population"; see SCSL, *Prosecutor v. Taylor*, Prosecution's Second Indictment, 2007, Count 1, pp. 2–3, *supra* note 47. The Special Tribunal for Lebanon (STL) is also dealing with acts of terrorism, and its Appeals Chamber has concluded that a customary rule of international law has evolved on terrorism, at least with respect to peacetime. See STL Appeals Chamber, *Interlocutory Decision on the Applicable Law: Terrorism, Conspiracy, Homicide, Perpetration, Cumulative Charging*, STL-11-01/I/AC/R176bis, Decision of 16 February 2011.

volume, the concept of gravity is not self-explanatory. How it is to be determined for the purpose of international criminal law, whether in theory or practice, remains to be investigated.

2.3.3. Crimes Committed, Organised, or Tolerated by Powerful Persons

Another characteristic feature of universal crimes is that they typically concern crimes committed, organised, or tolerated by powerful persons, that is, by persons who are part of central or dangerous power structures within a society.

The most obvious cases are those international crimes planned and organised by a government or by leadership of the ruling party in a particular state, for example, the genocides against the Jews and other groups in Hitler's Third Reich or against the Tutsis in Rwanda in 1994. Such crimes may involve participants from several powerful sectors of the state, for example, the military, the police, or other administrative bodies. In some cases, governments may use private militia groups to avoid clear evidence of state participation in the criminal acts. The strong relationship between organised power structures and universal crimes is further discussed in the section 2.3.4 on gravity assessment.

However, being powerful is not a characteristic limited to state actors. Non-governmental groups may have the weapons, economic resources, and personnel needed to commit large-scale international crimes. Even small terrorist groups may be capable of committing serious crimes, which in particular cases may shock humanity or entire societies. For example, the violent kidnapping and later execution by the Red Army Faction of the German industrial leader Hans-Martin Schleyer in 1977, an attack that also killed four other people, probably had such an impact. The same is true of the killing of 11 Israeli participants during the Munich Olympic Games in 1972 by members of the Palestinian organisation Black September. In the latter case, the actions of Black September were probably tolerated by the principal power structures within Palestinian society, including the Palestine Liberation Organization. In fact, most serious terrorist acts are not only tolerated but actively supported and even directed (albeit frequently under cover) by other powerful entities or groups, sometimes even with suspected ties to foreign governments and intelligence services. This has been particularly clear with respect to more recent internationally organised acts of severe violent terrorism, committed or supported by organisations such as al-Qaeda, which was tolerated by the former Taliban government of Afghanistan before September 11, 2001, and may have been secretly financed or abetted by state entities or powerful persons in other countries as well. In many cases, such acts may well be recognised as universal crimes.[139]

Thus a special feature of the crimes under inquiry is that they are – from an empirical point of view – usually committed, organised, and/or tolerated by powerful personnel. That, of course, is one reason why such crimes are so dangerous to societies and to many potential victims, and why they are often a threat to international peace and security within the meaning of the UN Charter.

It should be added, however, that universal crimes need not be part of a larger criminal conspiracy, plan, or policy in legal terms. This is not necessary even with respect to the crime of genocide: a general genocidal policy is not a legal requirement of the genocidal crime types of 'killing' and 'causing serious bodily or mental harm',[140] although it has been recognised in the jurisprudence of the ICTR and ICTY that "it frequently happens in practice that acts of genocide are accompanied by or are based on a plan or a sort of conspiratorial scheme".[141] According to the un-ambiguous wording of the genocide definition in the Genocide Convention, Article II, which was later transposed to the statutes of international criminal courts, genocide crimes are characterised by two (objective) legal ingredients: the material element of the offence, consisting of one or several enumerated acts, and the particular *mens rea* of such offences, consisting of the specific intent to destroy, in whole or in part, a national, ethnic, racial, or religious group as such. However, with respect to the genocidal crime types of 'deliberately inflicting on the

---

[139] See further Chapter 4, section 4.9.2, on the legal status of terrorist acts under international criminal law.

[140] Convention on the Prevention and Punishment of the Crime of Genocide, Article II(a) and (b). See the identical genocide definition in the Rome Statute, Article 6.

[141] Antonio Cassese, "Is Genocidal Policy a Requirement for the Crime of Genocide?", in Gaeta, 2009, p. 129, *supra* note 80. Cassese notes in particular the judgments of ICTR, Trial Chamber, *Prosecutor v. Clément Kayishema and Obed Ruzindana*, ICTR 95-1-T, 21 May 1999, paras. 94 and 276, and ICTY, Appeals Chamber, *Prosecutor v. Goran Jelisić*, IT-95-10, 5 July 2001, para. 48. In both cases the courts rejected the notion that the existence of a larger plan or policy was a necessary legal ingredient of the crime. In the literature the viewpoints have differed on this issue. For a contradictory opinion, see Schabas, 2010, pp. 124–125, *supra* note 18.

group conditions of life calculated to bring about its physical destruction', 'imposing measures intended to prevent births within the group', and 'forcibly transferring children of the group to another group',[142] it is perhaps harder to imagine such acts being committed without being part of a larger plan or policy organised or tolerated by powerful persons within a power structure. This does not mean, in the opinion of this author, that a third *legal* ingredient, by necessary implication, must be added to the clear wording of the genocide definition. Neither is there a requirement of any particular motive behind the acts or the specific genocidal intent.

The ICTY *Jelisić* case, for example, concerned a notorious mass murderer, a man who proclaimed himself the "Serbian Adolf". Jelisić said that he "hated the Muslims and wanted to kill them all", and had also killed and ill-treated many Muslims in Bosnia.[143] It had not been proven beyond reasonable doubt that his actions were part of an existing plan, drawn up by others, for the actual crime scenes. The ICTY Appeals Chamber underlined the difference between the legal requirements, on the one hand, and the evidentiary considerations that are often relevant, on the other:

> The Appeals Chamber is of the opinion that the existence of a plan or policy is not a legal ingredient of the crime [of genocide]. However, in the context of proving specific intent, the existence of a plan or policy may become an important factor in most cases. The evidence may be consistent with the existence of a plan or policy, or may even show such existence, and the existence of a plan or policy may facilitate proof of the crime.[144]

Accordingly, the existence of a policy set forth by actors within a dangerous power structure is not necessarily a legal requirement of universal crimes,[145] although it is an important feature of universal crimes in a

---

[142] Convention on the Prevention and Punishment of the Crime of Genocide, Article II(c),(d), and (e).

[143] ICTY, *Jelisić* case, paras. 60–63, *supra* note 141.

[144] *Ibid.*, para. 48. The Appeals Chamber concluded on the substance of the case that Jelisić fulfilled the elements of the crime of genocide (para. 69–77).

[145] On the same track, with respect to the genocide crimes of killing and causing serious harm, see Cassese, 2009, p. 136, *supra* note 141: "To hold otherwise is to confuse a requirement demanded by a legal rule with a factual occurrence in practice: one simply mixes up *quod plerumque accidit*, i.e. what in fact occurs very frequently in real

sociological and prosecutorial perspective and might be a legal requirement as well for some universal crimes.

While the murderer in the *Jelisić* case did not act outside any power
structure,[146] in very exceptional cases of universal crimes even a single
person acting alone may commit acts that fulfil all the legal requirements
of crimes such as genocide, crimes against humanity, and terrorism. The
notion of a 'one-man genocide mission' has thus been envisaged in
international jurisprudence.[147] This might be more likely in times of war
and serious social unrest, but it is in theory possible in all societies where
individuals have access to dangerous weapons and materials for

life, with a specific and distinct ingredient required by legal rules for a conduct to be
characterized as genocide". The 'Elements of Crimes' corresponding to Rome Statute
Article 6, enacted pursuant to Article 9, are not fully conclusive on this point; see,
e.g., element no. 4 of 'Genocide by killing': "The conduct took place in the context of
a manifest pattern of similar conduct directed against that group or was conduct that
could itself effect such destruction". ICC, *Elements of Crimes*, PCNICC/2000/1/
Add.2, 2000. While the first alternative seems to imply a policy requirement, the second alternative allows for the interpretation that a notorious perpetrator might have
acted on his own with the intent and to the effect of such group destruction, even
without being directed by a policy set forth by others. The ICTY Appeals Chamber
judgment in the *Jelisić* case, *supra* note 141, thus appears to be consistent with the
'Elements of Crimes' under the Rome Statute as well. In the *Bashir* case, 4 March
2009, para. 124, *supra* note 48, the ICC Pre-Trial Chamber noted that the crime of
genocide "is only triggered when the threat against the existence of the targeted
group, or part thereof, becomes concrete and real, as opposed to just being latent or
hypothetical". Whether this implies a wholly different interpretation of the 'Elements
of Crimes' alternative of "conduct that could itself effect such destruction", in relation
to notorious offenders on the ground, remains to be seen.

[146] Many of Jelisić's victims were detained in informal collection centres. See ICTY,
Jelisić case, *supra* note 141, paras. 60–63. See also the indication in the "Partial Dissenting Opinion of Judge Shahabuddeen" in this case, p. 52, para. 16, that it "would
be open to a reasonable tribunal to find [...] that the respondent, though not proved to
be the actual commander of the camp, had *de facto* authority over prisoners in matters
of life and death".

[147] This was also recognised by the ICTY in the *Jelisić* case, *supra* note 141, para. 60
(with reference to the Trial Chamber): "even if he could be regarded as capable of
committing genocide as a single perpetrator – which the Trial Chamber thought 'theoretically possible' – the evidence did not support the conclusion ['that he was acting
pursuant to a plan created by superior authorities' and] that he did so beyond reasonable doubt"). See also para. 66: "the respondent believed himself to be following a plan
sent down by superiors to eradicate the Muslims [...] and that, regardless of any such
plan, he was himself a one-man genocide mission, intent upon personally wiping out
the protected group in whole or part".

manufacturing large bombs, as well as to information about potential targets. A case in point is the apparently carefully planned and politically motivated bombing in Norway, on 22 July 2011, of the main government buildings in Oslo (8 dead, 91 wounded) and the massacre of defenceless children and others at a summer youth camp of the ruling Labour party at Utøya (69 dead, 62 wounded by illegal ammunition causing extra serious damage).[148] The bombing and the massacre also constituted attempted murder of several hundred other people, maybe as many as 800 civilians. The suspect was a self-proclaimed conservative Christian 'crusader' who appeared to have planned and executed the crimes alone. He was immediately charged with terrorism by the Norwegian police, and according to public statements by the Norwegian prosecutor general, would also be considered for charges of 'crimes against humanity'.[149]

If a notorious offender has not been linked to any power structure, a useful guideline might still be found in the underlying idea of 'universal crimes' as 'crimes that shock humanity and civilised societies'.[150] The implication would be that only especially grave individual crimes are possible candidates for the 'exceptional cases' category when the crimes are not linked to a power structure. A legal recognition of such exceptional cases is not incompatible with a theory that generally emphasises the 'crime level' as well as the 'responsibility level' (see the next section of this chapter). Furthermore, the notion that exceptional universal crimes cases may occur should not distract from the fact that universal crimes typically are organised or tolerated by powerful or dangerous power structures.

---

[148] See, *e.g.*, Norwegian Broadcasting Corporation (NRK), "Fortsatt alvorlig for de skadde" ["Still Serious for Wounded"], NRK homepage (video and article), 1 August 2011.

[149] With respect to crimes against humanity, the 'Elements of Crimes' under the Rome Statute is again open to interpretation on the issue of a policy requirement linked to a dangerous power structure. For example, the three formal elements of Article 7(1)(a) of the Rome Statute do not set forth any explicit policy requirement. However, the introduction to the Elements states, "It is understood that 'policy to commit such attack' requires that the State or organization actively promote or encourage such an attack against a civilian population". For a legal opinion similar to the one expressed in the introduction, see, *e.g.*, Schabas, 2010, pp. 149–152, *supra* note 18.

[150] See section 2.1.3. of this chapter.

2.3.4. Gravity Assessment

If 'gravity' is taken as a defining aspect of universal crimes, it is still necessary to further specify several distinct ways in which gravity may be relevant. Among the alternatives, which are complementary rather than mutually exclusive, are the following:

1) Gravity may be essential for the distinction between universal or international crimes and other offences, as further discussed in Chapter 4.

2) Gravity assessments may affect the classification, content, and applicability of the different modes of punishable participation under international criminal law. For instance, if a certain mode of high-level participation tends to result in large-scale universal crimes, this weighs in favour of criminalisation and might affect the interpretation of written provisions.

3) Gravity assessment is also important for practical enforcement of international criminal law. The suspected gravity of mass crimes may thus motivate the establishment of ad hoc criminal tribunals.

4) Gravity is important for prosecutorial decision-making once a tribunal has been established.

5) Gravity is a primary consideration at the sentencing stage at international tribunals, which must also take into account the specific aggravating and/or mitigating circumstances of each case.[151]

In fact, the need for a mixture of abstract and concrete gravity assessment seems to be an inherent feature of 'universal crimes'.

Practical enforcement includes the process of identifying situations in certain countries or regions where relevant crime scenes may exist. This is an important part of the work of the ICC, although the basis for exercise of jurisdiction may vary from case to case. Situations can be

---

[151] See Mark A. Drumbl, *Atrocity, Punishment and International Law*, Cambridge University Press, Cambridge, UK, 2007, p. 64. Drumbl concludes that according to the jurisprudence of the ICTY and ICTR, "the gravity and egregiousness of the crimes [can be] identified as the primary consideration in imposing sentence". A number of cases are cited in support of this proposition. Note that in his listing of aggravating factors, Drumbl includes certain aspects of gravity in a broader sense as distinct or partly overlapping additional factors, including "the breadth of the crimes (*e.g.*, numbers of victims) and the suffering inflicted" and "the nature of the perpetrator's involvement" and "position as a superior".

referred to the ICC prosecutor by a state party or by the Security Council, or the prosecutor may initiate investigations *proprio motu* on the basis of information about crimes within the jurisdiction of the Court.[152] The prosecutor may first initiate a preliminary examination, which may include information sent by individuals, groups, states, intergovernmental organisations, or NGOs.[153] In order to determine whether there is a "reasonable basis to proceed with an investigation", the prosecutor, among other requirements, needs to "assess the gravity of the crimes allegedly committed in the situation", taking into account "various factors including their scale, nature, manner of commission, and impact".[154] Note in this regard that the "manner of commission" presumably includes also the degree of participation and the intent in commission and the extent to which the crimes were systematic or resulted from a plan or organised policy.[155] This guideline implies that it might be necessary to consider the larger context to determine gravity, rather than only the gravity of each crime in isolation. It is not necessarily enough that identified individuals can be accused on a reasonable basis of having committed a genocide crime, a crime against humanity, or a war crime, and that the case falls within the jurisdiction of the Court. The 'case' presented to the ICC must also be of sufficient gravity to justify further action by the Court.[156] Therefore, a higher gravity threshold exists for investigation and prosecution before the ICC than for determination that a crime has occurred.[157] However, the ICC Appeals Chamber has declined to set an

---

[152] Rome Statute, Articles 13–15.

[153] *Ibid.*, Article 15(2). See also ICC Office of the Prosecutor (ICC-OTP), *Regulations of the Office of the Prosecutor*, ICC-BD/05-01-09 (entry into force: 23 April 2009), Official Journal Publication, Regulation 25.

[154] See ICC, *Regulations of the Office of the Prosecutor*, Regulation 29(2), *supra* note 153. See further ICC-OTP, "Policy Paper on Preliminary Examination", 4 October 2010, where these non-exhaustive factors are explained in more detail.

[155] See ICC-OTP, "Policy Paper on Preliminary Examination", p. 14, *supra* note 154.

[156] Rome Statute, Article 17(1)(d). See also Article 53(1)(b).

[157] Consider ICC-OTP, "Policy Paper on Preliminary Examination", p. 13, *supra* note 154: "Although any crime falling within the jurisdiction of the Court is serious, Article 17(1)(d) requires the Court to assess as an admissibility threshold whether a case is of sufficient gravity to justify further action by the Court. The Office will apply the same assessment in relation to gravity at the situation stage".

overly restrictive legal bar to the interpretation of gravity that would hamper the deterrent role of the Court.[158]

The process becomes more complicated, acquiring both political and legal dimensions, when the UN Security Council decides that a particular situation is a threat to peace and security and may thus warrant international intervention. Is it desirable to establish International Criminal Court jurisdiction? If the ICC does not have jurisdiction, should the Security Council take the additional step of referring a situation to the ICC? This possibility was clearly confirmed by the decision of the Security Council in 2005 to refer the situation in Darfur to the ICC, despite the fact that Sudan is not a state party to the ICC treaty. But it might also be determined that there is a need for further fact-finding and independent assessment of the gravity of the alleged crimes before any decision is taken on referral to the ICC. Perhaps the state concerned might be allowed more time to initiate national prosecutions. Such investigations are complicated and highly political and may involve several different UN bodies, as seen in 2009 when the Goldstone fact-finding mission appointed by the UN Human Rights Council scrutinised the Israel/Gaza situation. One may ask, however, to what extent the members of the Security Council may be obliged by international *jus cogens* and *erga omnes* norms[159] to ensure accountability at least for the "most senior leaders suspected of being most responsible for crimes".[160]

When a situation has been formally identified and investigations have been pursued, the next practical issue from a prosecutorial point of view concerns the prioritisation and selection of cases.[161] As pointed out by Bergsmo, the need for effective case selection and prioritisation is

---

[158] *Ibid.* See also ICC, Situation in the Democratic Republic of the Congo, *Judgment on the Prosecutor's appeal against the decision of Pre-Trial Chamber I entitled "Decision on the Prosecutor's Application for Warrants of Arrest, Article 58"*, ICC-01/04-169, 13 July 2006.

[159] See Chapter 1, section 1.2., and Chapter 3, sections 3.2., 3.3.4., and 3.4.2.

[160] The Security Council used this formulation in Resolution 1534 (2004) when calling on the ICTY and the ICTR to concentrate their efforts on the senior leaders suspected of being most responsible for serious crimes. One may ask why the same principle should not also apply to the work of the Security Council, presuming that such crimes regularly endanger international peace and security.

[161] See, *e.g.*, Morten Bergsmo (ed.), *Criteria for Prioritizing and Selecting Core International Crimes Cases*, 2nd ed., FICHL Publication Series No. 4, Torkel Opsahl Academic EPublisher, Oslo, 2010. The book contains a number of articles on the matter.

most acute in the criminal jurisdictions confronted with the highest number of crime cases.[162] Do prosecutors in such situations have unlimited discretion, given constraints of available resources, to refrain from prosecution of universal crimes and/or a duty to act in a non-discriminatory manner, or should there be binding criteria for case selection and prioritisation? Is there a duty to prosecute certain crimes or certain known suspects, once they meet concrete gravity thresholds? A number of different issues related to prosecutorial discretion may arise, making this a recurring theme in the ICL literature and to some extent for international jurisprudence generally.[163] For example, if states have a duty to either extradite likely offenders or prosecute universal crimes, which they may well have under current international law,[164] does the practical fulfilment of the duty to prosecute – and thus the content of the duty – also depend upon a further gravity assessment as well?

These questions are not addressed in any detail in this book.[165] But it is noteworthy that many of the practical problems concerning prosecution of large-scale crimes are not new, but already confronted the prosecutors at Nuremberg. Telford Taylor, the chief of counsel for war crimes at the Nuremberg trials held under the authority of Control Council

---

[162] Morten Bergsmo, "The Theme of Selection and Prioritization Criteria and Why It Is Relevant", in *ibid.*, p. 13.

[163] For an instructive article on lessons learned and best practices from international tribunals, see Xabier Agirre Aranburu, "Gravity of Crimes and Responsibility of the Suspect", in Bergsmo, 2010, pp. 205–234, *supra* note 161. See also James A. Goldston, "More Candour about Criteria: The Exercise of Discretion by the Prosecutor of the International Criminal Court", in *Journal of International Criminal Justice*, 2010, no. 8, pp. 383–406; Daniel D. Ntanda Nsereko, "Prosecutorial Discretion before National Courts and International Tribunals", in *Journal of International Criminal Justice*, 2005, no. 3, pp. 124–144; Hassan B. Jallow, "Prosecutorial Discretion and International Criminal Justice", in *Journal of International Criminal Justice*, 2005, no. 3, pp. 145–161; Luc Côté, "Reflections on the Exercise of Prosecutorial Discretion in International Criminal Law", in *Journal of International Criminal Justice*, 2005, no. 3, pp. 162–186; and Allison Marston Danner, "Enhancing the Legitimacy and Accountability of Prosecutorial Discretion at the International Criminal Court", in *American Journal of International Law*, 2003, vol. 97, pp. 510–552.

[164] See Orakhelashvili, 2008, pp. 288–319, *supra* note 15, with extensive references to international legal sources and arguments pro et contra. At page 307, he seems to conclude that states are not only entitled but also obliged *erga omnes* to try an offender or extradite him for breaches of *jus cogens* crimes – the latter concept presumably being similar to 'universal crimes'.

[165] See preface to this book.

Law No. 10, was responsible for the selection of defendants. He noted, "The individuals indicted under Law No. 10 were a small minority of those who, on the basis of the available evidence, appeared and probably could be proved to be guilty of criminal conduct". Looking back at the 12 trials as a whole, "four factors were basic in making the final selections of the individuals to be accused". First and foremost was "what the evidence showed concerning the activities of particular individuals".[166] This required, however, the second component of evidence collection, which had to be approached with some assumptions and according to a plan:

> In short it was necessary to use deductive as well as inductive methods of investigation. Accordingly, all professional staff members were expected to familiarize themselves as rapidly as possible with the organization and functioning of the Reich [...]. In addition, a special section was set up to compile a sort of register of "Who's Who" of leading German politicians, civil servants, military men, business men, etc.[167]

It might be added that the collection of evidence may also raise special problems in investigations of mass crimes, for example with regard to finding the actual crime scenes and mass grave exhumations.[168]

The third and fourth factors, according to Taylor, were the availability of crime suspects and the resources made available to the prosecutorial enterprise in terms of time, staff, and money.[169] In conclusion, the task had been

> to determine, in light of all the available information, where the deepest individual responsibility lay for the manifold crimes committed [...] [regardless] of any particular occupation, profession, or other category of persons. To preserve the integrity of the proceedings, it was necessary to

---

[166] Telford Taylor, *Final Report to the Secretary of the Army on the Nuremberg War Crimes Trials under Control Council Law No. 10*, Washington, DC, 15 August 1949, p. 74.

[167] *Ibid.*, p. 75.

[168] See Melanie Klinkner, "Proving Genocide? Forensic Expertise and the ICTY", in *Journal of International Criminal Justice*, 2008, no. 6, pp. 447–466. See also Clea Koff, *The Bone Woman: A Forensic Anthropologist's Search for Truth in the Mass Graves of Rwanda, Bosnia, Croatia, and Kosovo*, Random House, New York, 2005.

[169] Taylor, 1949, *supra* note 166, pp. 75–76.

scrutinize the conduct of leaders in all occupations, and let the chips fall where they might.[170]

This, it seems, is not very different from what most actors and commentators in international criminal law would still recommend. The following principles suggested by Agirre Aranburu are worth recalling for the purpose of this book as well:

> Based on the lessons learned and best practices from international tribunals, the use of the criteria of gravity and highest responsibility for selection of prioritization of cases would be best guaranteed by the following principles:
>
> a. Determine the substantive offences that are regarded as gravest (such as possibly killing and rape) and develop the selection process mainly around them.
>
> b. Define clear parameters of gravity, including quantitative and qualitative aspects (number of victims, manner, specific intent, etc.) and considering sentencing criteria.
>
> c. Adopt an explicit hypothesis of the case as the outline for selection and investigation.
>
> d. Adopt a clear definition of "most responsible", focusing on the primary causal actors and presuming that they are the same as senior leaders only under certain factual circumstances.
>
> e. Beware of the existence of multiple types of power structures, discrepancies between their formal definition and real functioning, and variations over time and space.
>
> f. Utilize systematically analytical techniques, including crime pattern databases, statistics, standard indicators checklists, mapping, chronologies, network analysis, etc. to determine both gravity and highest responsibility.
>
> [g.] Beware of the risk of confirmation bias in suspect-driven investigations and take measures to control it.[171]

Once it is concluded that the determination of gravity is important at several stages of the processes implementing international criminal law, it becomes critical for the international community to be aware of, and to agree on, the methods used to define gravity for each of the purposes set forth at the start of this section. This book advances the thesis that such

---

[170] *Ibid.*, p. 85.

[171] Agirre Aranburu, 2010, pp. 233–234, *supra* note 163.

methods are necessarily an inherent part of international criminal law. In addition, it proposes that the core meaning of 'gravity' in international criminal law can be usefully considered to be a function of two main parameters: the seriousness of each particular *universal crime scene*, defined by the underlying crimes committed within a certain socio-political context ('universal crime scenario'), and the *level of responsibility* for the crimes within the power structures which can be considered in empirical terms to be collectively responsible for the crimes.[172] A universal crime scene can be an exact location, for example a detention centre, a small village, a school or church, even a house, but it might also be taken as a wider geographic area, such as a town or even a city. The relevant sociopolitical context is considered in legal terms to be part of the definition of the crime category in question, for instance, a state of armed conflict with respect to war crimes or a "widespread or systematic attack directed against any civilian population" with respect to crimes against humanity.[173] Determining the level of responsibility requires a principal focus on the rank and role of the primary leader allegedly responsible and of other high-ranking personnel, and their concrete modes of participation. However, the most notorious offenders positioned at intermediate or low levels of the power structure may also, by the scale and cruelty of their involvement, be assigned a high level of responsibility. In other words, the 'responsibility level' is not necessarily determined only by a person's formal or *de facto* position within the relevant power structures, but in special cases wholly or primarily by the suspect's own conduct at the concrete crime scenes. In very exceptional cases, as argued in section 2.3.3. of this chapter, the crimes of notorious offenders who have been planning and executing crimes as if they were supported by a dangerous power structure, although they were actually not, might be considered for a high score on 'responsibility level' as well.

The strong causal relationship between organised power structures and 'collective crimes' was noted by Roxin in 1963 in a seminal article

---

[172] The concepts of 'universal crime scene' and 'universal crime scenario' are also discussed in Chapter 5, section 5.2.2., in relation to the gravity clauses and underlying crimes inherent in the concept of universal crimes.

[173] ICC, *Report of the Preparatory Commission for the International Criminal Court*, Addendum Part II, "Finalized draft text of the Elements of Crimes", PCNICC/2000/1/Add.2, 2, November 2000, Article 7(1)(a), Crime against humanity, of murder.

that applied the notion of 'indirect perpetration' to leaders.[174] In his opinion, one may understand the acts of leaders from the point of view of criminal law in two ways: as collective crimes or as individual acts, but "[n]either of the two viewpoints can, in isolation, entirely encompass the substantive criminality of the occurrences".[175] He highlighted in particular the feature of control over an organised power structure by actors who remain behind the scenes, suggesting that an absence of proximity to the crime in question might be "compensated by an increasing degree of organizational control by the leadership positions in the apparatus".[176] In other words, according to Roxin, the farther removed a punishable participant is, in structural terms, from the victim and the direct criminal act, the more responsibility he bears for the universal crimes committed.[177] Roxin underlined that the number of victims is not conclusive in determining perpetration at the highest level; "[if] only a single person had been persecuted, the person behind the scenes would still have to be convicted as a perpetrator".[178] The assumption underlying this principle is important with respect to the concept of universal crimes itself.[179]

Figure 1 provides a visual representation of the general elements in an assessment of gravity in international criminal law.

---

[174] Originally published in German, the article has recently been republished in translation. Claus Roxin, "Crimes as Part of Organized Power Structures", in *Journal of International Criminal Justice*, 2011, no. 9, pp. 193–205. See also Gerhard Werle and Boris Burghardt, "Claus Roxin on Crimes as Part of Organized Power Structures: Introductory Note", in *Journal of International Criminal Justice*, 2011, no. 9, pp. 191–193.

[175] Roxin, 2011, *supra* note 174, p. 194.

[176] *Ibid.*, p. 200.

[177] *Ibid.* "We can see that the objective elements of organizational control are very clearly delineated here: whereas normally, the farther removed a participant is from the victim and the direct criminal act, the more he is pushed to the margins of events and excluded from control of the acts, in this case the reverse is true".

[178] *Ibid.*, p. 201.

[179] See Chapter 4, section 4.9., *e.g.*, with respect to the category of 'excessive use and abuse of authorised power' set forth in section 4.9.3.

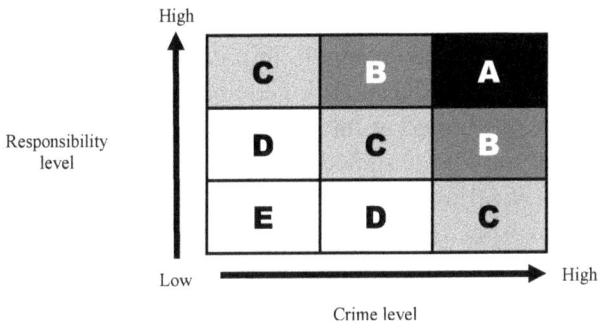

Figure 1: Gravity as a Function of Crime Level and Responsibility Level.

The horizontal axis shows the 'crime level' at a universal crime scene, with levels of seriousness increasing from low to intermediate to high. The vertical axis shows the 'responsibility level' of the person/group committing the crime, likewise increasing from low to high. An arrow could be drawn to show the effect of increasing seriousness of the crime level and level of responsibility, from cell E (low-low) to cell A (high-high). The underlying assumption is that for most purposes of international criminal law and justice, both factors are of approximately equal importance.

The matrix divides the set of options into nine different cells. If numerical indexes are provided for each axis, ranging from 1 to 3, the cell labelled A gets the maximum of 6 (3+3) points, the two cells labelled B get 5 (3+2) points, the three cells labelled C get 4 (3+1 or 2+2) points, the two cells labelled D get 3 (2+1) points, and the one cell labelled E gets the minimum of 2 (1+1) points.

Arguably, such a model is implicit in the concepts of international crimes, core crimes, and universal crimes alike, although it might be applied differently depending on the concept used. For example, the specific intent required for a crime of genocide (intent to destroy a group as such) forms part of the 'crime level' and moves that axis to 'high' for all such crimes. The responsibility level does not matter for the constitution of such crimes as universal crimes; that is, a crime meeting all the elements of the definition of 'genocide' is in principle a punishable crime under international law regardless of the level of responsibility for the underlying crime within a relevant power structure.[180] However, in

---

[180] See the discussions in section 2.3.3. of this chapter.

practice, genocide crimes seldom occur if there is no one at higher levels of the power structure who has planned, initiated, or consented to these or similar universal crimes. And as mentioned above, in the case of the most notorious offenders positioned at intermediate or low levels of the power structure, they may also be assigned a high level of responsibility. The existence of a high level of responsibility is thus *de facto* implicit in the 'gravity clause' of specific intent for genocide crimes, even if not formally part of the crime concept.

This is not the case for the crime of aggression. Under the definition adopted by the ICC, this crime explicitly requires the involvement of powerful individuals at the highest level, that is, of political and military leaders. The required level of gravity to constitute such a crime thus depends upon the 'crime level', that is, whether a violation of the UN Charter by the use of armed force is 'manifest' or not.[181] For other crime categories, the required gravity may depend upon specific combinations of the two parameters. For example, with regard to torture as a possible discrete crime under international law, and a serious act because of the consequences for the victim, it must at the very least be presumed that a high-ranking public official or other leader acting within an organisation is involved in order to reach the threshold required to designate it as an international or universal crime.[182]

With regard to prosecutorial discretion on issues of investigation, case selection, and prioritisation, the scale (number of victims), qualitative aspects (the substantive offences, specific intent, and manner), and impact of the crimes may all play an important role. It should be noted that Figure 1 is not meant to imply that all punishable universal crimes should be prosecuted regardless of resources, judicial capacity, and political considerations, or that some universal crimes should not be prosecuted. In other words, it is necessary to keep in mind the distinction between the crime elements, including the inherent gravity of typical universal crimes, and gravity assessments as part of prosecutorial decision-making, which may imply a higher gravity threshold for other reasons.

---

[181] See Chapter 4, section 4.7.2., on the definition of aggression in the Rome Statute.
[182] See Chapter 4, sections 4.9.2.2. and 4.9.3., and Chapter 5, section 5.2.2.

2.3.5. Universal Crimes Require Retributive Criminal Justice

The nature of universal crimes, particularly their damaging effects on entire societies, requires that offenders do not escape justice, either by receiving impunity in their own country or by finding a safe haven in another country. If universal crimes have been committed on a large scale, however, it might not be realistic for all suspects to be brought to comprehensive and fair 'retributive justice', with appropriate penalties imposed after a public trial before independent judges based upon substantive criminal law and criminal law procedures. Even with respect to universal crimes, there are other conceivable mechanisms of justice. There is, for example, the concept of 'restorative justice' for gross human rights violations, as exemplified by the South African Truth and Reconciliation Commission (TRC). This entails engaging those who were harmed, the wrongdoers, and the affected communities in search of solutions that repair and rebuild social relationships. The TRC had an expansive mandate: to go beyond truth-finding to promote national unity and reconciliation, to facilitate the granting of amnesty to those who made full factual disclosure, to restore the human and civil dignity of victims by providing them an opportunity to tell their stories, and to make recommendations to the president on measures to prevent future human rights violations.[183] Restorative approaches are said to seek balanced justice for victims, offenders, and the community through processes that preserve the safety and dignity of all. 'Restorative justice' is not easily defined, however, at least not in general terms.[184] It may include a wide range of mechanisms that are different from traditional criminal justice, offering alternatives to trials and penal sanctions. One form of restorative justice is economic compensation to victims, an element that is quite often incorporated into modern criminal law proceedings.

Important as different restorative mechanisms might be, under the rule of law they cannot be regarded as sufficient. While they may provide a useful supplement, they cannot fully replace ordinary retributive justice through the criminal court system, and especially not in the case of universal crimes. There are several reasons for this, but to a large extent

---

[183] See, *e.g.*, Audrey R. Chapman and Hugo van der Merwe, *Truth and Reconciliation in South Africa: Did the TRC Deliver?*, University of Pennsylvania Press, Philadelphia, 2008.

[184] For the specific definition set forth by the TRC, see *ibid.*, p. 27.

they are the same reasons that apply to ordinary criminal acts. The main tool used with respect to a serious crime is punishment in the form of a unconditional sentence to imprisonment for a fixed number of years prescribed by a court. Since universal crimes can be presumed to be of even greater gravity than other serious crimes, the reasons for using that tool are presumably much stronger.

The general purposes of and justifications for criminal sanctions enforced by public authorities have long been discussed from a variety of philosophical, historical, sociological, and legal perspectives. In terms of the distinction between *mala in se* (acts that are criminal because they are clearly morally wrong) and *mala prohibita* (acts that are criminal because they are proscribed), universal crimes are definitely a prime example of the former. The infliction of retributive punishment for serious crimes, based on individual guilt to be established only through a fair and public prosecution, has been perceived as necessary in modern societies for a number of different although interconnected reasons. A plausible synthesis of the consensus among the majority of criminal law experts and policy makers, insofar as this author is able to judge, is shown in Box 1.

Ten Arguments in Favour of Retributive Justice for Grave Crimes

- Retributive justice has deterrent effects on future crimes by the same offender and by others, effects which are presumably stronger than those of other ('restorative') mechanisms with regard to grave crimes.
- Retributive justice upholds and clarifies the norms underpinning the proscription of specific grave crimes.
- Retributive justice is morally justified and required by reference to serious violations of fundamental common values and interests.
- Retributive justice meets the expectation that justice will be done.
- Retributive justice monopolises the use of physical sanctions and helps discourage private justice or blood revenge.
- Retributive justice individualises guilt and makes proportional punishment possible.
- Retributive justice militates against the temptation to impose collective punishment and against exaggerated fear in a population or group of people caused by overly broad images of who the perpetrators are and what their crimes are.
- Formal, fair, and efficient retributive processes establish the truth. The 'right to truth' is a common community value and may be considered an inherent human right with regard to grave crimes.
- Retributive justice is a prerequisite for true community reconciliation, that is, between victims and the society. Such reconciliation restores respect for the victim's dignity and may restore the broken bond between society and the perpetrator, once the sentence has been served. Retributive justice thus has important 'restorative' effects. (Reconciliation between victims and perpetrators is laudable, but should not be expected and is usually not considered necessary from a victim's or community's point of view with regard to grave crimes.)
- Retributive justice with formal procedures is a precondition for establishing, reestablishing, or preserving the rule of law – the existence of which is dependent upon people's respect for public authorities and the legitimacy of the legal system at large – because it emphasises compliance with substantive legal and moral norms and addresses breaches of those norms.

Box 1: Ten Arguments in Favour of Retributive Justice for Grave Crimes.

It should therefore be clear that in principle, at least, retributive justice is recommended for grave crimes, although different reasons may weigh more heavily in different states or at different times. The ways and means of implementation, however, raise additional complex issues. The natural preference for retributive justice with regard to universal crimes does not rule out the use of complementary 'restorative' mechanisms.

Such alternatives may even be preferable in a specific historical or socio-political setting.

When universal crimes are committed within a particular state, the 10 reasons presented in Box 1 apply as much to such crimes as to other serious crimes that are exclusively based on national legislation and jurisdiction. That the crimes may be much graver and may be committed by leaders and other high-ranking personnel should in general make the justifications for retributive justice even more compelling. And if the state where the crimes took place is not willing and able to prosecute such crimes, other states or the international community through international tribunals should act in the interest of the populations concerned, thus honouring their obligations *erga omnes*.

The important point, for now, is that deterrent effects constitute a principal justification for prosecution and punishment. Such effects are both *individual*, relating to the perpetrator, and *general*, relating to potential new perpetrators in the population at large who may abstain from criminal behaviour because of the recognised risk of criminal sanctions. This general preventive effect applies to potential new perpetrators in the state in question, in particular to new leaders. Even more important, it applies to potential new perpetrators in *all* states of the world. Thus the prosecution of particular universal crimes being committed in a country is relevant not only for the population and leaders of that country, but for leaders and other powerful persons everywhere in the world. As a distinct feature of universal crimes, this provides a strong justification for the assertion that universal crimes require fair criminal justice actions regardless of the location, nationality, religion, or political affiliations of the offenders.

3

Legal Bases of Universal Crimes Norms

3.1. Methodological Challenges

The subject matter of universal crimes raises special methodological challenges. This is because of the fragmented nature of international criminal law, and because the concept of international crimes is not in itself sufficiently clear to define which crimes are included or even what the conditions for inclusion are.[1] The principal focus of the universal crimes project is on binding international law, making traditional methodological issues a pressing concern. With regard to interpretation of treaties, for instance, the principles set out in the Vienna Convention on the Law of Treaties (VCLT) apply (see in particular Articles 31–33).[2] Additional challenges posed by the specific subject matter of this book, which is primarily concerned with the *concept* of universal crimes, are briefly set forth below.

This analysis starts from the assumption that the concept of universal crimes in international law is essentially a legal concept, consisting of binding norms of international criminal law. Legal norms are taken to mean rules proscribing a type of conduct, or, to the contrary, prescribing a kind of conduct which should be followed, which in some way is upheld by sanctions or possible sanctions within a system of law.[3] Following the opinion of the International Law Commission, international law is considered to be a 'system of law'.[4] Therefore, the rules of particular interest to this study are legally binding norms, which originate from specific law-creating sources of international law.[5]

---

[1] See also Chapter 1, section 1.2.

[2] See section 3.3.2 in this chapter.

[3] See further Chapter 4, section 4.8.1.

[4] See International Law Commission (ILC), *Conclusions of the Work of the Study Group on Fragmentation of International Law: Difficulties Arising from the Diversification and Expansion of International Law*, 2006, conclusion no. 1, reprinted in *Yearbook of the International Law Commission, 2006*, vol. II, part II.

[5] See further section 3.3. in this chapter.

A feature of binding rules is their 'if-then' character: that is, singular norms often form part of a larger structural norm encompassing abstract legal conditions ('if') for certain abstract legal consequences ('then'). Legal norms thus consist of legal conditions and legal consequences that should follow when all the necessary and sufficient conditions are fulfilled ('if a, b, and c, then x and y'). These may concern rights, obligations (duties), procedures, or competences. The simplest legal norms consist of just one condition and one consequence. Other rules may consist of several conditions and one consequence, while the most complex legal norms consist of several cumulative and alternative conditions and a number of consequences. Legal concepts often seek to encompass whole clusters of such legal norms concerned with the same subject matter, such as property rights, freedom of expression, refugee status, and criminal liability.

Because of the complexity of universal crimes and the often-noted fragmentation of international criminal law, a broader theoretical perspective may be needed, consisting of overarching concepts covering the entire field. The concept of universal crimes, it is argued, is the pre-eminent candidate for such a concept. It provides a common legal mega-norm, although, of course, it needs to be analysed and discussed from different perspectives. In a very simplified form, the concept can be shown as follows:

If:

Universal crime *and*

Punishable participation

Then:

Individual criminal liability *and*

Prosecution or extradition *and*

Universal court jurisdiction

There are multiple legal consequences included in the diagram, including the issue of jurisdiction. Even so, it is arguably too simple a model, implying that all universal crimes may have legal consequences that are comparable in all respects. That would not be accurate. For example, prosecutorial discretion may insert another layer in the model that needs to be taken into account in relation to the 'duty to extradite or prosecute',[6] raising the broader issue of accountability and jurisdiction.[7]

In principle, it should be possible to trace and assess the legal basis of each universal crimes norm. Since many other rules of international law emerge from the same legal bases, the necessary and sufficient conditions for distinguishing universal crimes norms from other legal norms must be specified. Such criteria and their formulations are discussed in Chapter 4, taking the closely related but better-known concept of 'international crimes' as the point of departure. On this basis, the different types of international crimes are enumerated.[8] One of the proposed conditions necessary for constituting an international crime is that the proscriptive norm must be anchored in the law-creating sources of international law. The question of legal bases is therefore unavoidable.

Before discussing these possible legal bases, the next section considers the difficulties arising from the diversification and expansion of international criminal law.

3.2. The Fragmented Nature of International Criminal Law

Is international criminal law (ICL) really one body of law that is a coherent subset of public international law? Or, alternatively, is ICL a somewhat artificial term, comprising several more or less integrated and partly conflicting law regimes?

In the case of national law within a state, one can expect legislation and criminal courts to form a unified system. Jurisdiction is normally allocated geographically at the lower levels, but a uniform interpretation of the law is made possible through a hierarchical appeal system. In national criminal law, the principles of legality and equality before the law require uniform and foreseeable application of the law. In federal states, distinctions are made between 'state' and 'federal' matters, but otherwise the structures are similar. ICL, on the other hand, does not constitute such a hierarchical and unified system of law.

It may be argued that jurisdiction over universal crimes is delegated to and applied by all states, at least all those states where the various crime scenes occur. This is true in theory. In practice, however, ICL has

---

[6] See also Chapter 2, section 2.3.5.
[7] See preface to this book.
[8] See Chapter 4, sections 4.8 and 4.9.

not actually functioned this way, with a few possible exceptions related to post–World War II war crimes trials and, arguably, to present-day transitional and post-transitional justice trials in Latin America[9] and some other countries assisted by the international community.[10] One key reason is that quite often governments themselves are involved in the universal crimes; another is the lack of adequate mechanisms for judicial implementation of prosecutions of these crimes. Political scientists have pondered why universal crimes trials happen in some countries and not at all or to a significantly lesser extent in other countries, even when the violations are much the same.[11] Legally, there is no remedy for appealing such decisions at the national level to an international criminal tribunal.

With respect to uniformity at the international level, there is no single, authoritative list of universal crimes (or 'international crimes'),[12] nor are there uniform criteria for punishable participation in such crimes. Crimes against humanity have been included in all the statutes of the various international tribunals since World War II, but apart from these, the categories and underlying crimes included, as well as their exact formulations, have varied.[13] In addition to crimes against humanity,

---

[9] In 1985 Argentina became the first country in Latin America to bring to court criminal cases for gross human rights violations, comparable to universal crimes, committed during military rule. Argentina was only the second country in the world (after Greece in 1975) to take such action in the period following the World War II cases. The success of this effort was initially limited, since the five junta members convicted were pardoned in 1990 along with other military officials. However, prosecutions of former political and military leaders started again in the mid-1990s, principally in Argentina and Chile. There have subsequently been cases in Bolivia, Guatemala, Haiti, Mexico, Paraguay, Peru, Suriname, and Uruguay. See Elin Skaar, *Judicial Independence and Human Rights in Latin America: Violations, Politics, and Prosecution*, Palgrave Macmillan, New York, 2010, pp. 2–3.

[10] See Chapter 2, section 2.2.4, and Chapter 4, section 4.3., for references to the international hybrid courts or internationalised courts in Sierra Leone, Lebanon, Cambodia, East Timor, Bosnia and Herzegovina, Kosovo, and Iraq.

[11] Skaar, 2010, *supra* note 9, analyses both political and legal structures but emphasises the impact of judicial independence in explaining why some prosecutors and courts in Argentina and Chile eventually took the lead in retributive justice.

[12] On attempts made to identify 'international crimes', see generally Chapter 4.

[13] An example is the particular jurisdictional limitation of the Nuremberg Charter Article 6(c), which arguably could be understood as specifying that crimes against humanity come within the Tribunal's jurisdiction only when committed "in execution of or in connection with" other crimes, in practice crimes against peace and war crimes. The English wording of Article 6(c) did not support this interpretation, but the prose-

---

genocide, aggression, and war crimes have generally been included. Other crimes outside these 'core crimes' have generally not been included, with differing opinions on their legal status.[14]

Another possible factor leading to fragmentation is court jurisdiction. The International Court of Justice (ICJ) is a general court of international law but not a criminal court. Although it may offer important opinions on legal issues directly relating to universal crimes, its jurisdictional limitations and the fact that it is not concerned with individual responsibility for universal crimes makes it unlikely that the ICJ could comprehensively and regularly address universal crimes issues. Historically, the treaty-based Nuremberg and Tokyo tribunals were clearly *ad hoc* courts with confined personal and temporal jurisdiction. The jurisdiction of the International Criminal Tribunal for Rwanda (ICTR), established by the UN Security Council, was also limited temporarily and territorially. In the case of the International Criminal Tribunal for the former Yugoslavia (ICTY), also established by the Security Council, the jurisdiction was limited territorially. While no explicit, forward-looking temporal limitation was formally established, it was clear from the beginning that the ICTY would only function for a limited period. The same applies to the Special Court for Sierra Leone (SCSL) and the Extraordinary Chambers in the Courts of Cambodia (ECCC), arguably the principal hybrid international tribunals.

The only international criminal court with an unlimited forward-looking temporal jurisdiction (covering all crimes committed after 2002) is the treaty-based International Criminal Court (ICC). The ICC is therefore potentially the most important international court that has ever

---

cutors at Nuremberg had signed a special common protocol to this effect. See Roger S. Clark, "Crimes against Humanity at Nuremberg", in George Ginsburgs and V. N. Kudriavtsev (eds.), *The Nuremberg Trial and International Law*, Kluwer Academic, Dordrecht, Netherlands, 1990, pp. 190–192. This led the Nuremberg Tribunal to the conclusion that acts before the outbreak of World War II in 1939 were outside its jurisdiction with respect to crimes against humanity. See International Military Tribunal (IMT), *Trial of the Major War Criminals before the International Military Tribunal: Nuremberg, 14 November 1945 – 1 October 1946*, Nuremberg, 1947 (hereafter, *Trial of the Major War Criminals*), vol. I, p. 254.

[14] See Chapter 4, sections 4.2–4.7.

been established, although it has other jurisdictional limitations.[15] Prosecution usually depends upon a referral by the forum state where the crimes have been committed, as provided in the Rome Statute, Article 13(a), or *proprio motu* upon the forum state being judged unwilling or unable to prosecute.[16] In addition, the limited number of crime types included in operational terms from the start has left other possible universal crimes in limbo, including the crime of aggression.[17]

To date, the ICC has not been able to establish itself as an effective world criminal court for the most serious crimes. It remains to be seen whether it will overcome its legal, political, and financial constraints. Kaye points out that even though "the ICC may seem to have become an indispensable international player", a closer look suggests that it is "still struggling to find its footing almost a decade after its creation". In addition, considering that all six of its investigations involve abuses in Africa, "its reputation as a truly international tribunal is in question".[18]

Although it is unlikely that the ICC will ever be able to function as a comprehensive criminal court system for the enforcement of universal crimes, it is nonetheless probable that the Court will become the most important institution for consideration of universal crimes issues. It may be able to reinforce a concerted effort by some states to prosecute major leaders and notorious offenders earlier supported or protected by national power structures. If this were accomplished on a regular basis over many

---

[15] On the jurisdictional bases of the ICC, see the Rome Statute of the International Criminal Court (hereafter, Rome Statute), Articles 13, 14, and 15. See in this book further Chapter 2, sections 2.2.4. and 2.3.4.

[16] See Rome Statute, Article 13(c). Two other possibilities exist: referral by the United Nations Security Council, as provided in Rome Statute Article 13(b), and referral by a state party other than the forum state. The latter option has not yet been utilised, but it is clearly part of Article 13(a). See James Crawford, "The Drafting of the Rome Statute", in Philippe Sands (ed.), *From Nuremberg to The Hague: The Future of International Criminal Justice*, Cambridge University Press, Cambridge, UK, 2003: "[...] any state party to the Statute can refer a possible crime to the Prosecutor, irrespective of any lack of contact between the referring state and the crime" (p. 148).

[17] See, however, Chapter 4, section 4.7., on the new provision in the Rome Statute, Article 8 *bis*, with respect to the crime of aggression.

[18] David Kaye, "Who Is Afraid of the International Criminal Court? Finding the Prosecutor Who Can Set It Straight", in *Foreign Affairs*, May/June 2011, available at http://www.foreignaffairs.com/articles/67768/david-kaye/whos-afraid-of-the-international-criminal-court, last accessed 27 June 2011.

---

years, even for a limited number of cases, that would be a significant step forward in human history.

As noted earlier, the rise of international institutions in the twentieth century has changed our perceptions of what international law is and how it can serve common interests of the world community as a whole.[19] Within the UN paradigm of international law,[20] partly autonomous regimes have been allowed to operate within frameworks that are not entirely limited by the self-interests of sovereign states and their leaders. Although the distinct character of these regimes also makes it difficult to integrate them within the perspective of a unified international law, each represents a thoughtful response to real-life problems whose solution requires international cooperation. The International Law Commission (ILC) has identified three types of such 'special' or 'self-contained' regimes:[21]

- Regimes consisting basically of primary rules relating to a special subject matter, for example, a treaty on the protection of a particular river or the use of a particular weapon.

- Regimes established by secondary rules for the purpose of considering breaches and reactions to breaches of a particular group of primary rules.

- Regimes perceived as a collection of all the rules and principles that regulate a certain problem area, for example, 'law of the seas', 'humanitarian law', 'human rights law', and so on.

Where does international criminal law fit within this analytical framework? Most obviously, it seems to fit well within the last category, as a collection of rules and principles regulating a certain problem area and understood as a distinct field of international law. This is a coherent definition even though the underlying norms proscribing the relevant acts may originate in the related fields of humanitarian law and human rights law. However, each of the various international criminal courts may also fall within the second category, each thus constituting a special regime in its own right. Contemporary ICL thus shows an inherent dualism: from one perspective it is an almost unified body of law, while from another perspective it comprises several distinct bodies of law. A similar dualism

---

[19] See Chapter 2, in particular section 2.2.2.
[20] On this concept, see Chapter 2, section 2.2.3.
[21] ILC, 2006, conclusions nos. 11 and 12, *supra* note 4.

can be found in other parts of international law, such as international human rights law. But these contradictions with respect to the substantive norms become particularly problematic when the law directly concerns attribution of individual criminal liability and enforcement of severe punishment.

At the descriptive level, ICL is a special regime of international law with a polycentric appearance. It can be visualised as several 'circles of law' or 'sub-regimes' functioning independently but also interacting with each other. Among these sub-regimes, some are more important than others in the current practice and future development of ICL. For instance, the ICC is expected to become the centre of gravity, whereas institutions such as the Special Tribunal for Lebanon are at the periphery of the ICL system.[22] The treaty-based ICC regime occupies a central place largely because it was designed to fit well within the main structures of the UN paradigm of international law. Thus its statute clearly envisaged a formal relationship with the United Nations and concrete points of cooperation with several organs of the UN.[23] Of particular importance is the competence of the UN Security Council, under certain circumstances, to extend the jurisdiction of the ICC.[24] This effort to 'integrate' the ICC within the core structures of the UN can be seen as an attempt to avoid further fragmentation of international criminal law, but it may arguably

---

[22] The Special Tribunal for Lebanon (STL) may still contribute to the field on particular issues, for instance with respect to a clarification of the legal status of acts of terrorism under international law. In fact, it has already made a significant contribution on the status of terrorism under customary international law and modes of liability under international criminal law. See STL Appeals Chamber, *Interlocutory Decision on the Applicable Law: Terrorism, Conspiracy, Homicide, Perpetration, Cumulative Charging*, STL-11-01/I/AC/R176bis, 16 February 2011. On international terrorist crimes as universal crimes, see Chapter 4, section 4.9.2.

[23] See Rome Statute, Article 2, requiring a formal agreement with the United Nations; Article 13, allowing the Security Council to give the Court jurisdiction and to trigger proceedings; Article 16, providing that the Security Council may suspend or defer proceedings; and Article 119(2), providing a role for the International Court of Justice. In addition, the Rome Statute also assigns a role for the UN Secretary-General (see Articles 121, 123, and 125–128).

[24] This happened in the cases of Darfur, Sudan, in 2005 and Libya in 2011. See UN Security Council Resolution 1593 (2005), 31 March 2005, and Resolution 1970 (2011), 26 February 2011. See Chapter 2, section 2.2.4., and also section 3.3.2. in this chapter on the legal basis for this competence.

---

also have the effects of politicising the ICC and weakening the independence of the Prosecutor's Office and the Court.

In order to counter the negative effects of fragmentation, certain other mechanisms have been established as well, such as a common Appeals Chamber for the ICTY and ICTR. There is also an Appeals Division at the ICC and appeals chambers within the hybrid special courts such as the SCSL, ECCC, and Special Tribunal for Lebanon (STL). To the extent that the appeals judges rely on common principles, this could counter fragmentation. But in fact, since the different courts have their own statutes, the appeals judges would normally be expected to respect and give priority to their own constituting instruments, resulting in different jurisprudence regarding the same concepts. There are already some examples of this in differences between ICTY/ICTR case law and ICC jurisprudence in the area of substantive crimes against humanity, and on certain issues of extended liability for participants. This reality comes from the international legality principle, namely, that a court of law must adhere to the substantive rules in the statutes defining the crimes and thus the jurisdiction of a particular court.

With regard to crimes or penal sanctions not included in the statute of an international or internationalised court, this would be clear enough: they cannot form the basis of prosecution before the court. In that sense, the principle of legality is "a principle of justice whose enforcement is vital to the rule of law".[25] The legality principle provides less guidance with respect to the applicability of crimes under international law generally. Apart from the core crimes, inclusion of a certain crime in a court statute does not guarantee that it is an international or universal crime. Under certain conditions, non-international crimes can also be prosecuted by international or internationalised courts.[26] On the other hand, there might be international crimes which could be prosecuted in conformity

---

[25] Kenneth S. Gallant, *The Principle of Legality in International and Comparative Criminal Law*, Cambridge University Press, Cambridge, UK, 2009, p. 404. Gallant, however, goes one significant step further when he argues that the principle of legality "means that Nuremberg and Tokyo and the rest of the post–World War II prosecutions retroactively creating crimes against peace (aggressive war and conspiracy to wage it) should be a one-time event" (p. 405); he thus implies that the prosecutions were illegitimate and would have been illegal under the current state of international law (pp. 405–406). This author does not share these further points of view, see section 3.3.4. in this chapter.

[26] See Chapter 4, sections 4.2. and 4.3.

with the international legality principle, but which are not. Their possible status under international law is thus not really tested. This arguably allows for a particular kind of fragmentation of ICL: that international prosecution pays attention only to some universal crimes categories.

It is also not clear to what extent the international legality principle may impose limits on the interpretation by judges of the scope of a given crime, including the modes of punishable participation, that is, limits that go beyond the generally recognised general principles of treaty interpretation.[27] For example, the VCLT provides for 'systemic integration' in Article 31(3)(c).[28] It requires the interpreter of a treaty to take into account "any relevant rules of international law applicable in the relations between the parties", including other treaties, customary rules, and general principles of law. Furthermore, since the laws of a special regime – and any sub-regime within it – are by definition narrower in scope than the general laws, it might be that a matter is not regulated clearly by a special law. The International Law Commission has therefore suggested that the general law will apply in such cases and fill in the gaps.[29] How far this is possible in international criminal cases will probably always be contested when such issues of interpretation arise, with the international legality principle weighing in favour of more restrictive limits on interpretation.[30]

From the perspective of legal science, a study should aim at the ideal of completeness, considering all material relevant to the topic. Researchers thus are commonly advised to avoid overly broad topics and to narrow the scope to make such completeness possible. However, strict adherence to this ideal would be unfortunate. In contemporary international law, there are many important themes which do not lend themselves to such comprehensive treatment, not only because of their scope but because the legal systems are dynamic and open to new input from different law-creating and interpretative sources as well as from national systems of law. In such cases there is a need for analysis of broad themes, in both individual monographs and collective projects, in order to counter

---

[27] See section 3.3.2. in this chapter.
[28] On 'systemic integration', see also ILC, 2006, conclusions nos. 17 and 18, *supra* note 4.
[29] *Ibid.*, conclusion no. 15.
[30] See section 3.3.2. in this chapter on the legality principle as a means of treaty interpretation.

undesirable and unintended fragmentation of the law. The ideal of completeness must be complemented by consideration of other analytical, inductive, or synthetic approaches.[31] International criminal law is an area particularly in need of such consideration.

3.3. The Legal Bases

3.3.1. The Framework of International Law-Creating Sources

When the UN paradigm of contemporary international law was established after World War II, an important provision was set out in Article 38 of the Statute of the International Court of Justice of 26 June 1945 (hereafter, ICJ Statute), annexed to the UN Charter as Chapter XIV. According to Article 92 of the UN Charter, the ICJ Statute, and thus also its Article 38, was based upon the Statute of the Permanent Court of International Justice under the auspices of the League of Nations, the predecessor of the ICJ. Article 38 codifies the basic norm of international law,[32] as it was already known before the war.

Three law-creating sources are first mentioned in Article 38, paragraphs 1(a–c): (a) "international conventions" (treaties), (b) "international custom", and (c) "the general principles of law recognized by civilized nations". Paragraph 1(d) recognises the importance of two additional kinds of authoritative sources: "judicial decisions" (by independent judges) and "the teachings of the most highly qualified

---

[31] This has long been recognised by some authors. See, *e.g.*, Georg Schwarzenberger, *The Inductive Approach to International Law*, Stevens, London, 1965, p. 6, fn. 28: "In the vast majority of cases the classes of objects and events with which science is concerned are far too numerous to permit anything even distantly approaching exhaustive individual examination of all the members. All the important inductions of science are what used to be called imperfect inductions, that is to say, generalisations based on the examination of a bare sample of the whole class under investigation".

[32] The term 'basic norm' evokes notions that have been much discussed in legal philosophy. See, *e.g.*, the classical but not identical theories of Hans Kelsen, *Pure Theory of Law*, translation from the second German edition by Max Knight, Lawbook Exchange, Clark, NJ, 2008 ('grundnorm'), and H. L. A. Hart, *The Concept of Law*, 2nd ed., Oxford University Press, Oxford, UK 1994 ('rule of recognition'). Article 38 of the ICJ Statute, however, ought to be understood in more practical terms, as a fundamental direction to the Court (and by implication also to other international jurists) to consider certain compulsory law-creating sources as well as other authoritative sources of international law when deciding legal issues and disputes before it.

publicists of the various nations". They are both considered as "subsidiary means for the determination of rules of law" that are derived from the law-creating sources.

Other subsidiary sources for the determination of the content of a rule might often be useful as well. These include a long list of possibly relevant 'interpretative sources', the relevance of which depends both on the primary law-creating source in question and on the factual circumstances of the matter at hand.[33]

What the authors of the ICJ Statute arguably failed to recognise, however, was the full potential of the newly created powers of the UN Security Council (SC) to take actions and decisions "for the maintenance of international peace and security" (see UN Charter, Chapter V, Article 24(1), and Chapter VII, "Action with Respect to Threats to the Peace, Breaches of the Peace and Acts of Aggression"). By being granted those specific powers to act on behalf of all the members of the UN, the SC has implicitly been vested with a certain power to create binding legal norms, although this may not have been so clear at the outset, and especially not during the Cold War. Since then, the Security Council, acting on behalf of the international community, has repeatedly confirmed the linkage between peace and justice. It has "acted in a number of innovative ways that demonstrate a capacity and willingness to lay down rules and principles of general application, binding on all states, and taking precedence over other legal rights and obligations".[34]

Law-making by the SC can take various forms and produce various legal effects. One can distinguish, for example, among determinations with regard to illegality or competences in general,[35] interpretations of the UN Charter, establishment of UN courts, and exercise of legislative acts on matters relating to peace and security.[36] It is clear that formal SC resolutions must today be recognised as a fourth possible law-creating source in current international law, and one of particular relevance to the

---

[33] See section 3.4.1. in this chapter.
[34] Alan Boyle and Christine Chinkin, *The Making of International Law*, Oxford University Press, Oxford, UK, 2007, p. 109.
[35] Two controversial issues are whether the findings by the Security Council are conclusive or not and whether judicial review by the ICJ is possible and can override the opinion of the SC. See, *e.g.*, Christine Gray, *International Law and the Use of Force*, 3rd ed., Oxford University Press, Oxford, UK, 2008, pp. 13–17.
[36] In the same vein, see Boyle and Chinkin, 2007, pp. 110–115, *supra* note 34.

subject matter of universal crimes. Whether or not the decision-making powers of the SC include the power to 'legislate', in the proper sense of the term, has been disputed. But these discussions tend more to concern the definition of 'legislation' than to contest the fact that the SC in some cases has created binding legal norms of a general character within the field of international criminal law.[37]

These different law-creating sources have dynamic and sometimes intricate relationships. Thus a treaty-based rule may reinforce a similar rule which also emerged from the source of international custom, itself often gaining wider acceptance as a result of the treaty. Broadly ratified conventions may provide the necessary "evidence of a general practice accepted as law", in the terms of the ICJ Statute, Article 38(1)(b). In other words, a law-creating source of universal crimes norms may function as an 'interpretative source' with respect to another law-creating source as well, whereas sources other than treaties, international customs, general principles of law, and binding SC resolutions can be legally relevant but not 'law-creating' *per se*.[38]

Legal opinions expressed, for example, in judgments by international courts and/or consistently in the law literature, may influence state practice and thus indirectly contribute to new customary rules. Studies and analyses may clarify and in practice further develop the general principles of law. Soft law, such as formulations by the UN General Assembly of norms which are not legally binding,[39] may have similar effects. Thus 'soft' legal materials must also be taken into account in 'hard' law-making processes.

These intricate interrelationships, however, should not be interpreted as eroding the distinction between law-creating sources and interpretative sources. On the contrary, this distinction is important to maintain as part of the UN paradigm of international law, and is itself a component of the rule of law. An inherent feature of 'law' is that legal reasoning follows a certain commonly accepted methodology which

---

[37] See section 3.3.5. in this chapter.

[38] See further section 3.4. in this chapter on the interpretative sources of international law.

[39] See also Chapter 1, section 1.2., on soft law and hard law.

enables different legal experts to reach the same results, while distinguishing between binding rules and other normative expressions.[40]

The conclusion stands that a binding international rule has to
originate from a predefined law-creating source through a process that
fulfils certain criteria that are agreed in international law and controllable
by a judicial tribunal or supervisory body. This is true even though the
content of the rule is affected by other dynamic processes involving
additional actors and source materials. Since law is a social construct and
is to some extent open-ended, the underlying theories of international law
require ongoing review.[41] This chapter first considers the four separate
legal bases: treaties (see section 3.3.2.), customary law (3.3.3.), general
principles of law (3.3.4.), and Security Council legislative resolutions
(3.3.5.). A final section (3.3.6.) considers whether several unclear legal
bases, taken together, might provide a sufficient legal basis.

3.3.2. Multilateral Treaties

From a practical point of view, treaties constitute the single most
important law-creating source in the history of international law, and a
reliable legal means of developing peaceful cooperation among nations.
Only through treaties can all recognised states purposely and with a fair
amount of certainty create new international law. A 'treaty', according to
the definition laid down in Article 2(1)(a) of the VCLT, is "an international agreement concluded between States in written form and
governed by international law".

Many treaties are relevant to the subject matter of universal crimes.
Some concern, explicitly or implicitly, the primary material norms
proscribing certain acts. Others contain secondary rules for the establishment of international courts, their jurisdiction, and the procedural rules
and maybe competences for the courts to enact further rules. As possible
legal bases for universal crimes norms, *multilateral treaties* rather than
bilateral treaties are the most interesting, especially when adopted by the
United Nations and acceded to by many states in different parts of the
world. It is not decisive whether a treaty is actually called a 'treaty', a
'convention', or something else. For example, the ICC Rome Statute is a

---

[40]   See section 3.5. in this chapter.
[41]   See, *e.g.*, Brian D. Lepard, *Customary International Law: A New Theory with Practical Applications*, Cambridge University Press, Cambridge, UK, 2010.

treaty between the states parties although the word 'treaty' is not used in the Rome Statute itself. At the same time, this treaty is among several examples which illustrate that not only states may have treaty-making powers under the UN paradigm of international law. The ICC Rome Statute in Article 4 presupposes that the ICC shall have international legal personality and is thus empowered to conclude agreements in the form of treaties. The general definition of a 'treaty' under international law should therefore rather be corrected to 'an international agreement concluded between entities with legal personality, usually states, in written form and governed by international law'.

A particularly interesting feature of the treaty-based ICC regime is its relationship to the United Nations. According to the Rome Statute in Article 13(b), the Security Council may – acting under Chapter VII of the Charter of the United Nations – refer a 'situation' to the prosecutor of the ICC, typically when crimes within the *ratione materiae* (subject-matter) jurisdiction of the ICC are alleged to have been committed outside the territories of the states parties to the Rome Statute.[42] Such a referral by the SC is a binding decision, for which the competence seems to come from the ICC Rome Statute (treaty) and the UN Charter as legal bases taken in conjunction. However, since a treaty cannot directly bind others who are not parties to the treaty, the legal power (competence) in this case must originate in the UN Charter Chapter VII, whereas the specific, practical use of the power is facilitated by the ICC Rome Statute. In addition, the SC has the competence to establish another international criminal tribunal if it so prefers.[43]

Interpretation of treaties is conditioned on well-established methodological principles, such as those set out in VCLT Articles 31–33, where a distinction is made between principal (Article 31) and supplementary (Article 32) means of interpretation. This establishes a certain hierarchy of the interpretative sources specific to treaties. The basic rule is enshrined in Article 31(1), whereby a treaty must be construed "in good faith in accordance with the ordinary meaning to be given to the terms of the treaty in their context and in light of its object

---

[42] See UN Security Council Resolution 1593 (2005), 31 March 2005 (Darfur, Sudan), and UN Security Council Resolution 1970 (2011), 26 February 2011 (Libya).

[43] For instance, an 'International Criminal Court for the Middle East and Northern Africa' with a forward-looking mandate would have several advantages, since few countries in that region have acceded to the ICC Rome Statute.

and purpose". Although not explicitly mentioned in Article 32, which refers generally to all "supplementary means of interpretation" and especially to "the preparatory work of the treaty", jurisprudence – in particular international judgments and decisions – and scholarly publications are part of the supplementary means of interpretation. This system is consistent with the general rule of the ICJ Statute, Article 38. The principles of treaty interpretation are also anchored in customary law and thus generally binding on all legal subjects of international law. Hence they apply to treaties within international criminal law.[44] Furthermore, they apply to interpretation of international court statutes created by the Security Council by means of SC resolutions, such as the statutes of the ICTY and ICTR.[45]

Particular issues may arise with respect to special rules of interpretation, such as those set forth in Articles 21 and 22 of the ICC Rome Statute. Article 22(2) prescribes that within the statute the "definition of a crime shall be strictly construed and not extended by analogy". This rule – which had already been applied explicitly at Nuremberg in the Ministries Case[46] and the Justice Case[47] – has been re-

---

[44] See, *e.g.*, Gerhard Werle, *Principles of International Criminal Law*, TMC Asser Press, The Hague, 2005, p. 95. Upheld in Gerhard Werle, *Principles of International Criminal Law*, 2nd ed., TMC Asser Press, The Hague, 2009, pp. 59–60: "As expressions of customary law, these rules of interpretation must be applied in interpretation not only of the ICC Rome Statute, but 'any other norm-creating instrument', including the ICTY and ICTR Statutes". For support, see, *e.g.*, ICTY Appeals Chamber, *Prosecutor v. Duško Tadic*, Judgment, IT-94-1-R, 1999, para. 303.

[45] See, *e.g.*, ICTY Appeals Chamber, *Prosecutor v. Zlatko Aleksovski*, Judgment, IT-95-14/1, 2000, para. 98.

[46] Nuernberg Military Tribunals (NMT), "The Ministries Case" [Judgment], in *Trials of War Criminals before the Nuernberg Military Tribunals under Control Council Law No. 10*, vol. XIII, US Government Printing Office, Washington, DC, 1952, p. 100: "The principles of strict construction and against retroactive legislation should be applied [...] to words and phrases which are present and which must be interpreted and construed". See also pp. 103 and 115.

[47] NMT, "The Justice Case" [Judgment], in *Trials of War Criminals before the Nuernberg Military Tribunals under Control Council Law No. 10*, vol. III, US Government Printing Office, Washington, DC, 1951, p. 982: "We hold that crimes against humanity as defined in C.C. [Control Council] Law 10 must be strictly construed to exclude isolated cases of atrocity or persecution whether committed by private individuals or by a governmental authority".

---

ferred to as "the canon of strict construction".[48] In case of ambiguity, the same provision states that "the definition shall be interpreted in favour of the person being investigated, prosecuted or convicted". The latter rule can be credited to the principle of *in dubio pro reo*, which holds that ambiguity or doubt is to be resolved in favour of the accused.[49] These principles of interpretation form part of the legality principle (*nullum crimen sine lege*) and may lead to other results than a plain application of the VCLT principles. However, Rome Statute Article 22(1) applies directly only to cases before the ICC. It is not clear to what extent this provision expresses general principles of international criminal law. As observed by Schabas, it "stands in very marked contrast with the jurisprudence of the *ad hoc* tribunals which has, generally, accorded little significance to principles of strict construction".[50] In his opinion, several interpretative results of the ICTY and ICTR would have been impermissible if Article 22(2) had been applied.[51] In any case, both Article 22(1) and the general principles are themselves open to interpretation and further clarification. Note, for instance, that the *in dubio pro reo* principle may primarily concern the facts rather than the law,[52] and that the 'strict

---

[48] See William A. Schabas, *The International Criminal Court: A Commentary on the Rome Statute*, Oxford University Press, Oxford, UK, 2010, p. 410.

[49] *Ibid.*

[50] *Ibid.* Schabas refers to a number of international judgments, which this author agrees do not support strict interpretation. See ICTY Appeals Chamber, *Prosecutor v. Duško Tadic*, para. 73, *supra* note 44; ICTY Appeals Chamber, *Prosecutor v. Dražen Erdemović*, Judgment, IT-96-22-A, 1997, Separate and Dissenting Opinion of Judge Cassese, para. 49; ICTR Trial Chamber, *Prosecutor v. Jean-Paul Akayesu*, Judgment, ICTR-96-4-T, 1998, para. 319; ICTR Trial Chamber, *Prosecutor v. Kayishma and Obed Ruzindana*, Judgment, ICTR-95-1, 1999, para. 103; ICTR Trial Chamber, *Prosecutor v. Georges A. N. Rutaganda*, Judgment, ICTR-96-3, 1999, para. 51; ICTR Trial Chamber, *Prosecutor v. Alfred Musema*, Judgment, ICTR-96-13-A, 2000, para. 155.

[51] Schabas, 2010, pp. 410–411, *supra* note 48.

[52] See, *e.g.*, ICTY Appeals Chamber, *Prosecutor v. Fatmir Limaj et al.*, Judgment, IT-03-66-A, 2007, Declaration of Judge Shahabuddeen, para. 2, in which he disagrees but concedes that "the basis of previous jurisprudence of the Tribunal, [...] has held that the principle [of *in dubio pro reo*] does not apply to questions of law". For a broader view in line with the later opinion of Judge Shahabuddeen, see NMT, "The Ministries Case", 1952, p. 100, *supra* note 46: "We stated at the outset that, in any case of real doubt, the language of Law No. 10 should be construed in favour of the defendants". See also ICTY Trial Chamber, *Prosecutor v. Stanislav Galic*, IT-98-29-T, 2003, Judgment, para. 93: "The effect of strict construction of the provisions of a

construction' principle of Article 22(2) according to its terms is limited to the "definition of a crime", an expression that is itself open to interpretation. For example, it might be arguable whether the principle of strict interpretation applies to the same extent with respect to modes of participation that extend liability beyond commission of those acts defined as crimes within the jurisdiction of the court.

In terms of *lex ferenda*, it could be argued that although the international legality principle is an important safeguard for the defendant, it may also serve as an unintended means of creating loopholes in court statutes and arbitrary inconsistencies between different parts of ICL that were neither foreseen nor desired when these were drafted. In comparison to national criminal legislation, which can more easily be amended based on experience and evaluation, revision of international court statutes is relatively difficult. Judges may accordingly prefer to try to strike a fair balance between the opposing legitimate interests and values rather than relying mechanically on strict construction principles.

3.3.3. Customary International Law

International custom as law evolves from the practices or customs of entities with legal personality, usually states. Certain conditions must be met before a practice becomes law, as not all acts, practices, or customs of states and other international legal subjects can become binding law. In the ICJ Statute 'international custom' is explained as evidence of 'a general practice accepted as law'. The common term today for binding international law which originates from practice (custom) is 'customary international law'.

The criteria for distinguishing between customary international law and other practices and conduct have been elaborated by the international law experts and judges at international courts, especially in cases before the ICJ. These criteria have generally been accepted as part of inter-national law throughout the international community. From a logical point of view, this means that the definition of customary international law is circular: the criteria define the relevant customs and the criteria are ex-

criminal statute is that where an equivocal word or ambiguous sentence leaves a rea-sonable doubt of its meaning which the canons of construction fail to solve, the bene-fit of the doubt should be given to the subject and against the legislature which has failed to explain itself".

tracted from that relevant practice. The way to understand this dialectic relationship, therefore, is to take into account the time factor and the development of new customary international law, as well as the readiness of international law judges and experts to uphold and if necessary also refine the criteria in light of new experiences.

There are relatively few limitations on what kinds of customs may be relevant. However, a practice that is incompatible with a broader international custom (a regional custom contrary to a universal custom), or contrary to treaty-based obligations of the state involved, or in conflict with *jus cogens*, can never give rise to customary law. Both the latter two limitations are important with respect to the subject matter of universal crimes. Norms proscribing acts for which direct criminal liability under international law is established are often considered superior to other rules on account of the importance of their content as well as the universal acceptance of their superiority.[53] Hence no derogation is permitted, whether by means of a treaty or a common practice. For example, if torture of alleged terrorists is practised to a certain extent by some states, and *if* state-sponsored torture has already emerged as a discrete universal crime,[54] acts of torture against alleged terrorists, however customary, would simply constitute criminal acts under international law. Furthermore, if a state has agreed to be bound by the UN Convention against Torture, which is a treaty proscribing torture and other cruel, inhuman or degrading treatment or punishment, the state incurs state responsibility for any act of torture within the meaning of the convention which can be attributed to it – regardless of the current status of torture as a discrete crime under international criminal law.

Some norms of customary international law – notably the prohibitions against genocide and slavery – have clearly acquired this higher legal status (*jus cogens*) in the opinion of most commentators. For other norms, arising both nationally and internationally, it is not yet clear that this is the case.[55] There is disagreement on the character and legal status

---

[53] ILC, 2006, conclusion no. 32, *supra* note 4.

[54] See Chapter 4, sections 4.9.2.2. and 4.9.3. See also Chapter 5, section 5.2.2. Torture is clearly a relevant universal crime when committed in the context of crimes against humanity, genocide, or war.

[55] See, *e.g.*, High Court of the Hong Kong Special Administrative Region, Court of First Instance, HCAL 132/2006, 18 February 2008, paras. 126–129. See also Inter-American Court of Human Rights (IACHR), *Miguel Castro-Castro Prison v. Peru*,

of such norms, "with some authors arguing that all human rights enshrined in international treaties are norms of *jus cogens* while others advocate a far more stringent approach".[56] However, as noted in Chapter 1, section 1.2., the concept and scope of *jus cogens* is not essential to our *study* of universal crimes, since the norms underlying these crimes no doubt have the required character in terms of content and universality. Their superiority thus depends upon their international law status as 'hard' or 'soft' law, and this question needs to be discussed independently of the *jus cogens* concept. In other words, the *jus cogens* concept is not necessary for the discussion of legal bases, although the outcome of that discussion may have implications for the legal consequences of *jus cogens*.[57]

The principal criteria weighed in determining customary international law seem to be (1) a reasonably consistent practice with regard to the substance of the acts; (2) a fairly general practice (in the sense of being common to a significant number of states relative to the nature of the issue);[58] (3) a certain number of repetitions or a certain duration of the acts; and (4) *opinio juris*. The latter criterion means that it must be possible to infer from the acts of states, including their statements, that the practice is considered legally permissible or illegal, as the case may be, by the relevant group of actors.[59] As Lepard comments, it is a paradox that

---

Judgment, 25 November 2006, *Series C, no. 160*, para. 271; IACHR, *Bayarri v. Argentina*, Judgment, 30 October 2008, *Series C, no. 187*, para. 81.

[56] Maarten den Heijer, "Whose Rights and Which Rights? The Continuing Story of Non-Refoulement under the European Convention on Human Rights", in *European Journal of Migration and Law*, 2008, vol. 10, no. 3, p. 299.

[57] See sections 3.3.5., 3.4.2., and 3.5. in this chapter.

[58] See Frederic L. Kirgis, "Custom on a Sliding Scale", in *American Journal of International Law*, 1987, vol. 81, no. 1, pp. 146–151. Kirgis assumes a relationship between the amount of practice required and the nature of the norm involved: human rights norms need little state practice, while economic norms need more (pp. 147–148).

[59] The criteria and their content derive primarily from a series of decisions of the ICJ and its predecessor, the Permanent Court of International Justice (PCIJ). These include PCIJ, *The Case of the S.S. "Lotus"* (France v. Turkey), Judgment, 7 September 1927, *Series A, no. 10*; ICJ, *Anglo-Norwegian Fisheries Case* (United Kingdom v. Norway), Judgment, *I.C.J. Reports 1951*, p. 116; *ICJ North Sea Continental Shelf Cases* (Federal Republic of Germany/Denmark; Federal Republic of Germany/Netherlands), Judgment *I.C.J. Reports 1969*, p. 3; and ICJ, *Military and Paramilitary Activities in and against Nicaragua* (Nicaragua v. United States of America), Merits and Judgment, *I.C.J. Reports 1986*, p. 14.

---

the condition of *opinio juris*, as traditionally formulated, requires that states at the critical stage of creating new customary international rules are supposed to believe erroneously that they are legally bound to observe a rule that is not yet legally binding.[60]

Notably, the formulations and application of these cumulative criteria are to some degree flexible. They should be considered in conjunction as a whole, not as separate and very strict conditions. Requiring the full satisfaction of all criteria simultaneously might unduly obstruct the formation of new customary international law. This is crucial with regard to some issues explored in this study. Universal crimes, as discussed in Chapter 2, are often committed or condoned by state governments against groups or individuals that should be protected by modern international law. Such crimes are inherently in deep conflict with world community interests and values despite the fact that security and foreign policy concerns, and possibly economic calculations as well, may obstruct concerted statements and actions appropriate to their universal criminal character.

Under these circumstances, the criteria for the formation of international customary law should not be applied in such a manner that states, which are themselves responsible for large-scale human rights violations, can block the emergence of an international rule to benefit future victims and support responsible behaviour by governments and other powerful actors within a society. This is the underlying reason why an international custom prohibiting certain acts, maybe eventually conferring criminal liability on individual members of political and military leaderships for serious violations, has sometimes been recognised, even if all the conditions for formation of international custom may not have been fully satisfied.

Examples includes some of the findings by the Nuremberg Tribunal,[61] especially on the legal status of aggression and criminal lia-

---

[60] Lepard, 2010, pp. 8–9, *supra* note 41. Instead he argues that a customary law norm arises "when states generally believe that it is desirable now or in the near future to have an authoritative legal principle or rule prescribing, permitting, or prohibiting a certain conduct", and that this belief is sufficient to create the norm. State practice can, however, "serve as one source of evidence" of what states believe.

[61] See IMT, *Trial of the Major War Criminals*, 1947, vol. I, [Judgment], pp. 171–341, *supra* note 13.

bility for aggressive acts before World War II.[62] Another example is the *Nicaragua* case,[63] where, according to some commentators, the ICJ deviated from "its traditional approach of seeking state practice supported by opinio juris by finding first opinio juris in the form of UNGA resolutions and then looking for state practice".[64] The critique is that the Court did not establish whether the traditional criteria were met to support its opinion that Article 3 of the Geneva Conventions had become customary international law.[65] Instead of criticising the ICJ for inconsistency, however, and thus challenging its reasoning as unsound or illegitimate, one should recognise that independent judges at a court constituting the highest judicial authority within a legal system will tend to perceive themselves as servants of a broader concept of law that cannot be constrained by a single expectation, whether loyalty to the status quo or to other similar considerations. On balance, judges with effective review powers may over the years advance the essentials of the legal systems of which they are a part. In some cases, this may mean new interpretations of the law. In other words, the general criteria of customary international law are to some extent adjustable depending on the circumstances, including the *jus cogens* character of the emerging substantive norms in question.

3.3.4. General Principles as International Law

The "general principles of law recognised by civilised nations" as a law-creating source of international law (ICJ Statute, Article 38(1)(c)) is an ambiguous notion that has generated much academic debate and confusion, even apart from the unintended ethnocentric connotations of the term 'civilised nations', as noted in Chapter 2. There were divergent views already within the committee of jurists which prepared this statute, ranging from a concept based on natural law to one based on the principles demonstrably accepted in the domestic law of those states regarded as civilised,[66] that is, states based on the rule of law. While the

---

[62] See also section 3.3.6. in this chapter.

[63] ICJ, *Military and Paramilitary Activities in and against Nicaragua*, p. 14, *supra* note 59.

[64] See Boyle and Chinkin, 2007, p. 280, *supra* note 34.

[65] *Ibid.* See further Theodor Meron, *Human Rights and Humanitarian Norms as Customary Law*, Clarendon Press, Oxford, UK, 1989, p. 36.

[66] See, *e.g.*, Ian Brownlie, *Principles of Public International Law*, 4th ed., Clarendon Press, Oxford, UK, 1990, pp. 15–16.

precedents in domestic law are surely one valid and important part of the overall concept, fundamental principles of current international criminal law must also be included,[67] especially the norms considered "as overriding principles of *jus cogens* which may qualify the effect of more ordinary rules".[68]

This ambiguity has not been resolved, however. While it is commonly recognised that general principles of law are of considerable significance to ICL, the concept is still often exclusively equated with rules originating in domestic law and with the legal principles already recognised by the world's major legal systems.[69] In this context, the ICTY cautioned that "a mechanical importation or transposition from national law into international criminal proceedings has to be avoided".[70] This statement was probably intended to restrict access to the general principles of law, but the formulation could also be used to expand non-mechanical access, thus facilitating the formation of new general principles of ICL regardless of whether they are already fully recognised domestically. If such an approach is taken, the subject matter of universal crimes might advance a new legal trend of openly acknowledging that it is difficult to distinguish clearly between customary international law and the general principles as law, given that both sources are continuously evolving.

International tribunals might thus rely on multiple legal bases in cases for which their criminal law jurisdiction is not clear, perhaps without taking a definite stand on the exact status of the general principle being invoked.[71] The ICC Rome Statute Article 21(1) is sufficiently flexible for such a position. In the first place, the *Statute* itself, the particular *elements of crimes*, and the court's *rules of procedure and evidence* apply (1)(a). Second, "applicable treaties and the principles and rules of international law" may apply, including "the established principles of the international law of armed conflict" (1)(b). Third, "general principles of law derived by the Court from national laws of legal systems of the world" may also apply, provided that they are not

---

[67] See further Boyle and Chinkin, 2007, pp. 286–288, *supra* note 34.

[68] See Brownlie, 1990, pp. 19, 512–515, *supra* note 66.

[69] See, *e.g.*, Werle, 2009, p. 53, *supra* note 44.

[70] See ICTY Trial Chamber, *Prosecutor v. Anto Furundžija*, Judgment, IT-95-17/1, 1998, para. 178.

[71] See also section 3.3.6. in this chapter.

inconsistent with the ICC Rome Statute and with "international law and internationally recognized norms and standards" (1)(c). The latter point implies the existence of some overriding general international norms. Article 21(3), in the same vein, states that the application and interpretation of law pursuant to Article 21 "must be consistent with internationally recognized human rights". In other words, general principles of international law may provide a legal basis for deriving new rules under Articles 21(1)(b) and (c), and may *in addition* serve as a kind of a 'rule of recognition'[72] for evaluation of new 'principles of law' that might be proposed, possibly derived from national laws.[73]

This dual function makes the concept of general principles equivocal. Rules originating from another source may themselves be constituted as general principles. At the same time general principles, meaning a general rule, a principle, or a fundamental rule, can also be derived from customary international law and expressed in binding treaties. While this may be confusing, it is not in itself contradictory. Specific rules termed 'general principles' can be derived from all the different law-creating sources of international law, including from a particular source called 'general principles of international law' or a similar term. Properly understood, the meaning is that the latter law-creating source is especially concerned with rules characterised as 'general principles', and, by logical inference, that this source, just like treaties and international customary law, may contain substantial rules that have no exact parallel in the binding rules previously derived from the other law-creating sources.

In fact, any legal order necessarily requires general principles of law. This is quite clear when one looks at any given national legal system constituted by law in the profound sense of the term. A written constitution needs to be applied and adapted to changing circumstances, whether or not it is formally amended. If there is no written constitution, there is still a need for constitutive norms that are believed to be binding. Within most areas of substantial law and court procedures, a living body of law cannot do without some general principles that serve the underlying purposes of the legal order and make possible consistent application

---

[72] See Hart, 1994, *supra* note 32.
[73] On Article 21(1) of the Rome Statute, see further Schabas, 2010, pp. 381–394, *supra* note 48.

of specific rules that may conflict with each other. For example, the principles of free consent and good faith, and the *pacta sunt servanda* rule, are universally recognised in contractual law and in international treaty law (as in the preamble to the Vienna Convention on the Law of Treaties). Within national criminal law, principles such as *in dubio pro reo* (the defendant should have the benefit of reasonable doubt regarding the facts) and the legality principle (*nullum crimen sine lege, nulla poena sine lege*), including the prohibition of *ex post facto* laws, are generally recognised.

Whether they are codified by legislators or not, certain 'constitutive principles' exist in all legal orders, although they might be different in different countries. They are usually familiar to scholars and knowledgeable practitioners working within the various fields of law. Judges may sometimes need to seek interpretative guidance in such principles, especially in difficult cases. In rare cases the principles may be applied directly in a judgment, possibly for lack of more accessible, written sources.

The UN paradigm of international law contains a number of binding general principles. Several of these are expressed in the UN Charter itself and are constitutive of the current legal order. Others may exist more specifically within certain substantive parts of international law; they are what might be termed 'field-specific' constitutive principles, with a content similar to general principles existing internally within the law among 'civilised nations'. As noted earlier, the reference to 'civilised nations' should be taken to mean nations adhering to the rule of law in compliance with fundamental UN principles; the phrase does not point to a state's presumed level of cultural or economic development. Note also that not every rule found in most legal systems adhering to the rule of law is necessarily a general principle of law within the international legal order. The ICTY in *Furundžija* stated that certain criteria must be fulfilled before field-specific national law concepts of criminal law can be applied in international court proceedings:

> (i) [...] [I]nternational courts must draw upon the general concepts and legal institutions common to all the major legal systems of the world [...]; (ii) account must be taken of the specificity of international proceedings when utilising national law notions. In this way a mechanical importation

or transposition from national law into international criminal proceedings is avoided.[74]

Among the general principles of international law embodied in the UN Charter and the present order of international law are the principles of equal rights and self-determination of peoples, the sovereign equality and independence of all states, non-interference in the domestic affairs of states for purposes other than those admitted by international law, refraining from the use of force, and observance of human rights and fundamental freedoms for all.

A central question is whether general principles of law on direct criminal liability should also be included. The argument is that individual liability, for crimes undermining the international legal order, became a constitutive principle of the international legal order established after World War II. Implicit support for this can be found in the first paragraph of the preamble of the UN Charter, where the quest for justice and respect for international law is highlighted and explained:

> We the Peoples of the United Nations, determined to save succeeding generations from the scourge of war, which twice in our lifetime has brought untold sorrow to mankind, and to reaffirm faith in fundamental human rights, in the dignity and worth of the human person, in the equal rights of men and women and of nations large and small, and to establish conditions under which justice and respect for obligations arising from treaties and other sources of international law can be maintained [...].

This statement should be understood in conjunction with the post–World War II tribunals and the adoption of the Universal Declaration on Human Rights and the Genocide Convention, all of which took place within the first four years of the formal establishment of the United Nations.[75]

A perhaps more intriguing question is whether general principles on universal crimes existed as part of international law even *before* World War II and the establishment of the UN. The problem for prosecutors at the Nuremberg trials was that the legal basis for criminal liability based upon customary international law and treaties before the war did not seem clear with regard to the crime of aggression and crimes against humanity.

---

[74] ICTY Trial Chamber, *Prosecutor v. Anto Furundžija*, *supra* note 70.

[75] See also Chapter 2, section 2.2.3., on the UN paradigm of international law.

The possibility of invoking liability based on general principles of criminal law was also quite doubtful, since the international legal order before the war was much less clear in many respects than the new UN paradigm with regard to alleged existence of universal norms on human rights and the need for individual criminal liability and justice for victims. If relevant general principles of criminal law did not exist, or could not be identified, criminal liability might not be legally established without violating the prohibition of *ex post facto* laws. Prosecutors and judges at Nuremberg would then have had to rely exclusively on prior treaties and customary international law, under which the evidence of existing criminal liability for all the crimes charged was at best doubtful. The defendants were even more dependent upon the existence of general principles of criminal law when invoking the legality principle.

The jurisdiction of the Nuremberg Tribunal was defined in the London Agreement of 8 August 1945 and the Charter of the International Military Tribunal (IMT) in pursuance of the agreement. The IMT Charter (or Nuremberg Charter) was also based on the assumption that "the countries to which the German Reich unconditionally surrendered [...] [had a right] to legislate for the occupied territories".[76] But one should also note that the Nuremberg Tribunal went further and pointed implicitly to universal jurisdiction over the crimes:

> The Signatory Powers created this Tribunal, defined the law it was to administer, and made regulations for the proper conduct of the Trial. In doing so, they have done together what any one of them might have done singly; for it is not to be doubted that any nation has the right thus to set up special courts to administer law.[77]

The "law" referred to here is international criminal law, and the implication is that any nation had the right to administer it with regard to the crimes being committed, that is, on the basis of universal jurisdiction if no other kinds of jurisdiction existed.

Therefore, a *prima facie* legal basis for the prosecution of crimes against peace, war crimes, and crimes against humanity, committed by the German leadership, had been established through international agreements and presumed international criminal law. The defendants in

---

[76] See IMT, *Trial of the Major War Criminals*, 1947, vol. I, [Judgment], p. 219, *supra* note 13.

[77] *Ibid.*, p. 218.

Nuremberg thus needed to undermine it by means of other parts of international law. Paradoxically, perhaps, they resorted to general principles of criminal law. It was argued on their behalf "that a fundamental principle of all law – international and domestic – is that there can be no punishment of crime without a pre-existing [substantive] law".[78] The maxim *nullum crimen sine lege, nulla poena sine lege* was explicitly invoked.[79] Furthermore,

> [i]t was submitted that ex post facto punishment is abhorrent to the law of all civilized nations, that no sovereign power has made aggressive war a crime at the time that the alleged criminal acts were committed, that no statute had defined aggressive war, and that no penalty had been fixed for its commission, and no court had been created to try and punish offenders.[80]

Under the international legality principle, in general, it is one thing for a certain conduct to be considered unlawful and criminal in nature, and another for it to be formally criminalised in international or national law before the act is committed. A more limited legality requirement, that formal criminalisation in national legislation or in the statutes of an international or internationalised court enacted after the acts were committed must be set before indictments are issued and trials starts before the court, was adhered to in Nuremberg and has been an undisputed element of international criminal law ever since. Within the existing UN paradigm of international law, it has consistently been upheld that accessibility and foreseeability are also elements of the legality principle. But it is *not* a requirement that an act falling within the substantive scope of *international (universal) crimes* must have been formally criminalised and penalties defined before the act was committed. This position has also been upheld in international human rights law.[81] The international

---

[78] *Ibid.*, p. 219.

[79] *Ibid.*

[80] *Ibid.*

[81] See the International Covenant on Civil and Political Rights, Article 15(2): "Nothing in this Article [principle of legality] shall prejudice the trial and punishment of any person for any act or omission which, at the time when it was committed, was criminal according to the general principles of law recognized by the community of nations". At the regional level, the *Kononov* case decided by the Grand Chamber of the European Court of Human Rights is instructive; see ECHR, *Kononov v. Latvia*, 36376/04, Grand Chamber Judgment of 17 May 2010. The Court held that the legality

principle of legality thus "allows for criminal liability over crimes that were either national or international in nature at the time they were committed".[82] It "does not require that international crimes and modes of liability be implemented by domestic statutes in order for violators to be found guilty".[83] A number of domestic courts have thus rendered decisions applying a different standard of the legality principle for ordinary crimes and universal crimes. This is in line not only with the jurisprudence of international criminal courts, but also with international human rights instruments and the jurisprudence of international human rights courts.[84]

The Nuremberg Tribunal, however, faced a significant choice between formal and substantive justice. It was impossible to completely escape the impression based on facts that the Tribunal applied *ex post facto* laws. It handled the issue in an interesting way. First, it claimed that the Nuremberg Charter was "not an arbitrary exercise of power on the part of the victorious Nations", but an "expression of international law existing at the time of its creation; and to that extent is itself a contribution to international law".[85] It is interesting to note that the Tribunal here seems to have relied on the new UN paradigm of international law, although not entirely. Second, the principle of non-retroactive laws was rejected up front as an absolute shield against accountability,

---

principle enshrined in ECHR Article 7 is "an essential element of the rule of law", and that it follows that an offence must be "clearly defined in law" (*ibid.*, para. 185). When speaking of 'law', the Court explained that this concept "comprises written and unwritten law" and "implies qualitative requirements, notably those of accessibility and foreseeability" (*ibid.*). The applicant had been convicted in Latvia of war crimes committed in 1944, on the basis of a provision enacted in 1993 (*ibid.*, paras. 191–196). The Court examined whether there had been a sufficient clear legal basis with respect to the state of international law in 1944. In line with the Nuremberg Judgment, the Court concluded that the relevant acts (killing of nine prisoners) were crimes under international law when they were committed, and that the applicant could have foreseen that they constituted war crimes (*ibid.*, paras. 234–244). The Court thus held by 14 votes to three that there had been no violation of ECHR Article 7.

82 Extraordinary Chambers in the Courts of Cambodia (ECCC), Pre-Trial Chamber, *Decision on Ieng Sary's Appeal against the Closing Order*, 002/19-09-2007-ECCC/OCIJ (PTC75), D427/1/30, 11 April 2011, para. 213.

83 *Ibid.*

84 *Ibid.* For a thorough overview, see the discussion in paras. 203–265.

85 IMT, *Trial of the Major War Criminals*, 1947, vol. I [Judgment], p. 218, *supra* note 13.

referring to morality and the nature of the crimes in question.[86] Due to the grave crimes that had been committed, the defendants could not successfully invoke a principle flowing from the idea of justice, according to the judgment.[87] This latter argument is not immediately convincing from a human rights perspective. It was, however, arguably the best way out of a difficult problem of justification more than anything else.

For the Nuremberg Tribunal, alternative justifications must have appeared less appealing. It could have argued that certain crimes are so grave that they are punishable *ex post facto* within any legal order at any time. That would mean reliance on a far-reaching natural law doctrine. Instead the Tribunal emphasised the legal development that had already taken place before World War II. As underscored by the IMT, international law is never static, "but by continual adaptation follows the needs of a changing world".[88] Thus, "in many cases treaties do no more than express and define for more accurate reference the principles of law already existing".[89] Alternatively, the judges could have argued that criminal liability was embodied in general 'constitutive' principles of international law existing already under the classical inter-state period of international law, which could be taken as a reconstruction of former international law.[90]

---

[86] *Ibid.*, p. 217, with regard to the crime of aggression: "To assert that it is unjust to punish those who in defiance of treaties and assurances have attacked neighbouring states without warning is obviously untrue, for in such circumstances the attacker must know that he is doing wrong, and so far from it being unjust to punish him, it would be unjust if his wrong were allowed to go unpunished. [...] [T]hey must have known that they were acting in defiance of all international law when in complete deliberation they carried out their designs of invasion and aggression".

[87] *Ibid.*, p. 219: "[T]he maxim *nullum crimen sine lege* is not a limitation of sovereignty, but is in general a principle of justice".

[88] *Ibid.*, p. 221.

[89] *Ibid.*

[90] National courts have dealt differently with this issue in cases originating from World War II. Compare, *e.g.*, Supreme Court of Canada, *Her Majesty The Queen v. Imre Finta*, 1 *Supreme Court Reports* 701 (24 March 1994); and High Court of Australia, *Polyukhovich v. Commonwealth*, 101 *Australian Law Reports* 545, (1991), 172 *Commonwealth Law Reports* 501, and 91 *International Law Reports* 1. The Canadian court took the approach that while crimes against humanity were new, the issue of legality was not important, as the perpetrators must have known that the underlying crimes were wrong. The Australian court held that crimes against humanity had already entered the realm of ICL.

Given the formation of the United Nations, it turned out not to be necessary for the judges to determine whether criminal liability was clearly established in international law before the war. The *jus cogens* character of the norms in question reinforced the approach taken. Once a fundamental change of circumstance had occurred, and new overriding rules of justice had been accepted by the international community and concrete steps taken for implementation, the exact content of prior substantive norms became a less decisive consideration. This may be another reason why the Nuremberg Judgment made a general reference to treaties, customs, and general principles in justifying the legal basis for the crimes identified in the Nuremberg Charter.[91]

Although it may be doubtful whether individual liability for some universal crimes clearly existed before World War II, such liability was implicitly and instantly part of the constitutive principles of the new UN paradigm of international law established by 1945. The Nuremberg Tribunal was therefore right to apply the Nuremberg Charter and international criminal law in accordance with a substantive notion of justice. In other words, a purely formal notion of justice – *nullum crimen sine lege, nulla poena sine lege*, itself a general principle of law – could not take priority without conflicting with other parts of the existing law. It should be recognised, even so, that the Nuremberg Tribunal did in fact prove that most of the criminal acts in question were illegal under any relevant standard. The defendants thus could not have ruled out criminal liability, even when the acts were committed. With regard to most of the war crimes, such responsibility was clearly foreseeable and partly embodied in existing laws before World War II. With regard to crimes against peace, the illegality of the attacks on several countries at the time they occurred cannot be doubted. The same is also true with regard to most of the underlying crimes that constituted crimes against humanity, which to a large extent also overlapped with war crimes. In other words, only a very strict – and for many lawyers and ordinary people, grossly unreasonable – application of the legality principle could potentially exempt the Germans most responsible from justice before the court.

---

[91] IMT, *Trial of the Major War Criminals*, 1947, vol. I [Judgment], p. 221, *supra* note 13: "The law of war is to be found not only in treaties, but in the customs and practices of states which gradually obtained universal recognition, and from the general principles of justice applied by jurists and practised by military courts".

In hindsight, the Nuremberg Principles have been a major contribution to international law and still form an important part of current ICL.[92] Today the trial and the Judgment should not be regarded as illegitimate or mistaken,[93] or even as a one-time event that cannot serve as a model for emulation.[94] The UN has consistently upheld their legitimacy and importance.[95] Instead of rejecting the precedent, one ought to recognise that a well-founded choice was made after World War II between conflicting principles of justice. The results included support for a universal right under international law of any nation to seek accountability of political and military leaderships for grave crimes on the basis of a fair trial.[96]

A challenge that remains today is to elucidate the content and hierarchical status of the different general principles of international criminal law, including their legal consequences, in settings where parallel rules are founded in different law-creating sources and the jurisdiction of new international courts or national legislation on grave crimes is still being defined. These issues will recur in other books in this series.

It should be noted, however, that an international criminal court, once established, cannot abdicate its responsibility for determining guilt because its legal basis does not provide a clear-cut answer to an interpretive issue. The judges may have to make a decision on the legal matter before it, and presumably a correct one under its statute and general

---

[92] See ILC, *Principles of International Law Recognized in the Charter of the Nürnberg Tribunal and in the Judgment of the Tribunal*, 1950, reprinted in *Yearbook of the International Law Commission, 1950*, vol. II, para. 97.

[93] The Nuremberg and Tokyo trials have "generated much critical literature", as noted by Nina H. B. Jørgensen in *The Responsibility of States for International Crimes*, Oxford University Press, Oxford, UK, 2000, p. 28 (with further references). International lawyers, the UN, and international courts, however, generally regard the results favourably.

[94] See, *e.g.*, Gallant, 2009, p. 405, *supra* note 25.

[95] See UN General Assembly Resolution 95, 11 December 1946, endorsing "the principles of international law recognized by the Charter of the Nuremberg Tribunal and the Judgment of the Tribunal". See also UN General Assembly Resolution 177 (II), 21 November 1947, urging the ILC to "formulate" the Nuremberg Principles.

[96] See UN General Assembly, 1946, *supra* note 95. Principle I affirms individual responsibility for crimes under international law; Principle III, responsibility of a head of state or government official; and Principle V, the right to a fair trial on the facts and law.

international law. When the ICTY and the ICTR were confronted with the problem that the crime of rape had not been defined, the ICTY Trial Chamber, in *Kunarac*, first examined the criminal laws in many different countries in order to ascertain a general principle underlying the crime of rape in national laws.[97] The definition of rape it extracted from these national sources was then accepted as part of international law by the ICTY Appeals Chamber.[98] This indicates that general principles of law are particularly important at this stage of globalisation and development of international criminal law, and that law-creating mechanisms other than international customary law and treaty law are needed to meet the new legal challenges and seek harmonised universal crimes norms.[99]

3.3.5. Legislative Security Council Resolutions

An additional law-creating source, which is still controversial, consists of SC resolutions establishing binding rules of a legislative character. This is controversial for reasons relating both to the legal basis of the SC's action under Chapter VII of the UN Charter and to its legitimacy as a law-making organ. Since the end of the Cold War, the SC has interpreted and used its competence in this respect to adopt binding rules and principles of general application. Consequently, "it has asserted and extended its authority where the inadequacies of law-making by treaty might undermine the pursuit of its objectives".[100]

An example of this development, which has been much discussed, is the comprehensive Security Council Resolution 1373 (2001), aimed at combating terrorism. Whether terrorist crimes are also universal crimes is discussed later in this book.[101] The point here is that Resolution 1373 lays down universal and binding obligations for states. According to Husabø and Bruce, the content of Resolution 1373 "largely corresponds to what could be expected from a convention, the traditional instrument for

---

[97] ICTY Trial Chamber, *Prosecutor v. Kunarac et al.*, Judgment, IT-96-23, 2001, para. 439.

[98] ICTY Appeals Chamber, *Prosecutor v. Kunarac et al.*, Judgment, IT-96-23/1, 2002, para. 127.

[99] This may also include soft law, *e.g.*, statements of the law by the ILC and maybe even a comprehensive declaration by the General Assembly on universal crimes; see Chapter 5, section 5.3.

[100] See Boyle and Chinkin, 2007, pp. 109–110, *supra* note 34.

[101] See Chapter 4, section 4.9.2.4.

creating new obligations under international law".[102] But the legal effects are different, since while states are free to choose whether to sign and accede to or ratify a convention, a resolution adopted under Chapter VII by the SC – made up of a limited number of state representatives, and dominated by the five permanent members – is immediately binding upon all members of the UN without exception. Such a resolution, being imposed on its subjects, has a vertical legislative character, rather than being a horizontal agreement among equal and sovereign states.[103] Furthermore, SC Resolution 1373 provides for an enforcement mechanism, the Counter-Terrorism Committee, which is a body subordinate to the SC. In SC Resolution 1540 (2005), the SC again legislated in general terms, this time to ensure that non-state actors are prevented from obtaining nuclear, chemical, or biological weapons. These features have led commentators to use the term 'legislation'[104] or 'quasi-legislation'.[105] As Husabø and Bruce observe, from a functional point of view "Resolution 1373 satisfies even the strictest definitions of international legislation".[106] Normatively, they are more sceptical of its legal validity, at least at the time when it was adopted.[107]

Some authors maintain that a systematic interpretation of the UN Charter contradicts the power of the SC to impose general legislative measures on member states.[108] It is true that the decision-making powers of the SC with regard to "measures not involving the use of armed force" are not exhaustively specified or enumerated in the UN Charter (Article 41). But both the text and the context of the Charter support the position that adoptions of binding rules are not *per se* excluded. The limited competences of the General Assembly in Articles 11(1) and 13(1), with regard to the development of general principles of international law, may suggest an underlying assumption that only states can create new general rules of international law, by treaties or the formation of customs. How-

---

[102] See Erling Johannes Husabø and Ingvild Bruce, *Fighting Terrorism through Multi-level Criminal Legislation: Security Council Resolution 1373, the EU Framework Decision on Combating Terrorism and their Implementation in Nordic, Dutch and German Criminal Law*, Martinus Nijhoff /Brill, Leiden, Netherlands, 2009, p. 35.

[103] *Ibid.*, p. 36.

[104] *Ibid.*, pp. 36–39 (with further references).

[105] Boyle and Chinkin, 2007, p. 114, *supra* note 34, use both characterisations.

[106] Husabø and Bruce, 2009, p. 39, *supra* note 102.

[107] *Ibid.*, pp. 40–54.

[108] *Ibid.*, p. 46 (with further references).

ever, the 'threat to the peace', which constitutes both a specific legal basis and a limitation on SC powers (Article 39), read in conjunction with the broad discretion regarding peaceful measures to be employed to that end (Article 41), does not exclude the use of abstract norm creation. Legislative acts are a common way of achieving such goals in national law, and can be presumed to be options within international law as well.

The limitations stem not from any bar to legislation as such by the Security Council, but from the requirement that the measures employed must be sufficiently linked to the specific purpose "to maintain or restore international peace and security" (Article 39); from the limitations flowing from "the purposes and principles of the United Nations" (Article 24, as well as Articles 1 and 2); and from other parts of international law, including the proportionality principle. The UN purposes and principles include, but are not necessarily confined to, "respect for human rights", "the principle of equal rights and self-determination of peoples", "justice", and "settlement of international disputes". It is also important to note that *jus cogens* rules of international law bind the SC in the exercise of its functions. In order for the UN Charter to remain in harmony with the peremptory norms of general international law (*jus cogens*) and not become void as a treaty,[109] the Charter – including its Chapter VII – must be interpreted as not being in conflict with these norms.[110] SC resolutions cannot legitimise grave crimes or any other activity falling within the scope of proscriptive *jus cogens*. The ICTY Appeals Chamber acknowledged such limitations in the *Tadic* case. It concluded that "neither the text nor the spirit of the Charter conceives of the Security Council as *legibus solutis* (unbound by law)".[111] Whether respect for other binding international rules requires that the Security Council not create new conflicting norms is a more difficult question. A simple answer seems to be that this is unlikely. In their analysis of this issue, Boyle and Chinkin conclude that the jurisprudence of international courts suggests that SC resolutions "over-ride inconsistent international law".[112] SC resolutions

---

[109] See the Vienna Convention on the Law of Treaties, 1969, Articles 53 and 64.

[110] See, *e.g.*, Antonios Tzanakopoulos, *Disobeying the Security Council: Countermeasures against Wrongful Sanctions*, Oxford University Press, Oxford, UK, 2011, pp. 70–72, with further references.

[111] ICTY Appeals Chamber, *Prosecutor v. Duško Tadic*, para. 28, *supra* note 44.

[112] Boyle and Chinkin, 2007, pp. 232–233, *supra* note 34.

thus have great potential significance in future international law, not least within the field of ICL.

Still, it may be that further limitations on SC legislative power should be read into the UN Charter. Some restrictions seem necessary in order to prevent the legislative powers of the SC from expanding beyond peace and security issues. This set of issues, however, often coincides with the concerns of ICL because of the close relationships between peace, security, and justice. Note also that 'peace' and 'security', under current international law, are not narrowly defined terms. The acceptance of basic 'human security' as a fundamental universal value and/or interest, and of the complementary notion of a 'responsibility to protect',[113] has expanded the powers of the SC under Chapter VII with respect to measures undertaken with the aim of protecting civilians who are exposed to universal crimes. Alternatively, one may consider that this power is already inherent in Chapter VII but that its use has become politically feasible in the aftermath of the Cold War.[114] Within this more flexible framework, the SC may be able to rewrite or disregard provisions of international law in particular situations.[115] This is a significant change in traditional perceptions of the limitations of international law. Two SC resolutions on the situation in Libya in 2011 seem to be a case in point. In the first one, the SC considered that "the widespread and systematic attacks currently taking place in the Libyan Arab Jamahiriya against the civilian population may amount to crimes against humanity".[116] It then, in another resolution, authorised member states "to take all necessary measures [...] to protect civilians and civilian populated areas under threat of attack in the Libyan Arab Jamahiriya".[117] For the first time, the United Nations had in practice authorised an international humanitarian

---

[113] See Gareth Evans, *The Responsibility to Protect: Ending Mass Atrocity Crimes Once and For All*, Brookings Institution Press, Washington, DC, 2008. See also Chapter 2, section 2.3.1.

[114] See, *e.g.*, Jennifer M. Welsh, "The Security Council and Humanitarian Intervention", in Vaughan Lowe, Adam Roberts, Jennifer Welsh, and Dominik Zaum, (eds.), *The United Nations Security Council and War: The Evolution of Thought and Practice since 1945*, Oxford University Press, Oxford, UK, 2008, pp. 535–562.

[115] Boyle and Chinkin, 2007, pp. 232–233, *supra* note 34.

[116] UN Security Council Resolution 1370 (2011).

[117] UN Security Council Resolution 1373 (2011).

---

intervention, that is, started a regular universally authorised war, for the purpose of protecting human beings against grave (universal) crimes.[118]

In reference to the resolution on terrorism in 2001, Husabø and Bruce have argued that an "interpretation of Chapter VII as broad as that on which Resolution 1373 is based could easily serve as a precedent for Security Council legislation in other areas", an outcome which could ultimately turn the SC into "a world government".[119] The example of Libya in 2011 might provide additional grounds for such a fear. There are, however, several factors that make such a scenario unlikely in general terms: these include the internal political constraints of the SC, including the veto power held by the five permanent members, as well as the legal reasons mentioned above. In *Tadic*, the ICTY expressed the view that "there exists no corporate organ formally empowered to enact law directly binding on international legal subjects". [120] Considering that the court in *Tadic* accepted the legality of Resolution 827 (1993), which established the ICTY itself with such legal effects, this statement might at first seem contradictory. The court probably intended a more limited meaning, namely, that there exists no such organ with a *general* law-creating power, that is, outside the scope of threats to peace and security. Following this interpretation, *Tadic* confirmed that unrestrained use of legislative powers would not be legally acceptable, although the concrete legislative act establishing the ICTY did fall within the ambit of SC powers.

The case for there being implicit and necessary limitations on SC legislative powers is often linked with the fact that there is only limited scope for judicial review of SC resolutions. Although it might be legally possible for the General Assembly to exercise control of the legality of SC-created rules by means of a request for an advisory opinion from the ICJ,[121] for political reasons this would usually not be an option. Individual states directly affected by an SC resolution could not bring such a complaint themselves, but would be dependent upon the General Assem-

---

[118] See Chapter 4, section 4.9.2. However, under a somewhat narrower definition of 'humanitarian intervention', the Security Council authorised several earlier armed interventions, notably in Northern Iraq (1991), Somalia (1992), Haiti (1993), Rwanda (1994), and East Timor (1999). See Welsh, 2008, pp. 538–553, *supra* note 114.

[119] Husabø and Bruce, 2009, p. 39, *supra* note 102.

[120] ICTY Appeals Chamber, *Prosecutor v. Duško Tadic*, para. 43, *supra* note 44.

[121] See Article 96(1) of the UN Charter and Article 65(1) of the ICJ Statute.

bly to take the initiative. The issue of judicial review of SC resolutions may later arise in a contentious case between two or more states before the ICJ,[122] but that would not satisfy a need for an immediate judicial review of a controversial SC resolution.

Other courts, including international criminal courts, may also scrutinise particular Security Council resolutions, as seen in the *Tadic* case. Another example of indirect court review is the case of *Kadi and Al Barakaat* before the European Court of Justice (ECJ), which held that the European Community judicature does have jurisdiction to review the measures adopted by the Community to give effect to SC resolutions. Although the ECJ declined to expressly "review the lawfulness of a resolution adopted by an international body", it still reviewed norms resulting from the SC resolution by comparing them to "fundamental rights that form an integral part of the general principles of law whose observance the Court ensures".[123] These included the principle of effective judicial protection, which had been infringed on several points.[124] The same principle of judicial review was upheld by the ECJ in the case of *Hassan and Ayadi*.[125]

The main problem with SC legislative acts, therefore, is arguably not so much the legal basis or legitimacy of the legislative acts *per se*. More importantly, there is little assurance that the SC will act consistently or at all, when it should, and judicial control is uncertain in cases where specific legislative acts may go too far. Despite these problems, it is clear that the law-creating function of the SC needs to be taken into account and further explored, particularly with respect to the concept of universal crimes as part of current international law. In particular, the precedent of SC Resolution 1373 (2001) on terrorism, at least when considered in

---

[122] See, *e.g.*, Boyle and Chinkin, 2007, pp. 230–231, *supra* note 34, with references to ICJ, *Certain Expenses of the United Nations (Article 17, paragraph 2, of the Charter)*, Advisory Opinion, I.C.J. Reports 1962, p. 151; and ICJ, *Questions of Interpretation and Application of the 1971 Montreal Convention arising from the Aerial Incident at Lockerbie* (Libyan Arab Jamahiriya v. United States of America), Provisional Measures, Order, I.C.J. Reports 1992, p. 114.

[123] ECJ, *Yassin Abdullah Kadi and Al Barakaat International Foundation v. Council of the European Union and Commission of the European Communities*, C-402/05 P and C-415/05 P, Judgment, 3 September 2008, paras. 4–5.

[124] *Ibid.*, para. 8.

[125] ECJ, *Faraj Hassan and Chafiq Ayadi v. Council and Commission of the European Union*, C-399/06 P and C-403/06 P, Judgment, 3 December 2009.

---

conjunction with other sources, including other (non-binding) SC resolutions on the same subject matter, may have given birth to a new binding norm on direct criminal liability under international law.[126]

3.3.6. Establishing Universal Crimes Norms with Multiple Legal Bases

The proposition that a binding international rule has to originate from an identifiable law-creating source is closely related to the rule of law in international relations.[127] One may raise the question, however, whether there might be a modification of this clear point of departure which would still be acceptable under international law and particularly relevant for fundamental universal crimes norms. This modification would entail anchoring a legal norm in multiple legal bases, without specifying any one of them as the principal legal basis. While the weight of each specific legal basis might be uncertain, one could still argue that their cumulative weight was sufficient to establish a binding international rule.

At first glance, an approach relying on multiple legal bases might seem questionable, suggesting an arbitrary and subjective mixture of customary international law, treaties, and general principles of law. However, Nuremberg provides a classical illustration of the underlying dilemmas caused by unclear legal status of universal crimes norms and of the consequent need for such a combined approach. The main issues put before the Nuremberg Tribunal were (1) whether aggression was prohibited before and during World War II, and (2) whether individual criminal liability for aggressive acts ('crimes against peace') existed under international law. With regard to the former, the Tribunal could rely on a number of international treaties, including several treaties to which Germany was a party and which it clearly had breached,[128] notably the Kellogg-Briand Pact of 1928.[129] In that treaty, the parties had declared "in the names of their respective peoples that they condemn recourse to war for the solution of international controversies, and renounce it, as an

---

[126] See Chapter 4, section 4.9.2.

[127] See Chapter 2, section 2.2.2.

[128] IMT, *Trial of the Major War Criminals*, 1947, vol. I [Judgment], pp. 216–224, *supra* note 13.

[129] Signed at Paris on 27 August 1928, the Kellogg-Briand Pact was a treaty between several states providing for the renunciation of war as an instrument of national policy.

instrument of national policy in their relations with another".[130] Although Germany claimed a reservation to the Kellogg-Briand Pact with regard to preventive self-defence, this was dismissed by the Tribunal as non-operational on the basis of general principles of law.[131]

The next issue was an even more difficult one, since neither the Kellogg-Briand Pact nor any other treaty explicitly addressed criminal liability for future acts of aggression.[132] The Tribunal here seems to have adopted an approach combining different treaties, emerging customary international law, and general principles of law into a single *sui generis* legal basis. What makes the approach particularly innovative and interesting is that the Tribunal does not make clear which particular legal basis it regards as the principal law-creating source. The Tribunal instead justified its affirmative answer with respect to individual criminal liability by pointing to the dynamic character of international law concerned with fundamental principles, and to the needs of a changing world. In this process it also invoked an analogy, compelling at least in terms of *lex ferenda*, that certain methods of warfare had also first been prohibited and subsequently recognised as war crimes under international law. A longer citation is warranted:

> The Hague Convention of 1907 prohibited resort to certain methods of waging war. These included the inhumane treatment of prisoners, the employment of poisoned weapons, the improper use of flags of truce, and similar matters. Many of these prohibitions had been enforced long before the date of the Convention; but since 1907 they have certainly been

---

[130] Kellogg-Briand Pact, Article I. See also Article II, stating that the settlement or solution of disputes or conflicts "shall never be sought except by pacific means".

[131] IMT, *Trial of the Major War Criminals*, 1947, vol. I[Judgment], p. 208, *supra* note 13. The court rejected the notion "that Germany alone could decide, in accordance with the reservations made by many of the Signatory Powers at the time of conclusion of the Kellogg-Briand Pact, whether preventive action was a necessity, and that in making her decision, her judgment was conclusive". Instead the court held that "whether action taken under the claim of self-defence was in fact aggressive or defensive must ultimately be subject to investigation and adjudication if international law is ever to be enforced".

[132] In the Versailles Treaty of 28 June 1919, Article 228, the German government after World War I recognised "the right of the Allied and Associated Powers to bring before military tribunals persons accused of having committed acts in violation of the laws and customs of war". This treaty was not directly applicable to crimes committed in World War II.

---

crimes, punishable as offences against the laws of war; yet the Hague Convention nowhere designates such practices as criminal, nor is any sentence prescribed, nor any mention of a court to try and punish offenders. [...] In the opinion of the Tribunal, those who wage aggressive war are doing that which is equally illegal, and of much greater moment than a breach of one of the rules of the Hague Convention. [...] The law of war is to be found not only in treaties, but in the customs and practices of states which gradually obtain universal recognition, and from the general principles of justice applied by jurists and practiced by military courts. This law is not static, but by continual adaptation follows the needs of a changing world. Indeed, in many cases treaties do no more than express and define for more accurate reference the principles of law already existing.[133]

The horizontal structure of international law – the systemic fact that "international law is not the product of an international legislature"[134] – may justify a similar approach in other exceptional cases.

The International Law Commission may on certain issues also have proceeded on the implicit basis of such an underlying theory of the legal bases of international criminal law.[135] For example, on the 'obligation to extradite or prosecute' (*aut dedere aut judicare*),[136] the ILC special rapporteur in his first report in 2006 discussed the sources of the obligation. The Rapporteur admitted that one of the crucial problems to be solved was to "find a generally acceptable answer to the question if the legal source of the obligation to extradite or prosecute should be limited to the treaties which are binding the States concerned, or be extended to appro-

---

[133] IMT, *Trial of the Major War Criminals*, 1947, vol. I [Judgment], p. 221, *supra* note 13. The prosecutors at Nuremberg often invoked several legal bases for the same crime. See *ibid.*, [Indictment], p. 43, on the legal bases of war crimes norms ("violations of international conventions, of internal penal laws and of the general principles of criminal law"); p. 44, on the crime of murder and ill-treatment of civilians; and p. 51, on the crime of deportation ("contrary to international conventions, in particular to Article 46 of the Hague Regulations 1907, the laws and customs of war, the general principles of criminal law"); p. 53, on murder and ill-treatment of prisoners of war ("contrary to International Conventions, particularly [...] the laws and customs of war, the general principles of criminal law"). See also pp. 54, 56, and 61–65.

[134] *Ibid.*, [Judgment], p. 221.

[135] On various statements by the ILC concerned with international crimes generally, see Chapter 4, section 4.5.

[136] See Chapter 4, section 4.5.9., on this particular subject matter.

priate customary norms or general principles of law".[137] As a point of departure, based upon a preliminary analysis, the special rapporteur was "convinced that the sources of the obligation to extradite or prosecute should include general principles of law, national legislation and judicial decisions, and not just treaties and customary rules".[138] It remains to be seen whether his preferred approach to the subject matter will eventually receive the support of states.[139]

In general, international courts have declined to follow a rigorous methodology that would unduly restrict their freedom to facilitate, if necessary, what seems to be a necessary development of international law in light of world community interests and elementary considerations of justice. Judges of international courts have sometimes been viewed as conservative and restrained in their interpretation of the law in certain fields, while at other times they have been portrayed as radicals. Such a focus on the judges may open interesting debates, but it would be a mistake to lay too much weight on the role of judges while ignoring deeper issues. Because international courts operate within the UN paradigm of international law, they must internalise and be guided by a legal culture compatible with that paradigm, thus including certain basic principles that reflect fundamental, common international interests and values.[140] When different fundamental principles, such as justice, effect-

---

[137] ILC, Zdzislaw Galicki, Special Rapporteur, *Preliminary Report on the Obligation to Extradite or Prosecute ('aut dedere aut judicare')*, A/CN.4/571, 2006, p. 12, para. 40.

[138] *Ibid.*, p. 15, para. 48.

[139] In the first discussion in the Sixth Committee of the General Assembly on the issue of the legal nature of the obligation, more restricted views were expressed, as also acknowledged by the special rapporteur in his second report. See ILC, Zdzislaw Galicki, Special Rapporteur, *Second Report on the Obligation to Extradite or Prosecute ('aut dedere aut judicare')*, A/CN.4/585, 2007, pp. 8–9 and 12–13, paras. 25–28 and 50. Still, the ILC has proceeded on the assumption that several legal bases need to be explored, but in particular treaties and customary international law, including possible "regional principles". See, *e.g.*, ILC, *Report of the International Law Commission*, Supplement no. 10, A/64/10, 2009, pp. 344–345, para. 204.

[140] The same is not necessarily true of politicians concerned with foreign relations and the international community. They typically operate from a domestic platform and represent state interests, which in many concrete cases may contravene long-term common international interests. Thus it may be correct that state representatives comply with international law for instrumental reasons. See Jack L. Goldsmith and Eric A. Posner, *The Limits of International Law*, Oxford University Press, Oxford, UK, 2005, p. 225: "We have argued that the best explanation for when and why states comply with international law is not that states have internalized international law, or

---

iveness, and legal certainty, clash, the outcome may then depend upon the concrete circumstances and the individual preferences of the judges.

It is therefore realistic to assume that international courts dealing with universal crimes will sometimes make use of multiple legal bases in a discrete manner, taking one particular legal basis, for example, customary international law, as the point of departure and using materials from other law-creating sources as interpretative materials to support a conclusion that the norm is legally binding. Under such an approach, the distinction between legal bases and interpretative sources is maintained,[141] even though the distinction between soft law and hard law has less clear-cut boundaries.

3.4. Interpretative Sources, Priority Principles

3.4.1. Various Interpretive Sources

In contrast to the law-creating sources discussed above in section 3.3., an interpretative source of international law as such cannot create binding universal crimes norms. This is true even though the four principal law-creating sources may also be interpretative sources with regard to another possible legal basis. Treaties, customs, general principles, and legislative Security Council resolutions thus each play a double role in the machinery of international criminal law. These roles are, however, distinct.

Among many other possibly relevant interpretative sources, the jurisprudence of international courts is particularly prominent. Others include law literature, UN reports and studies, statements by organs of the UN and other international organisations, as well as state practice of different kinds, including national court decisions on international criminal law issues.

Historically, the commanding position of international courts within this field goes back to the Nuremberg and Tokyo tribunals. In addition, the ICJ has contributed over many years with important judgments and

---

have a habit of complying with it, or are drawn by its moral pull, but simply that states act out of self-interest". However, the instrumental reasons may also include compliance with the fundamental structures of the UN paradigm of international law. Furthermore, from a legal point of view, the motivation for compliance or non-compliance is usually irrelevant.

[141] See section 3.3.1. in this chapter.

advisory opinions of high quality. This has been followed by the work of more recent international criminal tribunals, which taken together have produced an enormous number of invaluable judgments and interpretations of the law, and have thus developed and reinforced it. Although some legal reasoning and judgments carry more weight than others, a study of universal crimes should ideally pay attention to any judgment of interpretative force, whether originating from the Nuremberg Tribunal, the ICC, or other international courts, and to some extent should also consider persuasive reasoning by domestic courts applying the same rules.

However, international jurisprudence also has its limitations with respect to some aspects of universal crimes, since courts are dependent upon the cases they receive and their particular jurisdictions.

3.4.2. The Priority Principles: *Lex Superior*, *Lex Specialis*, and *Lex Posterior*

In general, it may not be necessary to prioritise the rules produced on the basis of different law-creating sources. However, if there should be a conflict between two or more rules having incompatible content, principles for prioritisation are needed. This is a general aspect of law, also known in domestic law. The principles of *lex superior* (a superior rule takes priority over an inferior rule), *lex specialis* (a specific rule takes priority over a general rule) and *lex posterior* (a newer rule takes priority over an older rule) are presumably part of the general principles of international law as well as of domestic law.

The impacts of the *lex specialis* and *lex posterior* principles are often uncertain, and the application of these principles should be handled with a great deal of care. Thus, if one rule is newer and the other is more specific, there is no general rule for deciding which should prevail. In general, the scope of the *lex posterior* principle is rather limited,[142] applying to successive multilateral treaties with different parties on the same subject matter. Furthermore, the notion of *lex specialis* does not necessarily imply that the *specialis* rule pre-empts the application of a coexisting more general rule, although this would generally be true.[143]

---

[142] See ILC, 2006, conclusion no. 25, *supra* note 4.

[143] *Ibid.*, conclusion no. 5: "The maxim *lex specialis derogat legi generali* is a generally accepted technique of interpretation and conflict resolution in international law. It

Apart from superior general principles of law (*jus cogens*), there may also be other considerations that provide reasons for concluding that a general law should prevail.[144] For example, one should take into account the nature of the general law and the intentions of the parties, as well as whether the application of special law might frustrate the purpose of the general law or affect the balance of rights and obligations as established in the general law.[145] Such considerations, which are important to note within the fields of international humanitarian law and human rights law, are also relevant for ICL. This is due, in particular, to the general principle of complementary protection in international law, that is, that rules for the protection of fundamental rights and interests of human beings, although originating from different sources of law or different treaties, may supplement each other. Although one substantive rule may be considered the special rule by an adjudicator, the more general substantive rule may apply simultaneously.

For example, the ICJ in the Wall Case found that the wall built by Israel within the occupied Palestinian territories violated rules of both international humanitarian law (IHL)[146] and human rights law (HRL),[147] although it considered IHL to be *lex specialis*.[148] As the ICJ explained, "some rights may be exclusively matters of international humanitarian law; others may be exclusively matters of human rights law; yet others may be matters of both these branches of international law".[149] The ICJ confirmed its view in its judgment in the *Armed Activities* case.[150] This

---

suggests that whenever two or more norms deal with the same subject matter, priority should be given to the norm that is more specific". See also conclusions nos. 6–8.

[144] *Ibid.*, conclusion no. 10.

[145] *Ibid.*

[146] ICJ, *Legal Consequences of the Construction of a Wall in the Occupied Palestinian Territory*, Advisory Opinion, *I.C.J. Reports 2004*, p. 136, at paras. 134–135, finding violations of the Fourth Geneva Convention, as well as of Security Council resolutions.

[147] *Ibid.*, para. 134, finding violations of the International Covenant on Civil and Political Rights, the International Covenant on Economic, Social and Cultural Rights, and the United Nations Convention on the Rights of the Child.

[148] *Ibid.*, para. 106: "In order to answer the question put to it, the Court will have to take into consideration both these branches of international law, namely human rights law and, as *lex specialis*, international humanitarian law".

[149] *Ibid.*

[150] ICJ, *Armed Activities on the Territory of the Congo* (Democratic Republic of Congo v. Uganda), Judgment, *I.C.J. Reports 2005*, p. 166, at paras. 216–220.

debate on the relationship between IHL and HRL has continued in the wake of the Wall Case and has been described as "a renewed battle between the proponents of the theories of complementarity and separation".[151] There is only one plausible solution under 'horizontal' international law, where each convention makes up its own legal regime, namely that "IHL and HRL are two distinct, though complementary, branches of law".[152] There is no hierarchical relationship between these and related fields of law like international refugee law and ICL, and the concern should be to seek clarity on the ordinary meaning of the provision at hand, guided by the object and purpose of each regime or instrument or by the particular norm in question.[153] As has been noted, in grey areas such as military occupation, insurgencies, or the 'war on terror', complementary application of different branches of international law not only may be in accordance with law, but "may guarantee the respect of the rule of law".[154]

In an interpretative process where two rules seem to conflict rather than complement each other, the practical way to solve the problem might be to interpret the norms in light of the presumption that a conflict was not intended. As observed by the Appeals Chamber of the ICTY in *Tadic*, with respect to a possible conflict between customary law and an SC resolution:

> It is open to the Security Council – subject to peremptory norms of international law (*jus cogens*) – to adopt definitions of crimes in the Statutes which deviate from customary international law. Nevertheless, as a general principle, provisions of the Statute defining the crimes within the jurisdiction of the Tribunal should always be interpreted as reflecting customary international law, unless an intention to

---

[151] Noëlle Quénivet, "The History of the Relationship between International Humanitarian Law and Human Rights Law", in Roberta Arnold and Noëlle Quénivet (eds.), *International Humanitarian Law and Human Rights Law: Towards a New Merger in International Law*, Martinus Nijhoff/Brill, Leiden, Netherlands, 2008, p. 12.

[152] Roberta Arnold, "Conclusions", in Arnold and Quénivet, 2008, p. 591, *supra* note 151.

[153] See UN High Commissioner for Refugees and ICTR, *Expert Meeting on Complementarities between International Refugee Law, International Criminal Law and International Human Rights Law: Summary Conclusions*, Arusha, Tanzania, 11–13 April 2011, conclusions nos. 1–4.

[154] Arnold, 2008, p. 592, *supra* note 152.

---

depart from customary international law is expressed in the
Statute, or from other authoritative sources.[155]

It follows from the same statement that the *lex superior* principle
must be adhered to even by the Security Council. Thus a rule seen as
possibly conflicting with *jus cogens*, under one interpretation, may be
construed under another interpretation as being in compliance with the *jus
cogens* norm. In such a case, that alternate interpretation should be
preferred.

3.5. *Lex Lata* and *Lex Ferenda*

The universal crimes project has among its principal goals to plausibly
describe and interpret international universal crimes law as it actually
exists (*lex lata*).[156] The rule of law depends on the principle that it is
possible to determine the correct interpretation of a rule (*lex lata*) within a
legal order. Such an interpretation may be correct even when it is not the
preferred legal solution on moral or political grounds. Lawyers adhering
to the rule of law must accept a distinction between what the law is (*lex
lata*) and what it ought to be (*lex ferenda*). In principle, two independent
adjudicators should arrive at the same result with regard to the law if both
apply the law at the same time in accordance with the relevant sources
and established methodology.

In some cases, however, two different results might be equally
plausible and arguable, due to the relative openness of legal judgments. In
principle, the favoured interpretation of the law should be arguable in the
context of the highest legal authority within the legal order that might
decide on the issue. If a legal solution is only arguable within the context
of a power structure or a setting that is closed to independent judicial
review, the solution might be *de facto* correct within that structure but still
not form part of *lex lata*. In other words, the conception of *lex lata* is
closely linked to a substantive conception of the rule of law; that is, 'law'
must be distinguishable from political, religious, or military 'power'
expressed only formally in judicial disguise by quasi-judicial bodies.

When two different solutions to a legal question are plausible and
arguable, the result will then depend upon the discretion of the adjudi-

---

[155] ICTY Appeals Chamber, *Prosecutor v. Duško Tadic*, Judgment, para. 296, *supra*
note 44.
[156] See preface to this book.

cator, guided by community interests and other legally relevant values internalised by the adjudicator. At a given time, it might thus be correct that one solution is as much *lex lata* as the other. This uncertain situation can change, however, when one solution is preferred in practice, as in the jurisprudence of the highest courts within the system. In this sense it is correct that courts, by clarifying a rule, also to some extent create law.

With regard to universal crimes, it is still an open question which court should be 'the highest' or most authoritative court at the international level. The immediate candidates today would seem to be either the ICJ or the ICC. Within the sphere of the ICTY and ICTR, the joint ICTY/ICTR Appeals Chamber is the highest judicial authority. Its jurisprudence is formally not legally subordinated to new jurisprudence originating from the ICC. With regard to the interpretation *lex lata* of a rule originating from customary international law or the general principles of law, the ICC might in the future be considered 'the highest court'. However, to date, the jurisprudence of different international courts provides different interpretative sources rather than being capable in itself of defining *lex lata* of ICL.

Legal authors are not in a position to create law. Their task is to analyse the law and comment on legal developments. In order to do that, they must offer their own views of the law as it is at a given time (*lex lata*). Otherwise, legal discussions become either purely theoretical (which, if well done, may serve legal science if not practice) or meaningless (as the reader will not know what the author is trying to communicate). In some cases authors may criticise the law and suggest better laws for the future (*lex ferenda*), but that too presupposes some conception of what the law actually is. In addition, authors have the option to criticise pronouncements of the law in decisions and other parts of the literature, flagging disagreement with other experts in order to seek the best interpretation when arguments for different views of the law are presented.

The universal crimes project, while basing itself on traditional legal analysis, is intended to explore ways to specify the concept of international crimes and the potential usefulness of a companion concept of universal crimes. The detailed analysis in the remainder of this volume is based on analysis of *lex lata*. But it is also intended to inform debates about *lex ferenda*, looking towards the ongoing and future development of international criminal law.

4

Reconceptualising International Crimes

4.1. Identifying Crimes under International Law

This chapter discusses how substantive crimes under international law, for which individuals may incur direct criminal liability, can be identified more specifically. In proposing methods for such identification and assessment, the text will move from a purely stipulative definition towards a theoretical one. Or, more precisely, it will explore the possibility of a theoretical definition that implies a specific concept of universal crimes.

In light of the stipulative definition set forth in Chapter 2, section 2.1.2., and the special features discussed in that chapter, a working definition – not a final legal definition – can be summarised as follows:

> 'Universal crimes' are certain identifiable acts that constitute grave breaches of rules of conduct usually committed, organised, or tolerated by powerful actors; and that, according to contemporary international law, are punishable whenever and wherever they are committed; and that require prosecution and punishment through fair trials, or in special cases, some other kind of justice, somewhere at some point.

Compared to the definition in Chapter 2, section 2.1.2., this definition has been slightly but significantly moderated on one point. In light of the following discussions in Chapter II, it is no longer stipulated that all universal crimes necessarily have to be committed, organised, or tolerated by powerful actors. The linkage to a power structure is still considered a special empirical or contextual feature of universal crimes, and a connection between the underlying acts and a power structure usually exists. Furthermore, such a linkage appears to be a legal requirement for some universal crimes. In exceptional cases, however, even certain genocide crimes and crimes against humanity might be committed by a single, notorious offender acting alone without a specific plan or policy set forth by others.[1] In order to possibly serve as a theoretical definition, this formulation needs further refinement. In particular, it does not provide sufficiently clear criteria for identification of crimes under

---

[1] See Chapter 2, section 2.3.3.

international law. In order to provide additional specificity, it is useful to begin with the concept of international crimes. This has been the dominant concept within the international criminal law (ICL) concept, along with the arguably narrower notion of 'core crimes'.

Sections 4.2. through 4.7. of this chapter survey the concept of international crimes, making reference to the statutes and jurisprudence of international courts, selected analyses of the concept in scholarly literature, and positions taken by the International Law Commission over the last 60 years. Special consideration is given to a specific case in 1948 and to recent changes in the ICC Rome Statute. Following this survey, section 4.8. proposes a detailed classification of international crimes. Section 4.9. puts this classification in a universal crimes framework, laying out five necessary and sufficient criteria for the identification of relevant crimes under international law. The section concludes with an proposed enumerative list of international crimes. Section 4.10. sums up the relationship between international crimes and universal crimes.

This detailed treatment is intended to provide a basis for justifying use of the concept of universal crimes in ICL. If successful, it will provide tools not only for analysis of existing law but also for possible further development of the law through its impact on philosophical, legal, and political thought relevant to ICL and related fields such as transitional justice.[2]

It should be noted that related but distinct ideas have been advanced concerning the concept of 'universal jurisdiction', which in fact is part of the proposed concept of universal crimes in this book. These ideas are expressed, for example, by Stephen Macedo in *Universal Jurisdiction*.[3] This edited volume was a follow-up to *The Princeton Principles on Universal Jurisdiction*, formulated in 2001 as "a set of guidelines or

---

[2] As noted by Roht-Arriaza, "The universe of transitional justice can be broadly or narrowly defined". Even the narrower view includes "prosecutions and criminal investigations, truth missions, vetting or cleansing of security forces, and, to some extent, formal reparations programs". Naomi Roht-Arriaza, "The New Landscape of Transitional Justice", in Naomi Roht-Arriaza and Javier Mariezcurrena (eds.), *Transitional Justice in the Twenty-First Century: Beyond Truth versus Justice*, Cambridge University Press, Cambridge, UK, 2006, p. 2.

[3] Stephen Macedo (ed.), *Universal Jurisdiction: National Courts and the Prosecution of Serious Crimes Under International Law*, University of Pennsylvania Press, Philadelphia, 2004.

---

standards for the development and use of universal jurisdiction".[4] This project apparently was based on the assumption that some of the principles were arguably already *lex lata* of international law, whereas others were recommendable *lex ferenda*, with the potential to become legal norms through the law-creating sources of international law, including new treaties and emerging customary international law. This perspective suggests that even private formulations and conceptual clarifications of legal principles that are in flux may contribute to new legal developments. Our project, however, is focused most specifically on certain parts of ICL. The long-term effects of acceptance of a concept of universal crimes, in addressing the fragmented and polycentric character of contemporary ICL, go beyond our immediate goals.[5]

The stipulative definition set forth above suggests that when certain *legal conditions* (criteria) apply, then certain *legal consequences* follow. Recall the presentation in Chapter 3, section 3.1.:

If:

Universal crime *and*

Punishable participation

Then:

Individual criminal liability *and*

Prosecution or extradition *and*

Universal court jurisdiction

This approach is further refined below, making use initially of the concept of 'international crimes'.

4.2. Different Conceptualisations of International Crimes

This section begins with a general overview of the concept of international crimes as found in a number of representative works on ICL. As noted below in section 4.4., scholars differ in many respects on the details. However, most actors and commentators would agree that, within the existing United Nations paradigm of international law, aggression, war crimes, crimes against humanity, and genocide are 'international

---

[4] *Ibid.*, p. 5. Macedo was project chair of the Princeton Project on Universal Jurisdiction, which developed the principles.

[5] See Chapter 3, section 3.2.

crimes'. These crimes, often referred to as core crimes, have been made operational in the statutes of international institutions and are proscribed by customary international law. As a result, at a minimum, individuals committing or otherwise participating in these crimes are directly liable to punishment under international law and in international institutions, even when effective enforcement mechanisms may not be available. Beyond this limited set of crimes, however, there is no general agreement. Some analysts would explicitly limit international crimes to these four, while others are willing to consider the inclusion of additional crimes.

There is often disagreement on interpretation of the core crimes themselves, on which modes of participation in such crimes apply, and thus on their overall scope in various settings. Much of the jurisprudence of international institutions, especially the tribunals on the former Yugoslavia and Rwanda but now also the International Criminal Court, is devoted to addressing these issues. Largely due to the legality principle, such discussions are primarily related to the statutes of these institutions as well as to relevant national legislation. These issues, for core crimes as well as other international crimes, are discussed in a forthcoming volume II on punishable participation in international crimes.

Our immediate concern, however, is the disagreement on which crimes other than the core crimes, if any, should also be labelled 'international crimes'. Viewpoints on those proposed for inclusion, such as terrorism, torture, and piracy, vary considerably. While the issues raised are often theoretical, they may also often be specific and contextual, raising jurisdictional or procedural questions. Thus there may be a linkage between determination of criminal jurisdiction and identification of a crime as an international crime. Such a linkage is implied by the concept of universal jurisdiction, which suggests that certain crimes are punishable both by the international community and by individual states, regardless of any territorial link between the prosecuting agent (international or national) and the location of the crime scene or the nationality of the perpetrators or victims. The grave character of the crime itself is presumed to justify and even may require prosecution somewhere.

However, the logical and legal inferences from the occurrence of a grave international crime itself, at the normative level, are often unclear in practice. This is partly due to the fact that jurisdiction under international law to prosecute, or a duty to extradite or prosecute (the *aut dedere aut judicare* principle), can be treaty-based. This is true, for example, with regard to several crimes other than the core international crimes – for instance, different acts of terrorism, illicit trafficking in human beings, drugs, or weapons, money laundering, and piracy. The International Law Commission (ILC) in 2010 identified 61 relevant multilateral treaties that contain provisions combining extradition and prosecution as alternative courses of action for the punishment of offenders.[6] While such treaties are legitimate and important grounds for the suppression of certain crimes, this widespread international practice may have led to failure to consider universal jurisdiction as an autonomous jurisdictional legal basis under international law, that is, independent of treaty. Treaties for suppression of specific crimes, when allowing or proscribing jurisdiction, have tended to treat universal jurisdiction as a *residual jurisdictional category* with unclear content and status under general international law, except when activated by treaty. Consequently, the links of the jurisdictional question to the nature and gravity of the crimes in question may have been weakened despite their possible utility in international law.

From a theoretical point of view, this leads to two problems. First, the procedural *consequences* of the crimes (universal jurisdiction) may be used to legally identify the 'international crimes' rather than the special character of the crimes themselves justifying and implying universal jurisdiction *lex lata*. Second, because universal jurisdiction with respect to certain crimes is invoked only as a residual jurisdictional category, treaty-based recognition of extended jurisdiction cannot be trusted as compelling evidence of identification of international crimes. It is therefore not satisfactory to seek a definition of international crimes in theories and national jurisprudence dealing with universal jurisdiction based on treaties. The issues connected with universal jurisdiction, therefore, are not explored in detail in this book.[7]

If treaty law is considered for these reasons to be unsatisfactory as the sole legal basis for international crimes, an alternative basis which

---

[6] See International Law Commission (ILC), *Survey of multilateral conventions which may be of relevance for the Commission's work on the topic "The obligation to extradite or prosecute (aut dedere aut judicare)"* (hereafter, *Survey of multilateral conventions*), Study of the Secretariat, New York, 26 May 2010. See also section 4.5.9. of this chapter.

[7] See preface to this book.

naturally presents itself is customary international law.[8] This approach, at least, may allow for additional options other than the four 'core crimes'.

Such a limitation of international crimes to crimes that clearly form part of *customary international law*, and are therefore universally recognised, may on its face seem a better choice. Excluding crimes defined by treaty, however, would exclude what is arguably the single most important law-creating source in international law. Linking international crimes to only one of the recognised law-creating sources of international law is certainly a possibility, within a stipulative definition, but on reflection it seems far too restrictive.

As a *normative definition*, linking international crimes only to customary international law is highly problematic because it downplays the fact that other crimes with a different legal basis under international law can have much the same legal consequences (individual liability, sufficient criminal jurisdiction, obligations to extradite or prosecute, and so on) as those that are part of customary international law.

To draw a parallel to the international status of human rights, the drafters of the Universal Declaration of Human Rights did not rely on the customary law status of certain rights to determine the list of rights to be included in that document. Nor has subsequent discourse on human rights taken their status under customary law as the point of departure. Within the UN and as well as within some regional organisations like the Council of Europe and the Organization of American States, both a non-binding declaration of human rights and binding human rights treaties were considered legally necessary, regardless of whether corresponding customary legal norms were already in existence.

The analogy to the development of universal human rights is not perfect, however, because of the legality principle that requires a sufficient legal basis before a crime exists (no legal proscription, no crime). Human rights, by contrast, may exist as influential moral norms (*lex ferenda*) even though they may not be legally binding (*lex lata*). In other words, it usually does not make sense to speak of *lex ferenda* crimes, but rather of a possible and desirable 'criminalisation' of morally wrong or otherwise undesirable acts. In some instances, moreover, the legal basis for a certain proscription *lex lata* might be arguable under international law, or perhaps not fully defined. In that case, the relevant

---

[8]   See Chapter 3, section 3.3.3.

recommendation may be to clarify the legal basis of the crime in international law, for example, in the form of an authoritative international code or other legally binding documents, in order to avoid possible issues with the legality due to lack of clarity.

With regard to prosecutions undertaken at the international level, the test of legality would usually be closely tied to the legitimacy and interpretation of international statutes. There are two components of such a test: (1) whether the alleged crime is covered by the definitions in the statute, and (2) whether the crime included in the statute is a crime under international law (an 'international crime'). If the answer to the first question is 'no', the international legality principle rules that the alleged crime cannot be prosecuted before the international institution.[9]

If the answer to the second question is 'no', the legal situation is more complicated. In such cases, the inclusion of the crime in the statutes may not in itself provide the court with jurisdiction, since it is possible that inclusion of the crime type was based on a mistaken assumption about the international status of the crime. But if the crime could have been prosecuted under the national law of all parties to the statute, and if the intention of parties was to provide the international institutions with jurisdiction with regard to that specific crime, or if the territorial state where the crime was committed has agreed to establish an international court for the prosecution of the crime, then the institutions could act without violating the international legality principle, even if the crime were not classified as an international crime. This is illustrated by the international hybrid courts, the statutes of which contain both international and domestic crimes (see section 4.3. below).

At a general level, the concepts of 'crime' within a state and of 'international crime' within the international community are similar. Within a state, 'crimes' for domestic purposes can be defined as 'punishable acts or conduct proscribed by law'.[10] In the same vein, 'international crimes' can be defined as 'punishable acts or conduct proscribed by international law'. Such a general definition does not, of course, say which crimes are included. But it has the advantage of not excluding any law-creating sources of international law from the outset; that is, it

---

[9] On the international legality principle, see also Chapter 3, section 3.3.4.

[10] At the beginning of this book, a 'crime' was defined as 'an offence for which one may be punished by law'; see Chapter 2, section 2.1.1.

includes general principles of law and legislative Security Council resolutions as well as treaties and international customs.[11]

An important difference between domestic crimes and international crimes is that the law is more difficult to ascertain at the international level because of the lack of a common legislator or other institutions fully competent to make law. Even so, *uncertainty* about a norm is not the same as *non-existence* of a criminal law norm. This distinction between domestic and international law is, however, relative rather than absolute. In some national states the principle of legality does, for instance, require that a criminal law (or at least the criminal law sanction and the legal basis for authorised legislative power to proscribe certain acts) be embodied in statutes formally enacted by the parliament. Such countries thus limit the relevant legal sources to one specific legal basis. In other states, the relevant legal bases for proscription in domestic law may also include customary law and general principles, provided they are sufficiently accessible and foreseeable. And formal statutes might also require such specification to provide an adequate legal basis if they were initially framed in language that is too vague. If there is such uncertainly, a criminal law norm cannot in itself serve as a valid legal basis for a criminal charge. Thus definitions of the requirements for a legal basis for criminal charges in domestic law, specified, for example, in the jurisprudence of the European Court of Human Rights (ECHR),[12] are also applicable in general terms to international crimes as well.[13] Hence, international crimes with which a person is charged must essentially have been established in international law with sufficient accessibility and foreseeability so that the person could have known (foreseen) what kind of acts and omissions would make him criminally liable and thus regulated his conduct accordingly.[14] By necessary implication this means

---

[11] See Chapter 3, section 3.3.

[12] See *e.g.*, ECHR, *Kononov v. Latvia*, 36376/04, Grand Chamber Judgment, 17 May 2010, paras. 185–246 (with further references).

[13] See, *e.g.*, Extraordinary Chambers in the Courts of Cambodia (ECCC), Pre-Trial Chamber, *Decision on Ieng Sary's Appeal against the Closing Order*, 11 April 2011, paras. 203–265.

[14] See ECHR, *Kononov* case, *supra* note 12, para. 187, in conjunction with paras. 185 and 238–239. In ECCC, *Sary* case, para. 236, *supra* note 13, the Pre-Trial Chamber asserted that "the requirements of accessibility and foreseeability are in line with those asserted by other international courts of a regional nature such as the European Court of Human Rights", and made particular reference to the *Kononov* case. The Pre-

that international law has realised the fact that a fine line may exist between acts that are crimes under international law and acts that are not, and that the full substantive content of international criminal law has never been fixed once and for all.

As will be discussed below, authors differ on which crimes to include in the set of international crimes, with some opting to include torture, slavery, terrorism, and piracy, for example, in addition to the core crimes. Less restrictive options also emerge in the discussions of the International Law Commission, although the 1996 Draft Code of Crimes against the Peace and Security of Mankind might give an impression of a more restrictive view.[15] It is also not clear without further explication what the legal consequences may be of deciding that a particular crime is not an international crime. Does this mean simply that individual liability under international law for other crimes does not exist under customary international law, or that such liability cannot even be established by means of a treaty arrangement? Or does it mean that national legislation cannot legitimately punish such crimes on the basis of reciprocal, extended criminal jurisdiction? Or that universal jurisdiction cannot be exercised with regard to such crimes when a specific treaty basis is lacking? Answering such difficult questions, we contend, requires first a more extensive exploration of the conceptual issues involved.

It should be stressed that the identification of international crimes also evolves as a result of pressure from the international community. When the need to address certain crimes becomes urgent for the relevant political and legal actors, the legality principle provides a strong incentive for identifying those crimes by statute and thus determining the material jurisdiction of the court specified in such a statute. These processes arise, of course, not only from legal concerns, but also from the political needs of the relevant decision-makers, the factual context of possibly relevant acts on the ground, and practical decisions regarding the potential capacity of the particular institutions that might be involved.

Thus one should not necessarily draw general conclusions from what is not included in a particular statute. For instance, the absence of

Trial Chamber noted (fn. 456) that guidance could be found in the jurisprudence of the ECHR in relation to the principle of legality because Article 7 of the ECHR served as a model for the drafting of Article 15 of the International Covenant on Civil and Political Rights.

[15] See section 4.2.4. in this chapter.

aggression in the statutes of the ICTY and ICTR should not be interpreted as proof that the drafters intended to reject its status as an international crime or as a core crime.

Similarly, genocide was not included as a separate crime in the Nuremberg Statute, and nobody was convicted of genocide in the immediate aftermath of World War II, although the concept had been invented in 1944 by Lemkin,[16] and the word had already become internationally known before Nuremberg and was indeed used in the Nuremberg Indictment.[17] However, this does not establish that genocide was not already an international crime within the UN paradigm of international law before the adoption of the 1948 UN Genocide Convention. On the contrary, the Genocide Convention is premised on the assumption that genocide was a crime under international law wholly independent of the new convention. Consequently, Article I of that convention obligates the contracting parties to "confirm" that genocide, whether committed in peacetime or wartime, "is a crime under international law" and a crime that they as members thus agreed to "undertake to prevent and punish". Likewise, in the convention's preamble, the contracting parties are expected to accept – after having considered the earlier General Assembly declaration on genocide[18] – "that genocide *is* a crime under international law, contrary to the spirit and aims of the United Nations and condemned by the civilized world" (emphasis added).

If genocide had been included as a crime in the Nuremberg Statute and applied by the Nuremberg Tribunal, it would have been controversial whether this violated the legality principle, making this even more contested than was the inclusion of 'crimes against peace' and 'crimes against humanity'.[19] A few years later, however, in 1951, the International Court of Justice (ICJ) accepted the viewpoint that "the principles

---

[16] Raphael Lemkin, *Axis Rule in Occupied Europe: Laws of Occupation, Analysis of Government, Proposals for Redress*, Carnegie Endowment for International Peace, Washington, DC, 1944, pp. 79–95. Before Nuremberg, Lemkin had elaborated on the term in two other works: "Genocide: A Modern Crime", in *Free World*, April 1945, vol. 4, pp. 39–43, and "Genocide", *American Scholar*, April 1946, vol. 15, no. 2, pp. 227–230.

[17] See Chapter 3, section 3.3.4.

[18] UN General Assembly Resolution 96 (I), "The Crime of Genocide", 11 December 1946. See also Chapter 2, section 2.2.3.

[19] See remarks on the legality principle in Chapter 3, sections 3.2. and 3.3.4.

---

underlying the [Genocide] Convention are principles which are recognized by civilized nations as binding on States, even without any conventional obligation".[20] The ICJ further recognised that it had been the intention of the United Nations

> to condemn and punish genocide 'as a crime under international law' involving a denial of the right of existence of entire human groups, a denial which shocks the conscience of mankind and results in great losses to humanity, and which is contrary to the spirit and aims of the United Nations (Resolution 96 (I) of the General Assembly, December 11th 1946).[21]

Given that genocide was not included in the Nuremberg Statute, the prosecutors could not press that charge. They did, however, decide to include the concept, and characterisations of the acts concerned were employed in the explanatory part of the indictment.[22]

This preliminary examination makes clear that in crafting a list of international crimes, one needs to be cautious about including or excluding particular crimes, and about claims that the resulting list is an exhaustive definition of international criminal law *lex lata*.

4.3. International Crimes in the Statutes of International Institutions

International criminal courts established since 1945 comprise the Nuremberg and Tokyo tribunals set up after World War II; the International Criminal Tribunal for the former Yugoslavia (ICTY) and the International Criminal Tribunal for Rwanda (ICTR) established by the UN Security

---

[20] See International Court of Justice (ICJ), *Reservations to the Convention on the Prevention and Punishment of the Crime of Genocide*, Advisory Opinion, 28 May 1951, *I.C.J. Reports 1951*, p. 15, at p. 23.

[21] *Ibid.*

[22] See International Military Tribunal (IMT), *Trial of the Major War Criminals before the International Military Tribunal: Nuremberg, 14 November 1945 – 1 October 1946*, Nuremberg, 1947 (hereafter, *Trial of the Major War Criminals*), vol. I [Indictment], pp. 43–44: "They conducted deliberate and systematic genocide, Viz., the extermination of racial and national groups, against the civilian populations of certain occupied territories in order to destroy particular races and classes of people and national, racial or religious groups, particularly Jews, Poles and Gypsies and others".

Council in 1993 and 1994 respectively; and the International Criminal Court (ICC), a permanent and general criminal court established by treaty in 1998 and made operational from 2002. These courts have been established by different methods, but with the exception of the ICC, all have been framed with specific, ongoing factual situations in mind.

Some other tribunals can be characterised as 'internationalised courts' rather than international courts in a strict sense. These internationalised tribunals, or hybrid courts, have a mixed national and international foundation and participation. They include courts or court chambers set up and made operational in different countries, including Kosovo (1999), with jurisdiction over war crimes and genocide; East Timor (2000) with jurisdiction over genocide, war crimes, and crimes against humanity, in addition to serious ordinary criminal matters; Cambodia (2001), with jurisdiction over genocide, crimes against humanity, and grave breaches of the 1949 Geneva Conventions; Sierra Leone (2002), with jurisdiction over crimes against humanity, violations of Common Article 3 of the Geneva Conventions, and other serious violations of international humanitarian law; and Bosnia and Herzegovina (2005), with jurisdiction over genocide, crimes against humanity, and war crimes.

The Special Tribunal for Lebanon is an interesting case, with very specific limitations. It was established by an agreement between the UN and the Lebanese Republic, authorised by the Security Council in 2007.[23] That resolution was pursuant to an earlier Security Council resolution which had responded positively to the request of the Government of Lebanon to establish "a tribunal of an international character to try all those who are found responsible for this terrorist crime" (the February 2005 killing of former Lebanese prime minister Rafiq Hariri and 22 others).[24] The jurisdiction of the tribunal can be extended to other attacks as well if they are "of a nature and gravity similar to the attack" on Hariri.[25] The tribunal has jurisdiction to apply only "the provisions of the Lebanese Criminal Code relating to the prosecution and punishment of acts of terrorism, crimes and offences against life and personal integrity, illicit associations and failure to report crimes and offences, including the

---

[23] UN Security Council Resolution 1757 (2007), "Attachment: Statute of the Special Tribunal for Lebanon".

[24] UN Security Council Resolution 1664 (2006), "Security Council Requests Establishment of International Tribunal for Killing of Former Lebanese Prime Minister Hariri".

[25] *Ibid.*, Article 1.

rules regarding the material elements of a crime, criminal participation and conspiracy".[26] From our perspective, the most interesting point is that "acts of terrorism" are for the first time being pursued by an internationalised tribunal.[27]

In addition, Iraq has established a Supreme Iraqi Criminal Tribunal, without direct international involvement,[28] which allows a role for "non-Iraqi judges who have experience in conducting criminal trials stipulated in this law" [29] and for international advisors.[30] This tribunal has jurisdiction over genocide, crimes against humanity, war crimes, and other serious national crimes.

Cumulatively, these tribunals have indicted and convicted a substantial number of persons for international crimes. In addition, serious international crimes have been pursued in many domestic proceedings on war crimes (broadly understood), based on territorial jurisdiction or nationality jurisdiction as well as universal jurisdiction.[31]

For historical, political, and legal reasons, the most important tribunals are unquestionably the Nuremberg Tribunal, the ICTY, the ICTR, and the ICC. Inclusion of particular crimes in the statutes of these courts provides strong evidence that such crimes are international crimes under any reasonable definition of that concept.

A brief look at these statutes shows that the number of crimes and *ratione materiae* jurisdictions have generally been quite limited. The focus has been on the 'core crimes'. The statutes of the tribunals

---

[26] *Ibid.*, Article 2(a).

[27] The possibly broader consequences for the legal status of terrorist crimes under international law is discussed in section 4.9.2. in this chapter.

[28] See Iraqi Law No. 10, 2005, "Iraqi High Criminal Court Law", *Al-Waqa'l Al-Iraqiya* (Official Gazette of the Republic of Iraq), no. 4006, 18 October 2005.

[29] *Ibid.*, Article 3, Fifth.

[30] *Ibid.*, Article 7, Second. "The President of the Court shall have the right to appoint non-Iraqi experts to act in an advisory capacity for the Criminal Court and the Cessation Panel. The role of the non-Iraqi nationals shall be to provide assistance with respect to international law and the experience of similar Courts (whether international or otherwise)".

[31] See the detailed survey by Joseph Rikhof, "Fewer Places to Hide? The Impact of Domestic War Crimes Prosecutions on International Impunity", in Morten Bergsmo (ed.), *Complementarity and the Exercise of Universal Jurisdiction for Core International Crimes*, FICHL Publication Series No. 7, Torkel Opsahl Academic Epublisher, Oslo, 2010, pp. 7–81. See also Chapter 2, section 2.2.2.

---

mentioned above all include war crimes, crimes against humanity (the only exception is the lack of jurisdiction of the Kosovo internationalised courts over crimes against humanity), and genocide (the exceptions being the early Nuremberg and Tokyo tribunals). The crime of aggression was included in the statutes of the Nuremberg and Tokyo tribunals (as 'crimes against peace') and of the ICC (with a more detailed definition of aggression adopted at the 2010 review conference in Kampala).[32] In the drafting of the Rome Statute, the crimes of terrorism and trafficking in narcotics were considered for inclusion but were not included in the final statute.

While its inclusion would not likely be considered today, the signatory parties to the Nuremberg Statute preserved "the right to bring individuals to trial for membership" in "a group or organization [...] declared criminal by the Tribunal" (Article 10). It followed from the latter, read in conjunction with Articles 9 and 11, that membership in a criminal organisation in principle was also considered to be an independent criminal offence under international law. Under Law No. 10 of the Allied Control Council of Germany passed on 20 December 1945, such membership was also recognised as a crime, in addition to being a form of extended liability. As an independent crime, a conviction for membership in a criminal organisation would not in itself amount to complicity in the underlying crimes committed by other members of the group or organisation.

Such a qualified 'group crime' or 'membership crime' has not been reproduced in later international court statutes. In refugee law in some jurisdictions, however, membership in brutal or inherently criminal organisations has been considered a particular mode of participation (complicity) in international crimes, and members of such organisations have thus been liable to exclusion from refugee status under the 1951 Refugee Convention, Article 1F.[33] In a recent case, the UK Supreme Court expressed serious doubt about this approach and expressed a preference for using other modes of participation, such as the concept of

---

[32] See section 4.7. of this chapter.

[33] See Joseph Rikhof, *Exclusion at a Crossroads: The Interplay between International Criminal Law and Refugee Law in the Area of Extended Liability*, Legal and Protection Policy Research Series, PPLA/2011/06, Division of International Protection, United Nations High Commissioner for Refugees, June 2011, pp. 17–18.

joint criminal enterprise, or possibly aiding and abetting, in such decisions on exclusion.[34]

Since the internationalised or hybrid courts are partly national as well as international, their jurisdiction has not been confined to international crimes. The statutes of these courts have thus included crimes other than core crimes, that is, crimes whose status as international crimes is problematic. Among crimes included by one or more of these courts are terrorist crimes, murder, sexual offences, torture, abuse of girls, organised crime, manipulation of the judiciary, and religious persecution. The selection of the additional crimes for each tribunal is presumably related to their significance in the particular national situations the court has been called upon to remedy. Thus their inclusion is not in itself sufficient proof of a special status under international law.

Thus the international court statutes provide broad support for the conclusion that war crimes, crimes against humanity, genocide, and the crime of aggression are today generally considered to be international crimes by nearly all member states of the United Nations, and thus by the international community as a whole. This conclusion is, as we will see, also fully consistent with common understandings in the legal literature.[35] The label 'core international crimes', or just 'core crimes', seems well justified, even though it remains to be explained why these crimes rose to this status whereas others did not. Is it the inherent *gravity* of the crime types as such, or the underlying interests relating to international peace and security, or maybe a combination of both, that distinguish these core crimes from other crimes of international concern? Moreover, the status of the core crimes concept is unclear, in particular whether it should be regarded primarily as a legal concept, a social science concept, or a philosophical concept.[36]

The international court statutes, however, are sufficiently limited that the failure to include crime types other than the core crimes does not in itself disqualify them from inclusion as international crimes. In addition to the mention of other crimes by the hybrid international courts, evidence

---

[34] See UK Supreme Court, *R (on the application of JS) (Sri Lanka) (Respondent) v. Secretary of State for the Home Department (Appellant)*, [2010] UKSC 15, Judgment, 17 March 2010.

[35] See section 4.4. in this chapter.

[36] See section 4.8. in this chapter for additional discussion.

of additional international crimes might be sought in other interpretative sources of international law, including UN documents. The next two sections consider a variety of viewpoints in the scholarly literature on international law and in the ongoing work of the International Law Commission.

4.4. Concepts of International Crimes in the Literature

Given the wide range of scholarly literature on international criminal law, this survey makes no claim to be exhaustive. It is, however, intended to be representative, focusing particularly on recent books by established authors within the field and textbooks offering comprehensive surveys of ICL. Our focus includes the most common terms, including 'international crimes' and 'core crimes', and the related term 'transnational crimes', as well as other less frequent usages such as 'crimes of serious international concern'.[37] Some authors clearly explain their choice of terminology, while others do not. In either case, the results show markedly different concepts in terms of the number of crimes included, ranging from three or four to almost 30 recognised crimes. Our presentation, aimed at identifying both commonalties and differences, begins with works with more limited definitions and moves towards those with more inclusive definitions.

4.4.1. Zahar and Sluiter 2008

In *International Criminal Law: A Critical Introduction*,[38] Alexander Zahar and Göran Sluiter include only include three distinctive crimes: war crimes, crimes against humanity, and genocide. Despite the title, they do not provide a definition of international criminal law, but instead presuppose that its meaning is clear.[39] Nor, despite the subtitle, do they provide a critical assessment of the substantive scope of ICL. In fact, the book has a limited research focus, offering "an insider's perspective" on international criminal tribunals and their jurisprudence. It is therefore not

---

[37] On the various expressions that are being used for crimes relevant to international law, see Chapter 1, section 1.2.

[38] Alexander Zahar and Göran Sluiter, *International Criminal Law: A Critical Introduction*, Oxford University Press, Oxford, UK, 2008.

[39] *Ibid.*, p. 4.

possible to conclude with much certainty whether or not the authors recognise only those three crimes as 'international crimes'.

4.4.2. Cassese 2008

By contrast, Antonio Cassese, in *International Criminal Law*,[40] explicitly discusses the notion of international crimes. According to this author, international criminal law is "a body of international rules designed both to proscribe certain categories of conduct [...] and to make those persons who engage in such conduct criminally liable".[41] He recognises torture, aggression, and terrorism as international crimes, in addition to war crimes, crimes against humanity, and genocide.[42]

Cassese defines international crimes as "breaches of international rules entailing the personal criminal liability of the individual concerned".[43] He then identifies four cumulative elements that all must be present in order to constitute international crimes: (1) they consist of violations of international customary rules, (2) such rules are intended to protect values considered important by the whole international community, (3) a universal interest in repressing these crimes exists, in the sense that, subject to certain conditions, alleged perpetrators may in principle be prosecuted and punished by any state, and (4) if the perpetrator has acted in an official capacity, the state on whose behalf he has performed the prohibited act is barred from claiming immunity (with the exception for a serving head of state, foreign minister, or diplomatic agent).[44]

Three points are especially noteworthy and interesting for our purpose. First, Cassese requires a breach of international customary rules and community values. By doing so he explicitly rules out piracy, because it is "not punished for the sake of protecting a community value".[45] Traffic in drugs and psychotropic substances, unlawful arms trade, smuggling of nuclear and other potentially deadly materials, money laundering, and

---

[40] Antonio Cassese, *International Criminal Law*, 2nd ed., Oxford University Press, Oxford, UK, 2008.
[41] *Ibid.*, p. 4.
[42] *Ibid.*, pp. 4, 11–13, and 148–183.
[43] *Ibid.*, p. 11.
[44] *Ibid.*, pp. 11–12.
[45] *Ibid.*, p. 12.

slave trade or traffic in women are also ruled out, since these crimes are "only provided for in international treaties or resolutions of international organizations, not in customary law" and because "these offences are normally perpetrated by private individuals or criminal organizations".[46] Apartheid is excluded since "this offence has not yet reached the status of customary law crime".[47]

Second, Cassese does not provide reasons to justify the inclusion of each of the four elements, instead assuming them to be self-evident. Nor is it specified whether they apply to *lex lata* or to *lex ferenda* (the text appears to refer to *lex lata*). Yet, since other authors present different criteria, the choice of these four cannot be self-evident, but rather requires explanation. For instance, by always requiring a breach of a customary rule, Cassese may risk putting too much emphasis on this particular law-creating source.[48] His second requirement, a breach of a community value, seems reasonable, but he does not explain why it should be mandatory or indicate how such values may be identified and distinguished from others that are not community values. For example, it is not clear why piracy at some level of organisation, scale, and brutality – such as the piracy problem off the coast of Somalia – may not breach community values such as the safety of international shipping and the personal security of crews and passengers.

Third, Cassese's third and fourth elements logically concern the legal consequences of international liability, and not the constituting conditions of an international crime. While they may in fact always follow from the existence of an international crime, they do not constitute part of the definition in the same sense as the first two, which are defining conditions.

4.4.3. Werle 2009

In *Principles of International Criminal Law*, Gerhard Werle begins with a broad definition but ends up with a more limited set of crimes than does

---

[46] *Ibid.*

[47] *Ibid.*, p. 13.

[48] See Chapter 3, section 3.3., on the four law-creating sources that are (also) relevant to substantive ICL.

Cassese.[49] Werle defines ICL as "all norms that establish, exclude or otherwise regulate responsibility for crimes under international law".[50] He then supplies three additional criteria which narrow the field considerably. According to Werle, an offence falls under ICL only if it meets three conditions:

> First, it must entail individual responsibility and be subject to punishment. Second, the norm must be part of the body of international law. Third, the offence must be punishable regardless of whether it has been incorporated into domestic law.[51]

Like Cassese, Werle does not explain the source of the conditions he proposes or provide a justification for how they are formulated. For instance, the requirement that individual responsibility must be "subject to punishment" is not self-evident, at least not if one understands this to require, as Werle apparently does, an existing *international* court mechanism for trial and punishment of a certain crime. Implicitly, this means emphasis on the formal development of the constituting instruments of international institutions, and Werle's approach is similar in that way to the approach taken by Zahar and Sluiter.

In the end, Werle recognises only war crimes, crimes against humanity, genocide, and the crime of aggression as crimes under international law. These so-called core crimes Werle regards as 'the most serious crimes of concern to the international community', as specified in the Rome Statute (preamble and Article 5).[52] He reserves judgment as to whether other crimes may also involve direct criminal responsibility under international law, saying that "here the development of international law is in flux".[53] Although he does not recognise terrorism as such as an international crime (or other crime), he is inclined to include some acts of terrorism within the parameters of crimes against humanity or war crimes, rather than as separate crimes. He also recognises certain

---

[49] Gerhard Werle, *Principles of International Criminal Law*, 2nd ed., TMC Asser Press The Hague, 2009.

[50] *Ibid.*, p. 29.

[51] *Ibid.*

[52] *Ibid.*

[53] *Ibid.*, p. 30.

conduct during civil wars, not included in the Rome Statute, as crimes under customary international law.[54]

4.4.4. Bassiouni 2008

M. Cherif Bassiouni is probably the author who has engaged the conceptual problems at issue most consistently, as developed in volume I of *International Criminal Law*.[55] Compared to the fairly distinct approach to ICL exemplified by Cassese and Werle, Bassiouni's approach is broader and more complex. The core of his argument is summed up in this statement from that volume:

> International Criminal Law (ICL) is a complex legal discipline that consists of several components bound by their functional relationship in the pursuit of its value-oriented goals. These goals include the prevention and suppression of international criminality, enhancement of accountability and reduction of impunity, and the establishment of international criminal justice. Each of these components derives from one or more legal disciplines and their respective branches, including international law, national criminal law, comparative criminal law and procedures, and international and regional human rights law. These legal disciplines are distinguished on the basis, *inter alia*, of their subjects, contents, scope, values, goals, and methods. Thus, they cannot be easily reconciled. Nevertheless, the different components that make up ICL constitute a functional whole, even though lacking in the doctrinal cohesiveness and methodological coherence found in other legal disciplines whose relative homogeneity gives them a more defined systemic nature. Thus, there is something that can be called the system of ICL, which derives from the functional relationship that exists between the different components of this discipline and the value-oriented goals it seeks to achieve. This is evident in the scholarly writings on ICL.[56]

---

[54] *Ibid.*, p. 29.

[55] M. Cherif Bassiouni (ed.), *International Criminal Law*, vol. 1, *Sources, Subjects, and Contents*, 3rd ed., Martinus Nijhoff/Brill, Leiden, Netherlands, 2008.

[56] M. Cherif Bassiouni, "The Discipline of International Criminal Law", in *ibid.*, p. 3.

This approach has led Bassiouni to quite different results with regard to the identification of 'international crimes' than Cassese and many other authors.

Bassiouni is very much aware that there is a great deal of confusion in the writings of scholars as to what constitutes an international crime and how these crimes should be referred to.[57] He points out that

> the literature contains various undefined terms, such as: crimes under international law, international crimes, international crimes *largo sensu*, international crimes *stricto sensu*, transnational crimes, international delicts, *jus cogens* crimes, *jus cogens* international crimes, and even a further subdivision of international crimes referred to as 'core crimes', meaning genocide, crimes against humanity, and war crimes.[58]

He then attempts to clarify what constitutes an international crime in conventional international law,[59] an approach in direct contrast to Cassese's emphasis on customary international law. According to Bassiouni, this can be done on the basis of an empirical study, as he himself undertook to do in earlier works.

Bassiouni first identifies a list of 10 penal characteristics, any one of which, "if found, even singularly, in any convention, is sufficient to characterize the conduct prohibited by the convention as constituting an international crime".[60] He does not explain how these penal characteristics were identified or what criteria were used. All the items on the list, however, concern international cooperation by means of treaties, one of the four international law-creating sources, for the purpose of joint criminalisation or suppressing criminal conduct through common efforts.[61] Bassiouni found 267 relevant conventions, which he used to generate a list of 28 international crimes.[62] He further divided these into three categories: *jus cogens* crimes (10), potential *jus cogens* crimes (14), and other international crimes (4). *Jus cogens* crime include, for example,

---

[57] M. Cherif Bassiouni, "International Crimes: The *Ratione Materiae* of International Criminal Law", in Bassiouni, 2008, pp. 132–133, *supra* note 55.

[58] *Ibid.*, p. 133.

[59] *Ibid.*

[60] *Ibid.*

[61] *Ibid.* The penal characterisations are listed on pp. 133–134.

[62] *Ibid.* The international crimes are listed on pp. 134–135.

war crimes, crimes against humanity, aggression, genocide, and torture (Bassiouni includes other forms of cruel, inhuman or degrading treatment or punishment as part of the same crime as torture). Potential *jus cogens* crimes includes some acts of terrorism. Thus the six international crimes recognised by Cassese are also recognised by Bassiouni. Bassiouni, however, includes a number of other crimes as well. Although Bassiouni does not claim that such crimes are part of customary international criminal law, he considers piracy, slavery, apartheid, and mercenarism to be *jus cogens* crimes, that is, international crimes of the highest rank, whereas they are not even considered international crimes by Cassese.

Thus two distinguished scholars come to significantly different results in identifying crimes that should be recognised as international crimes. This is not because they differ on what is implied by specific sources of international criminal law, such as treaties or customary international law, but rather because they differ about the way in which these sources should be used to used to define the concept of international crimes. Similar disagreements recur when we consider the opinions of additional scholars.

4.4.5. Schabas 2010

In *The International Criminal Court: A Commentary on the Rome Statute*, William A. Schabas focuses principally on the existing ICC provisions and their pre-legal history, including the Statute's preamble on 'grave crimes' and 'the most serious crimes' and Article 5 on the actual crimes within the jurisdiction of the ICC.[63] Although he does not directly address the concept of international crimes,[64] his reasoning is nevertheless relevant for our subject matter. When discussing the preamble on the most serious crimes, Schabas notes that it "suggests a qualitative criterion for inclusion of crimes within the Rome Statute".[65] Furthermore, he makes the point that although there is a presumption that all crimes within the jurisdiction of the ICC are serious, and there is no express hierarchy of

---

[63] William A. Schabas, *The International Criminal Court: A Commentary on the Rome Statute*, Oxford University Press, Oxford, UK, 2010.

[64] *Ibid.* According to the book's index (p. 1232), a definition of the concept of 'international crimes' is provided at pp. 46–47. However, a 'definition' proper is not set out, although the concept is employed at pp. 45–47.

[65] *Ibid.*, p. 40.

crimes within the Statute itself, some crimes are arguably more serious than others.[66]

Schabas also holds that "some serious international crimes are not punishable by the Court: the missing provisions dealing with nuclear weapons and other weapons of mass destruction provide an example".[67] Thus he considers some other specific international crimes to be serious international crimes, just like the core crimes listed in Article 5, even though they are not at the same level of seriousness as those core crimes. He says that Article 5 limits the jurisdiction of the ICC to "the most serious crimes of concern to the international community as a whole". According to Schabas, Article 5 "seems to set a quasi-constitutional threshold for the addition of new crimes", that is, "those that are *ejusdem generis* with the four enumerated categories [genocide, crimes against humanity, war crimes, and the crime of aggression], belong in the Statute".[68] In contrast, he comments, the absence of treaty-based crimes dealing with terrorism and drug trafficking "speaks volumes".[69]

Schabas is principally concerned whether crimes meet – or might meet in the future – the particular threshold of the Rome Statute Article 5, rather than with classification of crimes as international crimes or not. In another book, he explained that whether and to what extent crimes are of concern to the international community is less dependent upon "the objective gravity of the crime" than on whether the national justice system acts effectively to address the crimes:

> Terrorist crimes are a good example. They may often involve hundreds of deaths, in appalling circumstances, and they feature in the headlines of the world's newspapers. But they are of little concern to international justice because the crime is adequately prosecuted by the domestic courts.[70]

This raises the question, to be addressed in more detail later in this work,[71] whether the lack of an effective national justice solution for a particular crime might also serve as a criterion for international crimes

---

[66]   *Ibid.* See discussions at pp. 40–41.

[67]   *Ibid.*, p. 40.

[68]   *Ibid.*, p. 108.

[69]   *Ibid.*

[70]   William A. Schabas, *An Introduction to the International Criminal Court*, 3rd ed., Cambridge University Press, Cambridge, UK, 2007, p. 83.

[71]   See section 4.9.2. in this chapter.

more generally. While Schabas does not focus on this more general question, it will be relevant to consider whether specific crimes, such as terrorism, should still be termed international crimes even when there is adequate prosecution of those crimes by domestic courts.

4.4.6. Cryer, Friman, Robinson, and Wilmhurst 2010

In the opening chapter of *An Introduction to International Criminal Law and Procedure*,[72] Robert Cryer and his co-authors note that different meanings of international criminal law are useful for different purposes.[73] In their book, they decide to consider international crimes as "those offences over which international courts or tribunals have been given jurisdiction under general international law".[74]

These authors thus consider 'international crimes' to be in effect "the so-called 'core' crimes of genocide, crimes against humanity, war crimes and the crime of aggression".[75] For them, therefore, the concept "does not include piracy, slavery, torture, terrorism, drug trafficking and many crimes which States Parties to various treaties are under an obligation to criminalize in their domestic law".[76] Their approach is quite similar to those of Werle (2009) and Zahar and Sluiter (2008), although the latter do not include aggression.

Nevertheless, Cryer *et al.* go on to say that "because a number of the practical issues surrounding the repression of these [core] crimes are similar to those relating to [other] international crimes [...], they are discussed in this book, although only terrorist offences and torture will be discussed in any detail".[77] They add that some crimes other than the present 'core' crimes may, depending on how the jurisdiction of the ICC develops, "constitute international crimes within our meaning at some time in the future".[78] They also say that a more substantive approach

---

[72] Robert Cryer, Håkan Friman, Darryl Robinson, and Elizabeth Wilmshurst, *An Introduction to International Criminal Law and Procedure*, 2nd ed., Cambridge University Press, Cambridge, UK, 2010.

[73] *Ibid.*, p. 4.

[74] *Ibid.*

[75] *Ibid.*

[76] *Ibid.*, pp. 4–5.

[77] *Ibid.*, p. 5.

[78] *Ibid.*

might decide that international crimes "are considered to be those which are of concern to the international community as a whole (a description which is not of great precision), or acts which violate a fundamental interest protected by international law".[79]

They go on to make a distinction between ICL and 'transnational criminal law'.[80] By the latter the authors mean "those parts of a State's domestic criminal law which deal with transnational crimes, that is, crimes with actual or potential transborder effects".[81] We shall return to the concept of transnational crimes later, because it is important for our own purpose.[82]

This definition of 'transnational crimes' provided by Cryer *et al.* in the first chapter, comprising one substantive element (actual or potential transborder effects) and one formal element (being part of domestic criminal law), does not seem sufficient. Actual or potential transborder effects are common to all international crimes, not least the 'core' crimes, whether or not they are also the subject of domestic criminal law. The key questions for international law should not be whether the crimes are also dealt with in domestic law, but whether they are crimes of only domestic concern (which are the least interesting) or crimes of international concern that may be added to a list of 'core international crimes'.[83] With the exception of some issues concerning extraterritorial jurisdiction and international police cooperation, it is quite straightforward that the former crimes, where the original source of proscription is national law, simply fall outside the scope of ICL, whereas the latter might meaningfully be included as substantive 'international crimes'.

Another important question is whether 'international crimes' should be equated only with 'core crimes' or should be considered to comprise both the core crimes and other crimes of international concern (which might be called transnational crimes of international concern). For a crime to be of 'international concern', it seems reasonable to require that prohibition of the crime, that is, the proscribed conduct, have a clear legal

---

[79] *Ibid.*, pp. 6–7.
[80] *Ibid.*, pp. 5–6.
[81] *Ibid.*
[82] See sections 4.4.8. and 4.8. of this chapter.
[83] See the distinctions set forth by Robert J. Currie in *International and Transnational Criminal Law*, Irwin Law, Toronto, 2010. The book is discussed further below.

---

basis in one of the law-creating sources of international law, or at least that one or more of the 10 penal characteristics proposed by Bassiouni have actually been made part of international law, typically by means of a multilateral treaty.

In Chapter 14, "Transnational Crimes, Terrorism and Torture", the authors take a different and more coherent approach than in Chapter 1, defining transnational crimes as "crimes which are the subject of international suppression Conventions but for which there is as yet no international criminal jurisdiction".[84] This definition resembles 'transnational crimes of international concern', as noted above. The authors highlight crimes such as "drug trafficking, piracy, slavery, terrorism offences, torture, apartheid, enforced disappearances, transnational organized crime including people trafficking, smuggling migrants and illegal arms trafficking, and corruption" as relevant to ICL.[85] They add that "[s]ome of these are also covered by customary international law or are international crimes when committed in certain circumstances (for example as crimes against humanity)".[86] The difference between international crimes and transnational crimes thus lies in the fact that transnational crimes have not been included as distinct crimes in any international court statute. Making the distinction in this way helps provide a method for the international community to move a crime from one umbrella (transnational crimes) to the other (international crimes) through its inclusion in a statute. It also allows for some international crimes to exist in international law even if they are not included in most of the international court statutes.

4.4.7. Ratner, Abrams, and Bischoff 2009

In *Accountability for Human Rights Atrocities in International Law*,[87] Steven Ratner, Jason Abrams, and James Bischoff define ICL as "the international law assigning criminal responsibility for certain particularly

---

[84]   Cryer *et al.*, p. 334, *supra* note 72.

[85]   *Ibid.*, pp. 334–335.

[86]   *Ibid.*, p. 335.

[87]   Steven R. Ratner, Jason S. Abrams, and James L. Bischoff, *Accountability for Human Rights Atrocities in International Law: Beyond the Nuremberg Legacy*, 3rd ed., Oxford University Press, Oxford, UK, 2009.

serious violations of international law".[88] Its scope thus not only extends to responsibility for violations of human rights and humanitarian law, but "is in fact far wider, to include, for instance, drug crimes and terrorism offences".[89] Their definition, then, includes what others may refer to as transnational crimes. The authors are aware, however, that their definition does not resolve what it means to say that international law assigns criminal responsibility.[90] They suggest that a further inquiry should take account of the legal need both to elaborate the specific crime and to prescribe the role for states in suppressing it. In their view, such an inquiry must examine three different strategies for prescribing international criminal responsibility: (1) direct provision for individual culpability; (2) obligating some or all states, or the global community at large, to try and punish or otherwise sanction offenders; or (3) by means of international law, authorising states or the global community to do the same.[91] This is an important reminder that criminal liability under international law is neither a self-explanatory concept nor a self-executing legal norm.[92]

In addition, they suggest that "[t]he methods by which the law provides for individual criminal responsibility can form the basis for various lists of international crimes".[93] As a descriptive proposition, this is surely true, as the present review of different positions and lists of international crimes in the literature reveals. To what extent the law is really that open-ended in normative terms is a more complex question which remains to be explored.

The authors note that, in practice, the world community relies on all three strategies mentioned above. Subsequently, "a violation of international law becomes an international crime if the global community intends through any of those strategies (regardless of whether they are implemented through treaty, custom, or other prescriptive method) to hold individuals directly responsible for it".[94] This approach, as the authors themselves admit, "contrasts with methods proffering strict doctrinal

---

[88] *Ibid.*, p. 10.
[89] *Ibid.*
[90] *Ibid.*, pp. 10–11.
[91] *Ibid.*, p. 11.
[92] See sections 4.8.–4.9. in this chapter.
[93] Ratner, Abrams, and Bischoff, 2009, p. 12, *supra* note 87.
[94] *Ibid.*

criteria that yield a small list of crimes under international law",[95] referring to, among others, Cassese and Werle.

The question that follows from their approach is under what circumstances international law will hold an individual responsible for violations. The authors take as a point of departure that states, courts, and others participating in the law-making process agree that most violations of international law do *not* incur individual criminal responsibility: "Yet the question of which violations of international law, including human rights and humanitarian law, do entail such accountability is somewhat unsettled".[96] They argue that the international community at least "must share a consensus on the gravity of these offenses and appropriate means of enforcement".[97] It is clear to the authors that ICL does not 'incorporate' all humanitarian and or human rights law, but, generally speaking, only those acts – by themselves referred to as 'atrocities' – that are characterised by the directness and gravity of their assault upon the human person.[98]

The corpus of offences might, in their opinion, be divided along different lines, for example, as "generic offenses" – genocide, crimes against humanity, war crimes, and apartheid – and "specific offenses" – slavery, forced labour, torture, forced disappearances, and terrorism.[99] They note, however, that the results of the international legal process of criminalisation are far from completely logical, and that arguably arbitrary distinctions may determine whether a particular assault on an individual does or does not incur individual responsibility.[100]

We shall return later to the issue of international criminalisation, which is very relevant to our project. This issue includes the question of whether crimes under international law should be identifiable according to set of common criteria and an authoritative international enumeration of such crimes.[101] One additional author, however, adds a new and thought-

---

[95]   *Ibid.*

[96]   *Ibid.*, p. 1.

[97]   *Ibid.*, p. 14.

[98]   *Ibid.*

[99]   *Ibid.*

[100]   *Ibid.*

[101]   See section 4.9. in this chapter and Chapter 5, section 5.3.

provoking model which offers a possible scheme for logically classifying international and related crimes.

4.4.8. Currie 2010

In his recent book, *International & Transnational Criminal Law*, Robert J. Currie presents an interesting analytical model developed primarily to explore "the interaction between domestic criminal law and the international law norms that both inform it and to some extent are incorporated into it".[102] According to the author, the model "stems in no small part from the fact that this text [...] is taking a view of international and transnational criminal law largely from the perspective of one state, Canada".[103] This perspective 'from below' might serve as a correction to the perception of ICL as a well-defined and coherent body of international law, clearly distinguishable from both domestic criminal law and transnational criminal law (TCL).

Currie notes that although domestic crimes can be defined as those crimes that are "criminalized solely at the election of the state and are not initiated through international treaty", such crimes may also have "international law implications and present unique problems with which governments, courts, and defence lawyers must wrestle".[104] Although this is true, it can be argued that the criterion 'international law implications' is unlike the criteria usually employed to define ICL and even TCL, namely, possibly existing international law-creating sources, international courts with appropriate jurisdiction, suppression conventions, and/or international law consequences connected to certain types of crime. An example provided by Currie illustrates the point:

> For example, a criminal operation located in Canada fraudulently sells securities by telephone to US residents, who send their money to other members of the operation located in Panama and Costa Rica; does Canada have the jurisdiction to prosecute, or should it cede jurisdiction to another affected state?[105]

---

[102] Currie, 2010, p. 13, *supra* note 83.
[103] *Ibid.*
[104] *Ibid.*, p. 16.
[105] *Ibid.*

The example concerns what might be termed 'organised', 'aggravated', or 'international' fraud. In a sense this is clearly a concrete 'transnational crime', at least in empirical sociological or criminological perspective. However, as a crime type, fraud falls within long-established domestic criminal law categories and thus has not attracted international law concern as such. The concrete fraudulent acts, as in the example, might be 'transnational' in scope. But, from a strictly legal point of view, of either domestic or international criminal law, the concrete crime in Currie's example is similar to organised domestic fraud, even if the fact that it involves activities in several countries and seems to be organised through transboundary criminal cooperation and channels may provide an additional aggravating factor. Therefore, whether this kind of crime warrants the label 'transnational crime' from a legal point of view would depend not on the crime itself but on whether there have been international agreements providing for cooperation in its suppression. If no legal cooperation exists with regard to its concerted suppression by means of international law mechanisms, the label 'transnational crime' would seem to be inappropriate in legal terms even if appropriate as an empirical description. If the existence of any 'international law implications' of a crime justifies such a label, then most crimes known in domestic law can in fact be 'transnational', depending on the facts of each case. This would detach the concept of TCL from association with specific crime types, instead directing attention to the set of legal, political, and practical problems due to its transnational origins or effects.

When defining TLC in general terms, however, Currie follows closely the precedent of Boister, who discussed this issue in an article in 2003.[106] TCL, according to both these authors, primarily covers "the indirect suppression by international law through domestic penal law of criminal activities that have actual or potential trans-boundary effects". It therefore focuses especially on the network of "suppression conventions that have developed since the nineteenth century in order to coordinate inter-state efforts to combat certain types of crime".[107] In contrast, "[t]rue international criminal law [...] usually emerges from customary international law, and individual criminal liability under international law

---

[106] Neil Boister, "Transnational Criminal Law?", in *European Journal of International Law*, 2003, vol. 14, no. 5, pp. 953–976.

[107] Currie, 2010, p. 15, *supra* note 83, with reference to Boister, 2003, p. 955, *supra* note 106.

can now be directly enforced by, *inter alia*, the International Criminal Court".[108] Furthermore, according to Currie, ICL "deals with conduct that is deemed to offend or threaten the most important interests of the international community or to 'shock the conscience of humankind' [...] international crimes can be prosecuted by any state regardless of where they occur under the principle of universal jurisdiction, whereas jurisdiction over transnational crimes is more limited".[109]

Currie stresses that the structure he presents is not meant to redefine international and transnational criminal law as a discipline "or to displace the significant work of Bassiouni and others".[110] But he still finds the concept of TCL suggested by Boister useful as a descriptive analytical phrase, separate from ICL.[111] It can serve, he argues, "to present the salient features of this emerging area of law in a way that highlights the distinguishing features but allows appreciation of the interplay between the various streams".[112] His analytical scheme, then, comprises four categories:[113]

1) International crimes in the strict sense ('core crimes')
2) Other international crimes
3) Transnational crimes of international concern
4) Transnational crimes of domestic concern

This model neatly draws a distinction between ICL and TCL, as well as dividing each main category into two subcategories.

Currie defines international crimes as "crimes that are deemed by the international community to transcend the domestic criminal law of any state, and that call for suppression and enforcement either directly under international law or by permissive use of the widest bases of state jurisdiction".[114] As additional characteristics that apply "variously or in combination", he notes that they have a "pernicious nature, or threaten international peace and security", that they "will often have an element of

---

[108] Currie, 2010, p. 15, *supra* note 83.

[109] *Ibid.*, p. 16.

[110] *Ibid.*, p. 17.

[111] *Ibid.*, pp. 14–17.

[112] *Ibid.*, p. 15.

[113] *Ibid.*, pp. 17–21. Each category is discussed in a separate chapter of the book, something that underlines the apparent usefulness of the analytical scheme.

[114] Currie, 2010, p. 17, *supra* note 83.

state involvement", that the perpetrators are *"hostis humani generis"* (enemies of humankind), and that "prohibition of an international crime will usually be a *jus cogens* norm under international law".[115] The difference between the core crimes and other international crimes is that core crimes imply the existence of direct liability of individuals under international law and the possibility of direct prosecution by an international court.[116] They include genocide, crimes against humanity, the crime of aggression, and war crimes. The other ICL category, according to Currie, consists of torture, piracy, apartheid, and slavery; these "have not attracted the status of core crimes, but are deemed to be sufficiently egregious to justify prosecution of the perpetrators wherever they may go, so as to ensure they can find no safe haven".[117]

The third category within his model, transnational crimes of international concern, covers all crimes regulated by "a treaty or set of treaties [...] between groups of interested states that deal with the crime". These include "narcotics smuggling and trafficking, corruption of foreign officials, fraudulent use of the mails, terrorism, and human trafficking".[118]

The fourth category, transnational crimes of domestic concern, are "crimes under domestic law which involve, in some way, more than one state", whereas "[t]he criminal prohibition involved does not arise from an international law source but is simply part of the state's own criminal law system".[119] The principal legal issue that arises, Currie notes, concerns the matter of jurisdiction in such 'transnational situations'.[120] However, at the level of practical international police and justice cooperation and mutual enforcement mechanisms, transnational crimes that are predominantly of domestic concern may involve a wide range of other legal issues.

Even so, Currie's detailed examination of this scheme shows that the dividing line between categories 2 and 3, that is, between ICL and TCL, is still difficult to draw. It depends on a complex discretionary judgment of law and facts relating to the specific crime types within the two categories. This problem, common to solutions proposed by other authors

---

[115] *Ibid.*, pp. 17–18.
[116] *Ibid.*, p. 18.
[117] *Ibid.*, pp. 18–19.
[118] *Ibid.*, p. 20.
[119] *Ibid.*
[120] *Ibid.*

as well, indicates the need for further refinement. The demarcation line between categories 3 and 4, on the other hand, seems more clear-cut from a legal point of view, as illustrated by Currie's example of fraud outlined above.

Despite the limitations of Currie's model, it provides a clear framework to show how important aspects of international and national criminal law interact, even when it may be difficult to fully separate the categories in practice. There may be interactions between any two of the categories, but each interaction has a distinct character. For instance, core crimes may be prosecuted at both the national and international levels. Transnational crimes of domestic concern, in contrast, may only be prosecuted at the national level, even if they involve international arrest warrants and requests for extradition. Other international crimes and transnational crimes of international concern are currently only prosecuted at the national level. But the hybrid international courts might provide exceptions, which might become more frequent in the future. This possibility is shown by current discussions about a possible special international court for piracy, or alternatively, an extraterritorial Somali anti-piracy court supported by the United Nations.[121]

An additional refinement that could be considered is splitting category 2 into two categories, one comprising 'other crimes against the peace and security of mankind' (other than the core crimes, that is), and the other being the residual category of 'other international crimes'. This would have the advantage of highlighting the extensive discussions in the International Law Commission on the concept of 'crimes against the peace and security of mankind', to be discussed in the next section. Categories 3 and 4 in Currie's model, by contrast, might well be merged for most analytical and normative purposes into a category labelled simply non-international crimes. The result would be the following schema, which may prove to be an even better analytical tool:

1) Core international crimes
2) Other crimes against the peace and security of mankind
3) Other international crimes
4) Non-international crimes

---

[121] See further Chapter 5, section 5.2.3.

The first three categories would then be part of ICL, whereas the category of non-international crimes would be clearly distinguished from international crimes, even if it were also divided into several sub-categories. This alternative classification scheme is further developed in section 4.8. of this chapter.

4.5. Statements of the International Law Commission

4.5.1. International Law Context

Notions of international crimes have a long history, arguably dating back to the writings of the Roman jurist Marco Tullio Cicerone (Cicero).[122] His conception of the 'common enemies of all' (*communis hostis omnium*) was later adopted as applying to those who commit the most serious crimes of international concern, using the term 'enemies of all humankind' (*hostis humani generis*).[123] During the 1800s the latter concept was applied to the perpetrators of piracy and other crimes like the slave trade and slavery.[124] Observers have noted, however, that a special characteristic of pirates was that "the pirate had no fatherland": he did not have any country to protect him but was "just a fellow who was taken at sea and prosecuted for his crimes" (usually hanged).[125] Within the United Nations paradigm of international law, the notion of *hostis humani*

---

[122] See Bassiouni, 2008, p. 129, *supra* note 57.

[123] *Ibid.*

[124] See, *e.g.*, *ibid.*

[125] These remarks were made by the Dutch international lawyer Röling in his discussions with the Italian international lawyer Cassese in 1977. See Bernard Victor Aloysius Röling and Antonio Cassese, *The Tokyo Trial and Beyond: Reflections of a Peacemonger*, Polity Press, Cambridge, UK, 1994, p. 97: "I doubt whether there is yet enough solidarity in the world today to allow us to say: there are some crimes that make a man *hostis humani generis*. You mentioned 'piracy'. But the pirate had no fatherland. That was one of the aspects of piracy. He hadn't a country behind him. He was just a fellow who was taken at sea and prosecuted for his crimes. Every seafaring country felt that its interests were jeopardized by the acts of pirates. So, if captured, they just hanged him, in accordance with their national laws. International law approved the universal application of those national laws. But piracy was a very special case. I [still] think there will come a moment when we shall be able to say: the time is ripe for this kind of jurisdiction in relation to other crimes as well, which also threaten the whole world".

---

generis was nevertheless accepted as a matter of principle, as in the post–World War II criminal trials, in conjunction with a deepened interest in a universal criminal code and the recognition of certain minimum ethical standards of international law.

When the Charter of the United Nations was drafted, however, the participating states were opposed to conferring direct legislative power to enact such norms as binding rules of international law.[126] They also rejected proposals to confer on the General Assembly the power to impose certain general conventions on states by some form of majority vote.[127] This decision has led to particular legal uncertainties within the field of ICL regarding such matters as the international legality principle and the prohibition of *ex post facto* criminal laws, or at least the duty of their careful and exceptional application, that is, their application in compliance with human rights principles as generally recognised in the UN Charter and later specified in several human rights instruments.[128] Although Article 15(2) of the 1966 International Covenant on Civil and Political Rights explicitly allows for "punishment of any person for any act or omission which, at the time when it was committed, was criminal according to the general principles of law recognized by the community of nations", this does not resolve the problem of which acts or omissions meet this standard.

There was, however, strong support for conferring on the General Assembly the more limited powers of study and recommendation.[129] This led to adoption of the Article 13, paragraph 1 of the UN Charter, according to which the General Assembly "shall initiate studies and make recommendations for the purpose of [...] encouraging the progressive development of international law and its codification". In November 1947, the General Assembly established the International Law Commission and approved its statute.[130] The statute was later amended several times, most recently in 1981.[131] According to Article 1, the ILC

---

[126] See United Nations, *The Work of the International Law Commission*, 6th ed., vol. 1, 2004, p. 4.

[127] *Ibid.*

[128] See, *e.g.*, the 1948 Universal Declaration of Human Rights, Article 11(2), and the 1966 International Covenant on Civil and Political Rights, Article 15(1) and (2).

[129] United Nations, 2004, p. 4, *supra* note 126.

[130] UN General Assembly Resolution 174 (II), 21 November 1947.

[131] UN General Assembly Resolution 36/39, 18 November 1981.

"shall have for its object the promotion of the progressive development of international law and its codification".

The ILC has worked on different parts of international law and "extensively in the field of international criminal law, beginning with the formulation of the Nuremberg Principles and the consideration of the question of international criminal jurisdiction at its first session, in 1949, and culminating in the completion of the draft Statute for an International Criminal Court at its forty-sixth session, in 1994, and the draft Code of Crimes against Peace and Security of Mankind at its forty-eighth session, in 1996".[132] More recently, starting in 2004, the ILC has worked especially on the related topic of 'the obligation to extradite or prosecute'. Its secretariat has conducted an extensive survey of multilateral conventions at both the universal and regional levels.[133]

In this section we survey the ILC's statements over the years with respect to international crimes and criminal liability under international law. Our aim is to tease out the thinking behind the idea of international crimes, including not only the viewpoints that prevailed, but also other opinions and proposals which were the subject of serious discussion. We highlight selected points from seven different portions of this history: (1) the work of the first special rapporteur, Jean Spiropoulos; (2) the 1954 Draft Code of Offences against the Peace and Security of Mankind; (3) some suggestions made by a later special rapporteur, Doudou Thiam; (4) the 1991 provisional Draft Code of Crimes against the Peace and Security of Mankind; (5) the 1994 Draft Statute for an International Criminal Court; (6) the 1996 Draft Code of Crimes against the Peace and Security of Mankind; and finally, (7) the ongoing work on the obligation to extradite or prosecute. This list is not intended to be comprehensive, but is rather representative of ILC discussions of relevance for our subject matter.

It is important to note that the United Nations has never adopted a truly comprehensive codification of international crimes, whether in the form of a General Assembly resolution or a convention. Thus the work of the ILC has still not been completed, despite several attempts to do so. As early as 1947, the General Assembly directed the ILC to "formulate the principles of international law recognized in the Charter of the Nürnberg

---

[132] United Nations, 2004, p. 8, *supra* note 126.
[133] See ILC, *Survey of multilateral conventions*, 2010, *supra* note 6.

Tribunal and in the judgment of the Tribunal" and to "prepare a draft code of offences against the peace and security of mankind".[134] The ILC, discussing the matter in 1949, judged that "the elaboration of the draft code was a matter of 'progressive development of international law'". As a first step, it decided to circulate a questionnaire to governments "inquiring what offences apart from those defined in the Charter and judgement of the Nürnberg Tribunal, should, in view of the governments, be comprehended in the draft code".[135]

4.5.2. The First Rapporteur, Jean Spiropoulos (1949–1951)

The ILC appointed Jean Spiropoulos as special rapporteur in 1949 and directed him to prepare a working paper on the draft code.[136] He suggested two methods of approaching the subject.[137] The first was "to elaborate a text with detailed substantive and procedural provisions, an 'ideal' draft, similar to the penal codes of municipal law, without paying any regard to the question whether such a draft would have any chance of obtaining the approval of the governments".[138] The other consisted of "the elaboration of a text which, based on a realistic approach to our task, could serve as a useful basis of discussion at an international conference".[139] The second option was chosen by the special rapporteur as being more in line with the intentions of the General Assembly, and this 'realistic' approach has by and large prevailed within the ILC.

Although the idea of a general international penal code surfaced on occasion within the UN and in the work of the ILC, especially at the early stages, the ILC clearly distinguished between such a possible code and the more immediate task of drafting a code directed especially towards offences against the peace and security of mankind.[140] The first rapporteur

---

[134] UN General Assembly Resolution 177 (I), 21 November 1947.
[135] See *Yearbook of the International Law Commission, 1949*, part I, 30th meeting.
[136] *Ibid.*, 33rd meeting.
[137] United Nations, *Draft Code of Offences Against the Peace and Security of Mankind – Report by J. Spiropoulos, Special Rapporteur*, A/CN.4/25, 26 April 1950, para. 1.
[138] *Ibid.*
[139] *Ibid.*
[140] *Ibid.* See, *e.g.*, the discussions by Spiropoulos in paras. 23–32.

focused on the latter.[141] According to Spiropoulos, such a code "is intended to refer to acts which, if committed or tolerated by a State, would constitute violations of international law and involve international responsibility".[142] He emphasised as their main characteristic "their highly political nature", inasmuch as they "normally would affect the international relations in a way dangerous for the maintenance of peace".[143] He concluded that the draft code to be elaborated by the ILC "cannot have as its purpose questions concerning conflicts of legislation and jurisdiction in international criminal matters".[144] This limitation was a practical rather than a logical consideration, based on actual international experience and consistent with his emphasis on the "highly political nature" of crimes relevant to the peace and security of mankind. He excluded from this draft code "such topics as piracy [...], suppression of traffic in dangerous drugs [...], in women and children (white slave traffic), suppression of slavery, of counterfeiting currency, protection of submarine cables, etc.".[145]

This distinction between two different categories of international crimes, as advanced by Spiropoulos, has been a constant thread in ICL. Although differences in the justifications for and definitions of the two categories have diminished the usefulness of the concept, it has remained a prominent feature of thinking in the ILC and among other commentators. For example, it is generally agreed today that non-state actors might commit a war crime, a crime against humanity, and even genocide, all of which constitute contemporary 'core international crimes' whether or not they are tolerated by the authorities of the territorial state concerned. As this example illustrates, the notion of 'core crimes' currently has in this regard a somewhat broader focus than that proposed by Spiropoulos, with a focus on the gravity rather than the political nature of the crimes in question. Despite these differences, these core crimes have consistently been considered by the international community to be a particular class of crimes of well-founded international concern.

---

[141] *Ibid.*, para. 29. The distinction had already been made by the French representative to the former Committee on the Progressive Development of International Law and Its Codification, Mr. Donnedieu de Vabres, as referred to by the rapporteur Spiropoulos.

[142] *Ibid.*, para. 35.

[143] *Ibid.*

[144] *Ibid.*, para. 36.

[145] *Ibid.*

The draft code suggested by Spiropoulos enumerated 10 "crimes under international law" – or, more precisely, nine crimes and one additional provision detailing five different modes of participation. The nine crimes included five different kinds of aggression (including "organized terroristic activities carried out in another State");[146] a crime called "manufacture, trafficking and possession of weapons the use of which is prohibited by international agreements"; genocide; crimes against humanity; and war crimes.[147] The modes of participation, each of which could apply to any of the nine crimes, comprised conspiracy; direct and public incitement; preparatory acts; attempt; and complicity.[148] A person committing any of the acts mentioned would be "responsible [...] under international law and liable to punishment".[149] Furthermore, the parties to the code would be obliged to enact the necessary legislation, in particular "to provide effective penalties for persons guilty of any of the acts declared punishable by the code", and "to try by a competent tribunal persons having committed on their territory any of the acts declared punishable by the present code".[150] In other words, a duty under international law for the territorial state to prosecute these crimes was envisaged. The draft code also had a provision on the duty to extradite perpetrators and another on compulsory jurisdiction of the International Court of Justice for disputes between the parties relating to the interpretation, application, or fulfilment of the code, and the responsibility of a State under international law for any of the acts declared punishable under the code.[151]

---

[146] *Ibid.*, Appendix, Basis of discussion No. 1. The other four aggression crimes were "Crime No. I: The use of armed force in violation of international law and, in particular, the waging of aggressive war. Crime No. II: The invasion by armed gangs of the territory of another State. Crime No. III: The fomenting, by whatever means, of civil strife in another State. [...] Crime No. VII: The annexation of territories in violation of international law".

[147] *Ibid.*

[148] *Ibid.*

[149] *Ibid.*, Appendix, Basis of discussion No. 2.

[150] *Ibid.*, Appendix, Basis of discussion Nos. 4 and 5.

[151] *Ibid.*, Appendix, Basis of discussion Nos. 6 and 7.

4.5.3. 1954 Draft Code of Offences against the Peace and Security of Mankind

In 1951 the ILC adopted a preliminary draft code which was submitted to the General Assembly[152] together with a commentary (hereafter, 1951 Comment). The ILC then drafted a revised version of the code and circulated it to governments for further comments. In light of their responses, the ILC adopted a final version of the 1954 Draft Code of Offences against the Peace and Security of Mankind (hereafter, 1954 Draft Code), together with additional ILC commentary (hereafter, 1954 Comment).

The 1954 Draft Code had only four articles. Article 1 stated:

> Offences against the peace and security of mankind, as defined in this Code, are crimes under international law, for which the responsible individuals shall be punished.[153]

According to the 1951 Comment, the principle was based upon the Nuremberg Charter and Judgment, generalised as follows: "any person who commits an act which constitutes a crime under international law is responsible therefor and liable to punishment".[154] It is noteworthy that there was no formal requirement that a defined penalty or criminal law sanction be set forth in any particular legal provision beforehand. The preliminary draft code of 1951, however, contained the following provision in Article 5:

> The penalty for any offences defined in this Code shall be determined by the tribunal exercising jurisdiction over the individual accused, taking into account the gravity of the offence.[155]

---

[152] See *Yearbook of the International Law Commission, 1951*, vol. II, p. 133.

[153] Draft Code of Offences against the Peace and Security of Mankind (1954). Text adopted by the ILC at its sixth session, in 1954, and submitted to the General Assembly as part of the Commission's report covering the work of that session. The report also contains commentaries on the draft articles. See *Yearbook of the International Law Commission, 1954*, vol. II, p. 149. See also Sir Arthur Watts, *The International Law Commission, 1949–1998*, vol. 3, *Final Draft Articles and Other Materials*, Oxford University Press, Oxford, UK, 1999, p. 1676. Watts provides some short overviews and background notes to accompany the reprinted ILC documents.

[154] Watts, 1999, p. 1676, *supra* note 153.

[155] *Ibid.*, p. 1685.

This provision was deleted in the 1954 Draft Code, as the ILC considered that the question of penalties could more conveniently be dealt with at a later stage, after it had been decided how the code was to become operative.[156] The wording of the deleted provision, as well as the reason for its deletion, show, however, that the definition of the crimes in question depended on the nature of the proscribed acts, that is, the universal values and interest they offend, rather than on the existence of formally prescribed sanctions against the responsible individuals. This point is still important for understanding the concept of 'crimes' within the UN paradigm of ICL.[157] In other words, in 1964 the ILC was of the opinion that, according to international law, a certain act may be punishable and should be punished at the national or international level, even when an international court with appropriate jurisdiction to enforce a penalty for the offence has not yet been established or does not yet have sufficient jurisdiction.

Article 2 of the 1954 Draft Code contained 13 sub-paragraphs. The first 12 listed different kinds of offences against the peace and security of mankind, while sub-paragraph 13 listed four different modes – nonetheless called "acts" – that would all apply to "any of the offences defined in the preceding [12] paragraphs": "conspiracy", "direct incitement", "complicity", and "attempts".

The use of the word "acts" here seems to imply that the ILC considered such acts as 'independent crimes' rather than only as different modes of participation. However, the mode of participation is not really an independent international crime (or offence against humankind) as such, but rather an aspect of the crime which may in itself constitute a specific crime for the individual participant. This follows from the fact that conspiracy, incitement, complicity, or attempt cannot give rise to individual responsibility under international law, unless there is a connection to a relevant international crime category or crime type such as genocide. The pragmatic reason for considering certain modes to be independent, or separate, crimes is that one single person might in some cases participate at different stages or in different ways, and thus his or her responsibility ought to reflect the exact and whole range of his or her actual participation. For example, a person who was part of a conspiracy

---

[156] *Ibid.*

[157] See section 4.8. in this chapter.

to commit genocide might then later directly incite others to commit the crime and/or contribute to its perpetration through his or her presence and authority at one or more crime scenes. Under such circumstances, it might be correct to indict this person for several crimes. Whether the different "modes" are considered independent crimes, at the individual level, or just as different and possibly aggravating aspects of the same crime might thus have two different answers, depending on the context and circumstances.

A related problem is what kind of behaviour at the initial preparatory stage ought to be criminalised, regardless of whether the crime itself later materialises or not. Because of the grave danger inherent in many offences against international peace and security, inchoate crimes such as conspiracy and certain kinds of incitement might be proscribed in addition to actual attempts to commit the crime. They might thus, for practical purposes, be treated as independent crimes as well. A prosecutor or a court may face the need to resolve such 'legal language problems' and find workable, practical solutions by deciding to prosecute 'one crime' or 'several crimes', which may differ depending on the statutes or national legislation concerned and the relevant interpretative sources of law under which they are operating.[158]

The 1951 Comment explicitly noted that the notion of conspiracy was inspired by the Nuremberg Charter on crimes against peace and was deliberately extended to all 12 listed offences against the peace and security of mankind.[159] It further noted that "complicity" was "not intended to stipulate that all those contributing, in the normal exercise of their duties, to the perpetration of offences against the peace and security of mankind, could on that ground alone, be considered as accomplices in such crimes". For example, in the opinion of the ILC, there could "be no question of punishing as accomplices in such an offence all members of the armed forces of a State or the workers in war industries".[160] Against this background it seems clear that under the 1954 Draft Code, membership in a 'criminal organisation' would not constitute an independent crime, a possibility suggested by the Nuremberg Charter,[161] nor

---

[158] These issues will be discussed in the second volume of this series, especially in regard to contemporary ICL theory and practice.

[159] See Watts, 1999, p. 1683, *supra* note 153.

[160] *Ibid.*

[161] See section 4.3. in this chapter.

could such membership constitute responsibility as an accomplice for the crimes committed by such an organisation as a whole. The 1954 Comment stated that "several governments had expressed fear that the application of Article 2, paragraph 13 (old paragraph 12), might give rise to difficulties"[162] – in other words, as it stood, it might be considered too broad. This did not, however, lead the ILC to modify the wording of this paragraph, "as it felt that a court applying the Code would overcome such difficulties by means of a reasonable interpretation".[163]

The 12 paragraphs on offences set out the following crimes:

1) Any act of aggression, including the employment by the authorities of a State of armed forces against another State for any other purpose other than national or collective self-defence or in pursuance of a decision or recommendation of a competent organ of the United Nations.

2) Any threat by the authorities of a State to resort to an act of aggression against another State.

3) The preparation by the authorities of a State of the employment of armed force against another State for any other purpose other than national or collective self-defence or in pursuance of a decision or recommendation of a competent organ of the United Nations.

4) The organization, or the encouragement of the organization, by the authorities of a State, of armed bands within its territory or any other territory for incursions into the territory of another State, or the toleration of the organization of such bands in its own territory, or the toleration of the use by such armed bands of its territory as a base of operations or as a point of departure for incursions into the territory of another State, as well as direct participation in or support of such incursions.

5) The undertaking or encouragement by the authorities of a State of activities calculated to foment civil strife in another State.

6) The undertaking or encouragement by the authorities of a State of terrorist activities in another State, or the toleration by the authorities of a State of organized activities calculated to carry out terrorist acts in another State.

7) Acts by the authorities of a State in violation of its obligations under a treaty which is designed to ensure international peace and security by means of restrictions or limitations on armaments, or on military training, or on fortifications, or of other restrictions of the same character.

---

[162] Watts, 1999, p. 1683, *supra* note 153.
[163] *Ibid.*

8) The annexations by the authorities of a State of territory belonging to another State, by means of acts contrary to international law.

9) The intervention by the authorities of a State in the internal or external affairs of another State, by means of coercive measures of an economic or political character in order to force its will and thereby obtain advantages of any kind.

10) Acts by the authorities of a State or by private individuals committed with intent to destroy, in whole or in part, a national, ethnic, racial or religious group, as such, including:

   i)   Killing members of the group;

   ii) Causing serious bodily or mental harm to members of the group;

   iii) Deliberately inflicting on the group conditions of life calculated to bring about its physical destruction in whole or in part;

   iv) Imposing measures intended to prevent births within the group;

   v)   Forcible transferring children of the group to another group.

11) Inhuman acts such as murder, extermination, enslavement, deportation or persecutions, committed against any civilian population on social, political, racial, religious or cultural grounds by the authorities of a State or by private individuals acting at the instigation or with the toleration of such authorities.

12) Acts in violation of the laws or customs of war.

Several comments are relevant for interpretation of these points. According to paragraph 1, "any act of aggression" was considered an offence against the peace and security of mankind. In the 1951 Comment, reference was made to General Assembly Resolution 380 (V), of 17 November 1950, which reaffirmed that aggression "is the gravest of all crimes against the peace and security of mankind throughout the world".[164] This provision does not enumerate such acts, and aggression can also be committed through some of the acts mentioned in other paragraphs of Article 2. In fact, the subsequent seven paragraphs all concern different kinds and levels of aggression by the authorities of a state.

Paragraph 10 concerned genocide, and the 1951 Comment clearly noted that this crime could be committed "both by authorities of a state and by private individuals".[165] Although the 1951 Comment said that the

---

[164] *Ibid.*, p. 1677.

[165] *Ibid.*, p. 1681.

paragraph "follows the definition of the crime of genocide contained in article II of the Convention on the Prevention and Punishment of the Crime of Genocide", the wording actually differs on one important point. The convention defines genocide as "[...] any of the following acts committed with intent to destroy [...] a [...] group, as such: [...]", whereas the 1954 Draft Code says "Acts [...] committed with intent to destroy [...] a [...] group as such, including: [...]". The difference is that while the 1954 Draft Code enumerates the same five types of acts as the Genocide Convention, it does not present the list of relevant acts as exhaustive.[166] This issue is not further discussed in the comments of the ILC. But considering that the Genocide Convention is a treaty, produced through a negotiating process, one might assume that the ILC was of the opinion that the crime of genocide under general international law might be somewhat broader than the definition set forth in the Genocide Convention, since the latter was contemplated for the specific purpose of obligating states parties to prevent and punish genocidal acts. As we shall see, however, the ILC has adhered to the wording of the Genocide Convention in its later draft codes.

The crime of "inhuman acts" committed against "any civilian population", cited in paragraph 11, is also quite interesting. This was meant to correspond to "crimes against humanity" in the Nuremberg Charter. In the 1951 draft, there was the additional requirement that such crimes be "committed in execution of or in connexion with other offences defined in this article", in other words, together with another offence against peace and security. If that requirement were maintained, the contextual scope of this crime would be expanded by reference to the additional crimes included in the list, and therefore would clearly be applicable outside a war context. In comparison, the *jurisdiction* of the Nuremberg Tribunal was limited to a war context. The 1954 Draft Code expanded the scope of this crime even further than the 1951 draft by deliberately dropping the requirement that it be 'annexed' to another crime.[167] It also inserted another requirement, however, that inhuman acts

---

[166] On the common perception of the 1948 Genocide Convention on this point, see, *e.g.*, Florian Jessberger, "The Definition and the Elements of the Crime of Genocide", in Paola Gaeta (ed.), *The UN Genocide Convention: A Commentary*, Oxford University Press, Oxford, UK, 2009, p. 94: "The list of acts is exhaustive".

[167] See Watts, 1999, p. 1682, *supra* note 153.

committed by "private individuals" would only be international crimes if they had been instigated or tolerated by state authorities.[168]

This touches a point of considerable importance to our conception of 'universal crimes', namely, that crimes against the peace and security of mankind must with few exceptions be linked to a powerful political or military structure.[169] Stated in this way as a more general point, the requirement still seems well-founded. In light of historical experiences with other kinds of organised, powerful entities, such as *de facto* governments, non-state parties to an armed conflict, and international terrorist organisations as well, this point in the 1954 Draft Code and its comments seems too narrowly confined to *de jure* state structures. In its commentary on the next draft code, of 1991, the ILC acknowledged this point by not ruling out "the possibility that private individuals with de facto power or organized in criminal gangs or groups might also commit the kind of […] violations of human rights covered by the article".[170] This broader although still quite careful statement seems compatible with current legal opinion on the material content and reach of contemporary international law *lex lata*.

Paragraph 12 is brief, simply citing "Acts in violation of the laws or customs of war" as the last kind of offences against the peace and security of mankind. The formulation highlights the fact that a certain 'international crime' may in fact be a 'crime category', consisting of many different crimes. The 1951 Comment explains that the paragraph did not include an enumeration of offences in violation of the laws or customs of war, "since no exhaustive enumeration has been deemed practicable".[171]

In reference to paragraph 12, the ILC also questioned whether every violation of the laws or customs of war should be regarded as a crime under the code "or whether only acts of a certain gravity" should be characterised as such crimes. As stated in the 1951 Comment, the ILC adopted the first alternative.[172] While this was a quite reasonable

---

[168] *Ibid.*

[169] See the discussions in Chapter 2, sections 2.3.3.–2.3.4.

[170] United Nations, *Report of the International Law Commission on the work of its forty-third session, 29 April – 19 July 1991*, A/46/10, Official Records of the General Assembly, Forty-sixth session, Supplement No. 10, pp. 103–104.

[171] See Watts, 1999, p. 1682, *supra* note 153.

[172] *Ibid.*

approach to a general code of international offences, the principle of legality would certainly require more precision and detail in the statutes of international criminal courts or in national legislation defining the scope of court jurisdiction. The 1954 Comment added that the provision should be construed as covering any act which violates the laws and customs of war "prevailing at the time of its commission". In other words, the 1954 Draft Code was not intended to prohibit *ex post facto* international court statutes or national legislation providing for retroactive jurisdiction, but was instead based on the proscribed acts being contrary to existing material international law when committed. This continues to be an important point for the proper understanding of ICL.[173]

The crime of "manufacture, trafficking and possession of weapons the use of which is prohibited by international agreements", as suggested by the special rapporteur Spiropoulos, was not included in the 1954 Draft Code.

The proposed 1954 Draft Code was tabled for a long time by the General Assembly, formally for technical reasons relating to the definition of the crime of aggression. The real reason for the delay, however, was the prevailing general distrust and lack of international cooperation due to the Cold War. Neither the Eastern nor the Western bloc wanted to pursue work on the matter during this period.[174] Thus, for the next quarter of a century, the subject matter "lay dormant".[175] In 1974, however, the General Assembly finally adopted a definition of aggression.[176]

4.5.4. Special Rapporteur Doudou Thiam (1981–1991)

When this work was resumed by the ILC in the 1980s, Mr. Doudou Thiam was appointed special rapporteur. Between 1983 and 1991, he submitted nine reports to the ILC.[177] In his second report, in February 1984, he stated that the purpose was "to formulate a list of offences today considered as offences against the peace and security of mankind, in other

---

[173] On the international legality principle, see Chapter 3, section 3.3.4.

[174] See Bassiouni, 2008, p. 131, *supra* note 57.

[175] See Watts, 1999, p. 1670, *supra* note 153.

[176] See UN General Assembly Resolution 3314 (XXIX), 14 December 1974.

[177] See Watts, 1999, p. 1670, *supra* note 153.

words to bring up to date the list prepared by the Commission in 1954".[178] Echoing the earlier decision by the ILC in the 1950s, this was a more limited task than preparing "an international penal code",[179] that is, a general code purporting to cover all types of international crimes. According to Thiam, "many offences which undoubtedly constitute international crimes will not, for that reason alone, be included in the proposed draft".[180] He described the relationship between the two categories in these terms: "all offences against the peace and security of mankind are international crimes, but not every international crime is necessarily an offence against the peace and security of mankind".[181]

In that second report from 1984, Thiam also defined international crimes as "all offences which seriously disturb international public order",[182] in the sense that "an international crime results from the breach of an international obligation so essential for the protection of fundamental interests that its breach is recognized as a crime by the international community as a whole".[183] It is noteworthy that the emphasis is on the presumed criminal character of an act, considered in light of its negative consequences for the protection of fundamental interests, and not on the possible pre-existence of formal legal sanctions.

The precise nature of an "offence against peace and security of mankind", on the other hand, was "yet to be defined".[184] The preferred criterion chosen by the ILC at the time, and referred to by Thiam in his report, was that offences against the peace and security of mankind constituted not only serious breaches of the international order but breaches of "extreme seriousness".[185] The approach implies an assessment of gravity of the relevant international crime types. In other words, the distinction between the two broad categories of international crimes is

---

[178] See United Nations, *Second Report on the Draft Code of Offences against the Peace and Security of Mankind, by Mr. Doudou Thiam, Special Rapporteur*, A/CN.4/377 and Corr.1, in *Yearbook of the International Law Commission, 1984*, vol. II, part I, para. 6.
[179] *Ibid.*, para. 7.
[180] *Ibid.*
[181] *Ibid.*
[182] *Ibid.*, para. 10.
[183] *Ibid.*, para. 11.
[184] *Ibid.*, para. 12.
[185] *Ibid.*, para. 8.

not clear-cut, but rather involves a discretionary classification made along a continuum ranging from generally serious to generally even more serious offences – by analogy not very different from the classification of offences in internal criminal law into "petty offences, less serious offences and serious offences".[186] According to Thiam, the international dimension of the crimes in question simply means that the offences here "have greater repercussions in that they affect peoples, races, nations, cultures, civilizations and mankind when they conflict with *universal values*", and that "*seriousness* is evaluated in terms of these elements" (emphasis added).[187]

The practical solution to the task facing Thiam, to identify the extremely serious crimes, was to take the list set forth by the ILC in the 1954 Draft Code as a point of departure (category A) and then add other offences presumably recognised thereafter (category B).[188] Nevertheless, the nine 'category A' offences listed by Thiam actually differ somewhat in both number and wording from Article 2 of the 1954 Draft Code, which comprised 12 crimes or crime types. Thiam's enumeration of category A included the following:

1) Aggression, and the threat of and preparation for aggression
2) The organization of armed bands by a State for incursions into the territory of another State
3) The undertaking or encouragement by a State of activities calculated to foment civil strife in the territory of another State
4) The violation of restrictions or limitations on armaments, on military training, or on fortifications
5) The annexation of the territory of a State by another State
6) Intervention in the internal or external affairs of a State by another State
7) War crimes
8) Genocide
9) Crimes against humanity.[189]

---

[186] *Ibid.*
[187] *Ibid.*
[188] *Ibid.*, para. 14.
[189] *Ibid.*, para. 79.

Thiam then consulted a number of UN resolutions, declarations, and conventions[190] for the purpose of identifying additional crimes and sorting out the most serious from the less serious ones. He identified eight additional offences against peace and security as "certain violations of international law recognized by the international community since 1954" (category B):

1) Colonialism
2) Apartheid
3) The taking of hostages
4) Mercenarism
5) The threat or use of violence against internationally protected persons
6) Serious disturbance of the public order of the receiving country by a diplomat or an internationally protected person
7) The taking of hostages organized or encouraged by a State
8) Acts causing serious damage to the environment.[191]

Notably, this second list includes some acts which do not seem to be crimes punishable *lex lata*, under current international law. It may be difficult to judge whether this is due to weaknesses in the list or to gaps which should be filled in a comprehensive code of offences against the peace and security of mankind. However, it does seem that some of these 'category B' crime types do not *per se* reach the threshold of "extreme seriousness", as do crime types such as genocide and crimes against humanity.

Neither this nor Thiam's subsequent reports resulted in adoption of a definitive code. In 1989, however, the General Assembly adopted a resolution in which it recalled its "belief that the elaboration of a code of offences against the peace and security of mankind could contribute to strengthening international peace and security and thus to promoting and implementing the purposes and principles set forth in the Charter".[192] This book takes up that same theme at the end of Chapter 5, with the suggestion of a possible code of 'universal crimes' in the form of a 'Universal Declaration on Universal Crimes'.

---

[190] *Ibid.*, paras. 43–46.
[191] *Ibid.*, para. 79.
[192] UN General Assembly Resolution 44/32, 4 December 1989.

4.5.5. 1991 Provisional Draft Code

The next substantial step came in 1991, when the ILC provisionally adopted, on first reading, a Draft Code of Crimes against the Peace and Security of Mankind.[193] This provisional draft set out a list of 12 categories of crimes:

1) Aggression
2) Threat of aggression
3) Intervention
4) Colonial domination and other forms of alien domination
5) Genocide
6) Apartheid
7) Systematic or mass violations of human rights
8) Exceptionally serious war crimes
9) Recruitment, use, financing and training of mercenaries
10) International terrorism
11) Illicit traffic in narcotic drugs
12) Wilful and severe damage to the environment.[194]

In comparison to Thiam's proposal from 1984, this list adds 'international terrorism' and 'illicit traffic in narcotic drugs' and drops 'the taking of hostages', 'the threat or use of violence against internationally protected persons', and 'serious disturbance of the public order of the receiving country by a diplomat or an internationally protected person'. Some situations covered by the deleted crimes might, however, be covered by other crimes, such as the new crime of 'international terrorism'. Another notable difference from Thiam's draft list is that 'aggression' and 'threat of aggression' are treated as two different crimes, and certain kinds of aggressive acts enumerated in Thiam's proposal as distinct crimes might not be fully covered under the concept of aggression in the new point 1.

With regard to the definition of genocide, the ILC decided to use the wording of the Genocide Convention, which, according to the ILC,

---

[193] See United Nations, 1991, *supra* note 170.

[194] *Ibid.*, pp. 95–97.

"makes the list of acts exhaustive in nature".[195] In its commentary, the ILC explained:

> The commission decided in favour of that solution because the draft Code is a criminal code and in view of the *nullum crimen sine lege* principle and the need not to stray too far from a text widely accepted by the international community.[196]

This reasoning makes sense, but it was not the only alternative. If the ILC had stuck with its earlier definition, consistently arguing that the definition of genocide under general international law may also include some acts other than those enumerated in the Genocide Convention, the *nullum crimen sine lege* principle could hardly have prevented a subsequent definition in international court statutes and national legislation including other specified acts as well. If a defendant before such a court were to raise objections, it is not clear that the additions would be struck down as unlawful under international law.[197] Their relevance could be supported, for example, by the statements in the Genocide Convention itself that genocide was already an international crime *before* the adoption of the convention, and thus before the negotiated limitation to the five enumerated acts, which are focused entirely on the physical or biological destruction of a particular group.

In general, this illustrates a persistent issue for the project of the ILC to identify and define the most serious offences against the peace and security of mankind. If they expand the definition too widely, the crimes identified may be rejected politically or struck down legally. If they make the definition too narrow, protection against crimes on which the international community has the political will to act might not have an adequate legal basis under international law, and the reasonable gradual development of ICL might be curtailed.

These comments by the ILC underscore the considerable weight its members usually put on what they believe to be acceptable to the governments represented in the UN. The ideal definition of a certain crime, from a legal and universal value-oriented point of view, may thus be adapted to suit political and pragmatic concerns. This is probably part

---

[195] *Ibid.*, p. 102.

[196] *Ibid.*

[197] On the international legality principle as a limitation on prosecutions, see Chapter 3, section 3.3.4.

of the reason why the lists and definitions of the international crimes against peace and security have varied so much in the work of the ILC over the years.

The crime of 'systematic or mass violations of human rights" in the 1991 provisional draft code corresponds to 'crimes against humanity' in the Nuremberg Charter, but its formulation differs both from the Nuremberg version and from the alternative formulation in the 1954 Draft Code. The ILC explained in its commentary that "since the acts covered by the draft Code must be of an extremely serious character, [...] only systematic or mass violations of human rights would be a crime".[198] It was made clear that "isolated acts of murder or torture, and so on, which are not systematic or on a mass scale, no matter how reprehensible as violations of human rights, do not come under the Draft Code". What is important to note, in this regard, is what the ILC is *not* saying. It is not saying that isolated acts of murder and torture might not be considered 'international crimes', only that they are not covered by *the draft code*. As noted above, the ILC has consistently distinguished between crimes (offences) against the peace and security of mankind and other international crimes. One cannot, therefore, interpret the absence of a crime from the various draft codes as evidence of its absence from a comprehensive list of 'international crimes'.

This issue recurs with respect to war crimes in the provisional draft code, where Article 22 refers to 'Exceptionally serious war crimes'.[199] The ILC made clear in its commentary that it had decided to stay faithful to the criterion that the draft code should cover "only the most serious among the most serious of crimes".[200] It therefore had selected only crimes of this nature. As the ILC clearly states, this would in no way affect the fact that other violations of humanitarian law "are crimes under international law applicable in armed conflicts".[201] The concept of war crimes laid out in draft Article 22 was clearly meant to apply "only for the purposes of the Code".[202]

---

[198] *Ibid.*, p. 103.
[199] *Ibid.*, p. 104.
[200] *Ibid.*, p. 105.
[201] *Ibid.*
[202] *Ibid.*

Compared to the 1954 Draft Code, the 1991 provisional draft formulated the scheme for individual responsibility and punishment slightly differently and in greater detail, but it did not change the content. In Article 3, paragraph 2, in the 1991 provisional draft, it is stated that one "who aids, abets or provides the means [...] or conspires in or directly incites" is liable to punishment, whereas paragraph 1 covers "commission" and paragraph 3 "attempt". These modes of punishable participation cover the same ground as Article 2, paragraph 13 of the 1954 Draft Code. The relevant modes of participation, however, including possible confinement to a "leader or organizer", are included in several of the articles defining the various crime types. This more detailed scheme might arguably not be necessary for the code itself, but it could prove useful for defining the jurisdiction of an international court in a statute that might include different crimes as well.

4.5.6. 1994 Draft Statute for an International Criminal Court

The work on the draft code after 1991 paralleled the work that the ILC pursued with a great deal of urgency on the related question of the establishment of an international criminal court and its jurisdiction. The ICTY and ICTR were established by the Security Council in 1993 and 1994 respectively, and the international community was also prepared finally to consider a general international criminal court. In 1992 the ILC received the 10th report of its special rapporteur Thiam, which was entirely devoted to the question of establishing an international criminal court.[203] The ILC follow-up efforts resulted first in the adoption of the Draft Statute for an International Criminal Court in 1994 (hereafter, 1994 Draft Court Statute), then in a discussion of it in the General Assembly's Sixth Committee in 1995,[204] and finally in the 1998 Rome Statute of the ICC.

---

[203] On the drafting history of the 1994 Draft Statute for an International Criminal Court, see Watts, 1999, p. 1448–1450, *supra* note 153.

[204] See, *e.g.*, UN General Assembly, *Report of the International Law Commission on the work of its forty-sixth session (1994): Topical summary of the discussion held in the Sixth Committee of the General Assembly during its forty-ninth session prepared by the Secretariat*, A/CN.4/464/Add.1, 22 February 1995.

The principal purpose of 1994 Draft Court Statute,[205] as set out in its preamble, was "to further international cooperation to enhance the effective prosecution and suppression of crimes of international concern".[206] The court was "intended to be complementary to national criminal justice systems in cases where such trial procedures may not be available or may be ineffective".[207] However, it was "intended to exercise jurisdiction only over the most serious crimes of concern to the international community as a whole".[208] According to the ILC commentary, this simply meant "crimes of concern to the international community as a whole".[209]

In its commentary to the preamble, the ILC did not further explain this apparent contradiction in terms or the qualification "the most serious" crimes. One possible explanation could be that the expression "serious violations" occurs in Article 20(c) in regard to war crimes, which might indicate a lower gravity threshold as compared to the "exceptionally serious" standard employed in the 1991 provisional draft. It might also be questioned whether the treaty crimes cited in Article 20(e) were in fact all among the most serious crimes of concern to the international community as a whole. In any case, the crimes within the jurisdiction of the court were set out by enumeration in Article 20, which states that the Court has jurisdiction in accordance with the Statute with respect to the following crimes:

a) The crime of genocide

b) The crime of aggression

c) Serious violations of the laws and customs applicable in armed conflict

d) Crimes against humanity

e) Crimes established under or pursuant to the treaty provisions listed in the Annex, which, having regard to the conduct alleged, constitute exceptionally serious crimes of international concern.[210]

---

[205] The 1994 Draft Court Statute and the ILC commentary to it is reprinted in Watts, 1999, pp. 1454–1552, *supra* note 153.

[206] Watts, 1999, p. 1454, *supra* note 153.

[207] *Ibid.*

[208] *Ibid.*

[209] *Ibid.*

[210] *Ibid.*

For the definition of genocide, the ICL referred to the Genocide Convention.[211] With regard to the crime of aggression, it is noteworthy that the ILC in the commentary to Article 20 admitted that a number of its members took the view that not every single act of aggression was a crime under international law giving rise to criminal responsibility of individuals.[212] According to this minority view, "the customary rule as it had evolved since 1945 covered only *the waging of war* of aggression" (emphasis added).[213]

Considerations of gravity were explicitly introduced with respect to war crimes, in letter (c) on "serious violations" of the laws and customs of armed conflict. The ILC commented that "not all breaches of the laws of war will be of sufficiently gravity to justify their falling within the jurisdiction of the court".[214] It was made clear that the classification of conduct as a "grave breach" under the Geneva Conventions will not by necessity also constitute a "serious violation". The qualification "serious violation" thus seems to have implied an autonomous, concrete evaluation of the gravity of the alleged war crime committed, before any individual would be liable to prosecution and eventually punishment before the international criminal court. This is a point which has particular relevance to our conception of 'universal crimes'.[215] The issue of gravity also is raised in letter (e), with regard to the treaty crimes, as noted in more detail below.

With respect to crimes against humanity, the ILC referred to Article 6(c) of the Charter of the Nuremberg Tribunal, Article 5 of the Statute of the ICTY, and Article 21 of the 1991 provisional draft. The latter covered the same field as the ICTY provision, according to the ILC.[216] The definition of crimes against humanity was held to encompass "inhumane acts of a very serious character", involving widespread or systematic violations aimed at the civilian population in whole or in part. According to the ICTY Statute, Article 5, the proscribed acts are listed as follows:

a) Murder

---

[211] *Ibid.*, p. 1478.
[212] *Ibid.*, p. 1479.
[213] *Ibid.*
[214] *Ibid.*, p. 1480.
[215] See section 4.9.1. in this chapter.
[216] Watts, 1999, p. 1481, *supra* note 153.

b) Extermination

c) Enslavement

d) Deportation

e) Imprisonment

f) Torture

g) Rape

h) Persecutions on political, racial and religious grounds

i) Other inhumane acts.[217]

The ILC was of the opinion, however, that "the particular forms of unlawful acts [...] are less crucial to the definition of crimes against humanity than the factors of scale and deliberate policy".[218] The "hallmarks" of these crimes thus lie in their large-scale and systematic nature.[219] It also underlined that the crimes are "targeted against a civilian population in whole or in part". The ILC stated that it preferred the formulation in the 1991 provisional draft on this particular point rather than the formulation provided in the first paragraph of Article 5 in the ICTY Statute ("directed against any civilian population").[220]

In addition to the four 'core crimes' in Article 20, letters (a) through (d), the "Annex" referred to in letter (e) listed nine other international crimes or crime types that should be included as crimes within the jurisdiction of the proposed court:

1) Grave breaches of selected provisions of the Geneva Conventions and Protocol I

2) The unlawful seizure of aircraft as defined in treaty

3) Crimes against the safety of civil aviation as defined in treaty

4) Apartheid and related crimes as defined in treaty

5) Crimes against internationally protected persons as defined in treaty

6) Hostage-taking and related crimes as defined in treaty

7) The crime of torture as defined in treaty

8) Crimes against the safety of marine navigation as defined in treaty

---

[217] Reproduced by the ILC in its Commentary. See *ibid.*, p. 1480.

[218] *Ibid.*, p. 1482.

[219] *Ibid.*

[220] *Ibid.*

9) Crimes involving illicit traffic in narcotic drugs and psychotropic substances that according to treaty are crimes with an international dimension.[221]

Compared to the 1991 provisional draft code on crimes against peace and security, five crimes or crime types were omitted: "intervention", "colonial domination and other forms of alien domination", "international terrorism", and "wilful and severe damage to the environment". On the other hand, five crimes were added: "unlawful seizure of aircraft", "crimes against the safety of civil aviation", "crimes against internationally protected persons", "hostage-taking and related crimes", and "the crime of torture". The most interesting development, perhaps, is the inclusion of torture as a distinct crime. With regard to terrorism, several of the mentioned new crimes under the 1994 Draft Court Statute covered acts of terrorism, but not terrorism on a general basis.

In its commentary on the Annex, the ILC discussed several other treaties and treaty provisions that were *not* included, explaining the reasons.[222] For example, piracy, as defined by Article 15 of the Convention on the High Seas and Article 101 of the United Nations Convention on the Law of the Sea, was seriously considered. Weighing against inclusion, however, was the fact that the said provisions only confer jurisdiction on the seizing state. That is, the treaties did not give other states parties jurisdiction over the pirates with an *aut dedere aut judicare* provision. "On balance, the ILC decided not to include piracy as a crime under general international law in article 20".[223]

The commentary to the 1994 Draft Court Statute, Article 20, also stressed that it was not the function of the statute to codify all crimes under general international law:

> [T]he statute is primarily an adjectival and procedural instrument. It is not its function to define new crimes. Nor is it the function of the statute authoritatively to codify crimes under general international law. With respect to certain of

---

[221] *Ibid.* The specific treaties and provisions referred to for each crime or crime type are scrupulously set forth in the Annex (*ibid.*, p. 1539). Furthermore, all the directly relevant treaty provisions were annexed to the 1994 Draft Court Statute, in Appendix II; see *ibid.*, pp. 1543–1549.

[222] *Ibid.*, pp. 1540–1542.

[223] *Ibid.*, p. 1540.

these crimes, this is the purpose of the draft Code of Crimes against the Peace and Security of Mankind, although the draft Code is not intended to deal with all crimes under general international law. To do so would require a substantial legislative effort.[224]

The implications of these remarks – that many different crimes are supposed to be inherently part of general international law – are crucial for the proper understanding of the legal status and range of 'international crimes' under international law, if the observation by the ILC is taken to be correct. For this reason, we shall address the proposition critically in more detail later.[225] This issue goes to the heart of the concept of 'universal crimes' as propounded in this book.[226]

It is already clear, however, that it cannot be inferred from the 1994 Draft Court Statute and the ILC commentary to its provisions that certain crimes, for example, piracy, were *not* considered by the ILC to be possibly existing 'international crimes', or even to belong to the more narrow category of 'crimes against the peace and security of mankind'. The ILC stressed this point several times in its commentaries, also with respect to the shortlist of explicit 'core crimes' of Article 20, letters (a) to (d).[227] If one follows this line of reasoning, the set of international crimes added in the 1994 Draft Court Statute is significant, but it cannot be taken as a complete list of international crimes.

The selection criteria employed by the ILC indicate a fairly elaborate understanding of the nature of international crimes and the methods the Commission applied to the task before it. In particular, the ILC highlighted three criteria or considerations taken into account in determining crimes for inclusion in the proposed shortlist in letters (a) to (d):

- The magnitude of the crimes
- The continuing reality of their occurrence

---

[224] *Ibid.*, p. 1478.

[225] See section 4.8. in this chapter.

[226] See sections 4.9.–4.10. in this chapter, see also Chapter 5.

[227] See, *e.g.*, Watts, 1999, p. 1483, *supra* note 153: "[I]t should be stressed again that article 20, subparagraphs (a) to (d), are not intended as an exhaustive list of crimes under general international law. It is limited to those crimes under general international law which the Commission believes should be within the jurisdiction of the court at this stage [...]".

- The inevitable international consequences.[228]

The ILC does not explain how these criteria were applied to each of the different crime types. But it appears that the magnitude of the crimes might have counted substantially for the crimes of aggression, genocide, and crimes against humanity. For war crimes and other core crimes, the continuing reality of the occurrence of the crimes and their inevitable international consequences may have weighed heavily. Although these criteria may not be exhaustive, they do seem likely to be useful for other similar processes of international criminalisation.[229]

With regard to the treaty crimes included under Article 20(e), the ILC made use of two other criteria:

- The crimes are themselves defined by the treaty, so that an international criminal court could apply that treaty as law in relation to the crime, subject to the nullum crimen sine lege guarantee, and

- The treaty created either a system of universal jurisdiction based on the principle *aut dedere aut judicare* or the possibility for an international criminal court to try the crime, or both, thus recognizing clearly the principle of international concern.

One might ask why the additional international crimes (other than the four core crimes) would have to be treaty-based rather than having other valid legal bases under international law such as customary international law. From a principled legal perspective, such exclusions are not necessary. However, the limitation to treaties was probably chosen to facilitate practical legal and political concerns. Legally speaking, the ILC probably took into account that the legality principle might more likely be an obstacle to prosecution of acts that were not already clearly recognised as crimes in binding treaties. Even more important, from a political point of view, ILC members may have thought that governments would not accept the inclusion of crimes other than those already proscribed in significant universal treaties and thereby already formally recognised to be of particular international concern by a substantial number of state authorities. The ILC, it seems most likely, decided to advance as expansive a definition as they thought to be realistic at the time.

Arguably, the most important innovation in the 1994 Draft Court Statute was the condition set forth in Article 20(e) with respect to the

---

[228] *Ibid.*, p. 1483.
[229] See section 4.9.1. in this chapter.

annexed treaty crimes. In this regard, jurisdiction of the court required that the criminal acts would constitute exceptionally serious crimes of international concern, "having regard to the conduct alleged". As was made clear in the ILC commentary, this meant that not all concrete crimes within the relevant crime types should be elevated to the level of an international jurisdiction. Instead they should be dealt with by national courts.[230] An assessment would then have to be made by the prosecutor and the court whether a particular crime, of a crime type included in the Annex, reached the necessary threshold of an "exceptionally serious crime". A similar exercise was embedded in Article 20(c) with regard to war crimes, with the lower threshold of a "serious violation". Although the ILC did not elaborate their reasons, the difference might be seen as based on the idea that violations of the laws and customs applicable in armed conflict are in themselves more serious to start with, so that a "serious violation" of these laws would be more or less equivalent to an "exceptionally serious" treaty crime.

The use of qualification standards in Article 20 to distinguish crime types is of theoretical significance. It suggests that while some international crime types are generally exceptionally serious *per se* and others are not, crimes of the latter type might, "in the context of an individual case", still constitute an exceptionally serious crime of international concern.[231] Although the expression "individual case" is not further explained by the ILC, its meaning would likely include both relevant underlying crimes committed at a particular crime scene and the contextual elements of a particular international crime type that might be attributable to an individual suspect.[232]

Applying such criteria to the concept of universal crimes, these crimes might in similar fashion be considered to include both particularly serious international crime categories and underlying crimes, which constitute universal crimes when judged to meet the required gravity threshold based on a concrete assessment of the facts. The relevant facts would usually include the parameters of a specific location, a specific time or defined time period, a particular victim or group of victims, or

---

[230] See Watts, 1999, p. 1483, *supra* note 153.

[231] *Ibid.*

[232] The notion of 'crime scene' and its relationship to other concepts relevant to international and universal crimes is discussed especially in Chapter 5, section 5.2.2.

particular perpetrators, as well as facts corresponding to the required contextual gravity.[233] The classification used by the ILC thus did not provide a straightforward distinction between the four core international crimes and other international crimes, since the "serious violation" requirement was used in the proposed Article 20(c) to qualify war crimes, themselves regarded as one of the core crime types. As explained in more detail later, the application of gravity thresholds for universal crimes and for international crimes can be considered as parallel ways of identifying the same set of crimes. Concrete assessments of crimes under international law are legally possible only in compliance with an existing law framework, not as freestanding exercises or *ad hoc* constitutions of international crimes. This is a consequence of the rule of law and the international legality principle of the contemporary UN paradigm of international law.[234] Key to understanding such identification processes, therefore, might be a general principle of law that requires the fulfilment of certain universal threshold criteria that can also be translated into specific gravity clauses for all international crimes.[235]

4.5.7. The Relationship between the Statute and the Code

Also of interest to our project are statements from the Sixth Committee of the General Assembly in 1995 on the relationship between the code and the 1994 Draft Court Statute on the criteria for crime inclusion. With regard to the former, "some delegations reaffirmed their view that the draft Code was an essential complement to the draft statute".[236] Within the ILC, the same view had been clearly expressed, for example, in the commentary to the 1994 Draft Court Statute.[237] The Sixth Committee obviously considered the code important in its own right (although some delegations also found it controversial), but in addition it would, in the view of many delegations, prove useful in "developing an applicable substantive law to circumscribe more clearly the jurisdiction *ratione materiae* of the Court so that the two fundamental principles of criminal

---

[233] See also Chapter 2, section 2.3.4., on gravity assessment.
[234] See Chapter 2, sections 2.2.2. (on the rule of law) and 2.2.3. (on the UN paradigm of international law), and Chapter 3, section 3.3.4. (on the international legality principle).
[235] See further section 4.9.2.2. of this chapter; see also Chapter 5, section 5.2.2.
[236] UN General Assembly, 1995, para, 80, *supra* note 204.
[237] See Watts, 1999, p. 1484, *supra* note 153.

law, *nullum crimen sine lege* and *nulla poena sine lege*, might be respected".[238] In other words, there was thought to be an intimate relationship between the work on the general code of crimes against the peace and security of mankind and the anticipated list of crimes to be included in the court statute.

This statement from the Sixth Committee indicates that its members understood that the legality principle in international criminal law has several dimensions, one concerned with court jurisdiction (the legal basis set forth in a specific international court statute) and another concerned with the substantive existence *lex lata* of a certain crime type as a 'crime' under international law. Generally speaking, a crime can only be prosecuted before an international court if both requirements are met, because of the international legality principle.[239] For that reason, a code of international crimes – whether limited to crimes against the peace and security of mankind or extended also to international crimes not dependent on the existence of threats to peace and security – would be a step towards clarification of legitimate and legally sustainable international criminal prosecutions. This point would apply equally to the concept of 'universal crimes', as will be discussed in Chapter 5.

The Sixth Committee also emphasised that "the Court should have jurisdiction over the most serious crimes of concern to the international community".[240] This would be the case "regardless of whether those

---

[238] UN General Assembly, 1995, para. 80, *supra* note 204.

[239] The second requirement of the international legality principle, the existence of a 'crime' under general international law, should not be confused today as a result of the contemporary introduction of international 'hybrid courts'. These are courts that may rely in part on distinct national criminal provisions as part of their jurisdictional basis, covering crimes that are not necessarily 'international crimes' (see Chapter 2, section 2.2.). In such cases the hybrid court would usually be established on the territory of the state where the crimes were committed, and the crimes would unconditionally have to be within the criminal jurisdiction of the concerned national state in the first place. In other words, the legality principle still applies, although here with a national twist. It might also be underlined that international law does not even prevent two or several states from establishing a common criminal court with a view to prosecuting (also) crimes within their jurisdiction that are not 'international crimes'. However, constitutional law and legal principles of the cooperating states might be an obstacle, for example, if a national version of the legality principle presupposes that a national who commits a crime within the state must be tried before a national criminal court.

[240] UN General Assembly, 1995, para. 81, *supra* note 204.

---

crimes were covered by treaties specified in the statute or by general international law".[241] In other words, the jurisdiction should in principle not be limited to treaty crimes, but should be identified by a common substantial requirement ("the most serious crimes of concern to the international community"), regardless of the relevant international legal basis for the proscribed criminal act. This point of view is fully in line with the understanding advocated in this book of the relationship between the law-creating sources of international criminal law and norms proscribing international crimes.[242] The Sixth Committee, however, proposed three additional criteria that would all have to be met for offences to fall within the Court's jurisdiction:

- The offences would have to constitute a violation of fundamental humanitarian principles and outrage the conscience of mankind;
- Prosecution would be more appropriate at the international than at the national level; and
- It would be possible to hold one or more individuals personally responsible for the offences.[243]

Based on these new criteria, which arguably implied a more restrictive approach than suggested by the ILC, the Sixth Committee concluded that only genocide, aggression, serious war crimes, and systematic and large-scale violations of human rights (crimes against humanity) would properly come under the Court's jurisdiction.[244] These would become the four 'core crimes' within the scope of the Rome Statute Article 5. These remarks, whether intentional or not, might have set a more restrictive tone for the continued work by the ILC on the draft code, concluded the following year as the 1996 Draft Code of Crimes against the Peace and Security of Mankind (hereafter, 1996 Draft Code). What seems to have been missing in the position of the Sixth Committee is the distinction between, on one hand, the most serious *crime types* (the four core crimes) that in general or *prima facie* may fulfil the conditions, and on the other hand, other international crimes that might fulfil the conditions only upon an assessment of the particular *concrete crimes* being committed, as was implied by the proposed 1994 Draft Court

---

[241] *Ibid.*

[242] See Chapter 3, section 3.3.

[243] UN General Assembly, 1995, para. 82, *supra* note 204.

[244] *Ibid.*

Statute.[245] The latter approach seems to imply the existence of certain 'gravity clauses'. For instance, following this logic, a single act of piracy with no connection to a larger power structure may not constitute an international crime, whereas similar acts of piracy might be considered a crime under international law "when committed as part of a widespread or systematic attack directed against a ship, aircraft, or persons or property on board a ship or aircraft, for economic or private ends".[246]

In adopting the 1996 Draft Code,[247] the ILC commented on its scope, which was substantially reduced compared to the 1994 Draft Court Statute and the 1991 provisional draft code. With a single exception, all the treaty crimes covered by the 1994 Draft Court Statute were gone, and so were eight of the 12 crimes or crime types included in the 1991 provisional draft. The ILC explained its position partly in terms of a wish to reach consensus within the ILC and partly in terms of the need to obtain support by governments. It acknowledged, however, that some members regretted the direction the work had taken:

> [W]ith a view to reaching consensus, the Commission has considerably reduced the scope of the Code. On first reading in 1991, the draft Code comprised a list of 12 categories of crimes. Some members have expressed their regrets at the reduced scope of coverage of the Code. The Commission acted in response to the interest of adoption of the Code and of obtaining support by Governments.[248]

The ILC underlined, however, that the inclusion of certain crimes in the 1996 Draft Code "does not affect the status of other crimes under international law, and that the adoption of the Code does not in any way preclude the further development of this important area of law".[249] This, it can be added, is encouragement also for the present project on 'universal crimes'.

---

[245] See section 4.5.6. of this chapter.

[246] See sections 4.9.2.–9.3. of this chapter and Chapter 5, section 5.2.4.

[247] ILC Draft Code of Crimes against the Peace and Security of Mankind, 1996, reprinted in *Yearbook of the International Law Commission, 1996*, vol. II, part II.

[248] See United Nations, *Report of the International Law Commission on the work of its forty-eighth session, 6 May – 26 July 1996*, A/51/10, Official Records of the General Assembly, Fifty-first session, Supplement No. 10, para. 46. Reprinted in Watts, 1999, p. 1671, *supra* note 153.

[249] *Ibid.*

4.5.8. 1996 Draft Code of Crimes against the Peace and Security of Mankind

As noted above, the five crimes included in the 1996 Draft Code – the crime of aggression (Article 16), crime of genocide (Article 17), crimes against humanity (Article 18), crimes against United Nations and associated personnel (Article 19), and war crimes (Article 20) – can by no means be taken as a full listing of international crimes, whether in 1996 or later. This point was also highlighted in the ILC's commentary to Article 1 of the 1996 Draft Code. Paragraph 1 states that the restricted scope of crimes against the peace and security of mankind set out in Part II of the code was "not intended to suggest that the present Code covers exhaustively all crimes against the peace and security of mankind".[250] These distinctions suggest a model of international crime types with three concentric circles: an inner circle of the 'core crimes', a middle circle comprising all crimes against the peace and security of mankind, and an outer circle comprising all international crimes (see Figure 2 below).[251]

It is noteworthy that the 1996 Draft Code, in Article 1, paragraph 2, expressly recognised the principle that certain crimes are crimes under international law and are punishable as such, whether or not they are also punishable under national law. Thus the ILC's legal opinion reinforced the principle coming from the Nuremberg trials of the direct applicability of international criminal law.[252] In Article 2, the principle of individual criminal responsibility is also confirmed with reference to the Nuremberg Judgment, which stated that "international law imposes duties and liabilities upon individuals as well as upon States" and that "individuals can be punished for violations of international law".[253] The ILC held this to be "the cornerstone of international criminal law" and the enduring legacy of the Nuremberg Charter and Judgment.[254] In addition, Article 3 stated that an individual who is responsible "shall be liable to punishment [...] commensurate with the character and gravity of the crime". Strangely enough, in light of the debate on the duty to prosecute serious

---

[250] See Watts, 1999, p. 1686, *supra* note 153.
[251] See section 4.8.2. in this chapter.
[252] See Watts, 1999, p. 1687, *supra* note 153.
[253] See IMT, *Trial of the Major War Criminals*, 1947 [Judgment], vol. I, p. 223, *supra* note 22.
[254] Watts, 1999, p. 1687, *supra* note 153.

international crimes, the meaning of the word "shall" was not further commented upon by the ILC.[255]

The ILC did, however, make a distinction between the "character" and "gravity" of the crime with respect to commensurate punishment. The Commission explained "character" to mean "what distinguishes that crime from another crime". It is clear from these comments that by "character" the ILC meant specific crime types or crime categories, for example, aggression as different from a war crime.[256] The "gravity" of a crime, on the other hand, would be "inferred from the circumstances in which it is committed and the feelings which impelled the author", as well as from "the motive" of the individual and "the way in which it was executed: cruelty or barbarity".[257] Gravity assessment should, however, also take into account the connections to a power structure, and thus the level of responsibility for the crime. As we shall see, the ILC also recognised this point.

The different applicable modes of punishable participation were set forth in the 1996 Draft Code in Article 2. Paragraph 3, in sub-paragraphs (a) to (g), describes seven categories of such participation with regard to the crime of genocide, crimes against humanity, crimes against the United Nations and associated personnel, and war crimes. Following this norm, an individual shall be responsible for such crimes if he:

a) Intentionally commits such a crime;
b) Orders the commission of such a crime which in fact occurs or is attempted;
c) Fails to prevent or repress the commission of such a crime in the circumstances set out in article 6;
d) Knowingly aids, abets or otherwise assists, directly and substantially, in the commission of such a crime, including providing the means for its commission;
e) Directly participates in planning or conspiring to commit such a crime which in fact occurs;
f) Directly and publicly incites another individual to commit such a crime which in fact occurs;

---

[255] *Ibid.*, pp. 1696–1698.

[256] *Ibid.*, p. 1697.

[257] *Ibid.* On gravity assessment, see also Chapter 2, section 2.3.4.

g) Attempts to commit such a crime by taking action commencing the execution of a crime which does not in fact occur because of circumstances independent of his intentions.[258]

Article 2, paragraph 2 specifies the particular rules on criminal responsibility for the crime of aggression, where criminal liability is limited to individuals with leadership functions, that is, "an individual who, as a leader or organizer, actively participates in or orders the planning, preparation, initiation or waging of aggression committed by a State".[259]

The comment in the ILC's 1996 commentary on the level of responsibilities is particularly interesting. The ILC noted that whereas the mode of "planning or conspiring" in paragraph 3(e) was intended to ensure that "*high-level* government officials or military commanders" could be held accountable, the criminal responsibility of the "*mid-level* officials who order their subordinates to commit the crimes" was provided for in letter (b), and the responsibility of the individuals in "*low-level* positions", that is, "the subordinates who actually commit the crimes",[260] was provided for in letter (a). This division of actors into high-level, mid-level, and low-level positions within a power structure resembles the suggestion in this book of an analytical scheme for the assessment of gravity of universal crimes, as shown in Figure 1 on gravity (Chapter 2, section 2.3.4.).

4.5.9. The Work of the ILC on the Obligation to Extradite or Prosecute (2004–2010)

Since 1996, the ILC has not done additional work on a general code of crimes against the peace and security of mankind. Its 1994 Draft Court Statute, however, served as the basis for preparatory work on the Rome Statute,[261] as was confirmed by the UN Conference of Plenipotentiaries.[262] The Rome Statute eventually became considerably longer, although it did not add more crime types.

---

[258] Watts, 1999, pp. 1688–1689, *supra* note 153.
[259] Compare the new definition of aggression in the ICC Rome Statute (see section 4.7. in this chapter).
[260] Watts, 1999, p. 1694 (emphasis added), *supra* note 153.
[261] See *ibid.*, p. 1450.
[262] See United Nations, *Final Act of the United Nations Conference of Plenipotentiaries on the Establishment of an International Criminal Court*, A/CONF.183/13, vol. 1,

Since 2004, however, the ILC has also identified and actively worked on a related topic of international criminal law, as formally approved by the General Assembly, namely the 'obligation to extradite or prosecute' (*aut dedere aut judicare*).[263] The 1996 Draft Code, in Article 9, contained a provision on that particular obligation,[264] with the assumption that the subject matter would require further analysis and discussion. As of 2011, this work is continuing, and it will probably continue for several more years. The current special rapporteur, Mr. Zdzislaw Galicki, has so far produced three reports on the matter, in 2006, 2007, and 2008,[265] and one discussion paper, in 2010.[266] The ILC has collectively submitted six reports, one per year, on the same subject matter over the period 2005–2010.[267] Governments submitted comments in 2007, 2008, and 2009 after they were invited to do so by the General Assembly in 2006 and 2007.[268] In 2008 the ILC decided to establish a working group on the topic under the chairmanship of Mr. Alain Pellet,

---

2002, p. 71. In Annex I, Resolution A, the Conference of Plenipotentiaries "Resolves to express its deep gratitude to the International Law Commission for its outstanding contribution in the preparation of the original draft of the Statute, which constituted the basis for the work of the Preparatory Committee".

[263] For an overview of the relevant documents and a brief history of ILC work on this topic, see the homepage of the ILC under 'Obligation to extradite or prosecute' (http://www.un.org/law/ilc/). The documents can be downloaded from the site.

[264] The 1996 Draft Code of Crimes, Article 9, on 'Obligation to extradite or prosecute', reads: "Without prejudice to the jurisdiction of an international criminal court, the State Party in the territory of which an individual alleged to have committed a crime set out in article[s] 17 [crime of genocide], 18 [crimes against humanity], 19 [crimes against United Nations and associated personnel] or 20 [war crimes] is found shall extradite or prosecute that individual".

[265] ILC, *Preliminary report on the obligation to extradite or prosecute ('aut dedere aut judicare')*, A/CN.4/571, 2006; ILC, *Second report on the obligation to extradite or prosecute ('aut dedere aut judicare')*, A/CN.4/585, 2007; ILC, *Third report on the obligation to extradite or prosecute ('aut dedere aut judicare')*, A/CN.4/603, 2008.

[266] ILC, *Bases for discussion in the Working Group on the topic – The obligation to extradite or prosecute (aut dedere aut judicare)*, A/CN.4/L.774, 24 June 2010.

[267] See also the overview in United Nations, *Report of the International Law Commission: Sixty-second session (3 May–4 June and 5 July–6 August 2010)*, A/65/10, Official Records of the General Assembly, Sixty-Second Session, Supplement No. 10, 2010, paras. 332–334.

[268] See, *e.g.*, the information posted on the ILC website (http://www.un.org/law/ilc/) under the item 'Obligation to extradite or prosecute', Analytical guide, Item H: Reports of the ILC.

---

the mandate of which was determined in 2009. In addition, the Secretariat of the ILC in 2010 prepared a comprehensive study on multilateral conventions which may be of relevance to this work.[269]

The working group prepared a general framework for the consideration of the topic, which was reproduced in the ILC annual report of 2009.[270] This framework consists of a detailed list of issues and questions to be addressed.[271] Item (b), on the material scope of the obligation to extradite or prosecute, is the most interesting for our purposes.[272] The material scope is supposed to be determined through the identification of "the categories of crimes (for example, crimes under international law; crimes against the peace and security of mankind; crimes of international concern; other serious crimes) covered by the obligation to extradite or prosecute according to conventional and/or customary international law".[273] This implies that different crime categories (or crime types)[274] might fall under this obligation, whether they are classified as 'crimes under international law', 'crimes against peace and security', 'crimes of international concern', or even other 'serious crimes' (whether typical international crimes or not).

For this book, it is particularly relevant that the ILC presumes such a process of abstract crime identification to be required and that it may indicate direct legal consequences under international law. The criteria given by the ILC imply a broader class of international crimes than those already having a secure status as 'core crimes' and/or a legal basis in

---

[269] See ILC, *Survey of multilateral conventions*, 2010, *supra* note 6.

[270] See ILC, *Report of the International Law Commission, Sixty-first session (4 May – 5 June and 6 July – 7 August 2009)*, A/64/10, 2009, Chapter IX: "The Obligation to Extradite or Prosecute (*aut dedere aut judicare*)" pp. 344–347, para. 204.

[271] One issue, mentioned earlier in this book, concerns the *sources* of the obligation to extradite or prosecute. See Chapter 3, section 3.3.6.

[272] See ILC, *Report of the International Law Commission, Sixty-first session*, 2009, p. 345, para. 204, *supra* note 270. The other items are (a) the legal bases of the obligation to extradite or prosecute; (c) the content of the obligation; (d) relationship with other principles (including *inter alia* the principle of universal jurisdiction); (e) conditions for the triggering of the obligation; (f) implementation; and (g) the "third alternative" of surrendering the alleged offender to an international criminal tribunal (pp. 344–347).

[273] *Ibid.*, p. 345.

[274] On the analytical distinction between 'crime categories' and 'crime types', see sections 4.8.–4.9. in this chapter.

customary international law. On the other hand, it is not implied that classifying an offence as an international crime would be sufficient to bring the offence within the material scope[275] of the obligation to extradite or prosecute. This interpretation is supported by the three sub-questions posed under item (b) of the proposed framework:

  i)   Whether the recognition of an offence as an international crime is a sufficient basis for the existence of an obligation to extradite or prosecute under customary international law;

  ii) If not, what is/are the distinctive criterion/criteria? Relevance of the *jus cogens* character of a rule criminalizing certain conduct?

  iii) Whether and to what extent the obligation also exists in relation to crimes under domestic laws?[276]

These questions are well articulated, but they also highlight the lack within ICL of an authoritative definition of 'international crimes' with predictable legal consequences. The first two questions allow for a possible gravity requirement, but they give no indication whether this is or will become the opinion of the ILC. It is clear, however, that the ILC is searching for a principled position that, if adopted, would have significant consequences for international criminal law. The questions underscore the need for a more coherent framework defining international crimes, in which the 'obligation to extradite or prosecute' would likely be one important piece in a larger puzzle. If there were an institution authorised to pass international legislation, such a problem could in principle be easily resolved. Since there is no such institution, the question for the ILC and others is what is desirable and possible to envisage as the next small steps for clarification and progressive development of international law.

This book outlines the contours of a possible common international crimes framework, with a particular focus on the conceptual relationship between 'international crimes' and 'universal crimes' (see particularly sections 4.8.–4.10. in this chapter). Question (ii) in the above scheme may be key to this puzzle, because it raises the issue of a possible criterion (or criteria) which may distinguish some international crimes from others in a

---

[275] The 'material scope' is distinguished from 'the triggering of the obligation' (*i.e.*, presence of an alleged offender within state territory) in the framework of the ILC. See ILC, *Report of the International Law Commission, Sixty-first session*, 2009, pp. 345–346, para. 204, *supra* note 270.

[276] *Ibid.*, para. 204(b).

principled manner. Before continuing this line of thought, however, it is useful to consider two other developments in the history of ICL, namely, remarks made on the definition of international crimes more than 50 years ago in the famous Hostage Case (section 4.6.) and the recently agreed definition of the crime of aggression for the purpose of the ICC Rome Statute (section 4.7.).

4.6. Anyone Better? The Hostage Case (1948)

In one of the subsequent Nuremberg trials known as the Hostage Case (*United States v. Wilhelm List et al.*), the tribunal proposed the following definition of an international crime:

> An international crime is such an act universally recognized as criminal, which is considered a grave matter of international concern and for some valid reason cannot be left within the exclusive jurisdiction of the state that would have control over it under ordinary circumstances. The inherent nature of a war crime is ordinarily itself sufficient justification for jurisdiction to attach in the courts of the belligerent into whose hands the alleged criminal has fallen.[277]

This statement implies three distinct general criteria:

A) The act or type of conduct must be universally recognised as inherently criminal.

B) The crime or crime type must be considered a grave matter of international concern.

C) The crime or crime type cannot for some valid reason be left exclusively to a particular state.

The wording of the three points reflects the ambiguity in the definition proposed by the tribunal; that is, it is unclear whether the definition included in the first sentence of the quotation refers to certain crime types or to the concrete acts constituting the international crimes, or both.

The first criterion, that an act be universally recognised as inherently criminal, goes to the heart of any discussion of what constitutes

---

[277] Nuernberg Military Tribunals (NMT), "The Hostage Case", in *Trials of War Criminals before the Nuernberg Military Tribunals under Control Council Law No. 10, October 1946 – April 1949*, vol. XI, US Government Printing Office, Washington, DC, 1950, p. 1241, see 'Judgment, 19 February 1948'. The case concerned war crimes.

an international crime. It is interesting that it seems to focus directly also on the concrete act as the point of departure, rather than just on a certain crime type. This interpretation is reinforced by the second sentence of the quotation, which, read in conjunction with the first sentence, seems to suggest that the inherent nature of some international crimes, like war crimes, implies *prima facie* status as international crimes, whereas other crimes might also be international crimes based upon concrete assessment. The statement does not make clear, however, how one determines whether or not an act is universally recognised as criminal. Which source or sources should one consult for the information required? More fundamentally, should one turn to the political venue where the actual crime problems are discussed and condemned and some steps taken, even if limited? Or should one turn to the legal field, where counteractive measures may be established by conventions? Or should one pay more attention to moral considerations, or empirical studies, if available, on the shocking effects of certain crimes? As should be clear from the discussion above, there is no consensus on an answer to this question. This does not mean, however, that this first criterion suggested in the Hostage Case is misconceived.

The other criteria supplied by the tribunal imply that the recognition of a crime as an international crime must be intimately linked to the nature and/or gravity of the act, which in turn makes it a matter of such serious international concern that it cannot be left up to the discretion of even the most directly affected state. The universal recognition process seems to flow from a common-sense approach to the relationship between national and international jurisdiction within the field of criminal law, within the perspective that fighting impunity for the most serious crimes is a universal value within the UN paradigm of international law. The point made by the tribunal was that some crimes are not likely to be prosecuted domestically, and they may also be too important or too dangerous to leave a decision about prosecution within the exclusive competence of national states which may be unwilling or unable to act. The crime categories in question may in principle contain *prima facie* universal crimes, or certain crimes that can only be considered universal crimes upon assessment of the concrete situation of gravity at the crime scenes, but in both cases the crimes as well as the failure to prosecute would typically be linked to powerful entities such as government institutions and officials.

The tribunal in the Hostage Case, by indicating that international crimes might be identified through a combination of certain universal criteria and concrete assessment, may have been ahead of its time. The relationship in principle between a concrete act and the relevant crime types was, however, elaborated only within the particular factual framework of the case at hand. The tribunal was concerned with a particular issue – the practice of 'taking hostages' and 'reprisals [against] prisoners' (including execution of innocent hostages and prisoners) as a possible war crime – and with what it entailed in practical terms under international law.[278] It is both interesting and consistent with its general approach in the definition above that the tribunal also paid attention to fundamental concepts of justice and the rights of individuals in its discussion of the criminal nature of the acts in question. The tribunal, placing international law in opposition to arbitrary executions as well as targeted killings of civilians, embraced the principle of a fair trial:

> It is a fundamental rule of justice that the lives of persons may not be arbitrarily taken. A fair trial before a judicial body affords the surest protection against arbitrary, vindictive, or whimsical application of the right to shoot human beings in reprisals. It is a rule of international law, based on these fundamental concepts of justice and the rights of individuals, that the lives of persons may not be taken in reprisal in the absence of a judicial finding that the necessary conditions exist and the essential steps have been taken to give validity to such action. [...] We have no hesitancy in holding that the killing of members of the population in reprisal without judicial sanction is itself unlawful.[279]

In so doing, the tribunal also linked its analysis to fundamental values and world community interests inherent in the established UN paradigm of international law.

---

[278] See *ibid.*, pp. 1249–1257.
[279] *Ibid.*, pp. 1252–1253.

4.7. The New Definition of Aggression in the Rome Statute (2010)

4.7.1. International Law and Statutory Context: The Most Serious Crimes

The crime of aggression has consistently been included among the crimes against the peace and security of mankind since the establishment of the UN paradigm of international law immediately after World War II. It has been also been consistently recognised as such by the ILC.[280] Most actors and observers have regarded aggression as one of the 'core crimes', and the Nuremburg Tribunal even listed it as the paramount crime, the "supreme international crime".[281]

Its legal bases in contemporary ICL have rested on customary international law, the general principles of international law, or a combination of both sources.[282] In the words of the former British senior law lord Tom Bingham in a case before the UK Supreme Court (then House of Lords) in 2006, "the core elements of the crime of aggression have been understood, at least since 1945, with sufficient clarity to permit the lawful trial (and, on conviction, punishment) of those accused of this most serious crime".[283] In his opinion, it is "unhistorical to suppose that the elements of the crime were clear in 1945 but have since become in any way obscure".[284] The UN Charter Article 2(4), read in conjunction with Article 51 and Chapter VII, prohibits non-authorised use of force by states other than in self-defence. And the right to self-defence according to Article 51 is, moreover, only a temporary right in effect 'until the Security Council has taken measures necessary to maintain international peace and security'. This has not stopped states from resorting to force, and a wide range of armed conflicts have taken place since 1945.[285]

---

[280] See section 4.5. in this chapter.

[281] IMT, *Trial of the Major War Criminals*, 1947, vol. I [Judgment], p. 186, *supra* note 22.

[282] See Chapter 3, sections 3.3.3, 3.3.4, and 3.3.6.

[283] See United Kingdom House of Lords, *Opinions of the Lords of Appeal for Judgment In The Cause R. v. Jones et al.(Appellant) v. Director of Public Prosecutions (Respondent)*, [2006] UKHL 16, Judgment, 29 March 2006, para. 19.

[284] *Ibid*. The Court was unanimous on the status of aggression as a crime under international law.

[285] See, *e.g.*, Christine Gray, "The Charter Limitations on the Use of Force: Theory and Practice", in Alan Vaughan Lowe, Adam Roberts, and Jennifer Welsh (eds.), *The*

Even so, judicial enforcement of the proscribed acts has turned out to be difficult at the national as well as at the international level, primarily because of the highly politicised nature of such alleged crimes. In general, it has been left to the Security Council to condemn concrete acts of aggression, but only rarely has the Security Council found an act of aggression or a 'breach of the peace'; findings of a 'threat to the peace', which is also outlawed by UN Charter Article 2(4), have been more common.[286] In a few instances the Security Council has authorised armed intervention to combat aggressive acts by a state towards another state. A clear example is the internationally authorised war against Iraq in 1991 because of its attack on, and occupation of, the neighbouring state of Kuwait.[287]

In the Rome Statute, a compromise was reached among the state representatives with regard to the crime of aggression, which was in principle recognised as one of four crime types relevant to the ICC. But in contrast to genocide, crimes against humanity, and war crimes, the crime of aggression was not defined and made operational at the time. One close observer of the treaty process stated that the compromise solution saved the proposal for the ICC from collapsing, but that it left the crime of aggression both in and out.[288]

Article 5 of the Statute establishes the principle that the subject-matter jurisdiction of the ICC shall be confined to "the most serious

---

United Nations Security Council and War: The Evolution of Thought and Practice since 1945, Oxford University Press, Oxford, UK, 2008, p. 87: "there have been over 100 major conflicts since 1945". See also Appendix 7 to the book.

[286] *Ibid.*, p. 89.

[287] See UN Security Council Resolution 678, 29 November 1990, S/RES/0678 (1990), para. 2: "*Authorizes* Member States co-operating with the Government of Kuwait, unless Iraq on or before 15 January 1991 fully implements, as set forth in paragraph 1 above, the foregoing resolutions, to use all necessary means to uphold and implement Resolution 660 (1990) and all subsequent relevant resolutions and to restore international peace and security in the area".

[288] In an interview, former Nuremberg prosecutor Benjamin Ferencz stated, "If they had not included aggression, I'm sure the whole thing would have failed, collapsed. So it was hanging by a thread, and the trick compromise was that sleight of hand. That's what they did; they said aggression is in but it's out. Hocus pocus. It's in, but the court can't act on it unless you stand on your head and do all kinds of impossible things". "The Prosecutor: Interview with Benjamin Ferencz", in Heikelina Verrijn Stuart and Marlise Simons, *The Prosecutor and the Judge*, Amsterdam University Press, Amsterdam, 2009, p. 43.

---

crimes of concern to the international community as a whole", implying that not all international crimes reach the threshold set by the 'most serious' standard. But it is not clear whether this requirement might also apply to the core crimes and in particular to the crime of aggression. The question might seem to be a contradiction in terms, since the core crimes by definition are 'the most serious crimes'. But the answer might prove to be more complicated than that.

Another question left unanswered was whether a future addition of new crime types (or categories) other than the four 'core crimes' mentioned in Article 5(a) to (d) – genocide, crimes against humanity, war crimes, and the crime of aggression – must meet a kind of 'constitutional threshold'.[289] This has been argued, for example, by Schabas,[290] who refers to the *ejusdem generis* principle of interpretation.[291] On this basis he questions the prudence of including crimes like terrorism and drug trafficking, given that the Statute "creates a presumption that such crimes do not belong to the most serious".[292] Obviously, the high threshold set by Article 5 cannot be ignored. However, there might arguably be another interpretation less restrictive than that of Schabas, namely that a concrete criminal act falling under other categories of international crimes in situations of particular gravity can reach the 'most serious' standard, in addition to the other crimes included in the Statute as crime types, and thus also trigger the jurisdiction of the ICC. This interpretation would be consistent with the inclusion of additional specific threshold or gravity clauses in the crime type definitions in the following articles. In principle,

---

[289] On the analytical distinction between 'crime categories' and 'crime types', see section 4.8. in this chapter. In the present discussion, the two concepts are used interchangeably.

[290] "Article 5 seems to set a quasi-constitutional threshold for the addition of new crimes. It is true of course, that the States Parties can always amend this, just as they could, theoretically at least, decide that genocide no longer belongs to the species. But in future debates about expanding the subject-matter jurisdiction, the Rome Conference has bequeathed a potent and influential standard. Only crimes that meet this high threshold, those that are *ejusdem generis* with the four enumerated categories, belong in the *Statute*" (emphasis in original). Schabas, 2010, p. 108, *supra* note 63.

[291] *Ibid.*, p. 108. The *ejusdem generis* principle is a general principle of law and legal methods. It usually means that an enumeration of samples in a legal text should be interpreted as equals or in the same manner, hence implying a certain coherence and excluding interpretations that would substantially expand the scope of the provision.

[292] *Ibid.*

there is nothing to bar application of similar standards of gravity to international crimes not already included in Article 5(a) to (d). For example, piracy crimes like killing of crew or passengers, hostage taking, and armed robbery might be included in the Rome Statute on condition that they are "committed as part of a widespread or systematic attack directed against a ship, aircraft, or persons or property on board a ship or aircraft, for economic or private ends" (see sections 4.9.2.–4.9.3. of this chapter).

In the Final Act of the Diplomatic Conference in 1998, it was recommended that a future review conference "consider the crimes of terrorism and drug crimes with a view to arriving at an acceptable definition and their inclusion in the list of crimes within the jurisdiction of the Court".[293] It was explicitly recognised that "terrorist acts, by whomever and wherever perpetrated and whatever their forms, methods and motives, are serious crimes of concern to the international community".[294] It was also recognised that "the international trafficking of illicit drugs is a very serious crime, sometimes destabilizing the political and social and economic order in States".[295] Both crimes were thus considered to pose "serious threats to international peace and security".[296] The lessons seem to be, first, that certain international crimes besides the core crimes may, as a matter of principle, reach the required threshold, as crime types – at least to the extent that there would be a presumption in favour of the threshold being reached when the crimes are committed on a large scale or within a particularly dangerous context. Second, other international crimes than terrorism and drug crimes could be considered for inclusion in the Statute at some point as well, without necessarily violating Article 5. It seems difficult to argue that terrorist acts and drug trafficking *per se* are more serious than certain other international crimes, as for example some of the other crime types identified and listed in the works of the ILC at different points over the years.[297] What needs to be taken into account, however, is that specific

---

[293] See United Nations, 2002, p. 72, Annex I, Resolution E, *supra* note 262.

[294] *Ibid.*, p. 71.

[295] *Ibid.*

[296] *Ibid.*

[297] See section 4.5. in this chapter on statements of the ILC.

threshold clauses would presumably be needed for each proposed additional crime type.

The threshold standard of Article 5 can be formally revised and lowered if need be, of course, but that is not the point here. Rather, the point is that a revision of the general threshold standard in Article 5 is not required in order to facilitate ICC jurisdiction over additional crimes, if specific threshold clauses are included as part of new crime definitions in the Statute.

4.7.2. The Definition Adopted at the Review Conference

The definition of aggression adopted at the Review Conference in Kampala in June 2010 shows how language can be added with reference to a specific crime type without changing the general threshold standard. Of course, this does not solve the threshold question posed above with regard to international crime types other than the core crimes, since the crime of aggression is not a new crime under the Rome Statute. According to Article 5, paragraph 2, however, the ICC would not be able to deal with the crime of aggression before that crime had been appropriately defined and the conditions set out with regard to the exercise of jurisdiction over it.[298] In addressing these initial shortcomings, the 2010 Review Conference modified the definition by adding additional elements to the threshold standard as applied to this specific crime type.

The crime definition is annexed to a resolution adopted by consensus[299] and reads as follows:

> **Amendments to the Rome Statute of the International Criminal Court on the Crime of Aggression**
>
> *1. Article 5, paragraph 2, of the Statute is deleted.*

---

[298] The issue of exercise of jurisdiction is not dealt with here; see preface to this book. In short, the ICC will have jurisdiction with regard to the crime of aggression from 2017 onward, provided that at least 30 states parties ratify the amendments and at least two-thirds of all states parties vote to approve them after 1 January 2017. For some interesting thoughts on the background and future prospects of the new provision, see Hans-Peter Kaul, *Is It Possible to Prevent or Punish Future Aggressive War-Making?*, FICHL Occasional Paper Series, Torkel Opsahl Academic EPublisher, Oslo, 2011. Kaul is a judge and vice president of the ICC.

[299] See ICC, "The Crime of Aggression", RC/Res.6, 28 June 2010, Annex I, "Amendments to the Rome Statute of the International Criminal Court on the Crime of Aggression".

2. The following text is inserted after article 8 of the Statute:

Article 8 *bis*

Crime of aggression

1. For the purpose of this Statute, "crime of aggression" means the planning, preparation, initiation or execution, by a person in a position effectively to exercise control over or to direct the political or military action of a State, of an act of aggression which, by its character, gravity and scale, constitutes a manifest violation of the Charter of the United Nations.

2. For the purpose of paragraph 1, "act of aggression" means the use of armed force by a State against the sovereignty, territorial integrity or political independence of another State, or in any other manner inconsistent with the Charter of the United Nations. Any of the following acts, regardless of a declaration of war, shall, in accordance with United Nations General Assembly resolution 3314 (XXIX) of 14 December 1974, qualify as an act of aggression:

> a) The invasion or attack by the armed forces of a State of the territory of another State, or any military occupation, however temporary, resulting from such invasion or attack, or any annexation by the use of force of the territory of another State or part thereof;
>
> b) Bombardment by the armed forces of a State against the territory of another State or the use of any weapons by a State against the territory of another State;
>
> c) The blockade of the ports or coasts of a State by the armed forces of another State;
>
> d) An attack by the armed forces of a State on the land, sea or air forces, or marine and air fleets of another State;
>
> e) The use of armed forces of one State which are within the territory of another State with the agreement of the receiving State, in contravention of the conditions provided for in the agreement or any extension of their presence in such territory beyond the termination of the agreement;
>
> f) The action of a State in allowing its territory, which it has placed at the disposal of another State, to be

used by that other State for perpetrating an act of aggression against a third State;

g) The sending by or on behalf of a State of armed bands, groups, irregulars or mercenaries, which carry out acts of armed force against another State of such gravity as to amount to the acts listed above, or its substantial involvement therein.

The core meaning of an "act of aggression" is defined in paragraph 2, and the relevant acts are set out in sub-paragraphs (a) to (g), in accordance with General Assembly Resolution 3314 (XXIX) of 14 December 1974. What is especially noteworthy, in the context of this book, is the qualification in paragraph 1 of "an act of aggression" as constituting "a crime of aggression", for the purpose of the Statute, only when the "character, gravity and scale" of the act amount to "a manifest violation of the Charter of the United Nations". The concrete act must, ultimately, justify the "manifest violation" threshold.[300] No single act of aggression reaches this threshold *per se*.[301] This type of specification could plausibly be generalised for the purpose of defining 'universal crimes'. One should note, however, that the language used in the new provision reserves the word "crime" for the aggravated (manifest) violations; lesser violations are not only excluded from the jurisdiction of the ICC, but are not even classified as "crimes". This distinction between "an act of aggression" and "a crime of aggression" for the purpose of the Statute, useful as the choice of language might be for that particular purpose, does not necessarily change the concept of the crime of aggression under general international law. Consequently, those acts of aggression mentioned in Article 8 *bis*, paragraph 2, letters (a) to (g) are subcategories of the 'crime of aggression" and are thus also subtypes of 'international crimes' under ICL, even when they may not in concrete cases reach the specific threshold requirement for ICC purposes ("a manifest violation of the Charter of the United Nations"). However, the definition adopted at the ICC Review Conference underlines the point that a similar kind of gravity threshold is required in relation to individual

---

[300] *Ibid.*, Annex III, "Understandings regarding the amendments to the Rome Statute of the International Criminal Court of Aggression", para. 7.

[301] *Ibid.* It can be argued, though, that a certain modification might be called for, insofar as the very concept of an "invasion" may imply an attack of a certain scale as well an aggravated intention to occupy or annex the territory of another State and thus *prima facie* constitute a manifest violation of the UN Charter.

criminal liability of political and military leaders under international law.[302] In other words, not all acts that are prohibited under UN Charter Article 2(4) and justify state responsibility may incur criminal liability.

Let us now consider the three threshold criteria employed in Article 8 *bis*, paragraph 1. The first criterion, the "character" of the relevant acts, seems to be defined by the descriptions of the various "acts of aggression" as set out in paragraph 2, sub-paragraphs (a) to (g). Hence some of the enumerated acts – as 'crime types' – are generally more serious than others. For instance, an "invasion" (a) is typically of a more serious character than a "blockade" (c). The criteria of "gravity" and "scale", on the other hand, relate to the aggressive acts as defined by the concrete factual circumstances in each case. The "scale" is probably the easiest to define, although not necessarily easy to apply with certainty, as it refers to the size or magnitude of an attack or other kind of aggressive act.

The provision employs "gravity" as a distinct parameter, separate from "character" and "scale", according to "the ordinary meaning to be given to the terms of the treaty in their context", within the meaning of the Vienna Convention on the Law of Treaties, Article 31(1). This concept must consequently be allocated an autonomous content within the new Article 8 *bis*, paragraph 1, *inter alia* with reference to the more or less sinister intention, brutality, and consequences of a certain attack. In a sense, the "character" and "scale" can also be seen as parameters that contribute to the cumulative gravity of a concrete act of aggression, which in turn determines whether the act oversteps the threshold of "a manifest violation of the Charter of the United Nations". The use of "gravity" as just one of three parameters at the same level is unfortunate and confusing from a conceptual point of view. One could instead have made reference to other aggravating or mitigating circumstances and replaced "manifest violation" with "grave violation" of the Charter of the United Nations.

Nevertheless, the most important point, despite the more limited use of the term "gravity", is that the definition includes a gravity clause requiring a concrete assessment of each particular act of unlawful aggression. We may therefore ask whether similar qualifications could serve to define other international crimes or whether the crime of aggression is distinctive in this respect. This issue can be most usefully

---

[302] See the proposed list of international crimes section 4.9.3. of this chapter (under 'crimes of aggression').

addressed after a more detailed examination of the concept of international crimes, based on the developments examined so far in this book.

4.8. Classifying International Crimes

4.8.1. Different Kinds of Definitions of International Crimes

The purpose of this section is to classify international crimes, that is, to arrange such crimes systematically in classes or groups.[303] This is also a necessary exercise for the purpose of discussing the relationship between 'international crimes' and 'universal crimes' as the latter concept is set forth in Chapter 5. This section therefore focuses on defining the concept of international crimes and grouping such crimes into categories.

A preliminary problem, however, is that the word 'definition' may have different meanings in different contexts, as well as for legal purposes. As a lexical point of departure, a 'definition' is a succinct statement of the assumed 'exact meaning' of a word or phrase.[304] However, some words or phrases may have an exact meaning only to certain persons in a certain setting. A definition may be descriptive of the general use of a particular term within a population as a whole or within a specific group of people, such as judges at international courts and/or legal experts or legal writers. While 'international crimes' is a frequently used term of art within ICL, as we have seen, there is no consensus among actors and writers of international law as to its exact meaning. A definition may also be stipulative of the meaning intended by a particular speaker or writer, often in the context of a particular work or act of communication. In practice, it is not always clear whether a particular definition of international crimes is descriptive or stipulative. A normative definition, on the other hand, seeks to lay out a recommended meaning of a term, that is, how it should be used.

Legal definitions are normative definitions of a special kind, insofar as they concern how legal terms should be interpreted or applied as parts of legal norms. By 'legal norm' is here meant – as a stipulated definition –

---

[303] A standard meaning of the word 'classify' is used here. See, *e.g.*, *Oxford Advanced Learner's Dictionary of Current English, Encyclopedic Edition*, Oxford University Press, Oxford, UK, 1992, s.v. 'classify'.

[304] *Ibid.*, s.v. 'definition'.

'a rule either proscribing or prescribing a kind of conduct, for all people or for a group of people in a special situation, or for officials in a particular role, which in some way is upheld by sanctions or possible sanctions within a system of law'. Complete legal norms thus typically consist of certain legal conditions along with certain legal consequences that should follow when all the necessary and sufficient conditions are fulfilled ('if a, b, and c, then x and y'). When legal terms are authoritatively defined, for example, in a statute or a treaty, the intention is to determine the content of the law (how things should be). The persons who define legal terms in this sense are in a special position: they are 'law-makers'.

It is necessary to ask, therefore, whether a particular attempt to define the legal terms of international law in concrete cases is based on sufficient legal authority and intent to make law. That would be the case if the normative definition enacted through a certain procedure has a basis in the law-creating sources of international law. If not, a particular definition put forward by someone is not a genuine 'legal definition', but something else. For instance, it might be a descriptive definition, as when a legal writer points to a legal definition set forth in a treaty to assert that this is the common use of that term among international lawyers. If the point is, rather, to assert that the author intends to use that definition in a particular academic work, it would then be a stipulative definition.[305]

In other words, only those actors with sufficient legal competence can really define how a legal term should be understood and applied for legal purposes. Others may accept the legal definition enacted as binding. The legal writer in the example above, if he or she discusses the legal content of a genuine legal definition *lex lata*, must for instance respect the formulation of the definition, and its object and purpose, in compliance with the established principles of treaty interpretation. Examples of legal definitions in international law are hence definitions of legal concepts or linguistic entities in international court statutes (whether enacted lawfully by the UN Security Council or by states), definitions in other binding UN resolutions, and definitions in international treaties. Other legal terms that are alleged to be parts of such instruments, customary international law,

---

[305] Stipulative definitions are normative definitions of the user's own language. It confuses the point, however, to say that a legislator or a state is also a 'user' of its own language and that normative legal definitions in a statute or a treaty are thus 'stipulated definitions' as well.

or the general principles of law, and which are defined by international courts in order to clarify the interpretation of disputed legal rules or principles, might also be considered 'legal definitions' (albeit indirect or implied definitions as compared to the explicit legal definitions).

Judicial (court) statements of international law (jurisprudence) constitute an 'interpretative source' of international law rather than a 'law-creating source'.[306] A principled interpretation of a legal term by an international court might nevertheless have semi-binding effects insofar as it may carry considerable legal weight for new cases, especially within the court itself. It may thus resemble a legal definition, although formally it is not. The interpretation by a court might in turn be considered persuasive by other actors of international law, perhaps even to the extent that the dividing line between interpretation and law-making becomes difficult to discern.

Legal writers, on the other hand, do not possess any competence under international law to normatively define or redefine legal terms. They cannot make law. If the term 'international crimes' does exist as a normative legal concept in ICL, then a legal writer cannot normatively define that term authoritatively, in the sense that others would have to adopt that definition in order to comply with the law or interpret it correctly.

What a legal writer is allowed to do, however, is to introduce a proposed normative definition for the purpose of enhancing discussion of the law, with a view to accurate communication of the law's content and its further clarification and development. Such a normative proposition can in principle be checked by testing the proposition against the arguments for the specific normative definition proposed.[307] In contrast, a descriptive proposition must be checked by comparing the proposition with reality, as in the case of a descriptive definition, by comparing the proposition with the use of the word.[308] Other descriptive propositions

---

[306] See Chapter 3, section 3.4.1.

[307] A 'normative proposition' can, in principle, be checked "by testing the proposition against those arguments that are deemed relevant for justification and criticism of normative propositions", as proposed by the Norwegian legal philosopher Svein Eng. *Analysis of Dis/agreement – with particular reference to Law and Legal Theory*, Kluwer Academic, Dordrecht, Netherlands, 2003, p. 8.

[308] *Ibid.*

may seek to describe the essential features of a social phenomenon, what we may refer to as empirical definitions.

Consequently, five kinds of definitions, identified by their different specific purposes (as compared to the common purpose of definitions as set forth above), seem to be relevant here:

- Descriptive definitions based on existing uses of the term (for example, the most common use)
- Stipulative definitions of the author's own use of the term
- Genuine legal definitions
- Empirical definitions
- Proposed normative definitions for the purpose of improving the exact meaning of the term

Definitions of the term 'international crimes' proposed by legal writers that are not simply describing the language of others, referring to a legal text, or stipulating the author's own use of the term for a specific purpose will usually be proposed normative definitions (or normative propositions), indicating how the term ought to be defined in order to reflect the underlying content of international law (*lex lata*) as exactly as possible and/or how the law ought to be developed (*lex ferenda*).

Legal writers may seek the normative truth, that is, the exact meaning of some part of international law, by elaborating and proposing normative definitions of international crimes. However, descriptive and stipulative definitions may also influence how the content of international law is perceived normatively by others, particularly since authors may not be sufficiently clear about the distinction between different kinds of definitions. And, of course, stipulative or descriptive definitions of international crimes can in principle be traced back to earlier 'proposed normative definitions', such as the one proposed and relied upon in the Hostage Case.[309] Such a key concept as international crimes, however, requires periodic systematic examination.

Whatever the specific purposes of a definition, it may also be form-ulated in two distinct ways, which are often considered to be two different classes of definitions making use of different methods:

1) An intentional definition that specifies the necessary and sufficient conditions for international crimes in abstract terms.

---

[309] See section 4.6. in this chapter.

2) An extensional definition in the form of an enumerative definition that gives an explicit and exhaustive listing of the crimes that fall under the term.

The two classes of definitions can be used independently but also in conjunction, providing complementary clarification of the exact meaning of a term. One may be better than the other, or simply more useful for different purposes. As we have seen, actors and authors of ICL have used both types of definition, sometimes combining them.[310] The following sections first consider several levels of generality in approaching the concept of international crime (4.8.2.), then a negative delimitation by the contrasting concept of non-international crimes (4.8.3.), followed by the 'necessary and sufficient conditions' that should be considered the essential features of the term (4.9.1.), and finally an enumerative definition (4.9.2.–4.9.3.).

4.8.2. Different Levels of Generality of Definitions of International Crimes

Before classifying international crimes, it is first necessary to determine the level of generality at which they are being defined. Any enumeration will, of course, depend on the units being counted, which can range from specific concrete crimes to crime types or categories.

For example, classification of 'genocide' as an international crime is no doubt justified, but is it 'one crime', a collective 'crime category', or a cluster of several 'genocide crime types'? Article II of the Genocide Convention enumerates five different *acts*, each of which may satisfy the requirements of genocide; these acts include, but are not limited to, "killing" members of a protected group. Furthermore, Article III lists five different modes of punishable participation in genocide. Does this mean that there are 5 x 5 (25) different genocide crime types according to the Genocide Convention? Or five different genocide crime types (corresponding to the five relevant 'acts' listed in Article II), or even just one all-encompassing crime ('genocide')? The question arises also with respect to other international crimes, such as war crimes, the crime of aggression, and crimes against humanity. In order to attribute criminal liability, one has to focus on the concrete crime scenes and the acts of individual perpetrators and participants. To apply the concepts of 'genocide' or 'war

---

[310] See sections 4.4.–4.6. in this chapter.

crimes' as the operational units applicable to the facts on the ground may be too general to be workable in practice. At the same time, an act of killing cannot be identified as a crime of genocide without taking the context into account. Thus international crimes, it seems, must be considered at different levels of generality at the same time, perhaps justifying characterisations both as broad 'crime categories' and as more specific 'crime types'.

A much discussed practical legal issue, for example, has been whether the policies of 'ethnic cleansing' during the wars in the former Yugoslavia from 1992 to 1995 amounted to genocide; and if so, in which specific distinct cases? Is it possible and meaningful to distinguish one particular genocide from another within the same state during the same period of time? According to international jurisprudence relating to the former Yugoslavia, the answer is yes, which must also in principle be the correct response.The specific contextual requirements of international crimes must always be fulfilled (the 'gravity clauses'),[311] but the legal concepts may in this respect differ from popular conceptions.[312]

At this point we suggest, more generally, that international crimes can be divided into four analytical classes reflecting different levels of abstraction:

1) International crime categories
2) International crime types
3) Concrete international crimes
4) Individual international crimes

Note that the crimes being committed in real life, what are here termed 'concrete international crimes' and 'individual international crimes', can only be considered 'crimes' within an existing framework of international law. This book is concerned with the criminal law norms, not the actual crime situations in different places. For that reason categories (3) and (4) above could be considered redundant for our purpose. But because of the inherent complexity of universal crimes, it might be useful here to point out that prosecutions – with the end goal of determining whether a person is individually responsible for an inter-

---

[311] On the notion of 'gravity clauses', see section 9.2.2 in this chapter and Chapter V, section 2.2.

[312] See the *Jelisić* case (ICTY Appeals Chamber, *Prosecutor v. Goran Jelisić*, Judgment, IT-95-10, 2001), discussed in Chapter 2, section 2.3.3.

national crime or not – might engage all four analytical classes.[313] Thus the more traditional analytical model of substantive criminal law, of subsumption of facts under a legal rule, may not suffice in universal crime cases.[314] The last chapter of this book attempts to further clarify this particular point in analytical and practical terms.

The crime of aggression, the crime of genocide, crimes against humanity, and war crimes can all be labelled 'international crime categories', in that each comprises different specified 'crime types'. For example, Article 8(2) of the Rome Statute, in sub-paragraphs (a), (b), and (c), defines war crimes by reference to three subcategories of war crimes, each subcategory containing a number of specified war crime types. Examples of war crime types are certain specific grave breaches of the Geneva Conventions in the context of war, such as "wilful killing", "torture or inhuman treatment, including biological experiments", "wilfully causing great suffering, or serious injury to body or health", and so on. The class of 'concrete international crimes' on the other hand, corresponds to concrete sets of facts that fulfil all the conditions of the crime type in question, that is, at particular international crime scenes. Within such a set of facts and law, the 'individualised international crimes' will finally be identified by reference not only to a crime scene determined by point in time, place, methods, and victims, but also with respect to the individual perpetrators/participants. For most purposes, however, this four-part analytical scheme can be collapsed into three parts, and in this book the term 'crime types' is often used to mean both crime types and broader crime categories.

Generally speaking, it can be useful to classify international crimes in different ways and at different levels of generality for communicative purposes. What is important is that each such classification be clearly specified, and that it be consistent with the legal norms that constitute the crimes in question as well as the language used by other actors and writers.

This section is at the highest level of generality, a bird's-eye view, so to speak. The enumerative definition set forth below in section 9.2 can

---

[313] See also Chapter 1, section 1.2., where it is submitted that the complexity of universal crimes raises particular challenges for decision-makers at the crossroads between law and facts.

[314] See also Chapter 2, section 2.3.4., on the importance and complexity of gravity assessment.

be seen as a low-level classification of international crimes, since it lists all the crime types, with familiar names so far as possible. The intentional definition presented in section 9.1 is at an intermediate level, since it focuses on the necessary and sufficient abstract criteria for identifying international crimes.

In addition to the distinction of four levels of generality noted above, another high-level classification might consist of three abstract classes, as follows:

1) Core international crimes
2) Other international crimes against the peace and security of mankind
3) International crimes not dependent on the existence of threats to international peace and security

Most often, as noted earlier, the concept of core crimes is defined by enumeration, with the list usually limited to the crime of aggression, war crimes, genocide, and crimes against humanity. A few writers even explicitly limit international crimes to core crimes, excluding any others.[315]

The concept of 'crimes against the peace and security of mankind' has been elaborated in particular by the ILC.[316] It has always been taken to include more international crimes than the four core crimes mentioned, with the 1996 Draft Code being the most limited in that respect.[317] On the other hand, the ILC has consistently underlined that the concept of 'crimes against the peace and security of mankind' does not include all international crimes. The logical implication is that there is a residual class of international crimes that includes what might be termed 'international crimes not dependent on the existence of threats to international peace and security' or, perhaps for some purposes, just 'plain international crimes' (see the crimes listed in section 4.9.3., including grave piracy crimes). In other words, international crimes can be enumerated as consisting of the three abstract classes set forth in the scheme above. In principle, enumerative definitions of the classes of 'crimes against the peace and security of mankind' and 'international crimes not dependent on the existence of threats to international peace and

---

[315] See section 4.4. in this chapter.
[316] See section 4.5. in this chapter.
[317] See in particular section 4.5.8. in this chapter.

security' could be given, just as 'core crimes' is enumeratively defined. We can thus move down the ladder of generality, as specified in section 4.9.2. below.

These three classes or categories are not, however, mutually exclusive sets, as might be required by Aristotelian logic. Instead, they can be represented as the areas delimited by three concentric circles, as shown in Figure 2.

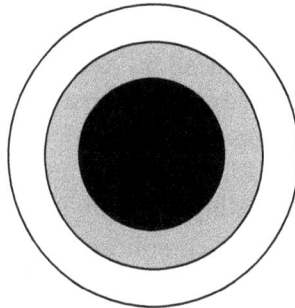

Figure 2:   Classes of International Crimes.

The inner circle, shaded black, indicates the core crimes. The middle circle encompasses all crimes against the peace and security of mankind; it includes both the core crimes (black) and other crimes against the peace and security of mankind (grey). The outer circle encompasses all international crimes, including the first two as well as international crimes not dependent on the existence of threats to international peace and security (white).

Before exploring in detail each of these groups, however, it is useful to address the area outside the circle, that is, non-international crimes.

4.8.3.   Delimitation by Non-international Crimes

This section lays out an abstract enumerative definition of 'non-international crimes'. As suggested in our earlier discussion of the categories proposed by Currie,[318] crimes that are not 'international crimes' might be termed 'non-international crimes'. These may be usefully divided into three classes, as follows:

1) Transnational crimes

---

[318]   See section 4.4.8. in this chapter.

2) Nationally imported international crimes

3) National (domestic) crimes

As these classes are ranked in descending order of complexity, let us first consider the most straightforward and familiar class. 'National crimes' here means crimes defined by the legal system of a state. In the case of the more serious acts, at least, their criminal character is typically justified by reference to national traditions and concerns, and the acts are made punishable by means of national legislation and courts decisions. Such crimes thus always have a national legal basis within the internal sources of law of the state in question. National criminal law furthermore delimits the criminal responsibility of persons (including legal persons) liable to punishment under the national laws, and provides rules, guidance, and limitations for sanctions and punishment. Such plain national crimes are easy to distinguish from international crimes.

The issue becomes more complicated with respect to what can be termed 'nationally imported international crimes', that is, recognised international crimes that are transposed – incorporated or transformed – into national criminal law. In such cases the criminal character of the proscribed acts has already been defined in international law, and the international norm has a legal basis in the law-creating sources of international law. For example, the new description of the 'crime of ag-gression', as amended in the Rome Statute Article 8 *bis*, might be incorporated word for word into national legislation.[319] Nonetheless, when it becomes part of a national criminal law statute, the norm also has a national legal basis as well, with applicable interpretative sources stemming from national preparatory works, national criminal law tradi-tions, and so on. Limitations on criminal responsibility and punishment would therefore also have both international and national bases.

In practice, it will vary from state to state how the 'imported crimes' are interpreted and implemented, and to what extent state author-ities and courts seek to apply autonomous ICL concepts as well as national standards. Therefore, the imported international crimes are usu-ally not equivalent in content with the international crimes on which they are based, and they should therefore be distinguished from the 'inter-national crimes' as such. Because of the fragmented character of ICL, a specific crime type at the international level may not even have the same

---

[319] See section 4.7.2. in this chapter.

material content under all the law-creating sources of international law. For each crime type, there might be several autonomous proscriptions under international law with slightly different formulations depending on the particular legal context (customary international law, specific treaty, and so on.).

Even so, nationally imported crimes are distinct in that they come under the control of national legal systems and thus run the risk of losing their original autonomous international law identity, especially if the national legislators and courts pursue their own *lex ferenda* interpretations of the international crimes as domestic *lex lata*. Similar processes are not unique to ICL, but are common to most areas of international human rights law as well, in particular where strong international supervision mechanisms are not in place to guarantee the minimum protection afforded by the international norm. In conclusion, therefore, imported types of international crimes at the national level are not considered international crimes as such for the purpose of the present analysis.

'Transnational crimes' as a class pose even more complicated issues.[320] This concept has not acquired a clear common meaning among international and domestic criminal lawyers, and arguably it is a social science rather than a legal concept. Often it is used to mean crimes which have transboundary effects but which are not clearly considered as international crimes. Some authors limit use of the term to organised transboundary crimes or 'transnational organized crimes'. In this book such crimes are considered a subclass of 'transnational crimes', a class which may also include a subclass of 'other transnational crimes'.

There are many criminal activities which may have actual or potential transboundary effects, either as implied by the crime type or in concrete cases. Examples include, but are not limited to, transboundary fraud, trafficking in human beings and drugs, corruption, and money laundering. Such crimes are of national and international concern, and attempts to suppress them both have national legal bases and are the subject of international cooperation and treaties at regional and global levels. An important international instrument in this regard is the United Nations Convention against Transnational Organized Crime and its protocols on trafficking in persons, smuggling of migrants, and illicit manu-

---

[320] See section 4.4.8. in this chapter.

facturing and trafficking in firearms.[321] The convention itself concerns in particular the crimes of 'participation in an organized criminal group' (Article 5), 'laundering of proceeds of crime' (Article 6), 'money-laundering' (Article 7), and 'corruption' (Article 8). Clearly, all these crimes fall under the subclass of 'transnational organized crimes'.

In some cases, however, a certain crime type labelled as a 'transnational organized crime' may appear to fit the criteria of both 'other (plain) international crimes' and 'transnational crimes'. If that is the case, it will, according to the logic of our classification system, be considered an 'international crime' only, since 'transnational crimes' is classified in our scheme as a subclass of 'non-international crimes'. For instance, if certain 'organised acts of terror' or 'organised drug trafficking' are 'international crimes' according to the normative definitions of international crimes set forth in sections 4.9.1.–4.9.2., it is only from an empirical point of view that such crimes would then be considered transnational crimes as well. Thus a crime considered in legal terms as a non-international 'transnational crime' may at some later time move into the category of 'international crimes', depending on the actual international legal developments. In this respect it is interesting that the United Nations Office on Drugs and Crime deals with a number of crimes that are usually classified as transnational crimes rather than international crimes, but also with crimes that might better be classified as international crimes, for example, organised and large-scale illicit trafficking in drugs, human beings, and firearms; piracy; and terrorism.

The second subclass of 'transnational crimes', in this book termed 'other transnational crimes', concerns offences criminalised under special

---

[321] United Nations, "Convention against Transnational Organized Crime", A/RES/55/25, 15 November 2000, in force from 29 September 2003. See United Nations, *Treaty Series*, vol. 2225, p. 209. As of 21 April 2011, the convention had 159 parties. The three protocols are as follows. (1) "Protocol to Prevent, Suppress and Punish Trafficking in Persons, Especially Women and Children, supplementing the United Nations Convention against Transnational Organized Crime", 15 November 2000, in force from 25 December 2003. See United Nations, *Treaty Series*, vol. 2237, p. 319. (2) "Protocol against the Smuggling of Migrants by Land, Sea and Air, supplementing the UN Convention against Transnational Organized Crime", 15 November 2000, in force from 28 January 2004. See United Nations, *Treaty Series*, vol. 2241, p. 507. (3) "Protocol against the Illicit Manufacturing and Trafficking in Firearms, Their Parts and Components and Ammunition, supplementing the United Nations Convention against Transnational Organized Crime", 31 May 2001, in force from 3 July 2005. See United Nations, *Treaty Series*, vol. 2241, p. 507.

international legal orders, that is, international organisations other than the United Nations. This includes certain specific crimes which have an international legal basis but which are applicable only for the more limited purposes of a particular international legal order. One such category could be labelled 'institutional crimes', consisting of violations of international proceedings which constitute punishable 'offences against the administration of justice' or the offence of 'misconduct' (see, for example, Rome Statute Articles 70–71). Another category would be the so-called 'eurocrimes', that is, crimes under European Union (EU) law.[322]

With regard to the eurocrimes, there are a number of EU instruments which criminalise, or at least prohibit, certain kinds of conduct.[323] These offences include 'crimes against fair competition', 'crimes against the financial sector', 'crimes against the financial interest of the Union', 'crimes against human dignity', 'crimes against the democratic society' (for example, terrorist activities), and many others.[324] However, some of these eurocrimes might be international crimes as well, for example, certain 'terrorist offences' criminalised in Articles 1, 2, and 3 of the EU's Council Framework Decision 2002/475 on Combating Terrorism. Another example is the criminalising of trafficking in human beings, in Article 1 of the Council Framework Decision 2002/629 on Combating Trafficking in Human Beings. Crimes such as these could be termed 'EU imported international crimes' and would thus constitute a special class of 'non-international crimes', at the same level as the classes of 'nationally imported international crimes' and 'transnational crimes' as set forth earlier in this section. However, since all the eurocrimes are closely related to a specific legal order, in this case the European Union, they might better be classified as a subclass of 'transnational crimes'.

Several of the eurocrimes resemble crimes that have been constituted as crimes or at least made the object of suppression by multilateral treaties adopted under the auspices of the United Nations as well as the Council of Europe. One example is money laundering (see the EU "Directive 2005/60 on Money Laundering"; the 2000 United Nations Convention against Transnational Organized Crime mentioned above, especially Article 7; and the 2005 Council of Europe Convention on

---

[322] The concept of 'eurocrimes' is used by André Klip in *European Criminal Law: An Integrative Approach*, Intersentia, Mortsel, Belgium, 2009, p. 197.

[323] *Ibid.*

[324] See, *e.g.*, *ibid.*, pp. 198–202.

Laundering, Search, Seizure and Confiscation of the Proceeds from Crime and on the Financing of Terrorism).[325] The eurocrimes are also implemented at the national level of each EU member state. Under the principle of legality, EU law "requires that criminal liability finds its basis in national criminal law".[326] Direct applicability of all the eurocrimes mentioned is thus prohibited without national transposition.[327] In other words, the EU obliges its member states to criminalise the said conduct in their own national legislation. The crimes become in that sense 'nationally imported transnational crimes', functionally quite similar to 'nationally imported international crimes'.

In conclusion, international crimes and non-international crimes can each be divided into three abstract classes, each class consisting of different crime types. The result is summarised in the following outline:

International crimes:
- Core international crimes
- Other international crimes against the peace and security of mankind
- International crimes not dependent on the existence of threats to international peace and security

Non-international crimes:
- National crimes
- Nationally imported international crimes
- Transnational crimes
  - ° Transnational organised crimes
  - ° Other transnational crimes
    - Institutional crimes
    - Eurocrimes

The next section focuses on establishing substantive criteria for this classification of international crimes, providing a corresponding enumerative list of international crimes, and relating this to a coherent concept of universal crimes.

---

[325] For the official text of the European convention, see *Council of Europe Treaty Series (CETS)*, no. 198, 2004.

[326] See Klip, 2009, p. 204, *supra* note 322.

[327] *Ibid.*

4.9. Classifying International Crimes within a Universal Crimes Framework

Throughout the preceding discussion of international crimes, we have pointed repeatedly to a gravity assessment of concrete crimes as well as to the inherent gravity of certain crime types as a central factor in justifying the designation of certain crimes as international crimes that require a response from the international community. Such a gravity assessment, rather than the mere fact of involvement of more than one nation, is critical to the need for an international response. While in the subsequent sections of this chapter we continue to use the term 'international crimes', we do so within a framework based on the systematic importance of such gravity assessments. This also warrants the use of the concept of universal crimes, and the two terms are used interchangeably towards the end of this section, the point being that international crimes classified within a 'universal crimes framework' might just as well be reconceived as universal crimes. So what is meant by a universal crimes framework? The first part of the answer is simply that crimes under international law as a matter of logic and principle should be identifiable according to a set of criteria. These criteria must be 'universal' in the sense that they can be applied equally to all crime candidates. Secondly, however, they should also be formulated on the basis of and in accordance with contemporary international law. Consequently, both the criteria and the results they produce, that is, the enumerated crimes, can be continuously discussed and evaluated in light of new developments of international law. Third, the framework should allow for pronouncements on the status of crimes *lex lata* and *lex ferenda*, as well as for expressions of doubt with regard to the one or the other.[328]

4.9.1. Necessary and Sufficient Conditions of International Crimes

4.9.1.1. General Remarks on the Conditions and Legal Consequences of International Crimes

As should be quite clear from the earlier discussion, there is no commonly accepted definition of international crimes, either in the legal literature or

---

[328] On the distinction between *lex lata* and *lex ferenda*, see Chapter 3, section 3.5. On the practical application of this distinction in relation to crimes under international law, see section 4.9.3. of this chapter.

within the international community. There is general agreement on inclusion of the four core crimes: the crime of aggression, war crimes, genocide, and crimes against humanity. But there is no agreement on either a comprehensive list or a conceptual definition.[329] This means that there is no agreed set of criteria for the identification of international crimes.[330]

One may thus conclude that no proposed comprehensive theory or normative definition of international crimes has been convincing enough to obtain a consensus within the international community. One can simply accept this situation, but it is also possible to offer new ideas as candidates for such consensus. This section attempts to provide an intentional definition that specifies the *necessary and sufficient conditions* for an international crime in abstract terms.[331] It is thus a 'proposed normative definition', offered with the purpose of presenting an improved exact meaning for the term.[332]

Focusing first on conditions, rather than also including legal consequences from the start, produces a limited definition of a legal norm. One should note, however, that it might be necessary at a later stage to include possible legal consequences as well. Such consequences of classification as an international crime might include the following:

1) Direct (individual) liability under international law applies
2) No statute of limitation applies
3) No *ex post facto* limitation on implementing statutes applies
4) Limited amnesty protection from prosecution applies
5) The territorial state of the crime scene has a right and a duty to investigate and prosecute
6) The nationality state of perpetrators/victims has a right to investigate and prosecute

---

[329] See sections 4.4.–4.6. in this chapter.
[330] Bassiouni, 2008, pp. 132–133, *supra* note 57, states, "The writings of scholars are uncertain, if not tenuous, as to what they deem to be the criteria justifying the establishment of crimes under international law. Moreover, there is a great deal of confusion in the writings of scholars as to what constitutes an international crime, and how these crimes should be referred to".
[331] See section 4.8.1. in this chapter.
[332] *Ibid.*

7) The nationality state of perpetrators may have a duty to investigate and prosecute

8) Third states may have universal jurisdiction to investigate and prosecute

9) States may have a duty to extradite or prosecute a suspected resident perpetrator

10) Prosecutions must adhere to the international legality principle

11) Prosecutions must adhere to international procedural standards of fair trial

12) The UN may facilitate prosecution in cooperation with the territorial state

13) The UN may establish criminal courts without consent of the territorial/national state

14) The UN may refer the situation to the prosecutor of the ICC

15) The UN may authorise armed intervention for the protection of civilians

Some of the listed consequences may apply to non-international crimes as well as to international crimes. For example, the fifth consequence should apply to any case of murder, which should be appropriately investigated by the appropriate territorial authority, according to human rights law, if practically possible. This is required by the positive obligation to secure the right to life, *inter alia* in the jurisprudence of the European Court of Human Rights.[333] In particular, in cases of suspicious death involving state agents or bodies, the ECHR will attempt to determine whether the investigation has been effective and capable of leading to the identification and punishment of those responsible for the crime.[334] This may include persons within a power structure who have planned, ordered, or otherwise participated in the crime, not

---

[333] See, *e.g.*, ECHR, *Öneryildiz v. Turkey*, 48939/99, Grand Chamber Judgment, 30 November 2004, para. 89, 93. See also ECHR, *Menson and Others v. United Kingdom*, 47916/99, Decision, 6 May 2003; and ECHR, *Angelova and Iliev v. Bulgaria*, 55523/00, Judgment, 26 July 2007.

[334] See, *e.g.*, ECHR, *Ramsahai and Others v. The Netherlands*, 52391/99, Grand Chamber Judgment, 15 May 2007, para. 324: "In order to be 'effective' as this expression is to be understood in the context of Article 2 of the Convention, an investigation into a death that engages the responsibility of a Contraction Party under that Article must firstly be adequate. That is, it must be capable of leading to the identification and punishment of those responsible. This is not an obligation of result, but one of means".

only the direct perpetrator. The investigation must thus have been fully independent of those alleged to have been involved in the alleged crime,[335] and it must have been pursued on the basis of objective evidence. The same duty of the territorial state to investigate and prosecute must apply to at least the same extent with respect to even more serious crimes.

The problem is that international crimes are often committed in situations of civil strife, armed conflict, and occupation, and in countries with limited resources, where there are practical, political, or economic obstacles to investigation and prosecution. This does not, however, release a state from its duties, unless a meaningful investigation and prosecution may prove impossible due to concrete constraints. This principle was clearly underlined by the Inter-American Court of Human Rights (IACHR) in 2005, in the *Mapiripán Massacre* case, which concerned the failure of Colombia to investigate a massacre of civilians carried out by a paramilitary group with the alleged assistance of state authorities.[336]

Furthermore, the European Court of Human Rights has held in several cases that the duty to investigate possible violations, including war crimes, is not limited to acts of its personnel committed on its own territory.[337] When state agents exercise authority and control over territories (for example, through occupation), or over buildings, aircraft, or ships, or physical power and control over a person, violations must be investigated.[338] In the *Al-Skeini* case, the ECHR thus held that the United Kingdom had violated "the procedural obligation under Article 2 of the [European] Convention to carry out an adequate and effective investigation" into the deaths of the relatives of four of the five

---

[335] *Ibid.*, para. 325. It was further added, "This means not only a lack of hierarchical or institutional connection but also a practical independence [...]".

[336] IACHR, *Case of the Mapiripán Massacre v. Colombia*, Judgment of September 15, 2005, Merits, Reparations, and Costs, para. 238: "In this regard, the Court recognizes the difficult circumstances of Colombia, where its population and its institutions strive to attain peace. However, the country's conditions, no matter how difficult, do not release a State Party to the American Convention of its obligations set forth in this treaty, which specifically continue in cases such as the instant one".

[337] See, *e.g.*, ECHR, *Al-Skeini and Others v. United Kingdom*, 55721/07, Grand Chamber Judgment, 7 July 2011, para. 136 (with further references to other ECHR judgments).

[338] *Ibid.*, para. 130–135 and 137–177.

applicants.[339] Although this obligation is based on a particular human rights treaty, it may imply the existence of a more general principle under international law of a duty of the nationality state to investigate and prosecute alleged perpetrators who are state agents (see point 7), no matter where the act was committed. In such cases, the territorial state and the nationality state may have concurrent jurisdiction (see point 5).

If either the suspected murderer or the victim in a non-international crime case is the citizen of a foreign state, that is, a state other than the one where the crime took place, both those states may also, according to international law, have concurrent jurisdiction to investigate and prosecute the crime (see point 6). If the perpetrator flees to a third state and is resident there, that state may be under an international treaty obligation to extradite the suspect upon request or to carry out an investigation itself (point 9). However, in an ordinary murder case, other third states do not have independent universal jurisdiction to investigate and prosecute the crime, that is, without consent of the territorial and/or national state with primary jurisdiction (see point 8). Likewise, the UN cannot establish a criminal court for the trial of suspected ordinary murderers without consent of the territorial/national state. The reason is that there must be a framework for respect of the criminal law sovereignty of states. An important part of that framework is the distinction between 'international crimes' and 'non-international crimes'.

In essence, international crimes may lead to direct liability under international law for concrete perpetrators, that is, individuals (physical persons), regardless of their position in society. In that sense, direct liability under international law (point 1) seems to be a necessary condition of international crimes for the purpose of a definition. Note that 'direct liability under international law' does not add specific legal consequences but rather is almost a restatement of the fact that a certain crime is an international crime. However, it can be taken to imply that having specific legal consequences is inherent in the notion of 'direct liability' and therefore also inherent in the concept of international crimes. One may therefore conclude that having international legal consequences is indeed required as a 'necessary condition' of the definition, although it is not appropriate to regard all the possible specific legal consequences as

---

[339] *Ibid.*, conclusion no. 6 (after para. 186). The underlying facts of the case concerned the suspected killings and ill-treatment of six civilians by personnel of the British Army in Iraq.

being among the 'necessary and sufficient conditions' of 'international crimes'. The consequential condition proposed, and included below as condition 5, can be worded as follows:

> The concept of 'international crimes' implies that direct international criminal liability and prosecution of such crimes before an international tribunal is legally independent of the consent of a concerned (territorial or nationality) state, whether or not consent has been provided before the crime (for example, by means of reciprocal treaties) or after the crime (for example, by means of subsequent agreement or extradition).

This may be shortened as follows: 'Criminal liability and prosecution is not dependent upon the consent of a concerned state'. This condition may serve as a convenient test of a correct application of the cumulative 'necessary and sufficient conditions' as a whole, since the first four conditions, focusing more on the substantive content of international crimes, are thus more difficult to determine objectively. This point will be illustrated in Chapter 5, using the crime of piracy as an example.[340]

4.9.1.2. Necessary and Sufficient Conditions

The normative proposition[341] for a legal definition of international crimes outlined here consists of five cumulative and interrelated conditions that need to be in place before any type of proscribed conduct (crime type) can be considered an 'international crime':

1) The type of conduct manifestly violates a fundamental universal value or interest.
2) The type of conduct is universally regarded as punishable due to its inherent gravity.
3) The type of conduct is recognised as a matter of serious international concern.
4) The proscriptive norm is anchored in the law-creating sources of international law.
5) Criminal liability and prosecution is not dependent upon the consent of a concerned state.

---

[340] See Chapter 5, section 5.2.3.

[341] The concept of a 'normative proposition' is earlier explained with reference to Eng, 2003, *supra* note 307. See section 4.8.1. of this chapter.

All five conditions are here considered to be necessary; that is, the offence is not considered to be an international crime if any one of them is absent. That said, it is also important to note that they may overlap and that each should be interpreted in light of the others. They are inductively obtained from the descriptive survey and classification typology set forth above, and they should be considered as a whole rather than as separate and fully independent conditions. Although they are formulated differently in several respects, they parallel the conditions identified by the tribunal in the Hostage Case for international crimes, which we paraphrased above as follows:[342]

A) The act or type of conduct must be universally recognised as inherently criminal.

B) The crime or crime type must be considered a grave matter of international concern.

C) The crime or crime type cannot for some valid reason be left exclusively to a particular state.

In our scheme, conditions 1 and 2 correspond to and clarify condition (A). Condition 3 corresponds to condition (B), and condition 5 to the final condition (C). Condition 4 stresses the place of the concept of international crimes within current ICL. The five-point scheme, we think, makes a systematic assessment easier and more transparent.

Condition 1

The type of conduct must *manifestly violate a fundamental universal value or community interest*, as recognised within the contemporary UN paradigm of international law. One can safely assume that if an international community with shared fundamental values and interests exists, it will seek to enforce manifest transgressions of the norms which embody those values and interests. The international community, as represented in particular by the United Nations, has in various ways and on many occasions proclaimed shared values and interests, and it has taken actions aimed at preventing serious violations of human rights and ensuring accountability for international crimes. This shows that an international community with shared values and interests exists as a

---

[342] NMT, "The Hostage Case", p. 1241, *supra* note 277.

reality rather than simply as an idea.[343] It follows – morally and politically – that the same community collectively, and in its singular units, must to some extent have an obligation towards community members to prevent and suppress crimes that adversely affect common fundamental values and interests.[344] If one accepts this premise, then one must ask which crime types serve to protect a fundamental value or interest, as recognised within the existing UN paradigm of international law, and therefore warrant being protected by punitive sanctions.

Accepting such a premise does not require most actors of international law to subscribe to the view that a more comprehensive 'united nations' or 'world society' of peoples and states with shared interests ought to be established to counterbalance the most negative consequences of a division of the world into states, or that the UN in fact already meets some of those expectations. Indeed, given the often contradictory actions and narrow self-interests pursued by states in their everyday foreign affairs, it is easy to conclude that "the present state of international relations is not yet conducive to [...] a shift of the center of gravity of international law away from states and towards a more abstract international community".[345] One should also be aware that to assume the existence and functioning of an international community may run "the risk of heightening expectations with corresponding risks that are bound to be disappointing".[346] Such assumptions may also encourage a rhetoric of universality that might become "a cloak for hegemonic tendencies by states with the power to decide what is and what is not a universal interest binding on all states".[347] These risks, however, should not deter us from the difficult journey towards an eventually much more consistent interpretation and enforcement of serious international crimes every-where, a concern which should outweigh the potential risks and disap-pointments.

To continue such a journey, it is sufficient that we ascertain that a clear normative foundation of the relevant values and interests has been adopted or expressed as representing the UN paradigm of international

---

[343] See M. Cherif Bassiouni, "The Subject of International Criminal Law: *Ratione Perso-nae*", in Bassiouni (ed.), 2008, pp. 23–30, *supra* note 55.
[344] See *ibid.*, p. 23.
[345] *Ibid.*, p. 30.
[346] *Ibid.*
[347] *Ibid.*

law. Numerous political statements and legal texts adopted since 1945, as well as consequential actions taken, point to such a normative foundation. These include, but are by no means limited to, the UN Charter, the Nuremberg Principles, the Universal Declaration of Human Rights, and ongoing work of the ILC and other international bodies.[348]

The point in our context is that a number of acts in contravention of these fundamental values and interests are easily identifiable. These acts fall into the following categories:

a) Acts that constitute a serious threat to international peace and security

b) Acts that are deemed to shock the conscience of humanity

c) Acts against the UN and associated personnel[349]

d) Acts violating other fundamental UN values or interests

e) Harmful organised transnational activities[350]

Any kind of conduct that offends officially proclaimed fundamental UN values and interests meets the requirement of letter (d) and thus our condition 1. But that would not, according to our scheme, by itself be sufficient to constitute an 'international crime', given that it must also meet conditions 2–5.

Conversely, conduct in compliance with the same fundamental interests and values does not meet the requirement, regardless of the labels used by others to characterise the conduct. For example, peaceful protesters who want regime change and who use their human rights of peaceful assembly and freedom of speech in contravention of repressive national laws cannot be deemed to constitute a threat to 'peace and security', even though such protests may indeed constitute a threat to a particular regime and even to international stability in the short term. Likewise, armed insurgents who fight foreign occupation or oppose a violent regime in civil war, and who are therefore labelled 'terrorists' or 'war criminals', cannot automatically for that reason be deemed to constitute a threat to peace and security or to any other fundamental UN value or interest. The definitions of international crimes and the concepts there embodied must be autonomous under international law, rather than

---

[348] See generally Chapter 2 and section 4.5. in this chapter.

[349] See, *e.g.*, the ILC 1996 Draft Code of Crimes, Article 19, *supra* note 247. Also see section 4.5.8. in this chapter.

[350] See section 4.8.2. in this chapter on 'organized transnational crimes'.

applied at will by particular national states. If protestors or insurgents do in fact engage in universally condemned acts, however, some of them may well have committed international crimes. In other words, condition 1, just like the other conditions, must be interpreted and applied 'objectively', that is, without discrimination for or against particular perpetrators, victims, or concerned states.[351]

This requirement of equality and non-discrimination is inherent in the definition of international crimes, in conformity with the general principles of law which are themselves an indispensable part of the fundamental values of the UN paradigm of international law. For that reason, any purported international crime designed to be applicable only to a situation-specific group of people *ex post facto* would not be an international crime.[352] The trials at Nuremberg and Tokyo after World

---

[351] The issue of *equal enforcement* of international crimes is a distinct question; see the next paragraph of the main text and the footnotes attached to it. In general, it cannot be expected that justice will be done with respect to all perpetrators of international crimes, especially since ICL is a relatively weak body of law. In 'failed states' and in states with significant defects in their domestic criminal justice systems, the same weaknesses apply to non-international crimes as well. In reality, equal enforcement of criminal law is impossible even in the most well-functioning states, if by equality one means that all guilty offenders – or even just suspected perpetrators of known crimes – are brought to justice. Equality in a more limited sense – meaning that particular groups are not singled out for prosecution while others enjoy impunity – is indeed possible, however, even in less well-functioning states. Enforcement of international crimes has been criticised for lacking equality in the second sense; in particular, some claim that the ICC has been unduly focused on crimes in certain African states. However, in order to evaluate such a proposition, a number of factors need to be taken into account, some of which might explain *prima facie* inequalities in the initial phase. For example, in the given example, a relevant factor might be – speaking hypothetically here, not asserting a truth – that some of the worst mass crimes have been committed in African states in recent years, compared to the totality of crimes for which the ICC has had jurisdiction and access to meaningful investigation.

[352] Consider the thoughtful remarks of Röling, one of the judges at the Tokyo Trial in 1946–1948, explaining why he dissented although he still upheld the charge of aggression: "My trouble with the majority was just that I didn't accept that what the Charter contained, as such, should be binding upon us. My argument was that, of course, you may set up an international tribunal; you can make a statute for it and that statute will set out the limits of the jurisdiction of the tribunal, beyond which it can never go. But that doesn't mean that whatever is considered a crime in the Charter should be eventually accepted as a crime by the Court. The victor in a war, even a world war, is not entitled to brand as an international crime everything he dislikes and

---

War II have often been criticised for dispensing 'victors' justice'. Leaving aside for a moment the issue of whether punishment for the 'crime of aggression' and other international crimes was inflicted in contravention of the legality principle,[353] this critique has some merit – given the suspicion that Allied forces may have committed war crimes, even crimes against humanity – but only insofar as the jurisdiction of the courts set up concerned personnel of the Axis states only.[354] The actual crime types, however, were defined in general terms at the outset, and this laid the ground for the general Nuremberg Principles adopted by the UN, as well as for the further development of ICL.

Condition 2

The type of conduct must be *universally regarded as punishable due to its inherent gravity*, allowing for punitive sanctions (retributive justice) as a legitimate response, regardless of the time and place of the crime scene. This means that the type of conduct should be widely condemned or considered clearly undesirable by the international community, and the criminal nature of the acts universally recognised, regardless of how it is characterised in social or political terms. In the Hostage Case,[355] the universal recognition of an act as 'inherently criminal' was considered to be essential, and the same thought underpins much, if not all, of the work of the ILC on international crimes and related subjects.[356]

In this book we have repeatedly emphasised that gravity assessment is essential to international criminal law and that the crimes we have in mind are usually linked to power structures, that is, organised or tolerated

---

wants to prosecute for. It is for the Court to verify whether pre-existing international law deems it a crime". Röling and Cassese, 1994, p. 65, *supra* note 125.

[353] See *ibid.* See also Chapter 3, section 3.3.4., for discussions of the legality principle.

[354] The critique has been rejected in various interesting ways. A sharp answer was provided by Benjamin Ferencz, prosecutor of the NMT (see NMT, "*The Einsatzgruppen Case*", in *Trials of War Criminals* [...], vol. IV, *supra* note 277). When asked whether he thought the Nuremberg trials were victors' justice, he replied, "No, they were not. If we wanted victors' justice, we would have gone out and murdered about half a million Germans. [...] [We] were not trying to get revenge, but to show how horrible it was, in order to deter others from doing the same. And to be just, not to convict anybody unless there was absolutely clear proof of their guilt. This was the main principle. It wasn't perfect". Stuart and Simons, 2009, *supra* note 288, p. 23.

[355] See section 4.6. in this chapter.

[356] See section 4.5. in this chapter.

---

by powerful institutions, organisations, or persons. Similarly, we have pointed to the underlying notion that some crimes have long been deemed capable of shocking humanity and societies guided by the rule of law. This may happen when clear violations of common values or interests are committed with malicious intent or as part of a plan or policy of large-scale commission, involve violence against especially protected or vulnerable persons, or constitute excessive use and abuse of power. The 'inherent gravity' is thus closely linked to these concepts and features of universal crimes, as set forth earlier.[357]

This does not imply that the proscribed conduct must have one standard characterisation in *legal* terms, whether internationally or in national jurisdictions. The key point is that the underlying conduct, which may be referred to by a set of closely related or associated terms, is generally considered illegal, unlawful, or criminal, and that punitive sanctions are widely considered to be an appropriate response. For example, punishment of murder is universally considered to be justifiable. Whether a murder in the context of an armed conflict constitutes a 'war crime', or whether a murder in a context of mass murder constitutes a 'crime against humanity' or even an act of 'genocide', is a complex legal question that cannot be solved by reference to condition 2 alone. The points are rather that (a) the underlying act, here murder, is a type of crime that fits the description of a universally punishable act, and (b) the political, military, or other social *context* of the underlying crime (act) defines the additional gravity, which in legal terms is required if the type of conduct shall qualify as an international crime. International crimes thus seem to consist of one or several underlying crimes plus a universally relevant social context. This contextual element implied in condition 2 points to the possible existence of distinct 'gravity clauses' of inter-national crimes.[358]

This does not necessarily imply that 'retributive justice' must be considered the only appropriate and justified *response* to universally punishable conduct, for example, war crimes or crimes against humanity. Exceptions might be made, for example, for less serious war crimes committed by low-ranking personnel in a civil war. As history has shown, societies in different 'transitional justice' situations have dealt differently

---

[357] See especially Chapter 2, sections 2.1.3. (shocking crimes), 2.2.2. (rule of law), 2.3.3. (linkage to power structures) and 2.3.4. (gravity assessment).

[358] On the notion of gravity clauses, see further section 4.9.2.2. in this chapter.

with such crimes. Some societies may, for different reasons, prefer alt-ernative or supplementary restorative justice mechanisms, including (at times reluctantly, as part of a political compromise) the use of blanket amnesties for the most serious crimes. In such cases the alternative option of prosecution and punishment would still, however, be considered justifiable from the perspective of universal norms, due to the inherent gravity of the criminal conduct, even long after the facts. An interesting illustration of this is the practice of 'post-transitional justice' in some Latin American countries.[359] Former high-ranking politicians and military personnel have been brought before national courts in countries such as Argentina and Chile and convicted of torture, extrajudicial killings, forced disappearances, genocide, and crimes against humanity, often many years after the initial regime change.[360] Far-reaching amnesties to bar pro-secution of gross human rights violations were circumvented or struck down by reformed and more independent courts, thus paving the way for universally justifiable punishment. The prosecutions before the Cambodian tribunal (the ECCC) might be another case in point, although different in many respects. Prosecutions of universal crimes long after the facts have also been initiated in many single cases around the world, many originating from World War II. The *Eichmann* case in Israel (1961–1962) is arguably the most famous,[361] and the far less spectacular Latvian *Kononov* case before the European Court of Human Rights (2010) one of the most recent.[362]

---

[359] On the concept of post-transitional justice, see, *e.g.*, Elin Skaar, *Judicial Independ-ence and Human Rights in Latin America: Violations, Politics, and Prosecution*, Pal-grave Macmillan, New York, 2011, pp. 2–4.

[360] Skaar (*ibid.*, pp. 199–202) suggests that the primary reason for these developments is to be found in the movement towards greater independence of courts and in legal re-forms that provided national judges with more tools to remedy gross human rights vi-olations, including increased opportunities to apply international law. Before military personnel can be prosecuted successfully, Skaar contends, "three preconditions must be met: the military must not present a credible threat to the democratic order, cases of human rights violations must be brought to court [by victims or human rights activ-ists], and there must be a sufficient legal basis for prosecution" (p. 190). In particular, "judges must have freedom from undue pressure if they are to exercise their constitu-tional guarantees of judicial independence" (p. 199).

[361] Jerusalem District Court, *The Eichmann Case* (Israel), Judgment of 12 December 1961, in *International Law Reports* 36, pp. 5–14 and 18–276, and Supreme Court Judgment of 29 May 1962, in *International Law Reports* 36, pp. 14–17 and 277–344.

[362] See ECHR, *Kononov* case, *supra* note 12.

Condition 3

The type of conduct proscribed must be *recognised as a matter of serious international concern*. A similar condition was floated in the Hostage Case,[363] and it has often – with some variations in language – been used by the ILC[364] and others in reference to the concept of international crimes. It is also used, in qualified terms, in Article 5 of the ICC Rome Statute for the purpose of distinguishing 'the most serious' international crimes from other crimes with respect to the negotiated jurisdiction of the ICC ("the most serious crimes of concern to the international community as a whole").[365]

There is, of course, a close relationship between condition 3 and condition 1 in our scheme (violations of fundamental values and interests). The element added here is the focus on actual serious international concern with preventing and suppressing the proscribed conduct and holding transgressors to account. Evidence of such concern can be found, for example, in UN-sponsored multilateral human rights and humanitarian conventions, in the establishment of international and hybrid criminal courts for the purpose of enforcing criminal liability, in the jurisprudence of international courts and the opinions of international supervisory bodies, and in binding resolutions by the Security Council authorising concrete protection measures and the use of force against perpetrators. One may ask how much 'serious international concern' must be demonstrated to determine when this particular condition is met. In most cases, however, this determination will not be difficult, since multiple international sources will concur that the proscribed conduct is indeed a matter of serious international concern.

Condition 4

The proscriptive norm must be *anchored in binding international law*, that is, in at least one of the four law-creating sources of international law.[366] Unlike the other four conditions, this condition has no clear foundation in the tribunal's proposal in the Hostage Case. The tribunal's first criterion – that the act or conduct must be 'universally recognised as

---

[363] NMT, "The Hostage Case", p. 1241, *supra* note 277.
[364] See generally section 4.5. in this chapter.
[365] The same formulation is also used in the preamble to the ICC Rome Statute.
[366] See Chapter 3, section 3.3.

inherently criminal' – might be construed to imply a legal basis in general principles of international law, universal customs, or multilateral treaties of near-universal accession. But that is not a compelling interpretation. A more plausible interpretation is that the tribunal was satisfied with a universal consensus on the criminal character of the act *lex ferenda*. A requirement that the proscriptive norm have a legal basis in one or more law-creating sources of international law, on the other hand, places international crimes within the sphere of *lex lata*.

Thus, condition 4 distinguishes current international crimes from possibly emerging proscriptive norms that have risen only to the level of international statements and declarations, for instance through condemnation of transgressions of the norm by the UN General Assembly, or through recommendations in international reports and similar non-binding (soft law) materials with a view to future criminalisation or suppression by means of treaties, or through condemnation in the Security Council. In comparison, the law-creating sources of international law are treaties, international custom, general principles of law, and legislative Security Council resolutions.[367]

Condition 4 must be seen in conjunction with conditions 3 and 5. Proscription of an offence in a single treaty may meet condition 4 while still not providing sufficient evidence that the conduct is 'recognised as a matter of serious international concern', per condition 3. For example, if a Latin American custom of constituting 'enforced disappearance' as a manifest crime has emerged at a certain time, that does not in itself prove that the same offence, when not part of a widespread or systematic practice such as crimes against humanity, is also recognised as a matter of serious international concern, that is, universally rather than only in Latin America. But if a UN convention on the subject matter were to be adopted and come into force (as indeed has happened)[368] for the purpose of criminalising the conduct and thus constituting it as a crime in a legally binding multilateral treaty,[369] and suppressing it,[370] and if, in addition, the

---

[367] See Chapter 3, sections 3.3.2–3.3.6.

[368] United Nations, International Convention for the Protection of All Persons from Enforced Disappearance, A/RES/61/177, 20 December 2006, in force from 23 December 2010. As of 3 May 2011 the convention had 25 parties and 88 signatories.

[369] According to the preamble of the Convention, enforced disappearance "constitutes a crime and, in certain circumstances defined in international law, a crime against humanity". Article 5 reinforces the notion that "widespread or systematic practice of en-

proscribed conduct were to be condemned in various other UN documents and statements, both conditions 3 and 4 would clearly be met.

Condition 5

Finally, *criminal liability and prosecution must not be dependent upon consent of a concerned state*. By a 'concerned state' is meant the territorial state where the offence was committed or the national state of any alleged offender or victim. If individual criminal liability and prosecution is preconditioned upon the consent of such a state, either in general terms by means of a reciprocal treaty concerned with the actual crime type or in a concrete case after the crime has been committed, then it follows that the offence cannot be considered an international crime. Hence, only the crime types that in principle can be enforced at the international level by an international criminal court, regardless of the consent or protest of a concerned state, can be taken as meeting condition 5.

If criminal liability can be enforced in third states by means of prosecution based on the doctrine of universal jurisdiction, that is, regardless of a concerned state's consent or protest, the conclusion must be the same. That is because the international law scope for the establishment of international prosecution of international crimes is at least as broad as that for universal jurisdiction, and possibly broader. A possible difference in scope might be explained by reference to one disputed requirement of universal jurisdiction for third states, namely, that the alleged offender has to be present in its territory before its authorities can lawfully investigate the crime, arrest the suspect or issue an arrest warrant, and, finally,

---

forced disappearance constitutes a crime against humanity as defined in applicable international law". Otherwise, however, the convention treats enforced disappearance as a discrete serious crime when committed "by agents of the State or by persons or groups of persons acting with the authorization, support or acquiescence of the State" (Article 2). This is similar to the framing of torture under the 1984 UN Convention against Torture.

[370] The preamble to the Convention states that the parties are determined "to prevent enforced disappearances and to combat impunity for the crime of enforced disappearance". Article 4 establishes a duty to criminalise the offence under national criminal law, Article 6 a duty to prosecute those criminally responsible, and Article 7 a duty to inflict "appropriate penalties which take into account its extreme seriousness". Article 8 limits the scope of statutes of limitation.

---

prosecute the crime before a court. These requirements are clearly additional to those attached to international court procedures.[371]

How, then, can one determine whether a particular crime type meets this final condition? The first and easiest step is to examine the crimes that have been included in international statutes.[372] With respect to the international hybrid courts, typically established by the UN in cooperation with a consenting concerned state, inclusion of a crime type in their statutes is not in itself proof of criminal liability and prosecution in the sense required by condition 5. Considering the Nuremberg, Yugoslavia, Rwanda, and Rome statutes leaves us the core crime categories of genocide, crimes against humanity, aggression, and war crimes as definitely included.

However, condition 5 may also apply to crime types other than those already included in the statutes of past or present international criminal courts: for example, any crime type for which there is lawful universal jurisdiction. If it is clear under international law that third states may exercise universal jurisdiction over a certain type of offence, no matter where the concrete crime was committed or the nationality of the alleged offender or victim (whether conditioned upon territorial presence of the alleged perpetrator or not in the third state), then condition 5, as well as conditions 1 through 4, can be assumed to be satisfied. That is, the existence of a material scope for genuine 'universal jurisdiction' implies that the conditions of an 'international crime' have been met. However, there is still the same unresolved issue, in that it is necessary to decide to which crimes the concept of universal jurisdiction applies. Whether the existence of an 'international crime' also implies 'universal jurisdiction', or whether this also depends on other factors, is another distinct issue.[373]

---

[371] Another possible difference might emerge if a guarantee of 'fair trial' has to be issued by the state proposing to exercise universal jurisdiction, if a concerned state asks for it. However, a fair trial guarantee is presumably considered inherent in the concept of an 'international criminal court' within the UN paradigm of international law.

[372] See section 4.3. in this chapter.

[373] With respect to issues of jurisdiction and accountability, see the preface to this book.

4.9.1.3. Formulating a Proposed Legal Definition of International Crimes

For determining whether crimes other than the core crimes (or new crime types within the established crime categories, such as new war crimes or new crimes against humanity) qualify as international crimes, it seems appropriate to take a descriptive-analytical approach based on multiple interpretative as well as law-creating sources. These may include the following:

1) Statements by UN bodies, including the Security Council and the General Assembly, which justify criminal liability and prosecution for the specific crime type in question; reports by the ILC and other UN experts on the need to enforce accountability for such offences; treaties aimed at suppression; new international court statutes; developments of customary international law; and legal opinions of international and national courts on the matters of criminal liability and prosecution under international law, including statements on the material scope of universal jurisdiction.

2) General principles of law in support of a consistent line of reasoning, for example, that there are additional offences which are in essence equally grave within the UN paradigm of international law as ones already included, unless this explicitly contradicts findings under (1).

The first point is similar to assessments of conditions 1–4, with a particular focus on statements or implicit language directly concerned with criminal liability and prosecutions accepted, initiated, or recommended independent of consent by a concerned state. Since this partly overlaps with the other conditions, it is important to remember that all five conditions must be understood in conjunction, and that all are required. Brief illustrations of the method are given in the next section, which deals with enumerated crimes. In conclusion, all five necessary and sufficient conditions can be incorporated within one comprehensive legal definition:

> The term 'international crimes' applies to conduct which (1) manifestly violates a fundamental universal value or interest, provided that the offence is (2) universally regarded as punishable due to its inherent gravity, (3) recognised as a matter of serious concern to the international community as a whole, and (4) proscribed by binding rules of international

> law, and provided that (5) criminal liability and prosecution
> is not dependent upon the consent of a concerned territorial
> state or the national state of an alleged perpetrator or victim.

If this proposed legal definition is correctly applied, it should naturally lead to the same results, in terms of including or excluding specific crimes or crime types, as the enumerative definition of international crimes presented in the next section.

4.9.2. Developing an Enumerative Definition of International Crimes

4.9.2.1. General Remarks on the Typology

This section and the next present an enumerative definition of international crimes, consolidated in the proposed list of separate international crimes presented in section 4.9.3.

'Separate international crimes' here refers to crime types that can be committed independently of other crimes. This contrasts to the various modes of punishable participation in a single international crime, which extend liability for the same type of crime beyond mere commission to other modes such as ordering, instigating, planning, aiding and abetting, and so on. The distinction may not always be clear. For example, a person might be indicted separately for "conspiracy to commit genocide",[374] "direct and public incitement to commit genocide",[375] or "attempt to commit genocide",[376] independently of any completion of physical genocidal acts by the suspect or by others. These are often referred to as 'inchoate crimes' in ICL terminology. One might argue, therefore, that similar inchoate crimes should generally be included among the enumerated international crimes. However, the relationship between modes of participation and independent crimes is itself a complicated matter, best left for separate consideration and therefore beyond the scope of this book.[377] Accordingly, modes of participation that might also be separate crimes are generally not included in the list. Still, such modes are

---

[374] Convention on the Prevention and Punishment of the Crime of Genocide (1948), Article III(b).

[375] *Ibid.*, Article III(c).

[376] *Ibid.*, Article III(d).

[377] The issue will be discussed in more detail in the forthcoming second volume in this series, dealing with punishable participation; see preface to the current volume.

explicitly included below in the case of three categories, namely crimes of genocide, terrorist crimes, and the *lex ferenda* category of crimes of group destruction not encompassed by the Genocide Convention. The dangerous specific intent to destroy a group or to provoke a state of terror that is characteristic of these categories provides a *prima facia* case for the existence of such separate crimes.

The enumerative definition set out in section 4.9.3. should be regarded as a working definition illustrating the method, rather than as a final extensional definition with an exhaustive listing of all international crimes.[378] Still, the list includes a large number of specific crime types. If one takes the ICC Rome Statute as the point of departure, the inclusion of most of these types should be uncontroversial,[379] and the relevant section of the Rome Statute is therefore indicated in the list. Alternatively, another presumably safe legal basis is provided, as in the case of the other modes of participation in genocide.

The list also includes crimes with an uncertain status under international law *lex lata*. In such cases a reference is given to international custom and/or the general principles of law (shortened to 'general international law'), sometimes combined with a more specific reference to a representative expression of the particular crime type under international law.[380] The precondition is always that the crime type is considered to meet the five conditions outlined in section 4.9.1. These crime candidates were identified among the proposed 'crimes against the peace and security of mankind' as set out in the works of the ILC,[381] or

---

[378] See section 4.8.1. in this chapter.

[379] However, this proposition is limited to the crime types as such. The exact formulation of any crime type can always be discussed, and the content of each crime type is even more open to debate. As noted earlier, ICL as a whole is fragmented and polycentric (see Chapter 3, section 4.2.). One should thus be aware that crime formulations made for the purpose of defining and delimiting the *material jurisdiction* of any international court, through the crime definitions in its statute and other sources of interpretation, may or may not also be an accurate reproduction of the same crimes as defined in other law-creating sources of ICL, *inter alia*, relevant multilateral treaties or customary international law. This does not undermine the correctness of the proposition that certain crime types are now an inherent part of general international law (customary international law and/or the general principles of law).

[380] The legal bases issue deserves further analysis in each case, but such analysis is beyond the scope of this book. For a general discussion of the underlying principles, see Chapter 3.

[381] See section 4.5. in this chapter.

---

otherwise by means of the descriptive-analytical approach of section 4.9.1. If the crime type was identified by the ILC at some point as a crime against the peace and security of mankind and thus as an international crime, reference to a relevant ILC document is sometimes made as well.

In addition, the list includes serious offences that do not meet all five conditions and are therefore not yet international crimes, but which might indeed constitute manifest violations of fundamental universal values or interests for which punishment is universally justifiable, thus satisfying conditions 1 and 2. Such offences ought to be considered *lex ferenda* as a matter of serious international concern (condition 3), which should be anchored in the law-creating sources of international (condition 4), and which should finally emerge as new international crimes for which criminal liability and prosecution is not dependent upon a concerned state's consent (condition 5). Although these are included in the list below, it should be stressed that they do not meet all five conditions and are therefore international crimes *lex ferenda* rather than actual international crimes *lex lata.*

It is often difficult to distinguish between the types which should be classified as uncertain crimes *lex lata* and those better classified as international offences *lex ferenda*. A prominent example is that of terrorist crimes, discussed further in section 4.9.2.4. in this chapter.

It is beyond the scope of this book to resolve all such uncertainties for every crime type. However, it organises the set of possible international crimes into crime categories and crime types, with each crime category containing a cluster of similar crime types.[382] War crimes, for example, is a crime category comprising several different war crime types, as previously noted in section 4.8.2.

Each crime category is assigned a capital letter (A, B, C, and so on). This organises the crime types by the same level of generality, thus providing a basis for enumerating the distinct crime types. The crime types are numbered sequentially (1, 2, 3, and so on). The description of the crime in the list is a shortened version, as a comprehensive description would go beyond the purpose of this list. The crime categories and crime types are also grouped into three broader classes of international crimes: (I) core international crimes, (II) other international crimes against the peace and security of mankind, and (III) international crimes not

---

[382] See section 4.8.2. in this chapter.

dependent on the existence of threats to international peace and security.[383]

The significance of which *class* of international crimes a particular crime type is deemed to belong to should not be overstated, since the most important distinctions with regard to general legal consequences under international law are presumably those between 'international crimes' and 'non-international crimes'[384], and between international crimes and internationally relevant offences that do not rise to the gravity level of an international crime. Those offences may be offences *lex ferenda* which may later emerge as new international crimes or international offences (that is, unlawful conduct) but clearly do not constitute manifest violations of fundamental values and interests. Examples would be breaches of humanitarian law which do not reach the level of the 'grave breaches' provisions of the Geneva Conventions. Typically, there are 'international offences' related to each international crime, consisting of offences that are unlawful but do not require criminal punishment. If one modified the earlier classification of international crimes and non-international crimes to include these two classes of 'international offences' as well, the result would be the following classification:[385]

International crimes:

- Core international crimes
- Other international crimes against the peace and security of mankind
- International crimes not dependent on the existence of threats to international peace and security

International offences:

- International crimes *lex ferenda*
- Non-grave international offences

Non-international crimes:

- National crimes

---

[383] See, *e.g.*, the graphic depiction of the three classes in Figure 2 in section 4.8.2. of this chapter.

[384] See section 4.8.2. in this chapter.

[385] See Figure 3, excluding the full listing of subclasses of 'non-international crimes', which is not reproduced here.

- Nationally imported international crimes
- Transnational non-international crimes

4.9.2.2. Requirement for a Gravity Clause

In accordance with the discussions of necessary and sufficient conditions in section 4.9.1., it is crucial that even the plain international crimes be aggravated or qualified types of offences under current international law, which fulfil, *inter alia*, the manifest violation requirement of condition 1 and the inherent gravity clause of any international crime.

The necessity of a gravity clause can be illustrated by an example. According to Article 8 *bis* of the new ICC Rome Statute on the "Crime of Aggression", an act constituting a violation of the "sovereignty" and/or "territorial integrity" of another state which is "inconsistent with the Charter of the United Nations" (that is, a 'fundamental universal interest' within the UN paradigm of international law) – such as "[a]n attack by the armed forces of a State on the land, sea or air forces, or marine and air fleets of another State"[386] – is not necessarily a *crime* of aggression. To qualify as such, an 'act of aggression' must "by its character, gravity and scale" constitute "a manifest violation of the Charter of the United Nations".[387] This raises the question of whether other proscribed types of offences should not also be accompanied by such a gravity clause, either explicitly or implicitly.

One possible answer might be that the crime of aggression is special in this respect, with the distinction between acts of aggression that are non-punishable international offences and the manifest offences that rise to crimes of aggression. However, crime categories such as genocide, crimes against humanity, and war crimes have also incorporated gravity clauses. The formulation and specific content of the gravity clause may differ, focusing either on a specific intent (genocide), on systematic or large-scale violations (crimes against humanity), or on the existence of war (war crimes). Furthermore, inherent gravity clauses are sometimes found in multilateral treaties concerning other international offences. For example, torture as a crime of serious international concern is pre-conditioned upon an act of torture being linked to an existing power structure within society, that is, on the intentional commission or

---

[386] ICC Rome Statute, Article 8 *bis* 2(d).
[387] See section 4.7.2. in this chapter.

participation in torture by state authorities or other persons acting in an official capacity.[388] The reason why this differs from the torture of one private individual by another, from the perspective of ICL, is not difficult to understand. While the latter might be just as serious for the victims concerned, the former implies that torture may have been institutionalised and/or might become an endemic problem of the society in question, especially if such acts of torture go unpunished. Such acts are thus of serious international concern and should be combated internationally *as crimes*.[389] The same line of reasoning applies, *inter alia*, to the crime of enforced disappearance, where the inherent gravity clause focuses on acts "by agents of the State or by persons or groups of persons acting with the authorization, support or acquiescence of the State".[390] The same principle might apply not only to the state but also to other power structures in society that include powerful non-state actors.

We therefore reject the argument that the crime of aggression is unique in requiring a gravity clause for its definition as an international crime. To the contrary, we argue that gravity clauses are a necessary requirement of all international crimes, and that a specific gravity clause must apply to each specific crime category. This requirement is implied by our definition in conditions 1 and 2, which prescribes that an international crime must be a manifest violation of a fundamental universal value or interest and universally regarded as punishable due to its inherent gravity.[391] In the enumerative definition of international crimes below, an implied gravity clause is taken to be an indispensable part of each crime type, even if such a clause may not be explicitly expressed in specific treaties, statutes, or other documents. Such a gravity clause does not apply only to core crimes and other crimes against the peace and security of mankind; it is, in fact, critical for the legal status of international crimes

---

[388] See the UN Convention Against Torture and Other Cruel, Inhuman or Degrading Treatment or Punishment, (1984). Article 1 defines 'torture' as "any act by which severe pain or suffering, whether physical or mental, is intentionally inflicted on a person" for certain purposes "when such pain or suffering is inflicted by or at the instigation of or with the consent or acquiescence of a public official or other person acting in an official capacity [...]".

[389] *Ibid.*, *inter alia*, Articles 4–8 and 12.

[390] See United Nations, International Convention for the Protection of All Persons from Enforced Disappearance, Article 2, *supra* note 368.

[391] See section 4.9.1.2. in this chapter.

that may exist independent of whether the offences constitute threats to international peace and security.[392]

4.9.2.3. The Relevance of Conditions of War or Peace

One particularly important variable that affects the identification of an international crime is whether the relevant act or conduct takes place under conditions of war or peace. Some international crimes require that the conduct take place in times of war, while others do not. While war crimes obviously must take place in wartime, all other international crime types, such as genocide and crimes against humanity, may occur during either war or peace.[393]

Some of the war crimes are further restricted in that they apply only during international wars ('international armed conflicts') and not during civil wars ('non-international armed conflict'). It has generally been assumed that the scope of humanitarian laws and the list of possible types of war crimes are significantly shorter with respect to civil wars that with respect to international wars, excluding not only those crime types which by definition only occur during international war, such as crimes committed by an 'occupying power',[394] but also others. The ICC Rome Statute, in Article 8 on war crimes, also makes this traditional distinction between 'international armed conflict' and 'armed conflict not of an international character'.[395]

To what extent the traditional assumption is correct *lex lata* and whether it should in any case be upheld *lex ferenda* under general

---

[392] See section 4.8.2. in this chapter on the three classes of international crimes. See also section 9.3 in this chapter and Chapter V, section 2.

[393] As noted earlier, the *jurisdiction* of the Nuremberg Tribunal with regard to 'crimes against humanity' was limited to such crimes when committed in connection with World War II, *i.e.*, after 1 September 1939. This crime category is, however, part of material ICL, regardless of how the jurisdiction of any particular international court is delimited. In fact, no subsequent international criminal court has included a require-ment that crimes against humanity be limited to those committed in wartime.

[394] See, *e.g.*, ICC Rome Statute Article 8(2)(b)(viii): "The transfer, directly or indirectly, by the Occupying Power of parts of its own population into the territory it occupies, or the deportation or transfer of all or parts of the population of the occupied territory within or outside this territory".

[395] Compare the Rome Statute Article 8(2)(b) on war crimes in armed conflict of an in-ternational character and Articles 8(2)(c) and 8(2)(e) on war crimes in armed conflict not of an international character.

---

international law are important issues.[396] Taking into account the general development of international law towards increasing normative protection of civilians in particular, as a result of the changing patterns of modern warfare which expose civilians to increasingly serious threats, our view is that war crimes should apply equally to all kinds of wars that are recognised as wars under international law (except for crimes which by their very nature are relevant only to international wars).[397] This conclusion would be consistent with the fundamental universal value of human dignity, and those portions of international human rights law, humanitarian law, and ICL which have obtained universal recognition within the international community. Thus in the list in section 4.9.3., the set of crimes applicable to international armed conflict is taken as more generally applicable. The crimes listed there, although grouped somewhat differently, are the crimes included in the ICC Rome Statute Article 8(2)(a) and (b).

The concepts of war and armed conflict are generally taken as identical for legal purposes. However, it is important to distinguish them from more general concepts such as violence and from other violent acts which do not qualify as 'war'. In descriptive terms, one may wish to apply the terms 'war' or 'armed conflict' to many acts of aggression, including less serious acts, as well as internal disturbances and violent tensions within a state, such as riots and more isolated or sporadic acts of armed violence. These, however, do not in themselves constitute armed conflict

---

[396] See Emily Crawford, *The Treatment of Combatants and Insurgents under the Law of Armed Conflict*, Oxford University Press, Oxford, UK, 2010, p. 173, concluding that "the next logical step would be the adoption of a harmonized regime that unifies the laws of war and bestows universal protection on all, in all situations of armed conflict".

[397] A step in this direction was undertaken at the ICC Review Conference in Kampala in 2010. See ICC, *Review Conference of the Rome Statute of the International Criminal Court, Kampala, 31 May – 11 June 2010*, RC/9/11, pp. 13–15. It was decided to amend Article 8(2)(e) of the ICC Rome Statute by making three more war crime types applicable also to 'armed conflict not of an international character' under the jurisdiction of the ICC: "(xiii) Employing poison or poisoned weapons; (xiv) Employing asphyxiating, poisonous or other gases, and all analogous liquids, materials or devices; (xv) Employing bullets which flatten easily in the human body, such as bullets with a hard envelope which does not entirely cover the core or is pierced with incisions". The three crime types were already included with respect to international armed conflicts. See Rome Statute Article 8, paragraph 2(b)(xvii–xix). See also the enumerative list of crime types in section 4.9.3. of this chapter.

or war in a legal sense. See, for example, the ICC Rome Statute Article 8 *bis* (1) with respect to the crime of aggression, which requires a 'manifest violation' before an *act* of aggression becomes a *crime* of aggression. Isolated small acts of aggression by themselves do not constitute war,[398] but they may begin a process of escalation which at a certain point becomes a war. Similarly, Article 8(2)(d) and (f) set a certain threshold for when armed violence within a state rises to the level of a 'non-international armed conflict' (civil war).[399]

A strong reason to set a relatively high threshold for war is that some acts which are usually illegal in times of peace may under certain conditions become lawful under international law in times of war. This includes, for example, intentional destruction of civil installations and property that are legitimate military objectives, according to the laws of war. The legal latitude for violent acts in war includes intentional killing of men and women who are regarded as enemy combatants under international law. War itself is a dangerous and destructive enterprise for the actors involved, for society at large, and not least for innocent victims of the violence. In addition, wars frequently threaten international peace and security. These are the principal reasons why acts of aggression are illegal under the UN Charter,[400] and why manifest acts of aggression are punish-

---

[398] Such minor acts of aggression could be termed 'international armed conflict short of war', 'armed conflict short of international war', or similar. See Gary S. Solis, *The Law of Armed Conflict: International Humanitarian Law in War*, Cambridge University Press, Cambridge, UK, 2010, p. 151: "Confusing the issue, there sometimes are armed conflicts involving two or more states that fall short of what might be termed 'war'. There is a long history of such events".

[399] ICC Rome Statute Article 8(2)(c) makes clear that serious violations of Article 3 common to the four Geneva Conventions constitute war crimes in cases of non-international armed conflicts, whereas sub-paragraph (d) states that the provision of sub-paragraph (c) "does not apply to situations of internal disturbances and tensions, such as riots, isolated and sporadic acts of violence or other acts of similar nature". Article 8(2)(e) concerns other serious violations in non-international armed conflicts, and sub-paragraph (f), according to its wording, sets a higher threshold for these violations (requiring also 'protracted armed conflict'). For a discussion of these thresholds, see Schabas, 2010, *supra* note 63, pp. 204–206. See also, *e.g.*, Knut Dörmann, *Elements of War Crimes under the Rome Statute of the International Criminal Court: Sources and Commentary*, Cambridge University Press, Cambridge, UK, 2003, pp. 384–389.

[400] See, *e.g.*, the UN Charter, Article 2(4), which prohibits "the threat or use of force against the territorial integrity or political independence of any state, or in any other manner inconsistent with the purposes of the United Nations".

---

able under the ICL provisions on the non-right to wage war (*jus ad bellum*).[401] This is also why grave transgressions of human rights in wartime and of humanitarian limitations on conduct in war,[402] including guarantees of civilised treatment of vulnerable groups during war, are punishable (*jus in bello*). Within contemporary international law, an effective balance must be struck between political war aims and military tactics on the one hand, and the protection of civilians and other vulnerable groups, on the other hand. Hence there has been development towards universal recognition of war crimes as an instrument to clarify and sanction the serious violations of values and interests that need to be respected in war, with eventual enforcement by criminal courts.[403]

There remains a significant distinction between the two main categories of war, that is, international war between states ('international armed conflict' or similar terms) and civil war within a state ('non-international armed conflict' or similar terms). But this distinction may be misleading, underplaying several factors. Although they are not definitively defined, a more fine-grained classification shows four distinct legal types of war within the UN paradigm of international law:

1) *Classic international war:* declared war or manifest armed conflict between states for any purpose.[404]

---

[401] See, *e.g.*, ICC Rome Statute, Article 8 *bis*, "Crime of Aggression". See also section 4.7.2. in this chapter.

[402] See, *e.g.*, the four 1948 Geneva Conventions and the 1977 Protocols. On the complementarity of human rights law and humanitarian law, see Chapter 3, section 3.4.2.

[403] Although such a development is legally logical and even necessary within the contemporary UN paradigm of international law, this is not to say that the developments that have taken place were inevitable. For example, without the vocal initiatives and prolonged support of a wide range of non-governmental organisations, and the efforts of many state officials, international legal experts, and politicians who as a matter of conviction and principle have supported the rule of law, a normative logic alone would have led nowhere, given the competing interests embedded in traditional state sovereignty and the strong additional interests of the major powers. During the Cold War those interests meant little progress in enforcement by international criminal courts.

[404] It is important to note the 'manifest' requirement. If this condition is not fulfilled, the armed hostilities and aggressive acts do not constitute a war or crimes of aggression in legal terms; see also Solis, pp. 151–152 *supra* note 398. Any such act, however, when not committed in legitimate self-defence (singularly or collectively) against an aggressive attack by another state or an imminent threat of such attack, is illegal and may incur state responsibility under international law. An attack by a state against an-

2) *Universally authorised war:* manifest armed intervention in a state authorised by the UN Security Council for the purpose of (a) maintaining or restoring international peace and security, or (b) protecting human beings against grave international crimes, that is, universal crimes.[405]

---

other state for the strict purpose of protection of human beings against attempted or ongoing grave international crimes might be lawful, however (see the doctrine of humanitarian intervention). The legality of an alleged humanitarian intervention by one or several states without UN authorisation will often be disputed. For example, note the NATO intervention in the former Yugoslavia in 1999, which was not authorised by the Security Council because Russia and China exercised their veto power.

[405] See the UN Charter, Articles 39 and 42. The authorisation itself is not equivalent to a declaration of war by the UN as such against the state. A subsequent armed intervention within the mandate prescribed by the Security Council, whether by a singular state or by several states in concert (organised, *e.g.*, within the framework of NATO), must reach the same threshold as a classic international war in order to constitute a war. An example of a 'universally authorised war' for the purpose of peace and security is the first Gulf War against Iraq (1990–1991), as mandated in Security Council Resolution 678 (1990). Authorised war for the purpose of protecting human beings against universal crimes is not explicitly stated in the UN Charter. However, authorisation on this basis is presumably inherent in the UN Charter, Chapter VII, insofar as the notion of humanitarian intervention and/or the doctrine of responsibility to protect can be seen as legal norms allowing for a specific kind of self-defence under international law, *i.e.*, a legitimate and proportional act of self-defence on behalf of a vulnerable third party (a state or group of people) under an imminent threat of universal crimes, anchored in the general principles of law and thus part of ICL. The notion of a lawful proportionate act of self-defence in favour of a threatened third person is common to most systems of domestic criminal law. For the application of a parallel principle in international law, Security Council Resolution 1973 (2011), of 17 March 2011, on the situation in Libya, is quite telling. In the preceding Resolution 1970 (2011), of 26 February 2011, the Security Council had considered "that the widespread and systematic attacks currently taking place in the Libyan Arab Jamahiriya against the civilian population may amount to *crimes against humanity*" (emphasis added). The Security Council, then, in Resolution 1973 (2011), "[a]cting under Chapter VII of the United Nations", authorised member states "to take all necessary measures […] to protect civilians and civilian populated areas under threat of attack in the Libyan Arab Jamahiriya". Despite "excluding a foreign occupation force", the resolution authorised armed intervention of other kinds, which would be tantamount to war. The military acts subsequently undertaken by NATO, including acts enumerated in the ICC Rome Statute, Article 8 *bis* (2)(b) ("bombardment […] against the territory of another State") and 2(d) ("attack […] on the land, sea or air forces, or marine and air fleets of another State"), have no doubt constituted a war under international law – lawful or just as this war presumably has been as an act of self-defence on be-

3) *Internationalised civil war:* manifest internal armed conflict of an international character, caused by armed intervention or other major interference for whatever purpose in a civil war by another state or other states, directly or through affiliates.[406]

---

half of the civilian population in Libya. The UN-authorised war against Libya in 2011 can thus also be described as a humanitarian intervention.

[406] It can be difficult to determine whether a civil war is sufficiently 'internationalised' when a foreign power is not directly and openly intervening through its own armed forces. As the ICTY Appeals Chamber noted in the *Tadic* case, "It is indisputable that an armed conflict is international if it takes place between two or more States. In addition, in case of an internal armed conflict breaking out on the territory of a State, it may become international (or, depending on the circumstances, be international in character alongside an internal armed conflict) if (i) another State intervenes in that conflict through its troops, or alternatively if (ii) some of the participants in the internal armed conflict act on behalf of that other State". ICTY, Appeals Chamber, *Prosecutor v. Duško Tadic*, Judgment, 15 July 1999, para. 84. The criterion to "act on behalf of" another state was clarified to refer to "a test of control" (paras. 95–97), which again must take into account "the general rules on State responsibility which set out the legal criteria for attributing to a State acts performed by individuals not having the formal status of State officials" (para. 98). In contrast to the high degree of 'effective control' suggested by the ICJ in the *Nicaragua* case (ICJ, *Military and Paramilitary Activities in and against Nicaragua* (Nicaragua v. United States of America), Merits and Judgment, *I.C.J. Reports 1986*, p. 14), the ICTY Appeals Chamber in the *Tadic* case did not agree that international law generally requires "a high threshold for the test of control" (para. 117). Instead, it suggested that the degree of control may vary according to the circumstances and that different situations may be distinguished (paras. 118–122). In the case of responsibility for war crimes through assistance to organised groups committing war crimes, the ICTY required that the intervening state exercise "overall control", "not only by equipping and financing the group, but also by coordinating or helping the general planning of its military activity", whereas "specific instructions" is a requirement with regard to "individuals or militarily unorganised groups" (para. 141). In the concrete case before it, the ICTY concluded that "the Yugoslav Army exercised in 1992 the requisite measure of control over the Bosnian Serb Army" (para. 147). Although this might be the correct approach to *attribution of accountability for war crimes* (and other international crimes during war), it could be argued that the criteria for determining when an internal armed conflict turns into an international war should be even more lenient. Any substantial assistance by another state to any party or group participating in a civil war increases the risk of intensifying the armed conflict, and it thus seems logical that the protective norms of international armed conflict should be extended accordingly *ipso facto*. Hence the criterion 'manifest interference' is preferred as the general term. If so, and if the 'Tadic test' is applied, many wars that have been classified as civil wars or 'internal armed conflicts' in the media and in the literature may actually have been international wars.

4) *Classic civil war:* manifest internal armed conflict not of an international character for any purpose between competing *de jure* and *de facto* state authorities, between *de jure* state authorities and organised armed insurgents or groups, or between organised groups within a state without necessarily involving state authorities.[407]

Each of these four war types may have different legal conditions and/or consequences attached, with respect to war crimes or other international crimes. The broadest conception of war crimes applies to the first three war types; they are all classes of international war. Only type (4) is a civil war proper.

The 'global war on terror' doctrine, launched by US authorities after 9/11, implies that a legally relevant war under international law can also exist between a state and a (self-proclaimed) 'terrorist organisation', even when the organisation is based or operating outside the borders of the state – in this case, the United States considering itself at war with al-Qaeda or with all alleged terrorists.[408] If accepted under international law, such a war on terror would constitute a fifth type of war within the scheme proposed above.

In the context of the 'war on terror', alleged terrorists have been considered neither lawful combatants nor civilians under international humanitarian law (IHL). They have also not been considered alleged criminals with ordinary due process rights under either human rights law or US national criminal law. Instead, the alleged terrorists and their supporters have been attributed a legal status *sui generis* under IHL as 'unlawful enemy combatants', 'enemy combatants', or 'unlawful combatants'. Such persons have been deemed not to enjoy protection under international law, or have been accorded very limited rights. Consequently, according to the 'global war on terror' doctrine of the first

---

[407] Classic civil wars must be distinguished both from internal isolated acts of armed violence that do not meet the threshold set by the ICC Rome Statute, Article 8(2)(d), and from international wars, especially 'internationalised civil wars'; see the preceding footnote.

[408] See the resolution passed by the US Congress on 18 September 2001, "Authorization for Use of Military Force Against Terrorists" (Pub. L. 107-40, 115 Stat. 224), stating that the president "is authorized to use all necessary and appropriate force against those nations, organizations, or persons he determines planned, authorized, committed, or aided the terrorist attacks that occurred on September 11, 2001, or harbored such organizations or persons, in order to prevent any future acts of international terrorism against the United States by such nations, organizations or persons".

George W. Bush administration, they could be targeted for killing even when not taking direct part in hostilities; they could also be detained without rights under either the Geneva Conventions or human rights law.[409]

This notion of a third IHL category not derives not from compelling legal logic but rather from alleged policy considerations.[410] Combatants who do not respect the international rules of engagement in war frustrate their enemies by, for example, not having a fixed distinctive sign recognizable at a distance or not carrying arms openly. They are thus in violation of the recognised rules of international warfare, and may for that reason alone be committing offences under IHL. However, it does not follow that they therefore become unlawful combatants in a normative sense and outlaws under international law, who should be deprived of all legal rights when captured, including human rights. Such a proposition echoes the position of the Nazi regime under Hitler with regard to partisans and civilians offering armed resistance to German occupation during

---

[409] President Obama decided, however, at the start of his presidency that "Common Article 3 of the Geneva Conventions" and "all applicable laws governing the conditions of such confinement" shall apply to any individual held in custody at Guantánamo or at any facility "owned, operated, or controlled by a department or agency of the United States". See "Closure of Guantanamo Detention Facilities", executive order, 22 January 2009, section 6. In another executive order, "Ensuring Lawful Interrogations", of 22 January 2009, Obama revoked an executive order of President George W. Bush (executive order 13440, 20 July 2007) on the interrogation of prisoners. The Obama order states, in section 3, that consistent with US national laws as well as the "[UN] Convention Against Torture, Common Article 3, and other laws regulating the treatment and interrogation of individuals detained *in any armed conflict*, such persons shall in all circumstances be treated humanely and shall not be subjected to violence to life and person (including murder of all kinds, mutilation, cruel treatment, and torture), nor to outrages upon personal dignity (including humiliating and degrading treatment), whenever such individuals are in the custody or under the effective control of an officer, employee, or other agent of the United States Government or detained within a facility owned, operated, or controlled by a department or agency of the United States" (emphasis added).

[410] The concept of 'unlawful combatants' originates from a 1942 US Supreme Court case, *United States ex rel. Quirin et al. v. Cox, Provost Marshal*, 317 US [Supreme Court Report] 1, stating that agents acting covertly are subject to trial and punishment as unlawful combatants "for acts which render their belligerency unlawful". The Court furthermore accepted that unlawful combatants may be detained without trial and without the privileges usually conferred on prisoners of war. For a discussion of the practice and problems with the category of unlawful combatants, see, *e.g.*, Crawford, 2010, pp. 53–61, *supra* note 396.

World War II, and it cannot be upheld as legitimate under the UN paradigm of international law. On the contrary, the most urgent problem of current IHL seems to be the limited protection for non-state actors in classical civil wars, including the fact that their acts of killing and destruction of property are not immune from the criminal laws of the state, while government forces do enjoy such immunity.[411] Even when they are regarded as criminals, however, and even during civil wars, they should enjoy core human rights,[412] including the right to a fair trial.[413]

Nevertheless, as has been pointed out, for example, by Cassese, there may be arguments to support the view that a new type of conflict – between certain states and international organisations committed to terror as means of achieving political purposes – is *de facto* developing as a historical phenomenon[414] that can be described in empirical terms. 'Terrorism' is a commonly used term with a relatively well-defined meaning, referring usually to non-state organisations and networks of dedicated terrorists and their supporters spread over more than one country. One

---

[411] See Crawford, 2010, p. 69, *supra* note 396: "Combatant status and the attendant POW rights are categorically denied to non-State participants in non-international armed conflicts. This goes to the heart of the IHL system, the idea of who may be 'permitted' to participate in an armed conflict. Thus, the fundamental difference between international and non-international armed conflict is that there is no systematic and comprehensive protection for non-State actors participating in non-international armed conflicts".

[412] *Ibid.*, p. 155. Crawford concludes that "the development of the law of non-international armed conflicts and IHRL [international human rights law] has effectively resulted in a convergence between the protections and guarantees afforded combatants and POWs in both international and non-international armed conflicts [...] Even the one remaining element that does not enjoy universality – that of combatant immunity – is increasingly accepted, at least for political if not legal reasons[,] in the form of post-conflict amnesties and transitional justice" (p. 152).

[413] See the UN Universal Declaration of Human Rights (1948), Articles 10 and 11. Under the 1966 International Covenant on Civil and Political Rights, states are permitted in time of 'public emergency which threatens the life of the nation and the existence of which is officially proclaimed" to derogate "to the extent strictly required by the exigencies of the situation" from some of their obligations, including fair trials (Article 14). The Human Rights Committee (HRC) has indicated that the right to trial by an independent and impartial tribunal is so fundamental that it must be considered "an absolute right that may suffer no exception". HRC, *González del Río v. Peru*, Communication 263/1987, Views, UN Doc. CCPR/C/46/D/263/1987, 2 November 1992, para. 5.1.

[414] See Antonio Cassese, *International Law*, 2nd ed., Oxford University Press, Oxford, UK, 2005, p. 420.

---

may well consider it universally justified to prevent terrorist crimes and combat terrorist organisations. But it is not clear whether a state of war between a state and terrorists in foreign states can exist *de jure* under contemporary international law.[415] The support for such a proposition in the law-creating sources of international law is not strong; innovative practice by powerful states in contravention of existing norms does not in itself create new law.[416]

---

[415] *Ibid.* Cassese rejects the idea completely.

[416] Wishful legal thinking on instant customary law or strained interpretations of Security Council resolutions cannot provide a legal basis for constituting the 'global war on terror' as a recognised type of war within the UN paradigm of international law. A further discussion of the matter should consider a wide range of different international sources and viewpoints, which, however, reach beyond the scope of this book. A separate question is whether the attack on Afghanistan and its Taliban government on 7 October 2001, by the armed forces of the United States and the United Kingdom, in cooperation with the Afghan United Front (Northern Alliance), was authorised by the UN Security Council in advance or after the fact. The answer to that is not obvious based on the language of the Security Council resolutions. On the one hand, Resolution 1377 (2001) clearly recognised that "acts of international terrorism constitute one of the most serious threats to international peace and security in the twenty-first century" and that such acts are "contrary to the purposes and principles of the Charter of the United Nations". The 9/11 terrorist attacks were condemned "in the strongest terms" the day after, and the Security Council expressed, in Resolution 1368 (2001), "its readiness to take all necessary steps to respond to the terrorist attacks". In Resolution 1373 (2001), it also reaffirmed "the need to combat by all means, in accordance with the Charter of the United Nations, threats to international peace and security caused by terrorist acts" and enacted a number of norms binding on all states for this purpose. On the other hand, the Security Council resolutions enacted before 7 October 2001 did not explicitly authorise any war against Afghanistan. Nevertheless, the Security Council on 14 November 2001 supported "international efforts to root out terrorism" and condemned "the Taliban for allowing Afghanistan to be used as a base for the export of terrorism by the Al-Qaida network and other terrorist groups and for providing safe haven to Usama Bin Laden, Al-Qaida and others associated with them, and in this context supporting the efforts of the Afghan people to replace the Taliban regime". No critique, explicit authorisation, or even mention of the attack by the US and UK armed forces was made, an absurdity that can presumably only be explained by reference to the veto powers of the two attacking states combined with the opposition by other states to providing explicit UN authorisation of the war. In conclusion, the attack on Afghanistan on 7 October 2001 was at best implicitly accepted *ex post facto* by the UN Security Council, and the legality of the attack remains unclear. It seems difficult to justify the attack on Afghanistan and the subsequent invasion as an act of self-defence within the framework of a classic international war. Most likely, the manifest attack constituted from the start an international war, whether authorised by the UN or not.

Should this type of war at some point form part of international law, the presumption would be that the most extensive list of normative war crimes protections should apply as a matter of principle.[417] A practical legal problem, however, would be to determine the relevant battlefields, since war under international law has traditionally been linked to specific geographic locations.[418] An absolute precondition for accepting war on terror as a separate kind of war under the UN paradigm of international law would be explicit UN Security Council authorisation and a formal

---

[417] Although the global war on terror since 2001 has not been a war as such in legal terms, it has partly been fought in war-torn countries, *inter alia*, in Afghanistan. Many acts by a wide range of different actors may thus have amounted to war crimes and other offences under international law. Even if we assume that the attack on Afghanistan by US and UK forces on 7 October 2001 did not initially rise to the level of an international war (see the preceding footnote), one can argue that the civil war between the Taliban insurgents, with the support of their foreign affiliates, and the Karzai regime, assisted by NATO countries, soon became internationalised. This process arguably began with the US-initiated 'Operation Enduring Freedom' in 2001, whose main purpose was to seek out and destroy al-Qaeda fighters and their leaders and affiliates and to reconstruct the government and society of Afghanistan. The military targets included initially the Afghan (Taliban) government, believed to be cooperating with al-Qaeda and shielding its leaders, including Usama bin Laden. The major international interference in the Afghan civil war, including the 'overall control' of the Afghan government and governmental forces by NATO, almost immediately transformed (internationalised) it into a continuous international armed conflict. Taliban and foreign voluntary fighters taking direct part in concrete armed conflicts in support of the Taliban, whether associated with al-Qaeda or not, must therefore be considered combatants under international law and thus legitimate enemy targets of the current Afghan regime and its partners in the war against Taliban. Even if it should wrongfully be regarded as a non-international armed conflict, international law is still relevant, as previously noted. The war on terror doctrine has to some extent, it seems, relied on fictions of international lawlessness. For an account of the consequences for prisoners, the rule of law, and criminal liability, see M. Cherif Bassiouni, *The Institutionalization of Torture by the Bush Administration: Is Anyone Responsible?*, Intersentia, Mortsel, Belgium, 2010. In 2011, in a 52-page document on national security posted on the website of the US White House, the concept of a war on terror does not appear ("National Security Strategy", May 2010). On the other hand, the Obama administration has not clearly distanced itself from the notion that the United States *in legal terms* is engaged in a global war with al-Qaeda, the Taliban, and associated forces.

[418] See Laurie R. Blank, "Where Is the Battlefield in the 'War on Terror'? The Need for a Workable Framework", in *Jurist Legal News and Research*, Forum, 1 December 2010, available at http://jurist.org/forum/2010/12/where-is-the-battlefield-in-the-war-on-terror-the-need-for-a-workable-framework.php, last accessed 20 June 2011. Even during the 'total war' of World War II, the Allied forces were not entitled to attack a neutral state for strategic or tactical reasons.

mandate, including clarification of the legitimate battlefields and legal consequences for the combatants and others under international law. If such action were taken, the war on terror doctrine could possibly be conceived as a new subclass of 'universally authorised war' in the scheme above, allowing for a 'manifest armed intervention in a state authorised by the UN Security Council for the purpose of … [c] *preventing terrorist crimes and combating international terrorist networks in the serious interest of international peace and security'*.

4.9.2.4. The Crime Status of Terrorism

An alternative approach to construing the international war on terror as a fifth type of war may be to consider 'terrorist crimes' as a separate category of 'international crimes' (see category F in the list below). Crimes characterised as terrorism, just like genocide and crimes against humanity, can be committed in times of peace or times of war. Precisely how to characterise and identify such crimes, however, is much disputed.[419] Different criteria have been used, including an emphasis on the distinct violent *acts of terrorism*, the preferred approach under the suppression treaties,[420] or, alternatively, on the *perpetrators* of such crimes (states, non-state actors, terrorist organisations), or on the *specific intent and purpose* which characterises terrorism.

In contrast to the core crimes, there is no general agreement as to the legal status of these crimes under international law,[421] that is, whether

---

[419] For an extensive discussion of the definition of terrorism under international law, see Ben Saul, *Defining Terrorism in International Law*, Oxford University Press, Oxford, UK, 2006.

[420] The UN Security Council's Counter-Terrorism Committee lists 16 legally binding United Nations instruments on its home page. They include, *inter alia*, the 2005 International Convention for the Suppression of Acts of Nuclear Terrorism; 1999 International Convention for the Suppression of the Financing of Terrorism; 1997 International Convention for the Suppression of Terrorist Bombings; 1988 Convention for the Suppression of Unlawful Acts Against the Safety of Marine Navigation and its 2005 Protocol; 1979 Convention on the Physical Protection of Nuclear Material; 1979 International Convention Against the Taking of Hostages; 1973 Convention on the Prevention and Punishment of Crimes against Internationally Protected Persons, including Diplomatic Agents; 1971 Convention for the Suppression of Unlawful Acts against the Safety of Civil Aviation; 1970 Convention for the Suppression of Unlawful Seizure of Aircraft; and 1963 Convention on Offences and Certain Other Acts Committed on Board Aircraft.

[421] See sections 4.4.–4.5. in this chapter.

---

they are international crimes for which the perpetrators incur direct liability under international law.[422] Acts of terrorism thus far have not figured as crimes in the statutes of international courts, with the exceptions of the Special Court for Sierra Leone (SCSL) and the Special Tribunal for Lebanon (STL).[423] It follows from Article 3(d) of the SCSL statute that the SCSL has the power to prosecute persons who committed or ordered the commission of acts of terrorism amounting to serious violations of Common Article 3 of the Geneva Conventions.[424] The STL also has jurisdiction with respect to terrorism under the Lebanese Criminal Code (see Article 2(a) of the STL statute). The "prosecution and punishment of acts of terrorism" in the latter case, it can be argued, derived from the consent of the concerned state and was thus not independent from such state consent, so that it would not meet condition 5 of the general criteria for international crimes laid out in the previous section.[425] The STL statute therefore cannot be used as conclusive evidence of an 'upgraded' legal status of terrorist crimes under international law. However, the Appeals Chamber has rendered a recent opinion on the issue, discussing the notion of terrorism in international law generally and concluding that the crime of terrorism today exists under customary international law.[426]

The language of the Security Council is also noteworthy insofar as it refers to "the demand of the Lebanese people that all those responsible for the terrorist bombing that killed former Lebanese Prime Minister Rafiq Hariri and others be identified and brought to justice"[427] and calls for the establishment of "a tribunal of an international character to try all those who are found responsible for the terrorist crime".[428] When this is

---

[422] See section 4.9.1. in this chapter on the legal consequences of international crimes.

[423] See section 4.3. in this chapter.

[424] The SCSL has charged and upheld charges against former president Charles Taylor for acts of terrorism. See, *e.g.*, SCSL, *The Prosecutor against Charles G. Taylor*, Case No. SCSL-03-01-T, Prosecution Final Trial Brief, 8 April 2011, paras. 702–754.

[425] See section 4.9.2. in this chapter.

[426] See STL Appeals Chamber, *Interlocutory Decision on the Applicable Law: Terrorism, Conspiracy, Homicide, Perpetration, Cumulative Charging*, STL-11-01/I/AC/R176bis, Decision of 16 February 2011, para. 83–113.

[427] UN Security Council Resolution 1664 (2006), *supra* note 24.

[428] UN Security Council Resolution 1757 (2007), "Security Council Authorizes Establishment of Special Tribunal to Try Suspects in Assassination of Rafiq Hariri", Attachment: "Statute of the Special Tribunal for Lebanon" (preamble).

read in conjunction with other Security Council resolutions on terrorism and the establishment and continuous work of the Security Council's Counter-Terrorism Committee, it is clear that grave acts of terrorism manifestly violate fundamental universal values and peace and security interests (condition 1), are universally considered punishable due to their inherent gravity (condition 2), and are repeatedly recognised as a matter of serious international concern (condition 3), and that many of the relevant norms are also proscribed in treaties and binding Security Council resolutions (condition 4). In addition, as indicated by the prominence of the war on terror and concerted international efforts to combat terrorism, including criminal legislation at multiple levels,[429] there is clearly a strong determination of the whole international community to deal effectively with such crimes.

This was reaffirmed in Security Council Resolution 1963 of 20 December 2010, which included a statement in the first paragraph that arguably can be interpreted as an expression of intent to constitute acts of terrorism as 'international crimes':

> [The Security Council reaffirms that] terrorism in all forms and manifestations constitutes one of the most serious threats to international peace and security and that any acts of terrorism are criminal and unjustifiable regardless of their motivations, whenever and by whomsoever committed and remaining determined to contribute further to enhancing the effectiveness of the overall effort to fight this scourge on a global level, […].[430]

By claiming that terrorism in all forms constitutes "one of the most serious threats to international peace and security and that any acts of terrorism are criminal", the Security Council places terrorism high in the hierarchy of crime categories of serious international concern, and firmly within the scope of crimes against the peace and security of mankind. In

---

[429] See, *e.g.*, Erling Johannes Husabø and Ingvild Bruce, *Fighting Terrorism through Multilevel Criminal Legislation: Security Council Resolution 1373, the EU Framework Decision on Combating Terrorism and their Implementation in Nordic, Dutch and German Criminal Law*, Martinus Nijhoff/Brill, Leiden, Netherlands, 2009, p. 35. The authors discuss in particular the legally binding UN Security Council Resolution 1373 (2001), the EU Framework Decision on combating terrorism (2002), and their implementation in certain countries.

[430] UN Security Council Resolution 1963 (2010).

addition, the resolution speaks of terrorism "in all forms". It would seem clear, then, that grave acts of terrorism must be international crimes.

The best argument for excluding terrorism from the status of international crimes has been the lack of a common definition of terrorism under general international law.[431] This reason might not be decisive, given that the lack of a legally binding comprehensive universal definition of aggression did not bar the existence of the crime of aggression as an international crime *lex lata*, long before the consensus reached at the ICC Review Conference in 2010 on a precise definition of aggression.[432]

Nevertheless, the analogy is not perfect. The crime of aggression, if not a detailed definition of the crime, was already authoritatively included in the Nuremberg Charter (as 'crimes against peace'), and it was confirmed and applied by the Nuremberg Tribunal in 1946. It formed part of the Nuremberg Principles adopted by the UN, and it was repeatedly accepted as part of international law by the ILC.[433] Relevant acts of aggression were comprehensively defined in a General Assembly resolution in 1974.[434]

In contrast, Security Council Resolution 1963 (2010) has significant weaknesses as a legal platform for definition of terrorism. On its face, the statement puts all acts of terrorism on an equal footing ("any acts of terrorism are criminal"), regardless of who the perpetrators are ("by whomsoever committed") or their motives. It is significant that the formulation does not confine acts of terrorism to specific actors, although most commonly it is limited to non-state actors, including, especially, proclaimed or alleged terrorist organisations. In addition, the resolution leaves several key issues unresolved: it does not define what characterises terrorism, it does not provide a gravity threshold for terrorist crimes, and it does not provide a comprehensive list of relevant terrorist acts. It is thus

---

[431] See Saul, 2006, p. 270, *supra* note 419, concluding that it is premature to accept the argument "that terrorism is a customary international crime", since the requirement of a fixed, common definition under customary law is not met. The question remains, however, whether that is a valid ground for denying the legal status of 'international crimes' to all terrorist crimes.

[432] See section 4.7.2. in this chapter.

[433] See section 4.5. in this chapter.

[434] See UN General Assembly Resolution 3314 (XXIX) of 14 December 1974, which is mentioned explicitly in the amended ICC Rome Statute, Article 8 (2) *bis*.

much too vague to constitute an effective proscriptive norm, as required by condition 4.

The suppression treaties partially fill this gap with respect to a list of acts, although the list of acts included in the universal treaties seems short and the acts overly specific: nuclear terrorism, financing of terrorism, terrorist bombings, acts against the safety of maritime navigation, acts committed on board aircraft, acts against the safety of civil aviation, acts of violence at airports serving civil aviation, seizure of aircraft, taking of hostages, and crimes against internationally protected persons. One could possibly conclude on this basis that a core of terrorist acts, at least, do fulfil the requirement of condition 4.

The EU has taken another approach through the EU Council Framework Decision on Terrorism in 2002. This is formulated in broader terms, including, *inter alia*, attacks on a person's life which may cause death, attack upon the physical integrity of a person, kidnapping or hostage taking and extensive destruction to a government or public facility, a transport system, or an infrastructure facility,[435] as well as a number of other acts.[436] It also includes the crime of threatening to commit any of the listed acts.[437] This sensible approach raises the question of how the relevant acts of terrorist crimes are different from comparable acts of crimes against humanity or war crimes, although there may be some acts which would be specific only to terrorism.

The Security Council, in Resolution 1566 (2004), took another approach, reserving terrorism for

> criminal acts, including against civilians, committed with intent to cause death or serious bodily injury, or taking of hostages, with the purpose to provoke a state of terror [...] *which constitute offences within the scope of and as defined in the international conventions and protocols relating to terrorism.*[438]

---

[435] See Council of the European Union, "Council Framework Decision of 13 June 2002 on combating terrorism", 2002/475/JHA, in *Official Journal of the European Communities*, Article 1(1)(a) to (d).

[436] See *ibid.*, Article 1(1)(e) to (h) on seizure of public or goods transport, weapons, dangerous substances, fires, floods, or explosions, and supply of water, power, or other natural resources necessary for human life.

[437] *Ibid.*, Article 1(1)(i).

[438] See UN Security Council Resolution 1566 (2004), para. 3, emphasis added.

However, when this is read in conjunction with later resolutions, *inter alia* Resolution 1963 (2010), it seems that the international community also accepted that the concept of terrorism under international law cannot be arbitrarily limited to some specific acts, while other acts bearing the same characteristics and endangering human life and integrity just as much are deemed legally irrelevant. Even if other acts might be added later, however, there is no reason that relevant types of terrorist crimes to be constituted as 'terrorist crimes' should not be first identified through descriptions of the unlawful acts, which, depending on reaching a gravity threshold, might then be identified as international crimes.

Accordingly, the tentative list of terrorist acts included in the consolidated list of international crimes below includes not only those acts of terrorism within the scope of international conventions and protocols relating to terrorism, but also others whose status may be uncertain. In either case, the relevant acts only qualify as terrorist crimes when they meet the necessity gravity threshold as well as satisfy the conditions for defining terrorism.

Since a gravity clause according to our theory is inherent in all international crimes, there should be no problem in principle in applying this requirement to possible terrorist crimes as well. The key question is how to identify and formulate such a gravity clause, as well as, of course, how to define what is meant by terrorism itself as a crime category. A list of acts presumed to be acts of terrorism is not sufficient, since many of those same acts could also be included in other crime categories, such as genocide, crimes against humanity, or war crimes. The definition first set forth by the UN General Assembly in 1994 seems to be a natural starting point:

> All acts, methods and practices of terrorism [...] [are] criminal and unjustifiable, wherever and by whomever committed [...]. [They] constitute a grave violation of the purposes and principles of the United Nations, which may pose a threat to international peace and security, jeopardize friendly relations among States, hinder international cooperation and aim at the destruction of human rights, fundamental freedoms and democratic bases of society [...]. [They] are] criminal acts intended or calculated to provoke a state of terror in the general public, a group of persons or particular persons for political purposes [and] are in any circumstances unjustifiable, whatever the considerations of a political,

philosophical, racial, ethnic, religious or any other nature that may be invoked to justify them [...].[439]

It clarifies that acts of terrorism are criminal acts intended to provoke a state of terror in the general public, a group of persons, or particular persons for a political purpose, typically aimed at the destruction of the fundamental bases of society, namely freedoms, human rights, and democracy. The core part of this definition has been repeated annually in General Assembly resolutions, referred to by the Security Council,[440] and adopted in legal theory as an acceptable definition under international law.[441] The proposition that a core definition can be sufficiently identified can also draw support from the 1999 International Convention for the Suppression of the Financing of Terrorism. Article 2 explains the acts whose financing shall be prohibited by referring to a list of nine treaties annexed[442] and by providing a general definition of other relevant acts:

> Any other act intended to cause death or serious bodily injury to a civilian, or to any other person not taking an active part in the hostilities in a situation of armed conflict, when the purpose of such act, by its nature or context, is to intimidate a population, or to compel a government or an international organization to do so or to abstain from doing any act.[443]

The general part of this definition is in many respect similar to the GA definition, although there are differences as well. It more clearly emphasises that acts of terrorism can also take place against civilians during armed conflict, a conclusion for which there is precedent in IHL[444] and in international court jurisprudence.[445] While the purposes of the acts

---

[439] See UN General Assembly, "Declaration on Measures to Eliminate International Terrorism", A/Res/49/60, 9 December 1994, Annex.

[440] See UN Security Council Resolution 1269 (1999) and Resolution 1373 (2001).

[441] See Husabø and Bruce, 2009, p. 19 (with further references), *supra* note 429.

[442] See UN General Assembly, "International Convention for the Suppression of the Financing of Terrorism" (1999), Article 2(1)(a) and Annex.

[443] *Ibid.*, Article 2(1)(b).

[444] See Saul, 2006, pp. 271–313, *supra* note 419, examining the emergence of the prohibition of terrorism in armed conflict, grounded in the first and second world wars and the interwar period, as well as in modern humanitarian law developed since 1945.

[445] Although terrorism was not established as a distinct crime in the Nuremberg Charter, many references to terrorism can be found both in the Nuremberg Indictment and in the Judgment itself. To take but one example, the Indictment states, "Throughout the

are more clearly formulated in this definition, the specific intent of provoking a state of terror or extreme fear is less explicit in this text, which refers only to "intimidat[ing] a population". The intent to "provoke a state of terror", however, can be found in Security Council resolution 1566 (2004).[446] The 2002 EU Framework Decision contains a similar definition with an implicit gravity clause.[447]

In conclusion, there is a need for an authoritative formulation of the gravity clause pertaining to terrorist crimes. However, that does not mean that grave acts of terrorism are not already international crimes under current international law. Just as international crimes of genocide existed before the Genocide Convention, as recognised in the Genocide Convention itself,[448] and just as international crimes of aggression existed before the 2010 Review Conference, many grave acts of terrorism must

---

period of their occupation of territories overrun by their armed forces the defendants, *for the purpose of terrorizing the inhabitants*, murdered and tortured civilians, and ill-treated them, and imprisoned them without legal process" (emphasis added). IMT, *Trial of the Major War Criminals*, 1947, vol. I, p. 43, *supra* note 22, 'Count Three on War Crimes', (A) 'Murder and Ill-treatment of Civilian Population of and in Occupied Territory and on the High Seas'. The term was also frequently employed in some of the subsequent Nuremberg cases, *e.g.*, "The Hostage Case" (*supra* note 277), and in a few war crimes cases before national courts in the aftermath of the war (see Saul, 2006, pp. 287–289, *supra* note 419). On the other hand, the concept, it seems, has more often than not been used to assist in the application of other provisions not directly concerned with terrorism as discrete crime. An important case is ICTY Trial Chamber, *Prosecutor v. Stanislav Galić*, IT-98-29-T, Judgment of December 2003. Here the ICTY concluded that 'a crime of terror against the civilian population' had been committed at Sarajevo, based on the Geneva Conventions, Protocol I, Article 51. It held that the distinctive feature of the crime of terror is "the primary purpose of spreading terror" (para. 597), thus regarding terror as a crime of specific intent. Terror was considered equivalent to 'extreme fear'; see para. 137 of the case on reference.

[446] See UN Security Council Resolution 1566 (2004), para. 3: "criminal acts [...] committed with intent to cause death or serious bodily injury [...] with the purpose to provoke a state of terror".

[447] See Council of the European Union, 2002, Article 1(1), *supra* note 435: "[I]ntentional acts [...] which, given their nature or context, may seriously damage a country or an organisation where committed with the aim of: [...] seriously intimidating a population [...] unduly compelling a Government or international organisation to perform or abstain from performing any act, or [...] seriously destabilising or destroying the fundamental political, constitutional, economic or social structures of a country or an international organisation".

[448] See the 1948 Geneva Convention, Article 1 and preamble, both *confirming* that genocide "is a crime under international law".

---

already be considered international crimes *lex lata*. The legal basis depends on a combination of several law-creating sources: treaties on the suppression of specific acts of terrorism, humanitarian law, general principles of law, and a contextual interpretation of the binding Security Council Resolution 1373 (2001).[449] Given these multiple sources, the existence of the proscriptive norm seems firmly grounded in ICL, although the final evidence leading to a definitive conclusion might still be lacking. That evidence could emerge in a number of different ways in the coming years. Possibly the ongoing work on a UN framework convention on terrorism may result in a commonly accepted, generally binding definition or gravity clause. Terrorist crimes may be incorporated into the ICC Rome Statute. Alternatively, the Security Council by resolution, or the international community by treaty, may establish an international court with statutory jurisdiction over terrorist crimes. Any of these options might establish definitely that criminal liability under international law and the lawful prosecution of terrorist crimes do not depend on the consent of a concerned state (condition 5), with all the legal consequences that may entail.[450]

In the consolidated list of international crimes below, the gravity clause offered for crimes of terrorism may be disputable, but it is formulated as far as possible in line with international law and consistent with the analysis undertaken in this book.

4.9.2.5. A Brief Note on the Status of Other Possible Crimes under International Law

The discussion of the crime status of terrorism serves to illustrate that whole crime categories may have an uncertain legal status under international law. A detailed analysis of other possible crime categories in the abstract is not necessary for our purpose here. However, it can be argued that since 'crime categories' are often not separated from 'crime types' in ICL analysis, this complicates comparison of different opinions by different analysts, for instance with regard to the crime (or crimes) of 'piracy'. Other possible crime categories may not have been sufficiently discussed from the perspective of *lex ferenda*. One such case could arguably be possible 'crimes of group destruction', relating to intended

---

[449] See Chapter 3, section 3.3.6.
[450] See section 4.9.2. in this chapter.

destruction of any identifiable civilian group (as opposed to a military or armed group) that is not encompassed by the Genocide Convention. The underlying crimes of group destruction could be formulated as more or less identical to the underlying crimes of the Genocide Convention, but they should preferably be stated in more appropriate language related to underlying crimes of other crime categories within ICL that may seem especially relevant. For instance, widespread or large-scale destruction of infrastructure, significant buildings, or monuments ought to be included as an underlying crime, because experience has shown that perpretrators targeting a particular civilian group (including ethnic or religious groups) may also seek to undermine the group's existence by destroying such objects.

The central question is whether the theory of implicit gravity clauses specific to each crime category, and the proposed legal definition of international crimes containing the previously noted five conditions, may lead to concrete results. The list of international crimes compiled by the author below may indicate only the potential in that regard, with respect to both the clarification of current ICL and future legal developments. Instead of further theoretical elaboration, this chapter now moves straight on to the list.

4.9.3. Consolidated List of International Crimes

The following list encompasses three classes of universal crimes, 10 universal crime categories, and 150 universal crime types. The classes of crimes are identified with Roman numerals (I, II, III) and the crime categories with capital letters (A, B, C). The individual crime types are numbered sequentially (1, 2, 3).

For each crime category, a proposed gravity clause, to be applied to all crime types in the category, immediately follows the name of the crime category. The formulations of the gravity clauses for the class of core international crimes (I) closely follow the Rome Statute with respect to crimes of aggression, genocide, crimes against humanity, and war crimes. The other gravity clauses presently lack authoritative formulations in international law, but they are formulated as far as possible in compliance with international law and consistent with the analysis undertaken in this book. The class of other international crimes against the peace and security of mankind (II) has three crime categories: crimes against the United Nations and other internationally protected persons, terrorist crimes, and crimes of group destruction not encompassed by the Genocide Convention. Finally, the class of international crimes that are not dependent on the existence of threats to international peace and security (III) also has three categories: grave piracy crimes, grave trafficking crimes, and excessive use and abuse of authorised power. These latter crimes may, depending on the concrete circumstances, also constitute a threat to international peace and security, but in many such cases the threat is as best indirect and the risk of serious escalation is low. But when the gravity of the crimes reaches a certain level, they constitute serious threats to universal values, human rights, or community interests supposed to be protected and enforced within the UN paradigm of international law.

The list includes both actual and potential international crimes, that is, international crimes *lex lata* and *lex ferenda*. The international crimes *lex lata*, moreover, include both those with fully confirmed legal status and those with uncertain legal status. Crime types with uncertain status as international crimes *lex lata* are marked with one asterisk (*), while those that are clearly still *lex ferenda* are marked with two asterisks (**).

References to the legal bases for any crime type clearly having *lex lata* status are given in parentheses in abbreviated form: for example, ICC 8.2.a refers to Article 8, paragraph 2, sub-paragraph (a) of the Rome Statute. In some cases, such references to possible legal bases are also given for crime types with uncertain *lex lata* status. Many of the crime types may have more than one established legal basis in the law-creating sources of international law.[451] Other crimes may only be considered to reach the threshold of a legal basis in international law when several legal bases are considered in conjunction,[452] or must be considered just potential crimes under current ICL. In the list only one source is usually indicated for each crime. Customary international law (CIL) is used as the common reference when the legal status of the crime type is debatable. No legal basis is provided with respect to crimes *lex ferenda*. The crimes included as *lex ferenda* typically fulfil the first two conditions of the five necessary and sufficient conditions *lex lata*, and maybe one or two of the other three conditions as well. The main point is that they concern conduct which (1) manifestly violates a fundamental universal value or

---

[451] See Chapter 3, section 3.3.
[452] On this possibility, see Chapter 3, section 3.3.6.

interest, and (2) is universally regarded as punishable due to its inherent gravity; thus they are potential international crimes where their possible legal status depends on the developments of international law. Of the 150 universal crime types on the list, 15 are considered crimes *lex ferenda*. With regard to all such underlying issues, however, the list should be considered preliminary and incomplete.

Hence the international crimes are enumerated tentatively in accordance with the conditions set forth in section 4.9.1., taking into account the explanatory remarks in section 4.9.2. Each crime type must be understood in the context of the particular gravity clause attached to it, as noted in the general criteria following each crime category (aggression, genocide, and so on). These conditions apply to each type within the category. Thus a full definition of Type 1 would be 'Invasion or attack by armed forces of another state's territory which constitutes a manifest violation of the UN Charter by the use of armed force against the sovereignty, territorial integrity, or political independence of another state'. Type 11 would be 'Killing with intent to destroy, in whole or in part, a national, ethnical, racial or religious group, as such'. Type 19 would be 'Murder (killing) when committed as part of a widespread or systematic attack directed against any civilian population, with knowledge of the attack'. And Type 36 would be 'Wilful killing of protected persons when constituting a grave breach of the Geneva Conventions or other serious violation of the laws and customs of international or non-international armed conflicts'.

International Crime Types and Potential International Crime Types

I) Core International Crimes

A) Crimes of aggression

(When constituting manifest violations of the UN Charter by the use of armed force against the sovereignty, territorial integrity, or political independence of another state)

1) Invasion or attack by armed forces of another state's territory (ICC 8 *bis* 2.a)

2) Military occupation resulting from invasion or attack (ICC 8 *bis* 2.a)

3) Annexation of territory by the use of force (ICC 8 *bis* 2.a)

4) Bombardment or the use of any weapons against another state (ICC 8 *bis* 2.b)

5) Blockade of the ports or coasts of another state (ICC 8 *bis* 2.c)

6) Attack on the land, sea, or air forces of another state (ICC 8 *bis* 2.d)

7) Attack on the marine and air fleets of another state (ICC 8 *bis* 2.d)

8) Use of armed forces within another state in breach of agreement (ICC 8 *bis* 2.e)

9) Allowing territory to be used for an act of aggression by a third state (ICC 8 *bis* 2.f)

10) Sending of armed bands, groups, irregulars, or mercenaries which carry out acts of armed force against another state amounting to an act of aggression (ICC 8 *bis* 2.g)

B) Crimes of genocide

(When committed with intent to destroy, in whole or in part, a national, ethnical, racial or religious group, as such)

11) Killing (ICC 6.a)

12) Causing serious bodily or mental harm (ICC 6.b)

13) Deliberately inflicting conditions of life calculated to physically destroy a group in whole or in part (ICC 6.c)

14) Imposing measures intended to prevent birth (ICC 6.d)

15) Forcibly transferring children of one group to another group (ICC 6.e)

16) Conspiracy to commit genocide (ICC 6) (Genocide Convention III.b)

17) Direct and public incitement to commit genocide (ICC 6) (Genocide Convention III.c)

18) Attempt to commit genocide (ICC 6) (Genocide Convention III.d)

C) Crimes against humanity

(When committed as part of a widespread or systematic attack directed against any civilian population, with knowledge of the attack)

19) Murder (ICC 7.1.a)

20) Extermination (ICC 7.1.b)

21) Enslavement (ICC 7.1.c)

22) Deportation or forcible transfer of population (ICC 7.1.d)

23) Imprisonment or other severe deprivation of liberty (ICC 7.1.e)

24) Torture (ICC 7.1.f)

25) Rape (ICC 7.1.g)

26) Sexual slavery (ICC 7.1.g)

27) Enforced prostitution (ICC 7.1.g)

28) Forced marriage* (CIL)

29) Forced pregnancy (ICC 7.1.g)

30) Enforced sterilization (ICC 7.1.g)

31) Any other form of grave sexual violence (see crimes 25–29) (ICC 7.1.g)

32) Enforced disappearance of persons (ICC 7.1.i)

33) Other grave inhumane acts (see crimes 19–31) (ICC 7.1.k)

34) Persecution, in the aggravated form of an intentional and severe deprivation of fundamental rights of any identifiable group on a universally impermissible ground (ICC 7.1.h)

35) Apartheid, in the aggravated form of grave inhumane acts (see crimes 19–33) committed in the context of an institutionalised regime of systematic oppression and domination

by one racial group over any other racial group or groups with the intention of maintaining that regime (ICC 7.1.j)

D) War crimes

(When committed in the context of war, in particular when committed as part of a plan or policy or as part of a large-scale commission of such crimes, and constituting grave breaches of the Geneva Conventions or other serious violations of the laws and customs of international or non-international armed conflicts)

a) Grave violations of personal integrity, rights, and freedoms

36) Wilful killing of protected persons (ICC 8.2.a.i)

37) Killing or wounding a combatant who has surrendered or has no means of defence (ICC 8.2.b.vi)

38) Killing or wounding treacherously individuals belonging to the hostile nation or army (ICC 8.2.b.xi)

39) Torture (ICC 8.2.a.ii)

40) Inhuman treatment (ICC 8.2.a.ii)

41) Rape (ICC 8.2.b.xxii)

42) Sexual slavery (ICC 8.2.b.xxii)

43) Enforced prostitution (ICC 8.2.b.xxii)

44) Forced pregnancy (ICC 8.2.b.xxii)

45) Enforced sterilization (ICC 8.2.b.xxii)

46) Any other form of grave sexual violence (ICC 8.2.b.xxii)

47) Subjecting persons to physical mutilation (ICC 8.2.b.x)

48) Biological experiments on human beings (ICC 8.2.a.ii)

49) Subjecting persons to unjustified medical or scientific experiments which cause death or serious danger to health (ICC 8.2.b.x)

50) Wilfully causing great suffering or serious injury to protected persons (ICC 8.2.a.iii)

51) Outrages upon personal dignity, in particular humiliating and degrading treatment (ICC 8.2.b.xxi)

52) Denial of fair and regular trial to a prisoner of war or other protected person (ICC 8.2.a.vi)

53) Denial of rights in a court of law of the nationals of the hostile party (ICC 8.2.b.xiv)

54) Unlawful confinement of people (ICC 8.2.a.vii)

55) Conscripting or enlisting children under the age of 15 years into armed forces or groups using them to participate actively in hostilities (ICC 8.2.b.xxv, ICC 8.2.e.vii)

56) Compelling nationals of the hostile party to take part in the operations of war against their own country (ICC 8.2.b.xv)

57) Forced military recruitment of prisoners of war or other protected persons (ICC 8.2.a.v)

58) Unlawful deportation of people (ICC 8.2.a.vii)

59) Unlawful transfer of people (ICC 8.2.a.vii)

60) Transfer by an occupying power of parts of its own population into occupied territory (ICC 8.2.b.viii)

61) Deportation or transfer of all or parts of the population of the occupied territory within or outside this territory (ICC 8.2.b.vii)

b) *Excessive use and abuse of war power*

62) Intentional attack against the civilian population as such (ICC 8.2.b.i)

63) Intentional attack against individual civilians not taking direct part in hostilities (ICC 8.2.b.i)

64) Intentional attack against civilian objects which are not military objectives (ICC 8.2.b.ii)

65) Intentional attack against hospitals and places where sick and wounded are collected (ICC 8.2.b.ix)

66) Intentional attack that will cause incidental loss of life or injury to civilians (ICC 8.2.b.iv)

67) Intentional starvation of civilians as a method of warfare (ICC 8.2.b.xxv)

68) Declaring that no quarter will be given (ICC 8.2.b.xii)

69) Attack or bombardment of places which are undefended and not military objectives (ICC 8.2.b.v)

70) Intentional attack that will cause incidental damage to civilian objects (ICC 8.2.b.iv)

71) Intentional attack that will cause incidental widespread, long-term, and severe damage to the natural environment not proportional to military advantage anticipated (ICC 8.2.b.iv)

72) Unjustified intentional attack against protected buildings or monuments (ICC 8.2.b.ix)

73) Unjustified destruction or seizing of the enemy's property (ICC 8.2.b.xiii)

74) Unjustified extensive destruction and/or appropriation of property (ICC 8.2.a.iv)

75) Pillaging a town or place, even when taken by assault (ICC 8.2.b.xvi)

c) *Excessive use and abuse of prohibited weapons or the means of war*

76) Employing poison or poisoned weapons (ICC 8.2.b.xvii)

77) Employing asphyxiating, poisonous, or other gasses, and all analogous liquids, materials, or devices (ICC 8.2.b.xviii)

78) Employing bullets which expand or flatten easily in the human body (ICC 8.2.b.xix)

79) Employing weapons, projectiles, and materials and methods of a nature causing superfluous injury or unnecessary suffering (ICC 8.2.b.xx)

80) Taking of hostages (ICC 8.2.a.viii)

81) Utilizing a civilian or other protected person as a human shield to render certain points, areas, or military forces immune from military operations (ICC 8.2.b.xxiii)

82) Improper use of a flag, emblems, or uniform of the enemy, resulting in death or personal injury (ICC 8.2.b.vii)

83) Recruitment, use, financing, and training of mercenaries**

d) *Attack on protected international personnel or materials*

84) Intentional attack against personnel or materials involved in humanitarian assistance or peacekeeping missions in accordance with the UN Charter (ICC 8.2.b.iii)

85) Intentional attack against buildings, material, medical units and transport, or personnel using the distinctive emblems of

the Geneva Conventions in conformity with international law (ICC 8.2.b.xxiv)

II) Other International Crimes against the Peace and Security of Mankind

E) Crimes against the United Nations and internationally protected persons

(When constituting serious acts of violence or serious threats)

86) Intentional attack against UN or associated personnel or materials involved in humanitarian assistance or peacekeeping missions in accordance with the UN Charter* (see ILC 1996 Draft Code, Article 19; see the similar crime type 84 and ICC 8.2.b.iii with regard to such attack in war)

87) Intentional attack against UN buildings, material, medical units and transport, or personnel using the distinctive emblems of the United Nations in conformity with international law* (see ILC 1996 Draft Code, Article 19; see the similar crime type 85 and ICC 8.2.b.xxiv with regard to such attack in war)

88) Intentional attack against other internationally protected persons* (CIL)

89) Threats against the United Nations, judges at international courts, and diplomats**

F) Terrorist crimes

(When intended or calculated to provoke a state of terror in the general public, a group of persons, particular individuals, or persons acting in an official capacity, regardless of the political, military, or any other motivation invoked to justify the crime)

90) Bombing or murder of civilians* (CIL)

91) Murder of public servants* (CIL)

92) Assassination of heads of state or political leaders* (CIL)

93) Extermination of a group* (CIL)

94) Execution of prisoners as reprisals* (CIL)

95) Execution of prisoners without a fair trial* (CIL)

96) Murder of hostages* (CIL)

97) Enforced disappearance of persons* (CIL)

98) Enslavement* (CIL)

99) Deportation or forcible transfer of a population* (CIL)

100) Imprisonment or other severe deprivation of liberty* (CIL)

101) Torture* (CIL)

102) Rape* (CIL)

103) Sexual slavery* (CIL)

104) Enforced prostitution* (CIL)

105) Forced pregnancy* (CIL)

106) Enforced sterilization* (CIL)

107) Any other form of grave sexual violence* (CIL)

108) Other inhumane or degrading acts* (CIL)

109) Persecution of any targeted group* (CIL)

110) Taking of hostages* (CIL)

111) Abduction of UN personnel, diplomats, or other protected personnel* (CIL)

112) Hijacking of ship, aircraft, or other means of public or goods transportation* (CIL)

113) Use of civilian aircraft or other means of public or goods transportation as a weapon* (CIL)

114) Destruction of aircraft or other means of public transportation* (CIL)

115) Destruction of infrastructure, significant buildings, or monuments* (CIL)

116) Bombing of embassies* (CIL)

117) Employment of poison, gas, or any other internationally prohibited weapons* (CIL)

118) Employment of other dangerous substances* (CIL)

119) Causing serious fires or floods or seriously interfering with natural resources* (CIL)

120) Employment of nuclear weapons* (CIL)

121) Threats of employment of nuclear weapons* (CIL)

122) Serious threats of other grave terrorist acts* (CIL)

123) Financing terrorist crimes* (CIL)

124) Conspiracy to commit terrorist crimes* (CIL)

125) Direct and public incitement to commit terrorist crimes* (CIL)

126) Attempt to commit terrorist crimes* (CIL)

G) Crimes of group destruction not encompassed by the Genocide Convention

(When committed with intent to destroy, in whole or in part, any identifiable civilian group, as such)

127) Killing**

128) Torture or other inhuman treatment**

129) Enforced disappearance of persons**

130) Enforced displacement, imprisonment, deportation, or forcible transfer of civilians**

131) Systematic or widespread destruction of infrastructure, significant buildings, or monuments**

132) Conspiracy, direct and public incitement, or attempt to commit group destruction**

III) International Crimes Not Dependent on the Existence of Threats to International Peace and Security

H) Grave piracy crimes

(When committed as part of a widespread or systematic attack directed against a ship, aircraft, or persons or property on board a ship or aircraft, for economic or private ends)

133) Killing of crew or passengers*

134) Armed robbery* (CIL)

135) Hostage taking* (CIL)

136) Torture or other inhuman treatment* (CIL)

137) Serious threats of violence * (CIL)

138) Destruction of ship or aircraft* (CIL)

139) Financing or profiting from piracy* (CIL)

I) Grave trafficking crimes

(When committed as part of organised large-scale transboundary crimes, with knowledge of the trafficking)

140) Illicit trafficking in human beings**

141) Illicit trafficking in drugs**

142) Illicit trafficking in weapons**

143) Money laundering**

J)   Excessive use and abuse of authorised power

(When committed, organised, or tolerated by a high-level public official or other high-level person acting as authorised within a power structure)

144) Isolated (non-systematic/widespread) acts of torture* (CIL)

145) Isolated (non-systematic/widespread) acts of enforced disappearance of persons* (CIL)

146) Isolated (non-systematic/widespread) acts of unlawful targeted killing of civilians* (CIL)

147) Serious acts of governmental corruption, theft, or embezzlement**

148) Serious acts of wilful destruction or pillage of national treasuries**

149) Serious acts of pillage of natural resources**

150) Serious acts of wilful damage to the environment**

4.10. From International Crimes to Universal Crimes

The extensive review of international crimes in this chapter has led us to five necessary and sufficient conditions for classification of an offence as an international crime and to the systematic employment of a related gravity clause, combined with references to the appropriate law-creating sources of international law (sections 4.9.1. and 4.9.2.). The result is the proposed enumeration of international crimes *lex lata* and international crimes *lex ferenda* in section 4.9.3.

In the next chapter we will argue that such a systematic approach, focusing on the universal characteristics of international crimes, justifies the use of an alternate term, namely, universal crimes. In contrast to the adjective 'international', which foregrounds the relationships between sovereign states or nations as a rationale for international criminal law, the adjective 'universal' emphasises the justification for international criminal law in common human values embedded in the UN paradigm of international law. It also has the advantage of clearly signalling the potential for the application of systematic criteria for identifying not only international crimes already agreed to be such (*lex lata*) but also others which share the same universal characteristics (*lex ferenda*) and should therefore be also confirmed as explicit *lex lata* by those institutions authorised to create international law in cooperation with states. Hence, the reconceptualizing of international crimes seems to require a terminological discussion, one that eventually may lead to the conclusion that the concept of universal crimes should gradually replace that of 'international crimes'.

5

Towards a Concept of Universal Crimes

5.1. Crimes with Uncertain Status under International Law

The Nuremberg and Tokyo trials laid the foundation for contemporary international criminal law (ICL). More than six decades later, there is still much uncertainty about which types of grave breaches of fundamental norms are defined as punishable crimes under international law. However, the most disputed areas today are not the ones that were contested initially, when the United Nations paradigm of international law was established. There is now widespread international consensus on violations classified as core international crimes: genocide, crimes against humanity, aggression, and war crimes. But there is a set of other crime categories and crime types whose status under international law remains uncertain. It is unclear whether these also constitute international crimes, and how they should be named, described, and grouped.

Examples of such disputed crime types include crimes of terrorism, crimes against the United Nations and internationally protected persons, crimes of group destruction not encompassed by the Genocide Convention, grave piracy crimes, grave trafficking crimes, and excessive use and abuse of authorised power.[1] The last category of so-called discrete crimes includes, but is not limited to, possible crimes under international law such as isolated acts of torture, enforced disappearance of persons, and unlawful targeted killing of civilians. Even though they are not systematic or widespread (if they were, they would constitute crimes against humanity), these singular acts are always serious. They are contrary to fundamental universal values and, furthermore, potentially dangerous to the rule of law when committed, organised, or tolerated by a high-level public official or other person acting as authorised within a power structure. It is unfortunate that current ICL appears to be still undetermined on many such critical issues.

As noted in earlier chapters, there is no common international legislature that can easily settle such issues by deciding which crimes are

---

[1] See the list of crimes presented in Chapter 4, section 4.9.3. See also Appendix I to this book, "Consolidated List of Universal Crimes".

currently crimes under international law. The thesis of this book is that some of this uncertainty – which is explainable and sometimes policy-driven – might be gradually reduced through careful analysis of the relevant 'crime criteria'. From the perspective of the rule of law as well as scholarship, these criteria must, in principle, be identifiable, to enable consistent application. Finding such common criteria and reaching consensus on specific crime categories, however, has been difficult, despite suggestions made by legal analysts and considered by the International Law Commission.

This suggests that the underlying theories of ICL may not be sufficiently developed. It is also possible that large gaps remain between common normative values of the world community and other interests affecting decisions on international law. Despite the lack of clear common theories and the presence of conflicting state interests, however, progress has been made in adapting international law to conform more adequately to proclaimed goals of the UN Charter and similar ideals. Since World War II, and particularly in recent decades, there have been some impressive results in using international law to combat grave crimes.[2] This is noteworthy since such crimes are most commonly committed, initiated, or tolerated by powerful persons, including heads of state. This gives us some confidence that improved analysis of ICL eventually may provide international actors with even better tools for ensuring systemic consistency and expanding the scope for legitimate changes in policy.

This book has had four research aims. The first was to give a contextual and comprehensive overview of the complex issue of which crimes are covered by international law, taking into account theoretical and historical perspectives, academic debates, the works of the International Law Commission, and the legal practice in international tribunals.[3]

The second aim was, on the basis of this survey, to examine different ways of classifying international crimes and to develop a set of necessary and sufficient conditions that should be used when defining and classifying punishable crimes under international law.[4] That analysis led

---

[2]   As reflected in the title of Chapter 1, "Universal Law versus Grave Crimes".

[3]   See Chapters 2 and 3, and Chapter 4, sections 4.2.–4.7.

[4]   See Chapter 4, sections 4.8.–4.9.

to the conclusion that all such crimes *lex lata* must meet five cumulative and interrelated conditions (listed here in abbreviated form):[5]

1) The type of conduct manifestly violates a fundamental universal value or interest.

2) The type of conduct is universally regarded as punishable due to its inherent gravity.

3) The type of conduct is recognised as a matter of serious international concern.

4) The proscriptive norm is anchored in the law-creating sources of international law.

5) Criminal liability and prosecution do not require consent of any concerned state.

These proposed normative criteria have general application within the field of ICL, and they apply regardless of how the set of international crimes is divided into groups for other purposes. Chapter IV discussed three such classes of relevance to international law: 'core international crimes', 'other crimes against the peace and security of mankind', and 'international crimes not dependent on the existence of threats to international peace and security'.[6] The criteria constitute a proposed legal definition of international crimes, and consequently of universal crimes as well. A legal definition forms part of a legal norm, as explained earlier.[7] But the particular legal norm in question here resembles a legal 'meta-norm'. It is a norm qualifying other norms *as legal norms*, like a norm setting forth the qualifying criteria of 'customary international law'. Such norms are grounded in the general constitutive principles of international law, that is, the basic norms of international law. No legal system can exist without some legal meta-norms. However, while the criteria of customary international law have general application within the whole field of international law,[8] the criteria of international crimes (universal crimes) are subject matter–specific, and thus less general in character. Their application is wide-ranging enough, however, that they constitute a 'basic universal crimes norm'. The identification of the proposed criteria

---

[5]   See further Chapter 4, section 4.9.1.

[6]   See Chapter 4, section 4.8.2.

[7]   See Chapter 4, section 4.8.1.

[8]   The criteria of customary international law might be applied with certain subject-matter modifications; see Chapter 3, section 3.3.3.

in this volume thus potentially has great significance for international criminal law.

With these criteria as a framework for identification and evaluation of relevant crimes, the book's third aim was to compile a comprehensive list of crimes under international law. These include crimes *lex lata* as well as crimes *lex ferenda* which fulfil some, but not all, of the criteria and which might merit later elevation to the status of *lex lata*.[9] This consolidated list, serving as an enumerative definition, thus includes both international crime types and potential international crime types.[10] Altogether, 10 crime categories and 150 crime types were identified for inclusion. The 150 crime types included 135 considered crimes *lex lata* and 15 considered crimes *lex ferenda*.

The fourth and final aim of this book has been to examine whether it may be useful to gradually replace the concept of international crimes with the concept of universal crimes in further academic analysis and legal debates, and whether this might provide a sound conceptual platform for extending our own legal analysis to other aspects of ICL.[11] This ambitious research aim is addressed by reflections in this final chapter.

One reason why this undertaking is so difficult is that it is obviously too soon to draw firm conclusions. Changing terminology in a field such as international criminal law is a process that involves considerable debate and reflection by a variety of stakeholders, which means that it inevitably takes time. This volume is intended not as a conclusion to such a process but rather as a beginning, in the hope that this will prove to be an opportune time for analytically rethinking the essentials of international criminal law and transitional justice. There are several grounds for thinking that the time is now ripe for such a process. First, the body of ICL has matured in recent decades. Second, ICL is now being implemented and enforced in many national jurisdictions. Third, practitioners are faced with substantial legal uncertainty which needs to be resolved, in a field of law that deals with fundamental issues of justice.

This volume thus begins a process of 'learning by doing'. Our thesis is that only by actually using the concept of universal crimes instead of international crimes in legal works can we gain relevant

---

[9]   See in particular Chapter 4, sections 4.9.2 and 4.9.3.
[10] See Chapter 4, section 4.9.3, as well as the parallel list in Appendix I.
[11] See preface to this book.

insights into the subject matter. This book shows that the terms 'international crimes' and 'universal crimes' can both be used in discussing several issues pertaining to ICL. For the first three research aims, the concept of international crimes was sufficient and appropriate, given its widespread use in the literature being examined.[12]

Nevertheless, as noted at the end of the preceding chapter, there may be particular advantages in employing the concept of universal crimes rather than international crimes. The first advantage is that the adjective 'universal' in 'universal crimes' highlights the justification for ICL in common fundamental values and interests that are embedded in the UN paradigm of international law, while the adjective 'international' in 'international crimes' implies a bias towards the sovereignty of states and the relationships between states. This bias is clearly problematic within this particular field of international law, which consists of so many *jus cogens* norms that states are obliged to respect.[13] Just as human rights are universal, so should substantive legal norms only be recognised as falling within the scope of international criminal law when they fulfil the full test of universality. Only then can the relevant crimes meet the common threshold in compliance with the general principles of the UN paradigm of international law. It follows that all crimes meeting these criteria should be recognised as universal crimes. It is important to underline that the defining criteria are closely linked to actual developments in international legal and political practice and that the crucial distinction between *lex lata* and *lex ferenda* is sustained within this universal crimes framework.

It is noteworthy that the first two of the five cumulative conditions constituting the proposed framework – that the type of conduct manifestly violates a fundamental universal value or interest and is universally regarded as punishable due to its inherent gravity – explicitly refer to *universality*, while the other three do not. However, when the third and fourth conditions – that the type of conduct is recognised as a matter of serious international concern, and that the proscriptive norm is anchored in the law-creating sources of international law – are considered in conjunction with the first two criteria, as they indeed should be, it

---

[12] Various terms are used to denote more or less the same phenomenon, but the term 'international crimes' has been dominant among them; see Chapter 1, section 1.2.

[13] On the meaning of *jus cogens* in this work, see Chapter 1, section 1.2, and Chapter 3, sections 3.3.4 and 3.4.2.

becomes clear that universality is implicit in this part of the framework as well. Insofar as the required legal basis is customary international law, binding Security Council resolutions, or binding general principles of law, or a combination of these three law-creating sources, this would be clear. Except in special cases, the substantive norms originating from these sources apply universally, given the nature of the law-creating source itself. With respect to treaties as a possible sole legal basis, the additional requirement of serious international concern means that normally only a multilateral treaty with significant and geographically broad state support will suffice. This will typically be a widely ratified UN treaty, although regional treaties may also support each other or a UN treaty with more limited accessions. As to the fifth condition, universality is clearly implied with regard to criminal liability and prosecutions which do not require the consent of a concerned state. That implies that it is not relevant who the perpetrator is, or which country the perpetrator comes from. In sum, it is exactly the universal character of the relevant crime types which best characterises the crimes under international law.

From this explanation it follows that the term 'universal crimes', while equivalent in content, is conceptually more appropriate than 'international crimes'. The implication is that the five necessary and sufficient criteria and the enumerative definition of international crimes set out in Chapter IV are just as relevant to the legal concept of universal crimes as they are to international crimes.

The next section briefly summarises and elaborates the findings from earlier chapters. It starts by proposing a theoretical definition of universal crimes (5.2.1.) and outlining essential features of universal crimes (5.2.2.). Taking the initial stages of international prosecution as the point of departure, section 5.2.3. then briefly illustrates how certain key conceptual building blocks can be related to each other, using the concept of gravity clauses and the crime of piracy as a case in point. The last section (5.3.) of this final chapter presents a proposal for developing a United Nations Declaration on Universal Crimes. Such an enterprise would be useful in clarifying crimes under international law and promoting further compliance with the international legality principle. A move toward universality and legal certainty could also serve as an effective remedy against the fragmentation of ICL.

5.2. Conceptualising Universal Crimes

5.2.1. Seeking a Theoretical Definition of Universal Crimes

Is it possible to formulate a theoretical definition of universal crimes, that is, a definition that may help us understand how the concept of universal crimes should be used in all cases, thereby also providing a theoretical argument for a particular conception of universal crimes?[14] A theoretical definition should clearly define 'universal crimes' in such a way that it includes all acts correctly identified as universal crimes while excluding all acts that are not universal crimes. In addition, a theoretical definition should help build a theory which informs a particular conception of universal crimes. It should lay out a certain way of thinking about crimes under international law and the essentials of international criminal law and transitional justice. The theory sketched here is closely linked to the principles and rules embedded in the UN paradigm of international law. It is also linked to the actual practices of international actors within the field of ICL when these actors confront the problems caused by grave crimes in real life. The underlying assumption is that some crime types are so inherently grave or dangerous that they concern all peoples and communities and are thus of universal concern.

In seeking a theoretical definition of universal crimes, both legal science and other fields of scholarship may be relevant. This is a challenge that also pertains to many other concepts of importance to the rule of law, 'human rights' being a particularly apt example. When the UN Charter and the Universal Declaration of Human Rights were adopted after World War II, the legal status and consequences of the rights proclaimed were still unclear under international law. In hindsight, one can see that the normative core of human rights immediately became part of the general principles of international law *lex lata*, whereas other human rights norms, and their softer edges, remained for a while in the sphere of *lex ferenda*. Over time, additional human rights have clearly become part of binding international law, as indicated by the term 'international human rights law'. In other words, the concept of human rights preceded its full legal content, and the legal development of human rights law continues. A similar process may apply to the concept of universal

---

[14] See Chapter 2, section 2.1.1., and Chapter 4, section 4.1.

crimes, covering both potential crimes *lex ferenda* and established crimes *lex lata* under international law.

This implies that a theoretical definition of universal crimes should be wide enough to cover universal crimes *lex ferenda*, precise enough to exclude acts that are not universal crimes, useful for the legal and other professions, and conceptually relevant for interdisciplinary fields dealing with the subject matter, such as transitional justice. A *theoretical* definition of universal crimes may be supplemented by an *operational* legal definition for the specific purpose of identifying and enumerating the universal crimes *lex lata*.

The theoretical definition below is derived from a combination of the empirical and legal definitions of universal crimes elaborated earlier in this book. Let us first recall the stipulative definition set forth at the beginning of Chapter IV:

> 'Universal crimes' are certain identifiable acts that constitute grave breaches of rules of conduct usually committed, organised, or tolerated by powerful actors; and that, according to contemporary international law, are punishable whenever and wherever they are committed; and that require prosecution and punishment through fair trials, or in special cases, some other kind of justice, somewhere at some point.[15]

This definition was 'stipulative' insofar as it was a preliminary definition of the author's use of the term, seeking to grasp the essentials of such crimes. On closer analysis, this is primarily an *empirical* definition rather than a *legal* definition; that is, it is a descriptive proposition that attempts to describe the essence of a social phenomenon. Its usefulness must be checked by comparing the definition with social reality.[16] Although presumably useful for empirical purposes, this definition does not provide sufficiently clear criteria for identifying crimes under international law. That, in contrast, requires a concise definition linked to the actual legal norms and practices within ICL. For example, the nexus between crimes and power structures is an important characteristic of universal crimes in empirical terms (this element can in principle be checked by comparing the proposition with concrete

---

[15] See Chapter 4, section 4.1., and Chapter 2, section 2.1.2.
[16] On different kinds of definitions relevant to this work, including 'empirical definitions', see Chapter 4, section 4.8.1.

universal crimes being committed in real life). But it is not necessarily a strict legal requirement for all universal crime categories or crime types.[17] Although the qualifier "usually" in the empirical definition with respect to offences "committed, organised, or tolerated by powerful actors" indicates room for exceptions, such language is not adequate as a general normative and legal definition. This would require an additional element, that is, identification of the grounds for exceptions in legal terms.

Because the legal status of several crimes under international law is apparently undetermined, this book has attempted to develop a set of necessary and sufficient criteria for recognising crimes in international law *lex lata*. Although these criteria were used to define 'international crimes' in Chapter IV,[18] they may, as already noted, equally well be applied to the concept of universal crimes:

> The term 'universal crimes' applies to conduct which (1) manifestly violates a fundamental universal value or interest, provided that the offence is (2) universally regarded as punishable due to its inherent gravity, (3) recognised as a matter of serious concern to the international community as a whole, and (4) proscribed by binding rules of international law, and provided that (5) criminal liability and prosecution is not dependent upon the consent of a concerned state (the territorial state where the crime was committed or the national state of an alleged perpetrator or victim).

This *legal* definition of universal crimes is precise enough to exclude acts that are not universal crimes, and thus potentially useful for the legal profession. The results it may produce when employed in legal analysis may also be useful for other professions and political actors in international law. It also provides a plausibly sound operational definition of universal crimes. But it is a bit too narrow as a theoretical definition with general application.

We can further specify this definition in the following way. By requiring only the first two criteria of the legal definition, we can define universal crimes *lex ferenda*, distinguishing these crimes from 'non-universal crimes'. Universal crimes *lex ferenda* are those with the potential of becoming universal crimes *lex lata*. 'Non-universal crimes' do not have

---

[17] See, *e.g.*, the discussion of 'crimes against humanity' in Chapter 2, sections 2.3.3. and 2.3.4.

[18] See Chapter 4, section 4.9.1.3.

that potential, at least not within a foreseeable future. By *not* including the three last criteria of the legal definition, we can adequately distinguish universal crimes *lex ferenda* from universal crimes *lex lata*, which must meet all five criteria. The relationship and boundaries between these classes are further illustrated below. Taking the first two criteria from the legal definition, adding two elements of the empirical definition to provide accessible descriptive content, and clarifying the typical relationship between the four different elements in the definition, we may offer the following *theoretical* definition of universal crimes:

> The term 'universal crimes' shall apply to any conduct which manifestly violates a fundamental universal value or interest, is universally regarded as punishable due to its gravity, and is usually committed, organised, or tolerated by powerful actors, and which therefore may require prosecution before international courts.

This theoretical definition is not meant to substitute for the operational *legal* definition of universal crimes, since the five required criteria of the legal definition are better suited for precise identification of universal crimes *lex lata*. Rather, the theoretical definition may supplement the legal definition as a tool for identifying the universal crimes *lex ferenda*. Conversely, the last three criteria of the legal definition not included in the theoretical definition may inform the theoretical definition; with the aid of these three criteria, one may discover the international legal and political implications emerging from the core parts of the theoretical definition. Hence, the two definitions serve different purposes, but reinforce each other. Their relationship and the delimitation from non-universal crimes can be illustrated in different ways. We may recall the classification of international and non-international crimes:[19]

International crimes:

- Core international crimes
- Other international crimes against the peace and security of mankind
- International crimes not dependent on the existence of threats to international peace and security

International offences:

- International crimes *lex ferenda*

---

[19] See Chapter 4, section 4.9.2.1.

- Non-grave international offences

Non-international crimes:

- National crimes
- Nationally imported international crimes
- Transnational non-international crimes

Applying the same scheme to the proposed theoretical definition of universal crimes produces the following reclassification:

Universal crimes:

- Core universal crimes *lex lata*
- Other universal crimes against the peace and security of mankind *lex lata*
- Universal crimes not dependent on the existence of threats to international peace and security *lex lata*
- Universal crimes *lex ferenda*

Non-universal crimes:

- Non-grave universal offences
- Transnational non-universal crimes
- Nationally imported universal crimes
- National crimes

This scheme is useful because it highlights the borderline between universal crimes and non-universal crimes by including potential universal crimes (*lex ferenda*) and by excluding non-grave international offences as well as other classes of non-universal crimes. The meaning and content of all these classes has already been discussed in Chapter IV, under the heading of international crimes, and thus needs no repetition. However, it might be useful to recall Figure 2 from Chapter IV, which was used to illustrate the relationship between the three abstract classes of 'core international crimes', 'other international crimes against the peace and security of mankind', and 'international crimes not dependent on the existence of threats to international peace and security'. These three classes of crimes under international law encompass all universal crimes, whether considered *lex lata* or *lex ferenda*. The relationship between universal crimes *lex lata*, universal crimes *lex ferenda*, and non-universal crimes is shown in Figure 3.

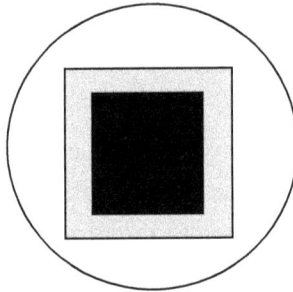

Figure 3: Universal Crimes *Lex Lata* and *Lex Ferenda*, and Non-Universal Crimes.

The black inner square represents universal crimes *lex lata*. These crimes meet all five criteria of the operational legal definition of universal crimes. The grey square represents universal crimes *lex ferenda*. They meet the first two of the five criteria, as they concern a conduct which manifestly violates a fundamental universal value or interest and is universally regarded as punishable due to its inherent gravity. In addition, these crimes may fulfil one or two of the other criteria as well. Their possible future legal status as crimes *lex lata* depends upon the development of international law. It is noteworthy that with regard to some universal crime types, uncertainty exists with respect to their legal status, so in reality the boundaries are not as clear as in Figure 3.

The same can be said for the boundaries between universal crimes *lex ferenda* and non-universal crimes. The outer white area represents all four classes of non-universal crimes in the scheme described just before Figure 3. Different assessments will also be made in the future by different analysts and actors regarding different crime types, in particular with respect to the boundaries between universal crimes *lex ferenda* and the two classes labelled 'non-grave universal offences' and 'transitional non-universal crimes'. This would be so whether or not the analysis and suggestions in this book are taken into consideration.

In conclusion, the proposed theoretical definition of universal crimes covers in principle the same ground as the legal definition extended to crimes *lex ferenda*. It explains concisely why a certain conduct ought to be considered a universal crime: because it clearly violates fundamental universal values or interests; is universally regarded as punishable due to its gravity; is usually committed, organised, or tolerated by powerful actors; and therefore may require prosecution before international courts. While the latter prosecutorial element is not a necessity as long as the crimes are fairly and effectively prosecuted in the concerned national jurisdictions, these crimes cannot, by their very nature, be left entirely to the discretion of individual states. Quite often, the incumbent administration, the military, or other public officials are implicated in universal crimes, or sufficiently competent and independent prosecutors and courts are not available. Sometimes both obstacles apply simultaneously.

The proposed theoretical definition illustrates a way of thinking about crimes under international law which implies a particular conception of universal crimes. It forms part of a theory on the essentials of international criminal law and transitional justice. While based on the existing UN paradigm of international law, the definition also provides a basis for further exploring the concept of universal crimes.

5.2.2. Distilling the Essentials of Universal Crimes

Taking into account the conceptual and contextual aspects of the proposed theoretical definition, one can list 10 overlapping kinds of acts that may constitute universal crimes:

1) Acts that shock humanity and civilised societies
2) Acts in conflict with the rule of law
3) Acts committed, organised, or tolerated by powerful persons
4) Acts manifestly violating a fundamental universal value or interest
5) Acts universally regarded as punishable
6) Acts constituting inherently grave breaches of universal norms
7) Acts recognised as a matter of serious international concern
8) Acts proscribed by rules of international law
9) Acts for which the international legality principle applies
10) Acts directly punishable under international law

These 10 elements should be considered when one constructs a proposed crime type in conformity with international law, which must then be tested for critical analysis and applied in concrete situations. We have already discussed how international crimes can be classified according to different schemes.[20] In the following we use only the term 'universal crimes', although the analysis would also be valid if the concept of international crimes were used. The argument presented here is

---

[20] See Chapter 4, sections 4.8. and 4.9.

that the same analytical distinctions earlier applied to international crimes also apply to the concept of universal crimes. For instance, universal crimes can be divided into four analytical classes reflecting different levels of abstraction:

1) Universal crime categories
2) Universal crime types
3) Concrete universal crimes
4) Individual international crimes

The last two analytical classes (3 and 4) are of interest with respect to certain specific issues that lie at the crossroads between law and facts in decision-making processes,[21] as discussed in the next subsection (2.3). The distinction between (1) *crime categories* and (2) *crime types*, however, is crucial to a proper understanding of what universal crimes are.[22] We may recall that the widespread notion of core crimes contains the four universal crime categories of genocide, crimes against humanity, crimes of aggression, and war crimes. Each crime category, in turn, contains several different universal crime types. A universal crime type is essentially a complete universal crime, setting forth all the necessary and sufficient material crime elements of a distinct universal crime. The relevant crime elements in this regard may include specific mental or subjective elements of certain crime types (apart from ordinary intent as contained more generally in criminal liability law, which is not discussed in this book). This is the case when such elements by necessity characterise the particular crime, as, for instance, with crimes of genocide and terrorism, and with certain types of war crimes. Whether or not such elements are included, however, each universal crime requires two elements: an *underlying crime* and a *gravity clause*.

Consequently, a crime type is not equivalent to an underlying crime as such, for example, an act of unlawful killing or torture. Rather, a specific universal crime type requires a combination of two components: (1) the underlying crime (for example, killing), and (2) the nexus to a particular gravity clause inherent in each particular crime category. When we listed the crime categories and crime types earlier, the formulations of the gravity clauses for the class of core crimes adhered closely to the Rome Statute with respect to crimes of (A) aggression, (B) genocide, (C)

---

[21] See Chapter 4, section 4.8.2., and Chapter 2, section 2.3.4.
[22] See Chapter 4, sections 4.8.2. (theory) and 4.9.3. (application).

crimes against humanity, and (D) war crimes.[23] Chapter IV discussed in particular the new definition of aggression in the Rome Statute, which clearly includes a gravity clause, and concluded that this crime category is not unique in requiring a gravity clause.[24] This general point was furthermore underpinned through the discussion of the status of the crime of terrorism, concluding that a specific gravity clause for this crime category can also be identified under international law, although the particular formulation is still disputable and thus remains a bit uncertain *lex lata*.[25]

All universal crimes included in this book follow the same scheme. It might be useful at this stage to explain how the gravity clauses generally relate to the other building blocks of universal crimes, especially the component of underlying crimes. Figure 4 illustrates this with reference to the early stages of investigation and prosecution, but it should be noted that the relationship between a gravity clause and an underlying crime is the same when the substantive rules of ICL are being applied by the judges at the next stages of the criminal law procedures.

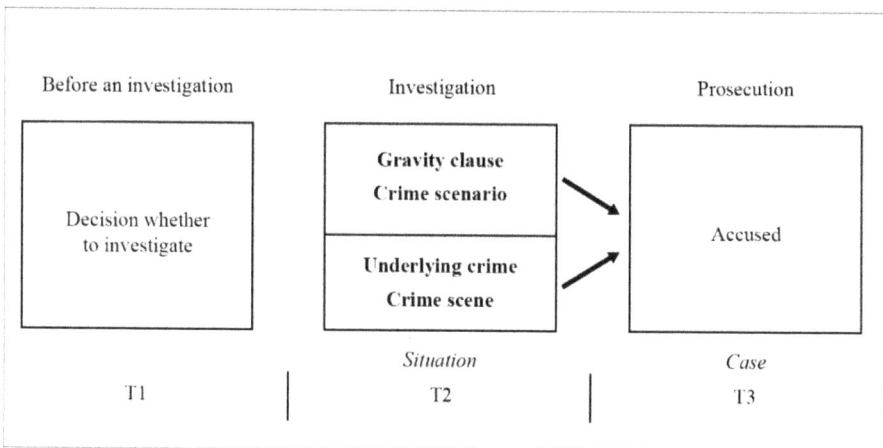

Figure 4: Investigating and Prosecuting Universal Crimes.

In principle the model is the same, regardless of the prosecutor, court, or universal crime type. At the outset (T1) one needs to determine

---

[23]   See Chapter 4, section 4.9.3.
[24]   See Chapter 4, sections 4.7.2., 4.9.2.2., and 4.9.3.
[25]   See Chapter 4, section 4.9.2.4.

whether there is sufficient reason to believe that universal crimes have been committed in a particular situation and that an investigation is warranted. If an international court with adequate jurisdiction has not already been established, the preliminary examination might be carried out by independent experts or a fact-finding mission appointed by the Security Council or other UN bodies. At the national level, if the prosecutors or courts do not have the required jurisdiction of competence to examine universal crime cases on their own initiative, a government may appoint a truth commission or similar body to examine the facts. Whether a formal investigation will ever be opened in such cases will also depend on various political and other factors.

If a preliminary examination leads to the conclusion that an investigation should be opened, for the purpose of potentially identifying individual suspects for prosecution, a factual and legal framework for the investigations and prosecutions should be utilised or considered for the relevant geographic areas and crime types. This might necessitate the establishment of a new *ad hoc* international criminal court with adequate jurisdiction and resources, if the International Criminal Court (ICC) does not have jurisdiction under the Rome Statute and the situation is not referred to the ICC by the Security Council.[26]

In the subsequent investigation of universal crimes (T2), a number of different prosecutorial considerations may apply with regard to selection and prioritisation, as discussed in earlier chapters.[27] Eventually, however, investigators must identify the underlying crimes and their nexus to a specific gravity clause with respect to individual suspects. In practice, this means that the concrete universal crimes must be identified by reference to a relevant 'universal crime scene', determined in relation to location, time, specific underlying crimes (for example, killing), and, as far as possible, individual victims and perpetrators. In addition, the underlying crimes must be linked to a legally relevant factual *context*, what might be termed a 'universal crime scenario'. A relevant crime scenario is determined by the possible facts corresponding to the normative elements of a gravity clause, for example, 'a widespread or systematic attack directed against a civilian population' in a particular situation, or the existence of 'intent to destroy' a concrete group. Only

---

[26] On the role of the Security Council in this regard, see Chapter 2, sections 2.2.4. and 2.3.4.

[27] See in particular Chapter 2, section 2.3.4.

when the underlying crimes committed (or planned) at the crime scene are sufficiently linked to a relevant universal crime scenario will it be legally possible to prosecute a person accused of universal crimes (T3).

In addition to the core universal crimes, six other crime categories have been included in our universal crime list (Appendix I), each constituted by a specific gravity clause. These other gravity clauses are presently lacking authoritative formulations in international law, but they are formulated as far as possible in line with international law *lex lata* or *lex ferenda* consistent with the analysis undertaken in this book. These categories are (E) crimes against the United Nations and internationally protected persons, (F) terrorist crimes, (G) crimes of group destruction not encompassed by the Genocide Convention, (H) grave piracy crimes, (I) grave trafficking crimes, and (J) excessive use and abuse of authorised power. The gravity clauses, and the different crime types in each category, as well as their legal status *lex lata* or *lex ferenda*, are indicated in Appendix I.

A distinct universal crime type therefore always consists of one underlying type of crime (for example, 'killing') and one contextual component in the form of a nexus to a specific gravity clause (for example, the gravity clause specific to genocide). A complete formulation of the crime type listed as number 11 in Appendix I would thus be: 'Killing with intent to destroy, in whole or in part, a national, ethnical, racial or religious group, as such'. This book argues that the same format, or design, applies to all other universal (international) crime types.

The theory of inherent gravity clauses has important repercussions for the classification and definition of several crimes that might be classified as universal or international crimes, but that currently have a disputed legal status under international law. Some of these crimes have received much scholarly and policy attention, for example, piracy, isolated acts of torture, and targeted killing.[28] The next subsection illustrates this briefly by focusing on piracy.

---

[28] See *e.g.*, UN General Assembly, Human Rights Council, *Report of the Special Rapporteur on Extrajudicial, Summary or Arbitrary Executions, Philip Alston, Addendum: Study on Targeted Killings*, A/HRC/14/24/Add.6, 20 May 2010. See also Nils Melzer, *Targeted Killing in International Law*, Oxford University Press, Oxford, UK, 2008.

5.2.3. Illustrating the Notion and Application of the Inherent Gravity Clauses

Acts of piracy are in a sense classic universal crimes, though they are not necessarily 'universal crimes' in terms of the concept proposed in this book. Piracy has been outlawed by nations and through international cooperation for a long time, since well before the UN paradigm of international law was established. Piracy is also clearly outlawed under current international law. The UN Convention on the Law of the Sea (UNCLOS),[29] in Article 101(a), defines piracy as "any illegal acts of violence or detention, or any act of depredation, committed for private ends by the crew or the passengers of a private ship or a private aircraft".[30] Article 100 of UNCLOS requires states to suppress piracy, whereas Article 105 recognises a particular kind of qualified universal jurisdiction for acts of piracy, allowing every state to "seize a pirate ship or aircraft, or a ship or aircraft taken by piracy and under the control of pirates, and arrest the persons and seize the property on board". Furthermore, according to Article 105, the "courts of the state which carried out the seizure may decide upon the penalties to be imposed, and may also determine the action to be taken with regard to the ships, aircraft or property, subject to the rights of third parties acting in good faith". With respect to its justification, this special right of seizure may have some similarities with an emergency right of self-defence in the interest of a third person, including the protection of human beings against grave crimes. Article 105 of UNCLOS provides full criminal law jurisdiction as well, but only for the courts of the state which carried out the seizure – implicitly, the flag state of the ship enforcing the seizure when this is carried out on the high seas, or in any other place outside the jurisdiction of any state.

A more difficult question is whether *other* states may have universal criminal law jurisdiction for *any act* of piracy as defined in UNCLOS, based on customary international law or general principles. If so, this means that states also have universal jurisdiction for isolated acts

---

[29] United Nations Convention on the Law of the Sea, 10 December 1982, in force from 16 November 1994. See United Nations, *Treaty Series*, vol. 1833, p. 3. As of 28 August 2011, the convention had 162 parties.

[30] UNCLOS Article 101(a) must be read in conjunction with the rest of Article 101, and with Articles 102–104, but Article 101(a) provides the general definition.

of piracy with no apparent connection to the prosecuting state. The main point to be made here is that any isolated act of piracy would not be a universal crime, since it may not fit any gravity clause inherent in the universal crime categories.[31] Put differently, in such cases of piracy there are relevant crime scenes, but a universal 'crime scenario' would presumably be lacking.[32] For example, an isolated act of armed robbery by a private ship may have more in common with non-international crimes of armed robbery than with universal crimes, even when committed on the high seas. This would be true even though taking place on the high seas would presumably be considered an aggravating circumstance in most national jurisdictions lacking a specific statute for piracy.

In our list of universal crimes (Appendix), we have suggested seven underlying crimes of piracy (killing of crew or passengers, armed robbery, hostage taking, torture or other inhuman treatment, serious threats of violence, destruction of ship or aircraft, and financing or profiting from piracy),[33] and the following gravity clause for the universal crime category (H) of 'grave piracy crimes':

> When committed as part of a widespread or systematic attack directed against a ship, aircraft, or persons or property on board a ship or aircraft, for economic or private ends.

This formulation resembles the gravity clause of crimes against humanity by requiring that the underlying crimes be committed in the context of a 'widespread or systematic attack' in order to constitute a universal crime. The proposed gravity clause is not limited to attacks directed against a civilian population, or to private ships or aircraft. A widespread or systematic pirate attack would usually be directed at

---

[31] Questions of universal jurisdiction generally are not addressed in this book (see the preface).

[32] See section 5.2.2. in this chapter, including Figure 4.

[33] The basis for selection is that these are presumably serious, common underlying crimes of widespread or systematic pirate attacks. For example, such attacks are usually organised for profit and require financing. Not included as separate crime types in our list (see category H in Appendix I) are the important and relevant punishable modes of planning, organising, and inciting piracy crimes. This does not, by any means, imply that prosecutions should not focus on these often high-level participants. To the contrary, the need to investigate and prosecute these persons should clearly be recognised, as has been pointed out by the Security Council in relation to the situation off the coast of Somalia; see UN Security Council Resolution 1976 (2011), para. 15.

private ships at sea for economic ends, but it could also target governmental ships in non-commercial service, ships employed in the official service of the United Nations, or coastal guards or military ships employed in the service of protecting against piracy. Arguably, it would be unreasonable under international law if attacks on such non-private ships, forming an integrated part of the overall attack, were not recognised as universal crimes on an equal footing with attacks on private vessels.[34]

The situation off the coast of Somalia provides a real-life example of 'widespread' pirate attacks, which are presumably also 'systematic' attacks. These attacks have threatened international shipping for several years. In legal terms, it is significant that the UN Security Council has adopted a number of resolutions on the matter. Acting under Chapter VII of the UN Charter, the Security Council has repeatedly expressed grave concern over the increase in piracy and has condemned all acts of piracy and armed robbery at sea against vessels off the coast of Somalia.[35] In other words, a clearly defined 'situation' has been identified by the world community for concerted action, including prosecutorial measures.

The gravity of the current situation is illuminated by data in a report submitted to the Security Council by the UN Secretary-General on 15 June 2011.[36] From 1 January 2011 until that date, a period of less than six months, there had been 177 attacks, of which 18 were successful.[37] As of May 2011, 26 ships were held by pirates, with a total of 601 hostages.[38] The increased range of attacks was achieved through the use of mother ships, with as many as a hundred pirates on board to guard hostages and deter rescue attempts. Hijacked crews were used as 'human shields' against military intervention and were threatened as a means to deter military attacks. One crew member was summarily executed and four other people were killed. The level of ransoms demanded continued to increase. Released crew members reported systematic threats and violence

---

[34] Although not directly applicable, the 'absurd result' principle of the Vienna Convention on the Law of Treaties, Article 32(b), might be an expression of a more general principle of law.

[35] See *e.g.*, UN Security Council Resolutions 1838 (2008), 1844 (2008), 1851 (2008), and 1976 (2011).

[36] UN Security Council, *Report of the Secretary-General on the Modalities for the Establishment of Specialized Somali Anti-piracy Courts*, S/2011/360, 15 June 2011.

[37] *Ibid.*, p. 27 (Annex I).

[38] *Ibid.*

during their captivity. Naval forces estimated that there were about 50 pirate leaders, around 300 leaders of pirate attack groups, and around 2,500 foot soldiers. It is believed that financing was provided by 10 to 20 individuals. In addition, there were a large number of armed individuals guarding captured ships and numerous ransom negotiators.[39] At the same time, the number of states prosecuting acts of piracy off the coast of Somalia in their courts had reached 20, and the total number of prosecutions nearly doubled from July 2010 to June 2011 (from 528 to 1,011), with 550 suspects convicted.[40] Presumably, there are not only relevant crime scenes at stake here, but universal crime scenarios as well. These statistics strongly indicate that the pirates systematically commit armed robbery in combination with the serious underlying crime of hostage taking, and that the crimes are widespread in this particular area of the world.

Against this factual backdrop, it seems clear that the situation off the coast of Somalia constitutes a textbook example of the universal crime of 'grave piracy crimes'. Any act of piracy within the meaning of the UNCLOS definition is considered illegal and punishable by the international community, and the Security Council has arguably accepted universal jurisdiction for such acts, extending even beyond the jurisdiction assigned to the seizing state by UNCLOS. Security Council Resolution 1976 recognised that "piracy is a crime subject to universal jurisdiction" and in that regard called on states to "favourably consider the prosecution of suspected, and imprisonment of convicted, pirates apprehended off the coast of Somalia, consistent with applicable international human rights law".[41]

However, this universal crime still has not been clearly established by international institutions in cooperation with states. The formulation in the Security Council resolution remains ambiguous insofar as it does not state clearly that the pirates can subsequently be prosecuted in any state, regardless of which state apprehends them, other links of the prosecuting state to the perpetrators or victims of piracy, or the consent of Somalia. There are at least two reasons for this. First, piracy as defined in UNCLOS encompasses singular (isolated) acts of piracy that do not meet

---

[39] *Ibid.*

[40] *Ibid.*, pp. 27–28 (Annex I).

[41] UN Security Council Resolution 1976 (2011), para. 14.

the gravity threshold for universal crimes.[42] Second, neither UNCLOS nor the Security Council seems to recognise that any act of piracy can be prosecuted by a state without the consent of a concerned state. Consequently, condition 5 of the five criteria is not met for considering any act of piracy a universal crime under international law.

The latter point is reinforced by certain wording in the June 2011 report submitted to the Security Council when discussing the possibility of establishing "an extraterritorial Somali specialized anti-piracy court to sit in another State in the region".[43] According to this analysis, this would have to be an extraterritorial *Somali* court. No other options for extra-territorial courts are suggested in the report. Such a court would thus be "an existing Somali court located extraterritorially in a third State, or a specially established new court or a new section of an existing court, either at the federal or regional level [of Somalia]".[44] By implication, as stated in the report, seemingly as a general proposition,

> An extraterritorial Somali anti-piracy court would require a legal basis in the constitutional and legislative framework of Somalia, a legal basis within the host State for its functioning in the territory of that State, and an agreement between Somalia and the host State to regulate the respective rights and obligations of the two States.[45]

Furthermore, as "an extraterritorial Somali court would be exercising Somali jurisdiction and applying Somali law, the judges, prosecutors, defence counsel and other legal professionals should ideally be Somalis, qualified in Somali law, and with professional experience of practising Somali law."[46] The report does envisage a degree of international participation, for example, by experts from other juris-dictions, or by judges or prosecutors selected by the United Nations.[47] What the report does not discuss, however, is perhaps more interesting. Notably, it does not mention the possibility that the Security Council

---

[42] Consider especially condition 2 of the five criteria of universal crimes *lex lata*, which is a necessary part of the legal definition and is also included in our theoretical defini-tion of universal crimes discussed earlier in this chapter.

[43] See UN Security Council, *Report of the Secretary General on the Modalities for the Establishment of Specialized Somali Anti-piracy Courts*, paras. 46–96, *supra* note 36.

[44] *Ibid.*, para. 61.

[45] *Ibid.*, para. 60.

[46] *Ibid.*, para. 80.

[47] *Ibid.*, para. 68.

might establish an international piracy court, or an *ad hoc* international court for the particular situation of piracy off the coast of Somalia, if necessary limited in scope, for example, to the prosecution of pirate leaders, notorious offenders, and financiers and planners of piracy. Instead the key question presented is whether an extraterritorial *Somali* anti-piracy court should have jurisdiction to prosecute large numbers of low-level perpetrators of acts of piracy, or a more limited number of financiers and planners, or both.[48]

Hence the situation off the coast of Somalia illustrates the problem caused by the uncertain legal status of piracy as a crime under international law, and similar issues concerning other crimes with an uncertain legal status. In the case of piracy off the coast of Somalia, the Secretary-General as well as the Security Council should ideally have recognised that such widespread and systematic piracy attacks fall in a particular crime category of international law, characterised by a widespread or systematic attack for economic or other private ends, and certain typical underlying crimes. This means that piracy *as a crime under international law* must meet a certain threshold, excluding isolated acts of piracy. Such acts are already illegal and proscribed by international law in accordance with the rules of UNCLOS. But not all acts of piracy encompassed by the UNCLOS definition should be considered crimes under international law. The notion of inherent gravity clauses applicable to all universal crimes may provide useful guidance in this regard.

Criminal liability and prosecution of grave piracy crimes, if recognised as international and universal crimes, would not require consent of any concerned state. Under such an understanding, the Security Council, or states in cooperation with the UN, might thus establish an international court with lawful and necessary subject matter jurisdiction for such crimes. The cooperation or consent of Somalia might therefore not be strictly necessary to establish an extraterritorial anti-piracy court with the purpose of prosecuting piracy crimes committed off the coast of Somalia. Whether this would be a wise political move is another question. But whatever decisions are made on political grounds, or on the basis of their perceived legitimacy in Somalia and the surrounding region, it is still essential for the international legal principles to be clear and not confused with political considerations.

---

[48]   *Ibid.*, para. 96.

In conclusion, therefore, the establishment of extraterritorial international anti-piracy courts may still appear too problematic for a mixture of political and legal reasons. In legal terms, as long as direct criminal liability under international law for grave piracy crimes remains uncertain, there is always the possibility that an international court, if one were to be established, eventually would find that it lacks jurisdiction under international law.

Similar underlying problems can also be illustrated by reference to the limited jurisdiction entrusted to the Special Tribunal for Lebanon (STL). As noted earlier in this book,[49] the STL was established by the UN Security Council in cooperation with the government of Lebanon for the principal purpose of prosecuting the terrorist attack resulting in the death of former Lebanese prime minister Rafiq Hariri. Its subject matter jurisdiction is entirely based upon domestic Lebanese law, including "acts of terrorism" within the meaning of the Lebanese Criminal Code.[50] To apply only the substantive criminal law of a particular country is a novel and questionable approach for international tribunals. But, as just discussed, the UN apparently seems inclined to follow a similar route with regard to an extraterritorial Somali anti-piracy court. It is thus noteworthy that, as of 2011, the STL still had not clarified the compatibility of domestic legal provisions on terrorism with the notion of terrorism under international law.[51]

The STL concluded that a crime of terrorism exists in international customary law, but that it was still confined to times of peace.[52] Never-

---

[49] See Chapter 4, sections 4.3. and 4.9.2.

[50] See the Statute of the Special Tribunal for Lebanon (STL), Article 2(a).

[51] See STL Appeals Chamber, *Interlocutory Decision on the Applicable Law: Terrorism, Conspiracy, Homicide, Perpetration, Cumulative Charging*, STL-11-01/I/AC/R176bis, decision of 16 February 2011.

[52] *Ibid.*, paras. 107–113. The STL held that with regard to terrorism in times of armed conflict, "a customary rule is [still] incipient (*in statu nascendi*)", and argued that the extension to armed conflict is dependent upon further international legal development (*ibid.*, para. 109). However, such a limitation of terrorist crimes to times of 'peace' is not convincing under a broader approach to ICL, taking into account all relevant legal bases, including treaties, Security Council resolutions, and general principles of law. Except for 'war crimes', which apply specifically in the context of war (armed conflict), all other universal crimes should generally be taken to apply regardless of the context of war or peace (see Chapter 4, section 4.9.2.3). In other words, if a certain universal crime type other than war crimes has achieved the status of *lex lata*, it should be applicable *also* in situations of war. The contrary view (that such a crime

theless, the STL cannot apply this concept of terrorism under international law directly to acts of terrorism prosecuted before it, due to its *statutory* constraints, in order to respect the international legality principle. The Lebanese definition of terrorism, on the other hand, cannot be applied in contradiction to binding international law, that is, to acts that are clearly not considered terrorism in international law. Thus the legal result is not fully satisfactory. For example, one may envisage a situation where there is sufficient proof of terrorist crimes under international law but where the acts are not sufficiently encompassed by the Lebanese Criminal Code. In that case, impunity for grave crimes may prevail, a result contrary to the object and purpose of the UN paradigm of international law and one that undermines the whole purpose of establishing and funding the STL.

Hence, given that the conclusion by the STL on the legal status of terrorism is correct *lex lata*,[53] in retrospect it seems unfortunate that the STL was not entrusted with concurrent jurisdiction over terrorist crimes under international law. This is yet another example of the problems caused by the uncertain status of important crime types under international law. How such problems might be overcome in a principled manner, and in compliance with the international legality principle, is the subject of the final section of this chapter.

5.3. Developing a United Nations Declaration on Universal Crimes

This book has made a number of references to the international legality principle and its implications.[54] Perhaps surprisingly, this principle as stated in international human rights law remains unclear with respect to which crimes, except for the core universal (international) crimes, actually constitute criminal offences under international law, as stated in Article 15(1) of the International Covenant on Civil and Political Rights

---

only applies during war) has been clearly rejected with regard to genocide crimes and crimes against humanity under current international law, and it is hard to see why the war/peace dichotomy should be reintroduced for terrorist crimes, piracy, or any other universal crime except for war crimes. Not even crimes of aggression fully depend upon the prior contextual status of war or peace, thus also confirming an initial legal presumption of general application. The failure of the STL to fully resolve this issue is another indication of the need to address such issues within the field of ICL.

[53] See the preceding note. On the crime status of terrorism, see also Chapter 4, section 4.9.2.4.

[54] See in particular Chapter 3, section 3.3.4., and Chapter 4, section 4.2.

(ICCPR). Hence it is also unclear to which other universal crimes the usual prohibition of *ex post facto* criminal liability and punishment may not apply, or rather, it is not legally relevant because the offences are already constituted as punishable crimes directly under international law. This latter point is reflected in Article 15(2), which states that nothing "shall prejudice the trial and punishment of any person for any act or omission which, at the time when it was committed, was criminal according to the general principles of law recognized by the community of nations".

Notably, the UN Human Rights Committee has not issued any general comment on the formulation of the legality principle as stated in Article 15 of the ICCPR, although the Committee by August 2011 had issued 34 general comments, covering almost all the civil and political rights enumerated in the ICCPR. A leading commentary on the ICCPR has only brief comments on the issue of the relevant international crimes referred to in Article 15.[55] A circular relationship may have occurred. That is, because international courts have lacked subject matter jurisdiction over certain possible crimes under international law, the international legality principle has not been clarified with respect to these crimes. And since its scope with regard to several crime types has not been clarified, states may not want to establish new international courts with adequate, but legally speaking uncertain, subject matter jurisdiction because of the international legality principle.[56]

This situation is unfortunate, particularly because international criminal courts are needed to avoid serious fragmentation of ICL. Within the circle of the core universal crimes, such fragmentation has largely been avoided, despite the existence of several international criminal tribunals operating under similar but differently framed statutes. Fragmentation has been counteracted by employing almost identical crime definitions in the courts' statutes; by having prosecutions before international courts focus mainly on genocide, crimes against humanity,

---

[55] See Manfred Nowak, *U.N. Covenant on Civil and Political Rights: CCPR Commentary*, 2nd ed., N.P. Engel, Kehl, Germany, 2005, p. 368. Nowak refers to customary international law and lists, without much discussion, "war crimes, crimes against peace and humanity, and similar provisions of international law, such as slavery and torture". He also finds treaty law relevant, referring to the Genocide Convention, the Apartheid Convention, the Third Geneva Convention, and the Rome Statute (p. 360).

[56] See section 5.2.3. in this chapter.

and war crimes; and by targeting the most responsible perpetrators. Prosecutors, defence lawyers, and judges at the international tribunals have thus also been able to learn from the experiences of their colleagues at other tribunals and to take account of the jurisprudence developed. Formal mechanisms such as appeals chambers have also contributed towards unity. Overall, most parts of ICL under international court jurisdiction have thus far developed harmoniously. According to one observer, ICL has – presumably insofar as the core crimes are concerned – now met the principal requirement of a legal system, that of being internally consistent and predictable.[57] That is particularly important since domestic legislators, prosecutors, and courts are also now more active in this arena, implying "a risk of unbridled and uncontrolled diversity".[58] This experience thus shows the importance of international jurisprudence of high quality, which can be achieved in relation to specific crimes when adequate international courts are entrusted with relevant and sufficiently clear subject matter jurisdiction.

As this chapter has made clear, the situation is less reassuring for other categories of universal crimes under international law. Paradoxically, the justified focus on the core universal crimes may have contributed to a particular kind of ICL fragmentation, which may persist if the focus is not broadened. At present, crimes satisfying the same universal crime criteria under international law are treated very differently in practice. This potentially creates a situation of inconsistency and unpredictability at the state level, for example with respect to whole categories of universal crimes, namely terrorism, crimes against the United Nations and internationally protected persons, crimes of group destruction not encompassed by the Genocide Convention, grave piracy crimes, grave trafficking crimes, and excessive use and abuse of authorised power in relation to especially serious underlying crimes.[59] It would be unfortunate if these other important universal crimes were not eventually also defined in

---

[57] See Joseph Rikhof, "Fewer Places to Hide? The Impact of Domestic War Crimes Prosecutions on International Impunity", in Morten Bergsmo (ed.), *Complementarity and the Exercise of Universal Jurisdiction for Core International Crimes*, FICHL Publication Series No. 7, Torkel Opsahl Academic Epublisher, Oslo, 2010, p. 78.

[58] *Ibid.*, p. 79. On the quantitative aspects of domestic prosecutions, see Chapter 2, section 2.2.2.

[59] See Appendix I, crime categories E through J. Whereas 85 universal crime types are classified as core crimes in the Appendix, 65 other universal crime types are also listed (of which 14 are considered universal crimes *lex ferenda*).

international instruments and prosecuted before competent international courts. We may recall here the proposition that inherently grave crimes require retributive justice through a fair and public prosecution, for at least 10 different although interconnected reasons.[60] These reasons include deterrent effects as well as the need to uphold and clarify the norms underpinning the proscription of the crimes. Retributive justice with formal procedures is a precondition for establishing, re-establishing, or preserving the rule of law because it emphasises compliance with substantive legal and moral norms and addresses breaches of those norms.

With respect to complex universal crimes, the experiences of recent decades with core crimes show that there are many advantages in having international courts lead the way with their procedures and eventually provide clear guidance to national prosecutors and courts on the same issues. When international guidance is more limited, fragmentation of universal norms, legal uncertainty, and even direct abuse of substantive criminal law concepts are likely to be more common at the national level. For example, the concept of terrorism under international law has probably been widely abused in some countries for the purpose of suppressing particular groups or persecuting political opponents rather than fairly prosecuting and preventing serious crimes. Such practices do a disservice both to the rule of law and to international relations more generally.

A recent example is the popular uprising in Middle Eastern and North African countries during the 'Arab Spring' of 2011. Demonstrators and rebels have sought freedom, opportunities for new generations, broader participation in the government, democracy, and human rights. Yet they have often been labelled terrorists or supporters of terrorism by the authorities, with the risk of being perceived by military and police forces as legitimate targets of violence and eventually severe punishment for terrorist crimes, even when the acts committed were only peaceful protest. By contrast, similar abuses of the concepts of genocide, crimes against humanity, and war crimes would be more difficult, in part because these concepts have been much more clearly defined in international law.

The lesson from successful international court actions on the core crimes is that it is possible to remedy fragmentation and the risk of abuse of international law through concerted actions. The threat of ICL fragmentation does not come from the establishment and works of competent

---

[60] See Chapter 2, section 2.3.5.

international courts, notwithstanding their particular legal basis and jurisdiction. What is required is that the crimes be sufficiently defined in the first place, in the court statutes, in accordance with already existing international law that is accessible and foreseeable to potential perpetrators in accordance with the international legality principle.

This brings us to the last point of this book: the need to develop a 'United Nations Declaration on Universal Crimes' that includes all universal crimes *lex lata* and places them on an equal footing. Such a declaration would put potential perpetrators around the globe on notice that the world community has identified a concrete and exhaustive list of universal crimes. Perpetrators of these universal crimes would be subject to prosecution and could not invoke domestic laws in their defence.

The substantive identification processes should be carried out in a principled and just manner, proceeding on the basis of common criteria, for example, the five criteria proposed in this book for the identification of universal crimes *lex lata*. When conducting new policy discussions anchored in the same agreed principles, it would be unproblematic for the UN to update the declaration regularly and thus elevate former universal crimes *lex ferenda* to the list. Taking such updates into account, it would be easy to determine whether a specific offence, when committed, "was criminal according to the general principles of law recognized by the community of nations".[61] For the crimes included in the initial declaration, it should be stated clearly in each case from which point in time the different crimes are supposed to have been sufficiently foreseeable, in accordance with the international legality principle. The crime would presumably be either (1) always a universal crime within the UN paradigm of international law, or (2) a universal crime at least from a certain point in time.

Would a broadly supported UN declaration meet the requirements of the international legality principle? Our contention is that it would, provided that the crimes included are identified using our five criteria and that the time frame for application is determined for each crime type. For this we have some precedents in international law, for example, with respect to the crime of genocide that was first declared a universal crime

---

[61]   International Covenant on Civil and Political Rights, Article 15(2).

by the General Assembly in 1946,[62] two years before the Genocide Convention was enacted. The Genocide Convention was thus premised on the normative fact that genocide was already a crime under international law, as noted in the preamble and in Article 1.[63] This point has been noted also by international courts. In its advisory opinion on reservations to the Genocide Convention, the International Court of Justice stated,

> The first consequence arising from this conception is that the principles underlying the Convention are principles which are recognized by civilized nations as binding on States, even without any conventional obligation. A second consequence is the universal character both of the condemnation of genocide and of the co-operation required "in order to liberate mankind from such an odious scourge" (Preamble to the Convention). The Genocide Convention was therefore intended by the General Assembly and by the contracting parties to be definitely universal in scope.[64]

On the basis of this precedent, a more comprehensive UN declaration on universal crimes could provide sufficient warning for states and individuals on inherently grave criminal conduct.[65]

A natural first step in the process toward such a UN Declaration on Universal Crimes would be for the General Assembly to entrust the International Law Commission with the mandate to prepare the first draft. Internal UN procedures ought to be complemented by broad and substantial public debate, which would be vital for the future legitimacy of such an important undertaking.

---

[62] See UN General Assembly Resolution 96(I), "The Crime of Genocide", 11 December 1946.

[63] See also Chapter 2, section 2.2.3.

[64] International Court of Justice (ICJ), *Reservations to the Convention on the Prevention and Punishment of the Crime of Genocide*, Advisory Opinion, 28 May 1951, *I.C.J. Reports 1951*, p. 15, at p. 23.

[65] This has recently also been recognised by the Extraordinary Chambers in the Courts of Cambodia (ECCC). See ECCC, Pre-Trial Chamber, *Decision on Ieng Sary's Appeal against the Closing Order*, 11 April 2011, paras. 246–249 (regarding genocide) and paras. 250–254 (regarding crimes against humanity).

APPENDIX I:
CONSOLIDATED LIST OF UNIVERSAL CRIMES

This list of universal crimes was compiled by the author based on the analysis and conclusions set forth in this book. The list encompasses three classes of universal crimes (I–III), 10 universal crime categories (A–J), and 150 universal crime types (1–150).

For each crime category, a proposed gravity clause, to be applied to all crime types in the category, immediately follows the name of the crime category. The formulations of the gravity clauses for the class of universal core crimes (I) closely follow the Rome Statute with respect to crimes of aggression, genocide, crimes against humanity, and war crimes. The other gravity clauses presently lack authoritative formulations in international law, but they are formulated as far as possible in line with international law *lex lata* or *lex ferenda* and consistent with the analysis undertaken in this book. A distinct universal crime type always consists of one underlying type of crime, for example 'killing', and a contextual component in the form of a link to one specific gravity clause, for example, the gravity clause specific to genocide. A complete formulation of crime type 11 would thus be: 'Killing with intent to destroy, in whole or in part, a national, ethnical, racial or religious group, as such'. The same format applies to all the other universal crime types.

The list includes both actual and potential universal crime types, that is, universal crimes *lex lata* and *lex ferenda*. Crimes types with uncertain legal status *lex lata* are marked with one asterisk (*), while those that are clearly still *lex ferenda* are marked with two asterisks (**).

References to the legal bases for any crime type clearly having *lex lata* status are given in parentheses in abbreviated form: for example, ICC 8.2.a refers to Article 8, paragraph 2, sub-paragraph (a) of the Rome Statute. In some cases, such references to possible legal bases are also given for crime types with uncertain *lex lata* status. Many of the universal crime types may have more than one established legal basis in the law-creating sources of international law. Other crimes may only be considered to reach the threshold of a legal basis in international law when several legal bases are considered in conjunction, or must be considered just potential crimes under current ICL. In the list only one source is usually indicated for each crime. Customary international law (CIL) is used as the common reference when the legal status of the crime type is debatable. No legal basis is provided with respect to crimes *lex ferenda*. With regard to all such issues, the list should be considered preliminary and incomplete.

I) Universal Core Crimes

A) Crimes of aggression

(When constituting manifest violations of the UN Charter by the use of armed force against the sovereignty, territorial integrity, or political independence of another state)

1) Invasion or attack by armed forces of another state's territory (ICC 8 *bis* 2.a)

2) Military occupation resulting from invasion or attack (ICC 8 *bis* 2.a)

3) Annexation of territory by the use of force (ICC 8 *bis* 2.a)

4) Bombardment or the use of any weapons against another state (ICC 8 *bis* 2.b)

5) Blockade of the ports or coasts of another state (ICC 8 *bis* 2.c)

6) Attack on the land, sea, or air forces of another state (ICC 8 *bis* 2.d)

7) Attack on the marine and air fleets of another state (ICC 8 *bis* 2.d)

8) Use of armed forces within another state in breach of agreement (ICC 8 *bis* 2.e)

9) Allowing territory to be used for an act of aggression by a third state (ICC 8 *bis* 2.f)

10) Sending of armed bands, groups, irregulars, or mercenaries which carry out acts of armed force against another state amounting to an act of aggression (ICC 8 *bis* 2.g)

B) Crimes of genocide

(When committed with intent to destroy, in whole or in part, a national, ethnical, racial or religious group, as such)

11) Killing (ICC 6.a)

12) Causing serious bodily or mental harm (ICC 6.b)

13) Deliberately inflicting conditions of life calculated to physically destroy a group in whole or in part (ICC 6.c)

14) Imposing measures intended to prevent birth (ICC 6.d)

15) Forcibly transferring children of one group to another group (ICC 6.e)

16) Conspiracy to commit genocide (ICC 6) (Genocide Convention III.b)

17) Direct and public incitement to commit genocide (ICC 6) (Genocide Convention III.c)

18) Attempt to commit genocide (ICC 6) (Genocide Convention III.d)

C) Crimes against humanity

(When committed as part of a widespread or systematic attack directed against any civilian population, with knowledge of the attack)

19) Murder (ICC 7.1.a)

20) Extermination (ICC 7.1.b)

21) Enslavement (ICC 7.1.c)

22) Deportation or forcible transfer of population (ICC 7.1.d)

23) Imprisonment or other severe deprivation of liberty (ICC 7.1.e)

24) Torture (ICC 7.1.f)

25) Rape (ICC 7.1.g)

26) Sexual slavery (ICC 7.1.g)

27) Enforced prostitution (ICC 7.1.g)

28) Forced marriage* (CIL)

29) Forced pregnancy (ICC 7.1.g)

30) Enforced sterilization (ICC 7.1.g)

31) Any other form of grave sexual violence (see crimes 25–29) (ICC 7.1.g)

32) Enforced disappearance of persons (ICC 7.1.i)

33) Other grave inhumane acts (see crimes 19–31) (ICC 7.1.k)

34) Persecution, in the aggravated form of an intentional and severe deprivation of fundamental rights of any identifiable group on a universally impermissible ground (ICC 7.1.h)

35) Apartheid, in the aggravated form of grave inhumane acts (see crimes 19–33) committed in the context of an institutionalised regime of systematic oppression and domination by one racial group over any other racial group or groups with the intention of maintaining that regime (ICC 7.1.j)

D) War crimes

(When committed in the context of war, in particular when committed as part of a plan or policy or as part of a large scale commission of such crimes, and constituting grave breaches of the Geneva Conventions or other serious violations of the laws and customs of international or non-international armed conflicts)

a) Grave violations of personal integrity, rights, and freedoms

36) Wilful killing of protected persons (ICC 8.2.a.i)

37) Killing or wounding a combatant who has surrendered or has no means of defence (ICC 8.2.b.vi)

38) Killing or wounding treacherously individuals belonging to the hostile nation or army (ICC 8.2.b.xi)

39) Torture (ICC 8.2.a.ii)

40) Inhuman treatment (ICC 8.2.a.ii)

41) Rape (ICC 8.2.b.xxii)

42) Sexual slavery (ICC 8.2.b.xxii)

43) Enforced prostitution (ICC 8.2.b.xxii)

44) Forced pregnancy (ICC 8.2.b.xxii)

45) Enforced sterilization (ICC 8.2.b.xxii)

46) Any other form of grave sexual violence (ICC 8.2.b.xxii)

47) Subjecting persons to physical mutilation (ICC 8.2.b.x)

48) Biological experiments on human beings (ICC 8.2.a.ii)

49) Subjecting persons to unjustified medical or scientific experiments which cause death or serious danger to health (ICC 8.2.b.x)

50) Wilfully causing great suffering or serious injury to protected persons (ICC 8.2.a.iii)

51) Outrages upon personal dignity, in particular humiliating and degrading treatment (ICC 8.2.b.xxi)

52) Denial of fair and regular trial to a prisoner of war or other protected person (ICC 8.2.a.vi)

53) Denial of rights in a court of law of the nationals of the hostile party (ICC 8.2.b.xiv)

54) Unlawful confinement of people (ICC 8.2.a.vii)

55) Conscripting or enlisting children under the age of 15 years into armed forces or groups using them to participate actively in hostilities (ICC 8.2.b.xxv, ICC 8.2.e.vii)

56) Compelling nationals of the hostile party to take part in the operations of war against their own country (ICC 8.2.b.xv)

57) Forced military recruitment of prisoners of war or other protected persons (ICC 8.2.a.v)

58) Unlawful deportation of people (ICC 8.2.a.vii)

59) Unlawful transfer of people (ICC 8.2.a.vii)

60) Transfer by an occupying power of parts of its own population into occupied territory (ICC 8.2.b.viii)

61) Deportation or transfer of all or parts of the population of the occupied territory within or outside this territory (ICC 8.2.b.vii)

b) *Excessive use and abuse of war power*

62) Intentional attack against the civilian population as such (ICC 8.2.b.i)

63) Intentional attack against individual civilians not taking direct part in hostilities (ICC 8.2.b.i)

64) Intentional attack against civilian objects which are not military objectives (ICC 8.2.b.ii)

65) Intentional attack against hospitals and places where sick and wounded are collected (ICC 8.2.b.ix)

66) Intentional attack that will cause incidental loss of life or injury to civilians (ICC 8.2.b.iv)

67) Intentional starvation of civilians as a method of warfare (ICC 8.2.b.xxv)

68) Declaring that no quarter will be given (ICC 8.2.b.xii)

69) Attack or bombardment of places which are undefended and not military objectives (ICC 8.2.b.v)

70) Intentional attack that will cause incidental damage to civilian objects (ICC 8.2.b.iv)

71) Intentional attack that will cause incidental widespread, long-term, and severe damage to the natural environment not proportional to military advantage anticipated (ICC 8.2.b.iv)

72) Unjustified intentional attack against protected buildings or monuments (ICC 8.2.b.ix)

73) Unjustified destruction or seizing of the enemy's property (ICC 8.2.b.xiii)

74) Unjustified extensive destruction and/or appropriation of property (ICC 8.2.a.iv)

75) Pillaging a town or place, even when taken by assault (ICC 8.2.b.xvi)

c) *Excessive use and abuse of prohibited weapons or the means of war*

76) Employing poison or poisoned weapons (ICC 8.2.b.xvii)

77) Employing asphyxiating, poisonous, or other gasses, and all analogous liquids, materials, or devices (ICC 8.2.b.xviii)

78) Employing bullets which expand or flatten easily in the human body (ICC 8.2.b.xix)

79) Employing weapons, projectiles, and materials and methods of a nature causing superfluous injury or unnecessary suffering (ICC 8.2.b.xx)

80) Taking of hostages (ICC 8.2.a.viii)

81) Utilizing a civilian or other protected person as a human shield to render certain points, areas, or military forces immune from military operations (ICC 8.2.b.xxiii)

82) Improper use of a flag, emblems, or uniform of the enemy, resulting in death or personal injury (ICC 8.2.b.vii)

83) Recruitment, use, financing, and training of mercenaries**

d) *Attack on protected international personnel or materials*

84) Intentional attack against personnel or materials involved in humanitarian assistance or peacekeeping missions in accordance with the UN Charter (ICC 8.2.b.iii)

85) Intentional attack against buildings, material, medical units and transport, or personnel using the distinctive emblems of the Geneva Conventions in conformity with international law (ICC 8.2.b.xxiv)

II) **Other Universal Crimes against the Peace and Security of Mankind**

E) **Crimes against the United Nations and internationally protected persons**

(When constituting serious acts of violence or serious threats)

86) Intentional attack against UN or associated personnel or materials involved in humanitarian assistance or peacekeeping missions in accordance with the UN Charter* (see ILC 1996 Draft Code, Article 19; see the similar crime type 84 and ICC 8.2.b.iii with regard to such attack in war)

87) Intentional attack against UN buildings, material, medical units and transport, or personnel using the distinctive emblems of the United Nations in conformity with international law* (see ILC 1996 Draft Code, Article 19; see the similar crime type 85 and ICC 8.2.b.xxiv with regard to such attack in war)

88) Intentional attack against other internationally protected persons* (CIL)

89) Threats against the United Nations, judges at international courts, and diplomats**

F) **Terrorist crimes**

(When intended or calculated to provoke a state of terror in the general public, a group of persons, particular individuals, or persons acting in an official capacity, regardless of the political, military, or any other motivation invoked to justify the crime)

90) Bombing or murder of civilians* (CIL)

91) Murder of public servants* (CIL)

92) Assassination of heads of state or political leaders* (CIL)

93) Extermination of a group* (CIL)

94) Execution of prisoners as reprisals* (CIL)

95) Execution of prisoners without a fair trial* (CIL)

96) Murder of hostages* (CIL)

97) Enforced disappearance of persons* (CIL)

98) Enslavement* (CIL)

99) Deportation or forcible transfer of a population* (CIL)

100) Imprisonment or other severe deprivation of liberty* (CIL)

101) Torture* (CIL)

102) Rape* (CIL)

103) Sexual slavery* (CIL)

104) Enforced prostitution* (CIL)

105) Forced pregnancy* (CIL)

106) Enforced sterilization* (CIL)

107) Any other form of grave sexual violence* (CIL)

108) Other inhumane or degrading acts* (CIL)

109) Persecution of any targeted group* (CIL)

110) Taking of hostages* (CIL)

111) Abduction of UN personnel, diplomats, or other protected personnel* (CIL)

112) Hijacking of ship, aircraft, or other means of public or goods transportation* (CIL)

113) Use of civilian aircraft or other means of public or goods transportation as a weapon* (CIL)

114) Destruction of aircraft or other means of public transportation* (CIL)

115) Destruction of infrastructure, significant buildings, or monuments* (CIL)

116) Bombing of embassies* (CIL)

117) Employment of poison, gas, or any other internationally prohibited weapons* (CIL)

118) Employment of other dangerous substances* (CIL)

119) Causing serious fires or floods or seriously interfering with natural resources* (CIL)

120) Employment of nuclear weapons* (CIL)

121) Threats of employment of nuclear weapons* (CIL)

122) Serious threats of other grave terrorist acts* (CIL)

123) Financing terrorist crimes* (CIL)

124) Conspiracy to commit terrorist crimes* (CIL)

125) Direct and public incitement to commit terrorist crimes* (CIL)

126) Attempt to commit terrorist crimes* (CIL)

G) Crimes of group destruction not encompassed by the Genocide Convention

(When committed with intent to destroy, in whole or in part, any identifiable civilian group, as such)

127) Killing**

128) Torture or other inhuman treatment**

129) Enforced disappearance of persons**

130) Enforced displacement, imprisonment, deportation, or forcible transfer of civilians**

131) Systematic or widespread destruction of infrastructure, significant buildings, or monuments**

132) Conspiracy, direct and public incitement, or attempt to commit group destruction**

III) Universal Crimes Not Dependent on the Existence of Threats to International Peace and Security

H) Grave piracy crimes

(When committed as part of a widespread or systematic attack directed against a ship, aircraft, or persons or property on board a ship or aircraft, for economic or private ends)

133) Killing of crew or passengers*

134) Armed robbery* (CIL)

135) Hostage taking* (CIL)

136) Torture or other inhuman treatment* (CIL)

137) Serious threats of violence * (CIL)

138) Destruction of ship or aircraft* (CIL)

139) Financing or profiting from piracy* (CIL)

I) Grave trafficking crimes

(When committed as part of organised large-scale transboundary crimes, with knowledge of the trafficking)

140) Illicit trafficking in human beings**

141) Illicit trafficking in drugs**

142) Illicit trafficking in weapons**

143) Money laundering**

J)   Excessive use and abuse of authorised power

(When committed, organised, or tolerated by a high-level public official or other high-level person acting as authorised within a power structure)

144) Isolated (non-systematic/widespread) acts of torture* (CIL)

145) Isolated (non-systematic/widespread) acts of enforced disappearance of persons* (CIL)

146) Isolated (non-systematic/widespread) acts of unlawful targeted killing of civilians* (CIL)

147) Serious acts of governmental corruption, theft, or embezzlement**

148) Serious acts of wilful destruction or pillage of national treasuries**

149) Serious acts of pillage of natural resources**

150) Serious acts of wilful damage to the environment**

APPENDIX II:
COURT CASES

European Court of Human Rights (ECHR)

ECHR, *Al-Skeini and Others v. United Kingdom*, 55721/07, Grand Chamber Judgment, 7 July 2011.

ECHR, *Angelova and Iliev v. Bulgaria*, 55523/00, Judgment, 26 July 2007.

ECHR, *Kononov v. Latvia*, 36376/04, Grand Chamber Judgment, 17 May 2010.

ECHR, *Menson and Others v. United Kingdom*, 47916/99, Decision, 6 May 2003.

ECHR, *Öneryildiz v. Turkey*, 48939/99, Grand Chamber Judgment, 30 November 2004.

ECHR, *Ramsahai and Others v. The Netherlands*, 52391/99, Grand Chamber Judgment, 15 May 2007.

European Court of Justice (ECJ)

ECJ, *Faraj Hassan and Chafiq Ayadi v. Council and Commission of the European Union*, C-399/06 P and C-403/06 P, Judgment, 3 December 2009.

ECJ, *Yassin Abdullah Kadi and Al Barakaat International Foundation v. Council of the European Union and Commission of the European Communities*, C-402/05 P and C-415/05 P, Judgment, 3 September 2008.

Extraordinary Chambers in the Courts of Cambodia (ECCC)

ECCC Pre-Trial Chamber, *Decision on Ieng Sary's Appeal against the Closing Order: Reasons for Continuation of Provisional Detention*, 002/19-09-2007-ECCC/OCIJ (PTC75), 24 January 2011.

Human Rights Committee (HRC)

HRC, *González del Río v. Peru*, Communication 263/1987, Views, U.N. Doc. CCPR/C/46/D/263/1987, 2 November 1992.

Inter-American Court of Human Rights (IACHR)

IACHR, *Bayarri v. Argentina*, Judgment, 30 October 2008, Series C, no. 187.

IACHR, *Mapiripán Massacre v. Colombia*, Judgment, 15 September 2005, Series C, no. 134.

IACHR, *Miguel Castro-Castro Prison v. Peru*, Judgment, 25 November 2006, Series C, no. 160.

International Court of Justice (ICJ)

ICJ, *Anglo-Norwegian Fisheries Case (United Kingdom v. Norway)*, Judgment, I.C.J. Reports 1951, p. 116.

ICJ, *Application of the Convention on the Prevention and Punishment of the Crime of Genocide (Bosnia and Herzegovina v. Serbia and Montenegro)*, Judgment, I.C.J. Reports 2007, p. 223.

ICJ, *Armed Activities on the Territory of the Congo (Democratic Republic of Congo (DRC) v. Uganda)*, Judgment, I.C.J. Reports 2005, p. 168.

ICJ, *Barcelona Traction, Light and Power Company, Limited (Belgium v. Spain)*, Judgment, I.C.J. Reports 1970, p. 3.

ICJ, *Certain Expenses of the United Nations (Article 17, paragraph 2, of the Charter)*, Advisory Opinion, I.C.J. Reports 1962, p. 151.

ICJ, *East Timor Case (Portugal v. Australia)*, Judgment, I.C.J. Reports 1995, p. 90.

ICJ, *Legal Consequences of the Construction of a Wall in the Occupied Palestinian Territory (Wall Case)*, Advisory Opinion, I.C.J. Reports 2004, p. 136.

ICJ, *Legality of the Threat or Use of Nuclear Weapons*, Advisory Opinion, I.C.J. Reports 1996 (I), p. 257.

ICJ, *Military and Paramilitary Activities in and against Nicaragua (Nicaragua v. United States of America)*, Merits and Judgment, I.C.J. Reports 1986, p. 14.

ICJ, *North Sea Continental Shelf Cases (Federal Republic of Germany/Denmark; Federal Republic of Germany/Netherlands)*, Judgment, I.C.J. Reports 1969, p. 3.

ICJ, *Reservations to the Convention on the Prevention and Punishment of the Crime of Genocide*, Advisory Opinion, I.C.J. Reports 1951, p. 15.

ICJ, *Questions of Interpretation and Application of the 1971 Montreal Convention arising from the Aerial Incident at Lockerbie (Libyan*

Arab Jamahiriya v. United States of America), Provisional Measures, Order, I.C.J. Reports 1992, p. 114.

International Criminal Court (ICC)

ICC Pre-Trial Chamber II, *Situation in the Central African Republic, Prosecutor v. Jean-Pierre Bemba Gombo*, Decision Pursuant to Article 61(7)(a) and (b) of the Rome Statute on the Charges of the Prosecutor Against Jean-Pierre Bemba Gombo, ICC-01/05-01/08, 15 June 2009.

ICC Pre-Trial Chamber I, *Situation in Darfur, Sudan, Prosecutor v. Omar Hassan Ahmad Al Bashir ("Omar Al Bashir")*, Second Warrant of Arrest for Omar Hassan Ahmad Al Bashir, ICC-02/05-01/09, 12 July 2010.

ICC Pre-Trial Chamber I, *Situation in Darfur, Sudan, Prosecutor v. Omar Hassan Ahmad Al Bashir ("Omar Al Bashir")*, Warrant of Arrest for Omar Hassan Ahmad Al Bashir, ICC-02/05-01/09, 4 March 2009.

ICC Pre-Trial Chamber I, *Situation in the Democratic Republic of the Congo, Prosecutor v. Thomas Lubango Dyilo*, Decision on Confirmation of Charges, ICC-01/04-01/06, 29 January 2007.

ICC Pre-Trial Chamber I, *Situation in the Democratic Republic of the Congo, Prosecutor v. Callixte Mbarushimana*, Warrant of Arrest, ICC-01/04-01/10, 28 September 2010.

ICC Pre-Trial Chamber I, *Situation in the Democratic Republic of the Congo, Prosecutor v. Bosco Ntaganda*, Warrant of Arrest, ICC-01/04-02/06, 22 August 2006.

ICC Pre-Trial Chamber I, *Situation in the Democratic Republic of the Congo, Prosecutor v. Germain Katanga and Mathieu Ngudjolo Chui*, Decision on Confirmation of Charges, ICC-01/04-01/07, 30 September 2008.

ICC Pre-Trial Chamber I, *Situation in the Libyan Arab Jamahiriya, Prosecutor v. Muammar Mohammed Abu Minyar Gaddafi et al.*, Decision on the "Prosecutor's Application Pursuant to Article 58 as to Muammar Mohammed Abu Minyar Gaddafi, Seif Al-Islam Gaddafi and Abdullah Al-Senussi", ICC-01/11, 27 June 2011.

ICC Pre-Trial Chamber III, *Situation in the Republic of Côte d'Ivoire*, Request for Authorization of an Investigation Pursuant to Article 15, ICC-02/11, 23 June 2011.

ICC Pre-Trial Chamber II, *Situation in the Republic of Kenya*, Decision Pursuant to Article 15 of the Rome Statute on the Authorization of an Investigation into the Situation in the Republic of Kenya, ICC-01/09, 31 March 2010.

ICC Pre-Trial Chamber II, *Situation in Uganda*, *Prosecutor v. Dominic Ongwen*, Warrant of Arrest, ICC-02/04, 8 July 2005.

ICC Pre-Trial Chamber II, *Situation in Uganda*, *Prosecutor v. Joseph Kony*, Warrant of Arrest as Amended, ICC-02/04-01/05, 27 September 2005.

ICC Pre-Trial Chamber II, *Situation in Uganda*, *Prosecutor v. Okut Odhiambo*, Warrant of Arrest, ICC-02/04, 8 July 2005.

ICC Pre-Trial Chamber II, *Situation in Uganda*, *Prosecutor v. Vincent Otti*, Warrant of Arrest, ICC-02/04, 8 July 2005.

International Criminal Tribunal for the former Yugoslavia (ICTY)

ICTY Appeals Chamber, *Prosecutor v. Dražen Erdemović*, Judgment, Separate and Dissenting Opinion of Judge Cassese, IT-96-22-A, 1997.

ICTY Appeals Chamber, *Prosecutor v. Duško Tadic*, Judgment, IT-94-1-R, 1999.

ICTY Appeals Chamber, *Prosecutor v. Fatmir Limaj et al.*, Judgment, IT-03-66-A, 2007.

ICTY Appeals Chamber, *Prosecutor v. Goran Jelisić*, Judgment, IT-95-10, 2001.

ICTY Appeals Chamber, *Prosecutor v. Kunarac et al.*, Judgment, IT-96-23/1, 2002.

ICTY Appeals Chamber, *Prosecutor v. Zlatko Aleksovski*, Judgment, IT-95-14/1, 2000.

ICTY Trial Chamber, *Prosecutor v. Anto Furundžija*, Judgment, IT-95-17/1, 1998.

ICTY Trial Chamber, *Prosecutor v. Kunarac et al.*, Judgment, IT-96-23, 2001.

ICTY Trial Chamber, *Prosecutor v. Stanislav Galić*, Judgment, IT-98-29-T, 2003.

International Criminal Tribunal for Rwanda (ICTR)

ICTR Trial Chamber, *Prosecutor v. Alfred Musema*, Judgment, ICTR-96-13-A, 2000.

ICTR Trial Chamber, *Prosecutor v. Clément Kayishema and Obed Ruzindana*, Judgment, ICTR 95-1-T, 1999.

ICTR Trial Chamber, *Prosecutor v. Georges A. N. Rutaganda*, Judgment, ICTR-96-3, 1999.

ICTR Trial Chamber, *Prosecutor v. Jean-Paul Akayesu*, Judgment, ICTR-96-4-T, 1998.

International Military Tribunal (IMT)

IMT, *Trial of the Major War Criminals* (Trial of the Major War Criminals before the International Military Tribunal: Nuremberg, 14 November 1945 – 1 October 1946, vol. I [Judgment], published at Nuremberg, Germany, 1947).

International Military Tribunal for the Far East (IMTFE)

IMTFE, *Araki et al.*, Judgment of 12 November 1948. Accessed through the ICC Legal Tools, available at the ICC homepage.

Nuernberg Military Tribunals (NMT)

NMT, *"The Einsatzgruppen Case"*, in Trials of War Criminals before the Nuernberg Military Tribunals under Control Council Law No. 10, October 1946 – April 1949, vol. IV [Judgment], US Government Printing Office, Washington, DC, 1950.

NMT, *"The Hostage Case"*, in Trials of War Criminals before the Nuernberg Military Tribunals under Control Council Law No. 10, October 1946 – April 1949, vol. XI [Judgment], US Government Printing Office, Washington, DC, 1950.

NMT, *"The Justice Case"*, in Trials of War Criminals before the Nuernberg Military Tribunals under Control Council Law No. 10, October 1946 – April 1949, vol. III [Judgment], US Government Printing Office, Washington, DC, 1951.

NMT, *"The Ministries Case"*, in Trials of War Criminals before the Nuernberg Military Tribunals under Control Council Law No. 10, October 1946 – April 1949, vol. XIII [Judgment], US Government Printing Office, Washington, 1952.

Permanent Court of International Justice (PCIJ)

PCIJ, *The Case of the S.S. "Lotus" (France v. Turkey)*, Judgment, 7 September 1927, Series A, no. 10.

Special Court for Sierra Leone (SCSL)

SCSL, *Prosecutor v. Charles Taylor*, SCSL-03-01-T, Prosecution Final Trial Brief, 8 April 2011.

SCSL, *Prosecutor v. Charles Taylor*, SCSL-03-01-PT, Prosecution's Second Amended Indictment, 29 May 2007.

Special Tribunal for Lebanon (STL)

STL Appeals Chamber, *Interlocutory Decision on the Applicable Law: Terrorism, Conspiracy, Homicide, Perpetration, Cumulative Charging*, STL-11-01/I/AC/R176bis, Decision, 16 February 2011.

Various National Courts

High Court of Australia, *Polyukhovich v. Commonwealth*, 101 Australian Law Reports 545, (1991), 172 Commonwealth Law Reports 501, and 91 International Law Reports 1.

High Court of the Hong Kong Special Administrative Region, Court of First Instance, *Yam, BF (Applicants) v. Director of Immigration (1st Respondent) and Secretary for Security (2nd Respondent)*, HCAL 132/2006, Judgment, 18 February 2008.

Israel Supreme Court, *The Eichmann Case*, Judgment, 29 May 1962, International Law Reports 36, pp. 14–17 and 277–344.

Jerusalem District Court, *The Eichmann Case (Israel)*, Judgment, 12 December 1961, International Law Reports 36, pp. 5–14 and 18–276.

Supreme Court of Canada, *Her Majesty The Queen v. Imre Finta*, 1 Supreme Court Reports 701, 24 March 1994.

UK House of Lords, *Opinions of the Lords of Appeal for Judgment in the Cause R. v. Jones et al.(Appellant) v. Director of Public Prosecutions (Respondent)*, UKHL 16, Judgment, 29 March 2006.

UK Supreme Court, *R (on the application of JS) (Sri Lanka) (Respondent) v. Secretary of State for the Home Department (Appellant)*, UKSC 15, Judgment, 17 March 2010.

US Supreme Court, *United States ex rel. Quirin et al. v. Cox, Provost Marshal*, 317 US [Supreme Court Report] 1, Per Curiam Decision filed 31 July 1942, Full Opinion filed 29 October 1942.

APPENDIX III:
FIGURES

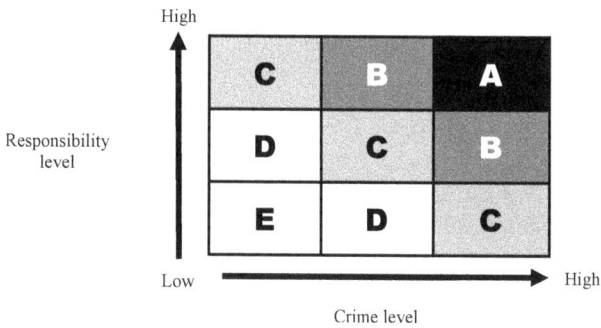

Figure 1: Gravity as a Function of Crime Level and Responsibility Level, p. 81.

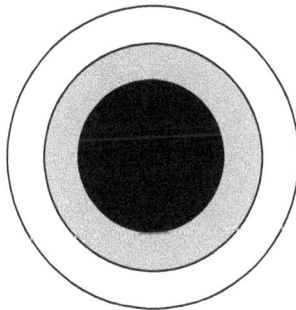

Figure 2: Classes of International Crimes (core crimes – black, all crimes against the peace and security of mankind – grey, all crimes – white), p. 225.

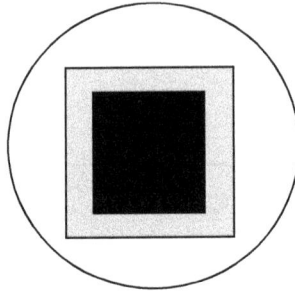

Figure 3: Universal Crimes *Lex Lata* (black) and *Lex Ferenda* (grey), and Non-Universal Crimes (white), p. 300.

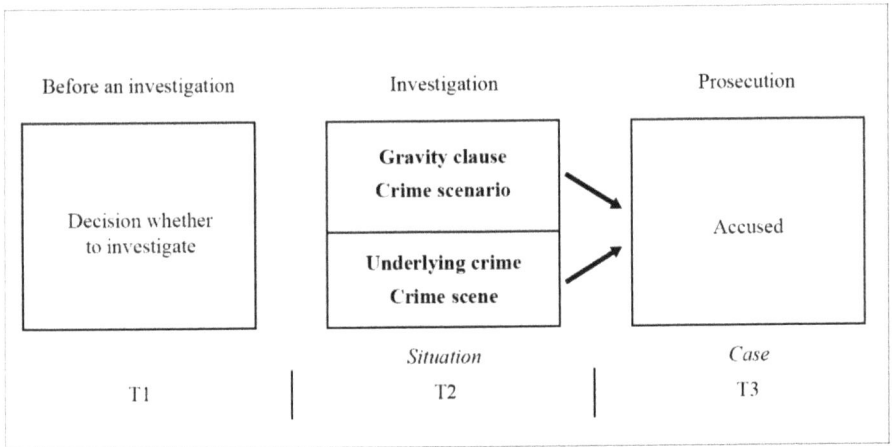

Figure 4: Investigating and Prosecuting Universal Crimes, p. 303.

BIBLIOGRAPHY

Agirre Aranburu, Xavier, "Gravity of Crimes and Responsibility of the Suspect", in Morten Bergsmo (ed.), *Criteria for Prioritizing and Selecting Core International Crimes Cases*, 2nd ed., FICHL Publication Series No. 4, Torkel Opsahl Academic EPublisher, Oslo, 2010.

Akhavan, Payam, "Are International Criminal Tribunals a Disincentive to Peace? Reconciling Judicial Romanticism with Political Realism", in *Human Rights Quarterly*, August 2009, vol. 31, no. 3, pp. 624–654.

Arnold, Roberta, "Conclusions", in Roberta Arnold and Noëlle Quénivet (eds.), *International Humanitarian Law and Human Rights Law: Towards a New Merger in International Law*, Martinus Nijhoff/Brill, Leiden, Netherlands, 2008.

Bassiouni, M. Cherif, "The Discipline of International Criminal Law", in Bassiouni, M. Cherif (ed.), *International Criminal Law*, vol. 1, *Sources, Subjects, and Contents*, 3rd ed., Martinus Nijhoff/Brill, Leiden, Netherlands, 2008.

Bassiouni, M. Cherif, *The Institutionalization of Torture by the Bush Administration: Is Anyone Responsible?*, Intersentia, Mortsel, Belgium, 2010.

Bassiouni, M. Cherif, "International Crimes: The Ratione Materiae of International Criminal Law", in *International Criminal Law*, vol. 1, *Sources, Subjects, and Contents*, 3rd ed., Martinus Nijhoff/Brill, Leiden, Netherlands, 2008.

Bassiouni, M. Cherif (ed.), *International Criminal Law*, vol. 1, *Sources, Subjects, and Contents*, 3rd ed., Martinus Nijhoff/Brill, Leiden, Netherlands, 2008.

Bassiouni, M. Cherif, "The Subjects of International Criminal Law: *Ratione Personae*", in Bassiouni, M. Cherif (ed.), *International Criminal Law*, vol. 1, *Sources, Subjects, and Contents*, 3rd ed., Martinus Nijhoff/Brill, Leiden, Netherlands, 2008.

Ben-Naftali, Orna, "The Obligations to Prevent and to Punish Genocide", in Paola Gaeta (ed.), *The UN Genocide Convention: A Commentary*, Oxford University Press, Oxford, UK, 2009.

Bergsmo, Morten (ed.), *Criteria for Prioritizing and Selecting Core International Crimes Cases*, 2nd ed., FICHL Publication Series No. 4, Torkel Opsahl Academic EPublisher, Oslo, 2010.

Bergsmo, Morten, "The Theme of Selection and Prioritization Criteria and Why It Is Relevant", in Morten Bergsmo (ed.), *Criteria for Prioritizing and Selecting Core International Crimes Cases*, 2nd ed., FICHL Publication Series No. 4, Torkel Opsahl Academic EPublisher, Oslo, 2010.

Blank, Laurie R., "Where Is the Battlefield in the 'War on Terror'? The Need for a Workable Framework", in *Jurist Legal News and Research*, Forum, 1 December 2010, available at http://jurist.org/forum/2010/12/where-is-the-battlefield-in-the-war-on-terror-the-need-for-a-workable-framework.php, last accessed 20 June 2011.

Boister, Neil, "Transnational Criminal Law?", in *European Journal of International Law*, 2003, vol. 14, no. 5, pp. 953–976.

Boyle, Alan, and Christine Chinkin, *The Making of International Law*, Oxford University Press, Oxford, UK, 2007.

Brownlie, Ian, *Principles of Public International Law*, 4th ed., Clarendon Press, Oxford, UK, 1990.

Brownlie, Ian, *The Rule of Law in International Affairs: International Law at the Fiftieth Anniversary of the United Nations*, Kluwer Law International, Alphen aan den Rijn, Netherlands, 1998.

Buchanan, Allen, *Justice, Legitimacy and Self-determination: Moral Foundations for International Law*, Oxford University Press, Oxford, UK, 2007.

Cass, Ronald A., *The Rule of Law in America*, Johns Hopkins University Press, Baltimore, MD, 2001.

Cassese, Antonio, *International Criminal Law*, 2nd ed., Oxford University Press, Oxford, UK, 2008.

Cassese, Antonio, *International Law*, 2nd ed., Oxford University Press, Oxford, UK, 2005.

Cassese, Antonio, "Is Genocidal Policy a Requirement for the Crime of Genocide?" in Paola Gaeta (ed.), *The UN Genocide Convention: A Commentary*, Oxford University Press, Oxford, UK, 2009.

Chapman, Audrey R., and Hugo van der Merwe, *Truth and Reconciliation in South Africa: Did the TRC Deliver?*, University of Pennsylvania Press, Philadelphia, 2008.

Clark, Roger S., "Crimes against Humanity at Nuremberg", in George Ginsburgs and Vladimir Nikolaevich Kudriavtsev (eds.), *The Nuremberg Trial and International Law*, Martinus Nijhoff /Brill, Leiden, Netherlands, 1990.

Côté, Luc, "Reflections on the Exercise of Prosecutorial Discretion in International Criminal Law", in *Journal of International Criminal Justice*, 2005, no. 3, pp. 162–186.

Crawford, Emily, *The Treatment of Combatants and Insurgents under the Law of Armed Conflict*, Oxford University Press, Oxford, UK, 2010.

Crawford, James, "The Drafting of the Rome Statute", in Philippe Sands (ed.), *From Nuremberg to The Hague: The Future of International Criminal Justice*, Cambridge University Press, Cambridge, UK, 2003.

Cryer, Robert, Håkan Friman, Darryl Robinson, and Elizabeth Wilmshurst, *An Introduction to International Criminal Law and Procedure*, 2nd ed., Cambridge University Press, Cambridge, UK, 2010.

Currie, Robert J., *International and Transnational Criminal Law*, Irwin Law, Toronto, 2010.

den Heijer, Maarten, "Whose Rights and Which Rights? The Continuing Story of Non-Refoulement under the European Convention on Human Rights", in *European Journal of Migration and Law*, 2008, vol. 10, no. 3.

Dodge, William S., "Alien Tort Litigation and the Prescriptive Jurisdiction Fallacy", in *Harvard International Law Journal Online*, 2010, vol. 51, pp. 35–46.

Donnelly, Jack, *Universal Human Rights in Theory and Practice*, 2nd ed., Cornell University Press, Ithaca, NY, 2003.

Dörmann, Knut, *Elements of War Crimes under the Rome Statute of the International Criminal Court: Sources and Commentary*, Cambridge University Press, Cambridge, UK, 2003.

Drumbl, Mark A., *Atrocity, Punishment and International Law*, Cambridge University Press, Cambridge, UK, 2007.

Drumbl, Mark A., "The Principle of Legality in International and Comparative Criminal Law, by Kenneth S. Gallant, Book Review", in *Human Rights Quarterly*, August 2009, vol. 31, no. 3, pp. 801–806.

Einarsen, Terje, "Drafting History of the 1951 Refugee Convention and the 1967 Protocol", in Andreas Zimmermann (ed.), *The 1951 Refugee Convention Relating to the Status of Refugees and Its 1967 Protocol*, Oxford University Press, Oxford, UK, 2011, pp. 37–73.

Enache-Brown, Colleen, and Ari Fried, "Universal Crime, Jurisdiction and Duty: The Obligation of Aut Dedere Aut Judicare in International Law", in *McGill Law Journal*, 1998, vol. 43, pp. 613–633.

Eng, Svein, *Analysis of Dis/agreement: With Particular Reference to Law and Legal Theory*, Kluwer Academic, Dordrecht, Netherlands, 2003.

Evans, Gareth, *The Responsibility to Protect: Ending Mass Atrocity Crimes Once and for All*, Brookings Institution Press, Washington, DC, 2008.

Fletcher, George P., *The Grammar of Criminal Law: American, Comparative, and International*, vol. 1, *Foundations*, Oxford University Press, Oxford, UK, 2007.

Futamura, Madoka, *War Crimes Tribunals and Transitional Justice: The Tokyo Trial and the Nuremberg Legacy*, Routledge, London, 2009.

Gaeta, Paola (ed.), *The UN Genocide Convention: A Commentary*, Oxford University Press, Oxford, UK, 2009.

Gallant, Kenneth S., *The Principle of Legality in International and Comparative Criminal Law*, Cambridge University Press, Cambridge, UK, 2009.

Gargarella, Roberto, "The Majoritarian Reading of the Rule of Law", in José M. Maravall and Adam Przeworski (eds.), *Democracy and the Rule of Law*, Cambridge University Press, Cambridge, UK, 2003, pp. 147–167.

Geis, Jacqueline, and Alex Mundt, "When to Indict? The Impact of Timing of International Criminal Indictments on Peace Processes and Humanitarian Action", paper prepared for World Humanitarian Studies Conference, Groningen, Netherlands, February 2009, available at http://www.brookings.edu/~/media/Files/rc/papers/2009/04_

peace_and_justice_geis/04_peace_and_justice_geis.pdf, last accessed 12 August 2011.

Gibney, Mark, *International Human Rights Law: Returning to Universal Principles*, Rowman and Littlefield, Lanham, MD, 2008.

Goldsmith, Jack L., and Eric A. Posner, *The Limits of International Law*, Oxford University Press, Oxford, UK, 2005.

Goldston, James A., "More Candour about Criteria: The Exercise of Discretion by the Prosecutor of the International Criminal Court", in *Journal of International Criminal Justice*, 2010, no. 8, pp. 383–406.

Goodwin-Gill, Guy, "Crime and International Law: Expulsion, Removal and the Non-Derogable Obligation", in Stefan Talmon and Guy Goodwin-Gill (eds.), *The Reality of International Law: Essays in Honour of Ian Brownlie*, Oxford University Press, Oxford, UK, 1999.

Gray, Christine, "The Charter Limitations on the Use of Force: Theory and Practice", in Vaughan Lowe, Adam Roberts, Jennifer Welsh, and Dominik Zaum (eds.), *The United Nations Security Council and War: The Evolution of Thought and Practice since 1945*, Oxford University Press, Oxford, UK, 2008.

Gray, Christine, *International Law and the Use of Force*, 3rd ed., Oxford University Press, Oxford, UK, 2008.

Hart Dubner, Barry, and Karen Greene, "On the Creation of a New Legal Regime to Try Sea Pirates", in *Journal of Maritime Law and Commerce*, 2010, vol. 39, no. 3, pp. 439–464.

Hart, Herbert L. A., *The Concept of Law*, 2nd edition, Oxford University Press, Oxford, UK, 1994.

Husabø, Erling Johannes, and Ingvild Bruce, *Fighting Terrorism through Multilevel Criminal Legislation: Security Council Resolution 1373, the EU Framework Decision on Combating Terrorism and Their Implementation in Nordic, Dutch and German Criminal Law*, Martinus Nijhoff /Brill, Leiden, Netherlands, 2009.

International Center for Transitional Justice, "What Is Transitional Justice?", 2009, available at http://ictj.org/publication/what-transitional-justice, last accessed 13 July 2011.

International Commission on Intervention and State Sovereignty, *The Responsibility to Protect*, International Development Research Centre, Ottawa, 2001.

Jackson, Robert H., "Notes on Proposed Definition of 'Crimes,'" London, 31 July 1945, available at http://avalon.law.yale.edu/imt/jack55.asp, last accessed 21 September 2011.

Jallow, Hassan B., "Prosecutorial Discretion and International Criminal Justice", in *Journal of International Criminal Justice*, 2005, no. 3, pp. 145–161.

Jessberger, Florian, "The Definition and the Elements of the Crime of Genocide", in Paola Gaeta (ed.), *The UN Genocide Convention: A Commentary*, Oxford University Press, Oxford, UK, 2009.

Jørgensen, Nina H. B., *The Responsibility of States for International Crimes*, Oxford University Press, Oxford, UK, 2000.

Kaul, Hans-Peter, *Is It Possible to Prevent or Punish Future Aggressive War-Making?*, FICHL Occasional Paper Series, Torkel Opsahl Academic EPublisher, Oslo, 8 February 2011.

Kaye, David, "Who Is Afraid of the International Criminal Court? Finding the Prosecutor Who Can Set It Straight", in *Foreign Affairs*, May/June 2011, available at http://www.foreignaffairs.co m/articles/67768/david-kaye/whos-afraid-of-the-international-criminal-court, last accessed 27 June 2011.

Kelsen, Hans, *Pure Theory of Law*, translation from 2nd German ed. by Max Knight, Lawbook Exchange Ltd., Clark, NJ, 2008.

Kirgis, Frederic L., "Custom on a Sliding Scale", in *American Journal of International Law*, 1987, vol. 81, no. 1, pp. 146–151.

Klinkner, Melanie, "Proving Genocide? Forensic Expertise and the ICTY", in *Journal of International Criminal Justice*, 2008, no. 6, pp. 447–466.

Klip, André, *European Criminal Law: An Integrative Approach*, Intersentia, Mortsel, Belgium, 2009.

Koff, Clea, *The Bone Woman: A Forensic Anthropologist's Search for Truth in the Mass Graves of Rwanda, Bosnia, Croatia, and Kosovo*, Random House, New York, 2005.

Kontorovich, Eugene, and Steven Art, "An Empirical Examination of Universal Jurisdiction for Piracy", in *American Journal of International Law*, 2010, vol. 104, no. 3, pp. 436–453.

Lemkin, Raphael, *Axis Rule in Occupied Europe: Laws of Occupation, Analysis of Government, Proposals for Redress*, Carnegie Endowment for International Peace, Washington, DC, 1944.

Lemkin, Raphael, "Genocide", in *American Scholar*, April 1946, vol. 15, no. 2, pp. 227–230.

Lemkin, Raphael, "Genocide: A Modern Crime", in *Free World*, April 1945, vol. 4, pp. 39–43.

Lepard, Brian D., *Customary International Law: A New Theory with Practical Applications*, Cambridge University Press, Cambridge, UK, 2010.

Lutz, Ellen L., "Prosecutions of Heads of State in Europe", in Ellen L. Lutz and Caitlin Reiger (eds.), *Prosecuting Heads of State*, Cambridge University Press, Cambridge, UK, 2009.

Lutz, Ellen L., "Transitional Justice: Lessons Learned and the Road Ahead", in Naomi Roht-Arriaza and Javier Mariezcurrena (eds.), *Transitional Justice in the Twenty-First Century: Beyond Truth versus Justice*, Cambridge University Press, Cambridge, UK, 2006, pp. 325–341.

Macedo, Stephen (ed.), *Universal Jurisdiction: National Courts and the Prosecution of Serious Crimes under International Law*, University of Pennsylvania Press, Philadelphia, 2004.

Mallinder, Louise, *Amnesty, Human Rights and Political Transition: Bridging the Peace and Justice Divide*, Hart Publishing, Oxford, UK, 2008.

Mann, Itamar, "The Dual Foundation of Universal Jurisdiction: Towards a Jurisprudence for the 'Court of Critique'", in *Transnational Legal Theory*, 2010, vol. 1, no. 4, pp. 485–521.

Marston Danner, Allison, "Enhancing the Legitimacy and Accountability of Prosecutorial Discretion at the International Criminal Court", in *American Journal of International Law*, 2003, vol. 97, pp. 510–552.

Melzer, Nils, *Targeted Killing in International Law*, Oxford University Press, Oxford, UK, 2008.

Meron, Theodor, *Human Rights and Humanitarian Norms as Customary Law*, Clarendon Press, Oxford, UK, 1989.

Nollkaemper, André, and Harmen van der Wilt (eds.), *System Criminality in International Law*, Cambridge University Press, Cambridge, UK, 2009.

Nowak, Manfred, *U.N. Covenant on Civil and Political Rights: CCPR Commentary*, 2nd ed., N.P. Engel, Kehl, Germany, 2005.

Ntanda Nsereko, Daniel D., "Prosecutorial Discretion before National Courts and International Tribunals", in *Journal of International Criminal Justice*, 2005, no. 3, pp. 124–144.

Orakhelashvili, Alexander, *Peremptory Norms in International Law*, Oxford University Press, Oxford, UK, 2008.

Power, Samantha, *A Problem from Hell: America and the Age of Genocide*, Perennial, New York, 2002.

Quénivet, Noëlle, "The History of the Relationship between International Humanitarian Law and Human Rights Law", in Roberta Arnold and Noëlle Quénivet (eds.), *International Humanitarian Law and Human Rights Law: Towards a New Merger in International Law*, Martinus Nijhoff/Brill, Leiden, Netherlands, 2008.

Ratner, Steven R., Jason S. Abrams, and James L. Bischoff, *Accountability for Human Rights Atrocities in International Law: Beyond the Nuremberg Legacy*, 3rd ed., Oxford University Press, Oxford, UK, 2009.

Rikhof, Joseph, *Exclusion at a Crossroads: The Interplay between International Criminal Law and Refugee Law in the Area of Extended Liability*, Legal and Protection Policy Research Series, PPLA/2011/ 06, Division of International Protection, United Nations High Commissioner for Refugees, June 2011.

Rikhof, Joseph, "Fewer Places to Hide? The Impact of Domestic War Crimes Prosecutions on International Impunity", in Morten Bergsmo (ed.), *Complementarity and the Exercise of Universal Jurisdiction for Core International Crimes*, FICHL Publication Series No. 7, Torkel Opsahl Academic Epublisher, Oslo, 2010, pp. 7–81.

Rikhof, Joseph, "War Criminals Not Welcome: How Common Law Countries Approach the Phenomenon of International Crimes in the Immigration and Refugee Context", in *International Journal of Refugee Law*, 2009, vol. 21, no. 3, pp. 453–507.

Roht-Arriaza, Naomi, and Javier Mariezcurrena, "The New Landscape of Transitional Justice", in Naomi Roht-Arriaza and Javier Mariezcurrena (eds.), *Transitional Justice in the Twenty-First Cen-*

tury: Beyond Truth versus Justice, Cambridge University Press, Cambridge, UK, 2006.

Roht-Arriaza, Naomi, and Javier Mariezcurrena (eds.), *Transitional Justice in the Twenty-First Century: Beyond Truth versus Justice*, Cambridge University Press, Cambridge, UK, 2006.

Röling, Bernard V. A., and Antonio Cassese, *The Tokyo Trial and Beyond: Reflections of a Peacemonger*, Polity Press, Cambridge, UK, 1994.

Roxin, Claus, "Crimes as Part of Organized Power Structures", in *Journal of International Criminal Justice*, 2011, no. 9, pp. 193–205.

Saul, Ben, *Defining Terrorism in International Law*, Oxford University Press, Oxford, UK, 2006.

Schabas, William A., *Genocide in International Law*, 2nd ed., Cambridge University Press, Cambridge, UK, 2009.

Schabas, William A., *The International Criminal Court: A Commentary on the Rome Statute*, Oxford University Press, Oxford, UK, 2010.

Schabas, William A., *An Introduction to the International Criminal Court*, 3rd ed., Cambridge University Press, Cambridge, UK, 2007.

Schwarzenberger, Georg, *The Inductive Approach to International Law*, Stevens, London, 1965.

Shue, Henry, *Basic Rights: Subsistence, Affluence, and U.S. Foreign Policy*, Princeton University Press, Princeton, NJ, 1980.

Skaar, Elin, *Judicial Independence and Human Rights in Latin America: Violations, Politics, and Prosecution*, Palgrave Macmillan, New York, 2011.

Smith, Karen E., *Genocide and the Europeans*, Cambridge University Press, Cambridge, UK, 2010.

Solis, Gary S. *The Law of Armed Conflict: International Humanitarian Law in War*, Cambridge University Press, Cambridge, UK, 2010.

Taylor, Telford, *Final Report to the Secretary of the Army on the Nuremberg War Crimes Trials under Control Council Law No. 10*, U.S. Government Printing Office, Washington, DC, 15 August 1949.

Ticehurst, Rupert, "The Martens Clause and the Laws of Armed Conflict", *International Review of the Red Cross*, 1997, no. 317.

Totani, Yuma, *The Tokyo War Crimes Trial: The Pursuit of Justice in the Wake of World War II*, Harvard University Press, Cambridge, USA, and London, First paperback edition, 2009.

Tzanakopoulos, Antonios, *Disobeying the Security Council: Counter-measures against Wrongful Sanctions*, Oxford University Press, Oxford, UK, 2011.

van Krieken, Peter J. (ed.), *Refugee Law in Context: The Exclusion Clause*, TMC Asser Press, The Hague, 1999.

Verrijn Stuart, Heikelina, and Marlise Simons, *The Prosecutor and the Judge*, Amsterdam University Press, Amsterdam, 2009.

Watts, Arthur, *The International Law Commission, 1949–1998*, vol. 3, *Final Draft Articles and Other Materials*, Oxford University Press, Oxford, UK, 1999.

Weiss, Thomas G., and Sam Daws, "World Politics: Continuity and Change since 1945", in Thomas G. Weiss and Sam Daws(eds.), *The Oxford Handbook on the United Nations*, Oxford University Press, Oxford, UK, 2008.

Welsh, Jennifer M., "The Security Council and Humanitarian Intervention", in Vaughan Lowe, Adam Roberts, Jennifer Welsh, and Dominik Zaum (eds.), *The United Nations Security Council and War: The Evolution of Thought and Practice since 1945*, Oxford University Press, Oxford, UK, 2008.

Werle, Gerhard, *Principles of International Criminal Law*, 2nd ed., TMC Asser Press, The Hague, 2009.

Werle, Gerhard, and Boris Burghardt, "Claus Roxin on Crimes as Part of Organized Power Structures: Introductory Note", in *Journal of International Criminal Justice*, 2011, no. 9, pp. 191–193.

Wheeler, Nicholas J., *Saving Strangers: Humanitarian Intervention in International Society*, Oxford University Press, Oxford, UK, 2000.

Zahar, Alexander, and Göran Sluiter, *International Criminal Law: A Critical Introduction*, Oxford University Press, Oxford, UK, 2008.

Zimmermann, Andreas, and Wennholz, Philipp, "Article 1 F", in Andreas Zimmermann (ed.), *The 1951 Refugee Convention Relating to the Status of Refugees and Its 1967 Protocol*, Oxford University Press, Oxford, UK, 2011, pp. 579–610.

INDEX

A

Abrams, Jason S., 160
accountability, 1, 2, 28, 29, 35, 41, 43, 60, 89, 154, 160, 162
  and the legality principle, 115
  for grave crimes, 118
  for participation in universal crimes, 50
  to ensure accountability for international/universal crimes, 56
  universal accountability for serious crimes, 3
accountability principle, 2, 35, 37
Afghanistan, 55, 69, 75, 264 (fn. 416), 265 (fn. 417)
African Union, 53
aggression, 177, 185, 253, 257, 278, 320
  definition by the UN General Assembly 1974, 269
  definition in the Rome Statute, 209–216
  "the gravest of all crimes", 178
  threat of, 185
Agirre Aranburu, Xabier, 78
aiding and abetting, 149, 249
Allied Control Council Law No. 10, 42, 77, 148
al-Qaeda, 69, 264 (fn. 416), 265 (fn. 417)
Al-Skeini Judgment, 234
amnesty, 62, 83, 232
  blanket amnesties, 51, 243
amnesty laws, 58, 59
anti-piracy courts, 167, 308 (fn. 36), 310–312
apartheid, 152, 156, 160, 162, 166, 184, 191
  crimes against humanity, 279
  crimes against the peace and security of mankind, 185
  international crimes, 191
  jus cogens norms, 8
  universal crimes, 322
Arab Spring, 316

arbitrary executions, 208, 305 (fn. 28)
Argentina, 90 (fn. 9), 243
Aristotle, 29, 225
Armed Activities Case, 131, 260 (fn. 406)
armed conflict, 8, 27, 65, 187, 190, 195, 209, 257, 260, 263 (fn. 411–412), 265 (fn. 417), 277
  classic civil war, 261
  classic international war, 258
  internal armed conflict of an international character, 260
  international armed conflict, 255
  in a legal sense, 256–257
  in descriptive terms, 256
  Martens Clause, 26
  not of an international character, 255
  relevance for international (universal) crimes, 255
  terrorism during armed conflict, 272
armed intervention, 210, 266
  authorised by the UN, 233, 259
  for the protection of civilians, 233
  humanitarian intervention, 122–123
  manifest armed intervention, 259, 266
Armenian massacres, 25
asylum from persecution, 46
  exception in the case of serious crimes, 46
  UDHR Art. 14, 46
attempted crimes under international law, 173, 175, 188, 201, 202
  genocide, 249, 279, 321
  group destruction, 285, 327
  terrorist crimes, 72, 285, 327
aut dedere aut judicare, 65, 127, 138, 192, 194, 203
autonomous international criminal law concepts, 226, 239

B

basic norm, 97
  "basic universal crimes norm", 291
  "grundnorm", 97 (fn. 32)

of international law, 97, 291
Bassiouni, M. Cherif, 154–156, 160, 165
Bergsmo, Morten, 75
binding international law, 6–7, 9, 87, 98–
    100, 104, 110, 119, 125, 129,140, 169,
    218, 244–245, 268, 274, 294–295,
    313, 318
    if-then character, 88
    superior legal norms, 62
Bingham, Tom, 209
Bischoff, James L., 160
Black September, 68
Boister, Neil, 164, 165
Bosnia, 54, 70, 146, 330, 342, 361
Boyle, Alan, 121
Brownlie, Ian, 31–33, 35

C

Cambodia, 54, 91, 146, 243, 329
Canada, 163
Cassese, Antonio, 20, 151–156, 162, 263
Central African Republic, 54
Chile, 243
China, 3
Chinkin, Christine, 121
Cicero, 168
civil war (see also armed conflict), 53,
    154, 255, 257–258, 260–261, 263
civilians protected under international
    law, 261, 270, 281, 289
civilised nations, 42, 108, 111
classic civil war, 261, 263
classic international war, 258
collective crimes, 79–80
Colombia, 55, 234, 330
colonial domination, 185, 192
colonialism, 184–185, 192
combatants, 257, 261–262, 266
complicity in the commission of crimes,
    45, 148, 173, 175–176
    different from membership crime, 148
concurrent jurisdiction, 233, 235
conspiracy, 27, 45, 69, 147, 173, 175,
    176, 249, 279, 284–285, 321, 327
constitutive principles, 111
    of international law, 112, 116–117,
    291
core crimes, 138, 147, 158, 166, 209

as a class of international crimes, 225,
    230
concept, 149
core international crimes, 11, 67, 159,
    167, 172, 224, 230, 252, 289, 298
core universal crimes, 299
gravity clauses, 302
the most serious crimes, 211
Côte d'Ivoire, Republic of, 54, 331
Council of Europe, 140, 229
Counter-Terrorism Committee, 120, 268
crime
    definition, 19
crime categories, 222, 251
crime categories and crime types
    the distinction, 302
crime of aggression
    crime category, 278, 320
    crime types, 278, 320
    different from act of aggression, 253
    gravity clause, 253
    ICL Draft Code, 185
    Rome Statute Article 8 bis, 214–215
    Rome Statute Review Conference, 66,
    213
crime of genocide
    affirmed in the Genocide Convention,
    48, 318
    at Nuremberg, 49
    concept invented by Lemkin, 48
    crime category, 278, 320
    crime types, 221, 278–279, 320–321
    definition in the Genocide Convention,
    179
    International Court of Justice, 145, 318
    UNGA Resolution 96(I), 48
crime of group destruction
    crime category, 285, 305, 327
    crime types, 285
    ICL Draft Code, 178
    lex ferenda, 274–275
    not encompassed by the Genocide
    Convention, 250, 276, 289, 315
    underlying crimes, 275
crime of persecution
    crimes against humanity, 279, 321
    in the Nuremberg Judgment,
    46, 48 (fn. 80), 49 (fn. 85)
    ICL Draft Code, 178

ICTY Statute, 191
  terrorist crimes, 284, 326
crime scenario, 79, 303, 305, 307, 309
  figure, 303
crime scene, 73, 77, 79, 81, 138, 195, 223,
  232, 303–305, 307, 309
  figure, 303
crime types, 222–223, 251
  examples, 277
crimes against humanity
  core crimes (see also core international
    crimes), 224
  crime category, 279, 321
  crime types, 279–280, 321-322
  crimes that shock humanity, 24
  ICL 1950, 45
  ICL Draft Code, 190-191, 200
  ICTY Statute, 190–191
  in the Nuremberg Judgment,
    49 (fn. 85)
  included in all statutes, 66, 90
  jurisdiction, 49, 179
  Norway 2011, 72
crimes against peace (see also *crime of
  aggression*), 45, 66, 144
crimes against the peace and security of
  mankind, 167, 170–171, 174, 176,
  182, 193, 220, 225, 230, 252, 283,
  298–299, 325
  crime categories and crime types, 283
crimes against the UN and internationally
  protected persons, 201, 275, 283, 289,
  305, 315, 325
crimes *lex ferenda*, 251–252, 276, 286,
  292, 296-300, 317, 320
  figure, 300, 336
crimes *lex lata*, 231, 251, 274, 276, 286,
  291–292, 296–299, 319
  figure 300, 336
crimes that shock civilised societies, 41
crimes that shock humanity and civilised
  societies, 23–24, 72
crimes with uncertain status, 289
criminal law
  definition, 19
Cryer, Robert, 158–159
current international crimes, 245
Currie, Robert J., 163–167, 225
customary international law, 104–108

crimes deviating from or part of, 112,
  132, 134, 140, 154, 164
and *jus cogens*, 64, 108
and universal crimes, 104
principal criteria, 106

D

definitions
  descriptive, 21, 218–220
  empirical, 220
  enumerative, 221, 249
  extensional, 221, 250
  legal, 218, 220
  normative, 219, 220
  stipulative, 21, 135, 137, 140, 217–
    218, 220, 296
  theoretical, 22, 135, 295–301
democratic law state, 29
Democratic Republic of the Congo, 54
descriptive definitions (see *definitions*)
descriptive propositions, 161, 219, 296
deterrent effect, 59, 84 (box 1)
direct criminal liability (responsibility), 4,
  12, 105, 112, 125, 135, 153, 236, 246,
  312
direct incitement, 175
Donnelly, Jack, 26, 28
Drumbl, Mark, 34
duty to extradite or prosecute (see also *aut
  dedere aut judicare*), 89, 138, 233
duty to investigate and prosecute, 232–
  234

E

East Timor, 54, 146
Eichmann case, 243
ejusdem generis, 157, 211
enemies of humankind (*hostis humani
  generis*), 166, 168
enemy combatants (see also *combatants*),
  257
  lawful, 261
  unlawful, 261
enforced disappearance, 245
  crimes against humanity, 279, 321
  excessive use and abuse of authorised
    power, 268, 328

group destruction, 285, 327
terrorist crimes, 283, 326
equality, 3, 28, 30–31, 35, 89, 112, 240
erga omnes, 8, 43, 63, 75, 86
ethnic cleansing, 222
EU Framework Decision, 120 (fn. 120), 229, 270, 273
eurocrimes, 229–230
ex post facto, 30, 111, 113–116, 169, 181, 232, 240, 314
excessive use and abuse of authorised power, 276, 286, 289, 305, 315, 328
exclusion from refugee status, 47, 148
extended liability, 95, 148, 249
membership crime, 148

F

fair trial, 14, 22, 45, 45–46, 63, 118, 135, 208, 233, 247 (fn. 371), 263, 296
figures in the book
Figure 1, 81, 335
Figure 2, 225, 335
Figure 3, 300, 336
Figure 4, 303, 336
fragmentation, 5, 17, 87 (fn. 4), 88, 95–97, 294, 314–316
fragmented character of ICL, 15, 137, 226
France, 42
Friman, Håkan, 158, 159
Führerprinzip, 30
fundamental universal value or interest, 34, 40, 85 (box 1), 122, 128, 208, 236–239, 244, 248, 251–254, 268, 276, 291, 293, 297–298, 300–301
Furundžija Judgment, 109 (fn. 70), 111, 112 (fn. 74)

G

Galicki, Zdzislaw, 203
Gaza Strip, 3, 55, 64 (fn. 126), 75
general principles as international law, 108–118
general principles of (international) law, 7, 23, 32, 42, 50, 64–65, 96–97, 99, 109–110, 112, 119–120, 124–126, 128, 130, 134, 142, 169, 209, 219, 245, 248, 250, 274, 294–295, 314, 317

in the UN Charter, 112
superior (*jus cogens*), 131
genocide
against the Jews, 68
accepted as a crime by the International Court of Justice, 144
concept invented by Lemkin, 144
confirmed as a crime in the Genocide Convention, 48, 144–145, 318
crime category, 278, 320
crime types, 278–279, 320–321
declared a crime by the General Assembly, 144
declared a universal crimes by the General Assembly, 317
definition, 179, 186
ICL Draft Code, 185–186
in the Nuremberg Indictment, 49, 144
multiple foundations within ICL, 64
not a separate crime in the Nuremberg Statute, 144
prevention and punishment obligations, 64
genocide crimes
one-man genocide mission, 71
two (objective) legal ingredients, 69
without being part of a larger plan or policy, 69–70, 82
Georgia, 55
Germany, 68, 91, 148
global war on terror (see also *war on terror*), 261, 265
Goldstone fact-finding mission, 75
grave acts of terrorism, 268–269, 273
grave breaches, 47, 191, 223, 252
grave breaches of international law, 66–68
grave crimes, 24, 41, 53–54, 58, 85
retributive justice, 84
grave piracy crimes, 276, 305, 307, 311, 312, 315
crime types, 285
grave trafficking crimes, 276, 305, 285, 315
gravity, 242
as a function of crime level and responsibility level, 80
relevance, 73

gravity assessment, 10, 14, 73–82, 182, 201–202, 216, 231, 276
gravity clauses, 10, 82, 199, 211, 242, 273, 277, 294, 302, 303
 and crime categories, 305
 and piracy, 307, 311
 and torture, 254
 implicit, 275
 inherent, 253, 254, 305, 306, 311
 inherent in all universal (international) crimes, 271
 the concept, 253
gravity threshold, 74, 76, 82, 189–190, 195–196, 211–212, 215–216, 271, 293, 319
 aggression, 215
 piracy, 310–311
 Rome Statute Article 5, 157
 terrorism, 269
Guinea, 55

H

Hassan and Ayadi Case, 124
Holocaust, 25
Honduras, 55
horizontal structure of international law, 127
Hostage Case, 17, 206–208, 220, 237, 241, 244
hostages, 184–185, 191, 208, 270, 282–283, 304, 308, 324–326
hostis humani generis (enemies of humankind), 166, 168
human dignity, 24–28, 41, 229, 256
human rights, 26–27, 41, 112, 131, 140, 295
 and customary international law, 140
 lex lata and *lex ferenda*, 140, 295
human security, 122
Husabø, Erling Johannes, 119, 120, 123
hybrid (international) courts, 54, 56, 91, 95, 141, 146, 149, 167, 247

I

illicit trafficking
 in human beings, 139, 227–228, 285, 327

 in drugs, 139, 192, 212, 227–228, 285, 328
 in weapons (firearms), 139, 228, 285, 328
impunity, 4, 58, 154, 207
 for grave crimes, 27, 313
in dubio pro reo, 103, 111
inchoate crimes, 176, 249
international armed conflict (see also *armed conflict*), 255
international community, 1, 3, 186, 232, 237
 as a whole, 63, 149, 157, 189
 important interests, 165
 shared values and interests, 237–238
international crime categories, 195, 222–223
international crimes
 a general definition, 141
 a proposed legal definition, 248
 accessibility and foreseeability, 142
 and non-international crimes, 225
 and the International Law Commission, 143
 as compared to international offences and non-international crimes, 252
 as compared to non-international crimes, 230
 categories and types, 222, 223
 concept, 6, 150
 definition in the *Hostage* Case, 206
 different conceptualisations, 137–144
 distinctive criteria, 205
 four analytical classes, 222
 gravity matrix, 81
 ILC selection criteria, 193
 lack of an authoritative definition, 205
 legal consequences, 232
 lex lata and *lex ferenda*, 231, 276
 necessary and sufficient conditions, 231, 236, 291
 relevance of war or peace, 255
 three abstract classes, 224, 225
International Criminal Court
 international legal personality, 101
 relationship to the UN, 101
 Review Conference, 17, 213–217, 269, 273
 subject-matter jurisdiction, 101

international criminal law
    as a branch of international law, 20
    fragmentation, 88, 94
    fragmented nature, 4, 89
    inherent dualism, 93
    polycentric character, 94, 137, 250 (fn.
        579)
international criminalisation, 162, 194
international humanitarian law and
    international human rights law
    relationship, 132
international hybrid courts (see *hybrid
    courts*)
international law
    as a system of law, 87
    horizontal structure, 32
    interpretative sources, 98
    law-creating sources, 87, 97
International Law Commission, 168–206
    fragmentation, 5
    Nuremberg Principles 1950, 44
    statements on international crimes, 168
international legality principle (see also
    legality principle), 95, 96, 104, 114,
    141, 197, 233, 294, 313, 317
    and crimes under international law,
        314
    and universal crimes, 115
International Military Tribunal for the Far
    East, 36 (fn. 45), 42
international offences, 13, 181, 251–253,
    298–299
international peace and security, 98
    UN powers and limitations, 121
international terrorism, 185, 192, 264 (fn.
    416)
international war, 255, 258, 260 (fn. 406),
    261, 264, (fn. 416), 265 (fn. 417), 266
internationally protected persons, 184–
    185, 191–192, 270, 275, 283, 289,
    305, 325
interpretation of ICL treaties
    strict construction, 103, 104
interpretation of treaties, 87, 96
    Rome Statute, 102–103
    VCLT, 101–102
interpretative sources, 129–130, 219
intervention
    as a crime, 178, 183, 185, 192

authorised by the UN, 233, 259, 266
for whatever purpose, 260
humanitarian, 62 (fn. 172), 123 (fn.
    118)
intransgressible principles, 43
investigation of universal crimes, 304
Iraq, 54, 147, 210
Israel, 55, 75, 131, 243

J

Jackson, Robert H., 30
Japan, 91, 148
Jelisić Case, 70, 71
joint criminal enterprise, 149
jus ad bellum, 258
jus cogens, 8, 9, 11, 43, 51, 75, 105, 108,
    109, 117, 131, 155, 166, 205
    and interpretation, 133
    and the Security Council, 121
    character of, 62
    relevant to legal processes, 9
jus cogens crimes, 155, 156
jus cogens norms, 293
    status as hard or soft law, 106
jus in bello, 258
justice and peace, 56
Justice Case, 102

K

Kadi and Al Barakaat Case, 124
Kaye, David, 92
Kellogg-Briand Pact, 125–126
Kenya, Republic of, 54
Kononov case, 243
Korea, 55
Kosovo, 54, 146, 148, 342
Kunarac Judgment, 119
Kuwait, 210

L

Latin America, 243, 245
    trials, 90
law-creating sources, 87, 129, 219
    ICJ Statute Article 38, 97
lawful combatants (see also *combatants*),
    261

Lebanon, 54, 94, 95, 146, 267, 312, 313
legal bases
  and interpretative sources, 129
  customary international law, 104
  general principles as international law,
    108
  law-creating sources, 97
  multilateral treaties, 100
  multiple legal bases, 125
  Security Council resolutions, 119
  universal crimes norms, 87
legal concepts, 88
legal conditions and consequences, 137
legal definition, 217, 218, 296
  lex lata, 218
legal meta-norms, 291
legal writers, 219, 220
legality of Security Council rules, 123
legality principle, 16, 33–35, 51, 95, 138,
  140, 143, 144, 194, 241
  and the definition of genocide, 186
  EU law, 230
  unreasonable application, 117
legibus solutis, 121
Lemkin, Raphael, 48, 144
level of responsibility, 79, 81–82, 201
lex ferenda, 15, 133, 134, 137, 220, 227,
  245, 250, 251
  15 crime types, 292
  and legal authors, 134
  international crimes, 276
lex lata, 15, 133, 134, 137, 180, 220, 227,
  245
  135 universal crime types, 292
  and international courts, 134
  legal authors, 134
  terrorism, 274
  uncertain crimes, 251
lex posterior, 130
lex specialis, 5, 130, 131
lex superior, 130, 133
Liberia, Republic of, 36
Libya, 2, 53, 54, 122, 123

M

Macedo, Stephen, 136
mala in se, 84
mala prohibita, 84

Mapiripán Massacre Judgment, 234
Martens Clause, 26
mass grave exhumations, 77
mass violations of human rights, 185, 187
membership in a criminal organisation,
  148, 176
mercenarism, 184
Ministries Case, 102, 103 (fn. 52)
modes of participation, 34, 43, 50, 79,
  104, 138, 148, 173, 175, 249–250
  punishable participation, 188, 201
  and independent crimes, 249
money laundering, 139, 151, 227, 229,
  285, 328
multilateral treaties
  and universal crimes, 100
multiple legal bases, 125
  and international courts, 129
  and the ILC, 127
  and the *Nuremberg Judgment*, 126
Munich Olympic Games, 68

N

national crimes, 226
nationality jurisdiction, 147
nationally imported international crimes,
  226
nationally imported universal crimes, 299
nexus to a particular gravity clause, 302
Nicaragua Case, 108
Nigeria, 55
non-discrimination, 240
non-grave universal offences, 299
non-international armed conflict, 257
non-international crimes, 95, 168, 225,
  228
non-universal crimes, 299
Norway, 72
notorious offender, 72, 79, 135
nulla poena sine lege, 111, 114, 197
nullum crimen sine lege, 103, 111, 114,
  186, 197
*nullum crimen sine lege, nulla poena sine
  lege*, 114, 117, 197
Nuremberg Judgment, 29, 42–43 46, 50,
  117
  and multiple legal bases, 126
  conflicting principles of justice, 118

crime of genocide not elaborated, 64
general principles of (international)
    law, 65, 114
the dynamic character of international
    law, 116
the principle of non-retroactive laws,
    115–116
the UN paradigm of international law,
    115
universal jurisdiction, 113
Nuremberg Principles, 45, 46, 170, 239,
    241, 269
    as a contribution to international law,
    118
Nuremberg trial, 35, 42–43, 49 (fn. 85),
    91 (fn. 13)

O

Obama, Barack, 1–3, 40, 52 (fn. 90), 262
    (fn. 409), 265 (fn. 417)
    Nobel lecture, 63
obligation to extradite or prosecute (see
    also *aut dedere aut judicare*), 127, 205
obligations *erga omnes*, 8, 43, 63, 86
opinio juris, 65, 106–108
organised crimes, 227, 230
Organization of American States, 140

P

pacta sunt servanda, 111
Palestine, 3 (fn. 10), 55, 68
peace and justice, 56, 98
peace and security of mankind, 143, 170–
    172, 174, 178, 180, 182, 185–186,
    198, 251
Pellet, Alain, 203
peremptory norm, 8, 28, 51, 63, 121, 132
persecution
    in the definition of a refugee, 46
    in the Nuremberg Judgment, 46
pillage, 286, 328
piracy
    and universal jurisdiction, 306, 309
    as a universal crime, 307, 310
    definition in UNCLOS, 306
    duty to suppress, 306
    jurisdiction of the seizing state, 192

not necessarily a universal crime, 307
off the coast of Somalia, 67, 308–309,
    311
outlawed by nations, 306
right to seize a pirate ship, 306
single act or as part of a widespread or
    systematic attack, 199
Plato, 29
polycentric laws, 94, 137
post-transitional justice, 90
power structure, 13, 43, 55, 70–72, 79,
    80–82, 133, 135, 199, 201–202, 233,
    253, 286, 289, 328
preventive effect, 86
prima facie, 113, 198, 207
priority principles, 129
proportional punishment, 84
proprio motu, 74, 92
prosecutorial discretion, 17, 76, 82, 88
protection of civilians, 256, 258
punishable participation, 88, 96

R

Ratner, Steven R., 160
reconciliation, 27, 57–58, 83–85
Red Army Faction, 68
Red Cross, 47
refugee status
    exclusion in the case of serious crimes,
    37, 47
research aims, iv, 290
responsibility to protect, 62, 122
restorative justice, 58, 83, 243
retributive justice, 58, 83, 85, 316
    deterrent effects, 84
    individualises guilt, 84
    restorative effects, 84
    ten arguments, 84
    upholds and clarifies the norms, 84
right to truth, 84
Rikhof, Joseph, 37
Robinson, Darryl, 158, 159
role of international law, 59
Roxin, Claus, 79, 80
rule of law, 63, 84, 289, 290, 316
    and *lex lata*, 133
    and power, 133
    and universal crimes, 8

in international affairs, 30
in international relations, 31
obligations, 32
standards, 33
subjects, 32
substantive notion, 34
the concept, 28
rule of recognition, 110
Russia, 3
Rwanda, 36, 68, 138

S

Schabas, William A., 103, 156, 157, 211
self-contained regimes, 93
Sevres, Treaty of, 25
Sierra Leone, 36, 54, 91, 146, 267
Sluiter, Göran, 150, 153, 158
soft law, 99
and hard law, 6, 129
Somalia, 152, 308, 309, 310, 311, 312
South African Truth and Reconciliation
Commission, 83
Soviet Union, 42
special regimes, 32, 93
specific gravity clause, 303
Spiropoulos, Jean, 170, 171, 172, 173
Sri Lanka, 55
Sudan, Republic of, 36, 53, 54, 61
system criminality, 52
systemic integration, 96

T

Tadic Case, 121, 123–124, 132
Taliban, 69
targeted killing, 305
targeted killings, 208
Taylor, Telford, 76, 77
territorial jurisdiction, 147
terrorism
against civilians during armed conflict,
272
crime status under international law,
266
definition by the EU, 273
definition by the General Assembly
and Security Council, 272
definitions, 269, 270, 271-273

EU, 270, 273
European Court of Justice, 124
General Assembly, 271
gravity clause, 271, 273, 303
international customary law, 312
Security Council, 123, 124, 268, 269,
270
Special Tribunal for Lebanon, 313
specific intent and purpose, 266
war, 263
terrorist activities in another State, 177
terrorist crimes, 305
crime types, 283
outlawed by the UN Security Council,
67
Thiam, Doudou, 170, 181, 182, 183, 184,
185
threat to peace and security
determination by the UN Security
Council, 75
threshold clauses (see also *gravity
threshold*), 213
Tokyo trial, 36, 42, 91
torture
discrete crime, 82, 105
distinct crime, 192
requirement for being an international
(universal) crime, 254
transitional justice, 56, 57, 242, 292
after World War II, 43
as an academic field, 57
in Germany and Japan, 60
trials in Latin America, 90
transnational crimes, 161, 164, 166, 167,
225, 227, 230
eurocrimes, 229–230
institutional crimes, 230
organised crimes, 227, 228, 230
transnational criminal law, 163
transnational non-universal crimes, 299
treaty
definition, 100, 101
treaty interpretation (see *interpretation)*

U

Uganda, 54, 148, 330, 332

UN Charter, 97–98, 111–112, 120–121, 169, 209–210, 216, 239, 257, 277–278, 282–283, 320, 324–325
UN paradigm of international law, 38, 41, 47, 50, 62, 63, 93, 94, 97, 101, 111, 137, 196, 207, 208, 209, 237, 239, 248, 253, 258, 263, 265, 276, 289, 293, 295, 301, 317
   accessibility and foreseeability as elements of the legality principle, 114
   and impunity, 313
   and international courts, 128
   distinction between law-creating and interpretative sources, 99
UN Security Council resolutions as a possible law-creating source, 98
United Kingdom, 42, 148, 209, 234
United States of America, 2–4, 40, 42, 261
universal crimes
   10 crime categories and 150 crime types, 292, 305
   a UN Declaration, 313, 317–318
   consolidated list, 319
   essentials, 301
   gravity matrix, 81
Universal Declaration of Human Rights, 45–46
universal jurisdiction, 11, 12, 88, 136, 147, 165, 194, 233, 235, 246, 247
   and piracy, 306, 309
   as a residual jurisdictional category, 139
universal law, 1
universal rights, 4
universal values, 183
universality, 7, 237–238, 241, 242, 254, 277, 293–294, 318
   as a counterweight to fragmentation, 17

unlawful combatants (see also *combatants*), 262

V

Versailles, Treaty of, 25
victors' justice, 241 (fn. 354)

W

Wall Case, 43 (fn. 66–67) 131, 132
war
   and terrorism, 263
   as a means of protecting against universal crimes, 259
   as a means of restoring international peace and security, 259
   between a state and terrorists, 264
   classic civil war, 261
   classic international war, 258
   four distinct legal types, 258
   in a legal sense, 257
   internationalised civil war, 260
   universally authorised war, 259
war crimes
   crime category, 280, 322–325
   crime types, 280
   exceptionally serious, 187
war on terror, 261, 264–265, 268
Werle, Gerhard, 152, 153, 154, 158, 162
Wilmshurst, Elizabeth, 158, 159

Y

Yugoslavia, 36, 91, 138, 222

Z

Zahar, Alexander, 150, 153, 158

TORKEL OPSAHL ACADEMIC EPUBLISHER

Research Professor J. Peter Burgess, PRIO
Judge Advocate General Arne Willy Dahl, Norway
Professor Emeritus Yoram Dinstein, Tel Aviv University
Professor Jon Elster, Columbia University and Collège de France
Mr. James A. Goldston, Open Society Institute Justice Initiative
Mr. Richard Goldstone, former Chief Prosecutor,
    International Criminal Tribunal for the former Yugoslavia
Judge Hanne Sophie Greve, Gulating Court of Appeal, formerly
    European Court of Human Rights
Dr. Fabricio Guariglia, Senior Appeals Counsel, Office of the Prosecutor,
    International Criminal Court
Dr. Franz Guenthner, Ludwig-Maximilians-Universität
Mr. Christopher Keith Hall, Amnesty International
Professor Emeritus Frits Kalshoven, Leiden University
Judge Hans-Peter Kaul, International Criminal Court
Judge Erkki Kourula, International Criminal Court
Dr. Claus Kress, Director of the Institute for Criminal Law and Criminal Procedure,
    Cologne University
Professor David Luban, Georgetown University
Mr. Juan E. Méndez, Special Adviser to the ICC Prosecutor on Crime Prevention, former
    President, ICTJ
Dr. Alexander Muller, Director, The Hague Institute for the Internationalisation of Law
Judge Erik Møse, Norwegian Supreme Court, former President,
    International Criminal Tribunal for Rwanda
Dr. Gro Nystuen, International Law and Policy Institute and Norwegian Defence Command
    and Staff College
Mr. William Pace, Convener, Coalition for the International Criminal Court
Ms. Jelena Pejić, International Committee of the Red Cross
Mr. Robert Petit, former International Co-Prosecutor,
    Extraordinary Chambers in the Courts of Cambodia
Maj-Gen (ret'd) Anthony P.V. Rogers, Cambridge University
Professor William A. Schabas, National University of Ireland, Galway
Professor James Silk, Yale Law School
Professor Emeritus Otto Triffterer, Salzburg University
Professor Marcos Zilli, University of Sao Paulo

ALSO IN THE
FICHL PUBLICATION SERIES

Morten Bergsmo, Mads Harlem and Nobuo Hayashi (editors):
Importing Core International Crimes into National Law
Torkel Opsahl Academic EPublisher
Oslo, 2010
FICHL Publication Series No. 1 (Second Edition, 2010)
ISBN 978-82-93081-00-5

Nobuo Hayashi (editor):
National Military Manuals on the Law of Armed Conflict
Torkel Opsahl Academic EPublisher
Oslo, 2010
FICHL Publication Series No. 2 (Second Edition, 2010)
ISBN 978-82-93081-02-9

Morten Bergsmo, Kjetil Helvig, Ilia Utmelidze and Gorana Žagovec:
The Backlog of Core International Crimes Case Files in Bosnia and Herzegovina
Torkel Opsahl Academic EPublisher
Oslo, 2010
FICHL Publication Series No. 3 (Second Edition, 2010)
ISBN 978-82-93081-04-3

Morten Bergsmo (editor):
Criteria for Prioritizing and Selecting Core International Crimes Cases
Torkel Opsahl Academic EPublisher
Oslo, 2010
FICHL Publication Series No. 4 (Second Edition, 2010)
ISBN 978-82-93081-06-7

Morten Bergsmo and Pablo Kalmanovitz (editors):
Law in Peace Negotiations
Torkel Opsahl Academic EPublisher
Oslo, 2010
FICHL Publication Series No. 5 (Second Edition, 2010)
ISBN 978-82-93081-08-1

Morten Bergsmo, César Rodríguez Garavito, Pablo Kalmanovitz and Maria Paula Saffon (editors):
Distributive Justice in Transitions
Torkel Opsahl Academic EPublisher
Oslo, 2010
FICHL Publication Series No. 6 (2010)
ISBN 978-82-93081-12-8
Also available in Spanish:
Justicia distributiva en sociedades en transición
ISBN 978-82-93081-10-4

Morten Bergsmo (editor):
*Complementarity and the Exercise of Universal Jurisdiction
for Core International Crimes*
Torkel Opsahl Academic EPublisher
Oslo, 2010
FICHL Publication Series No. 7 (2010)
ISBN 978-82-93081-14-2

Morten Bergsmo (editor):
Active Complementarity: Legal Information Transfer
Torkel Opsahl Academic EPublisher
Oslo, 2011
FICHL Publication Series No. 8 (2011)
ISBN 978-82-93081-55-5

Sam Muller, Stavros Zouridis, Morly Frishman and Laura Kistemaker (editors):
The Law of the Future and the Future of Law
Torkel Opsahl Academic EPublisher
Oslo, 2011
FICHL Publication Series No. 11 (2011)
ISBN 978-82-93081-27-2

Morten Bergsmo, Alf Butenschøn Skre and Elisabeth J. Wood (editors):
Understanding and Proving International Sex Crimes
Torkel Opsahl Academic EPublisher
Beijing, 2012
FICHL Publication Series No. 12 (2012)
ISBN 978-82-93081-29-6

Morten Bergsmo (editor):
Thematic Prosecution of International Sex Crimes
Torkel Opsahl Academic EPublisher
Beijing, 2011
FICHL Publication Series No. 13 (2012)
ISBN 978-82-93081-31-9

All volumes are freely available as e-books on the FICHL homepage www.fichl.org.
Printed copies may be ordered online from distributors such as www.amazon.co.uk.